Duet with tl

Duet with the Past

A Composer's Memoir

DARON HAGEN

Foreword by BERNARD JACOBSON

for Joel —
Love & gratitude
(and GOOD TUNES)

forever,

Daron Aric Hagen

20 Jan 2020
Rhinebeck, NY

McFarland & Company, Inc., Publishers

Jefferson, North Carolina

LIBRARY OF CONGRESS CATALOGUING-IN-PUBLICATION DATA

Names: Hagen, Daron, 1961– author.
Title: Duet with the past : a composer's memoir / Daron Hagen ;
foreword by Bernard Jacobson.
Description: Jefferson, North Carolina :
McFarland & Company, 2019 | Includes index.
Identifiers: LCCN 2019012609 | ISBN 9781476677378
(paperback : acid free paper) ∞
Subjects: LCSH: Hagen, Daron, 1961– | Composers—
United States—Biography. | LCGFT: Autobiographies.
Classification: LCC ML410.H102836 A3 2019 | DDC 780.92 [B] —dc23
LC record available at https://lccn.loc.gov/2019012609

BRITISH LIBRARY CATALOGUING DATA ARE AVAILABLE

ISBN (print) 978-1-4766-7737-8
ISBN (ebook) 978-1-4766-3587-3

Front cover: Daron Hagen, photograph by Karen Pearson, 2017

Printed in the United States of America

*McFarland & Company, Inc., Publishers
Box 611, Jefferson, North Carolina 28640
www.mcfarlandpub.com*

For Gilda, because this was our time;
and for Atticus and Seamus, because now it's your time.

I wake to sleep and take my waking slow.
I learn by going where I have to go. —Theodore Roethke

And as they were afraid, and bowed down their faces to the earth,
They said unto them, Why do you seek the quick among the dead?
                                                            —Luke 24:5

Table of Contents

Acknowledgments

Gilda Marie Lyons, for the love of a lifetime and a lifetime of love. I would not be alive today without you and our sons, Atticus and Seamus. You lead me to grace.

Inspiring writing mentors: Diane C. Doerfler, Gwen Hagen, Tim Page, and Emily Wallace.

I am deeply grateful for the steadfast support of my wife's parents Gilda Alemán Lyons and Bernard John Lyons, who read nearly every new draft of the manuscript. My thanks also to Juhi Bansal, Hortense Calisher, Joel Conarroe, Jocelyn Dueck, JoAnn Falletta, Daniel Felsenfeld, Barbara Grecki, Kevin & Ryan Hagen, Curtis Harnack, James Holmes, Cheryl Kaplan, Paula Kimper, Slavko Krstic, Timothy Lewis, Romulus Linney, Allison & Christopher Lyons, J.D. McClatchy, Russell Platt, William Rhoads, Ned Rorem, Nina & Michael Sundell, Michael Torke, Craig Urquhart, Elaine Valby, and Matthew Wright who, over the years, have given me valuable advice about the manuscript.

I have occasionally quoted lightly from correspondence with my brothers, my father, David Diamond, Speight Jenkins, Richard McKeon and Ned Rorem to provide context. I have also quoted a few passages from my mother's (and my own) unpublished journals. Thanks to Gardner McFall for allowing me to quote from her "Afterword" to the published libretto of *Amelia*.

My gratitude to David Alff, my editor at McFarland and Company; Bernard Jacobson for his foreword; and thanks to Karen Pearson for her photographic portraits.

I am grateful for the support of the American Academy of Arts and Letters; the Barlow Endowment for Music Composition; the Guggenheim Foundation; the American Society of Composers, Authors, and Publishers; Broadcast Music, Incorporated; the National Endowment for the Arts; the Rockefeller Foundation Bellagio Center, Como, Italy; the Camargo Foundation, Cassis, France; the Virginia Center for the Creative Arts; the MacDowell Colony; and the staff, my fellow Members of the Corporation of Yaddo, and the numerous gifted, inspiring, and generous fellow artists with whom I have shared thoughts, dreams, love, and work there over the past thirty-five years.

Foreword
by Bernard Jacobson

Berlioz was a great composer—but even if he had never written a note of music, the libretto he wrote for *The Trojans*, along with his *Memoirs,* would have entitled him to be celebrated as one of the greatest masters of French poetry and French prose. His was neither nor the last manifestation of such a union of musical and literary gifts. It had been evidenced more than two centuries earlier in England in the careers of Thomas Campion—not only a distinguished composer, but one of the leading poets of his time, and a lawyer and physician to boot!—and Thomas Morley. Later examples that come to mind, in varying ways and degrees, include, Rameau, Schumann, Debussy, Busoni, and Michael Tippett (not to mention, though with sadly different ethical connotations, Wagner).

Recent American history offers a similar case in the person of Daron Hagen's mentor Ned Rorem. And putting my experience of a sizeable proportion of Hagen's own copious and often profound musical output side by side with the impression created by this vividly expressive memoir and by his polished work as a librettist and co-librettist, I feel I can confidently conclude that he too belongs in that distinguished tradition.

Thinking about Rorem and Hagen, I am irresistibly reminded of a proverb propagated by Isaiah Berlin after Tolstoy—and the Russians in their turn took it from the Greek fabulist Archilochus: it holds that the fox knows many small things, but the hedgehog knows one big thing. Composers come in both shapes. Stravinsky, for instance, was a fox, whereas Schoenberg was a hedgehog, and among the leading figures in the Polish musical renaissance of the last hundred years, Lutosławski surely ranks as a fox and Panufnik indubitably as a hedgehog.

In similar terms, the highly urbane variety of Rorem's compositions and of his entertaining and frequently acerbic books of memoirs, along with a decided bias against "profundity," marks him out as a fox. Hagen, on the other hand, despite his restlessly questing intellectual curiosity and the bold eclecticism of his musical language, embracing the influence of styles ranging from high to low, classical to popular, nevertheless reveals a consistent attitude to life, an unwavering commitment to the moral and social responsibility of the artist, that is no less clearly characteristic of the proverbial hedgehog.

The difference between the two men, one might say, is the difference between the secular and the religious temperaments. What seems on the other hand to unite them is the preponderance of vocal over instrumental music in their respective outputs, but that is perhaps a deceptive judgment. Besides several operas and some of the most arresting songs of the past hundred years, Rorem has produced a substantial catalog of instrumental works

1

for both large and small forces. And for Hagen a similar accounting must set five symphonies, as well as many concertante and other orchestral works and chamber music including six piano trios, in balance with around a dozen operas, several choral works, and more than 300 songs.

It was one of his orchestral works that played a role in my acquaintance and longtime friendship with Daron, and thereby hangs a tale. Early in 2010, he was in Seattle, and my wife and I were living nearby on the other side of Puget Sound. In addition to serving as the Pacific Northwest correspondent for *Opera* magazine, I was writing regularly about music for the *Seattle Times,* and one of my assignments was to interview Daron, who was attending rehearsals for the premiere of his groundbreaking opera *Amelia,* the product of a commission from Seattle Opera. We arranged that I would pick him up for a working lunch from the company's rehearsal hall at the end of a morning rehearsal, and by way of greeting he remarked that it was the first time we had met since a precise date in 1990—a date I had no specific recollection of, but which was firmly fixed in his mind. "Well, you see," he explained, "it was the day you called me from the Philadelphia Orchestra offices and told me that the orchestra was going to perform my Symphony No. 1. How could I ever forget that?"

The clarity of memory that this showed goes to illustrate the intellectual acuity and sharp focus that have characterized both Hagen's music and his written English consistently throughout his career. Certainly, there are differing views about how far the appreciation of a composer's music may be intensified by acquaintance with his own perspective on it, or more broadly with details of his life outside music, can help us to enjoy his works. After all, to take just two examples that may appear to argue against those who think that it can, Mozart and Beethoven composed some of their most emotionally positive music at highly stressed moments in their lives. Mozart wrote one particularly sunny and lighthearted work while his wife was giving birth in the next room; and the composition of Beethoven's exhilarating and dynamic Second Symphony was roughly contemporaneous with the crisis of encroaching deafness that led him to write the heart wrenching "Heiligenstadt Testament." But it seems to me that simply knowing such biographical facts can indeed enhance our musical understanding and gratification. And even readers who take the opposing view, as well as any who are perhaps not particularly interested in the musical side of the matter, can scarcely fail to derive much pleasure, illumination, and mental enrichment from the contact with a well-stocked and sensitive mind that Daron Hagen's *Duet with the Past* offers.

Bernard Jacobson was born in London and now lives in Philadelphia, where he served for eight seasons as the Philadelphia Orchestra's program annotator and as musicological adviser to Riccardo Muti. He is the author of A Polish Renaissance *(Phaidon Press), a study of the music of Panufnik and three of his compatriots, of a memoir titled* Star Turns and Cameo Appearances *(University of Rochester Press), and of books on conducting and on Brahms.*

Prelude
Three Sunsets

New Berlin, Wisconsin, Summer 1970

Mother's hair was the color of spun gold the summer of my ninth year, and cut short, like Amelia Earhart's. The late afternoon sun made it glow as she worked clay with her expressive hands one afternoon, smoking Pall Mall cigarettes and drinking coffee on the patio of the Big Cedar House in which we lived. New Berlin was just a newly laid out suburb west of Milwaukee, and still practically farmland then. The shrill metallic burr of dog-day cicadas mingled with the purling of Paganini Violin Concertos, to which we listened—she had played the violin well into her teens—one after another.

"The Lord God formed man out of the dust of the ground," she told me, smiling rue-fully. "Now, I am just making a little boy," she said. "Would you like to be my model?" Her wry, knowing smile was dazzling. My brothers were off playing with their friends. If I said yes, then I'd have her all to myself for the rest of the afternoon. When my buddies had stopped by earlier to ask me to join them in playing *Last of the Mohicans*, or *Star Trek*, or *Rat Patrol* in the woods, she had said, "Listen, go ahead if you like. But if you want it to look like you, you have to stick with it; don't be surprised if this thing starts looking a lot like your brother Britt."

I was proud to serve as her model, and I tried very hard to sit still on the high stool. But my feet—the more I tried to stop them, the more they swung. Frustrated, she took a length of wire and sliced the boy's feet off and tossed them into the clay pail. Astonished, I fished them out, saying, "Mama, I'm sorry, I'm *sorry!* I'll sit *still!* They look fine to me." "Honey, I'm not angry with you," she reassured me. "I'm just frustrated by my lack of skill. Yes, they're okay," she paused, thinking, "but they're not *right*." "But nobody will know that except us," I protested. "But *we'll* know," she sighed. "Where's the satisfaction in not getting it exactly *right*?" she asked, draping a wet cloth over the statue. "Go and play. I'm going to start dinner."

For the next few days she made charcoal sketches of feet—first copies of Michelangelo drawings from a large art book, then her own feet, and then mine: "I must *feel* what a foot looks like, not just *see* it" she explained. Resuming her sculpting, she was happier with the results: "Let's roll up his pants a bit, like Tom Sawyer," she said. "Now that I've captured your feet, I want people to *see* them."

As far as I was concerned, we were done. But there was more. "Inspiration is the secret," she said. "Otherwise, this will just be another statue of a little smiling boy. What do you want his secret to be?" I was a serious child. "How can a statue have a secret?" I asked. She didn't answer. "He could be hiding something behind his back," I ventured. "Good," she laughed. "Don't peek; I'll put something in his hands behind his back when we're done working on the front." She promised to reveal the boy's secret when we picked him up.

She used me as her model because she needed a subject, she loved me, and because I was available. In due course, she drove us to the place in whose kiln the boy had been fired. After a few pleasantries with the potter, she stubbed out her cigarette and placed her cool hands over my eyes. I listened to the sound of the bricks being removed from the furnace's mouth and smelled the still slightly warm terra-cotta figure as it was slid out. Mother grinned as she slid her hands from before my eyes to my shoulders. Her sudden smile, as she observed my delight the first time that I saw the big green bullfrog clasped between the boy's hands, mirrored the boy's.

Seattle, Washington, 8 May 2010

I stood, forty years later, in my tuxedo at the orchestra pit's rail, gazing up into the slowly filling 2800 seat McCaw Opera House in Seattle. The seats formed a wine dark sea of plush red velvet. The susurrus of the audience's pre-performance chatter washed over me. Happy, confident, I turned my back on the audience, considered the pit, reached down, and shook the concertmistress' hand. "Thank you, Emma," I said. "My pleasure, really," she smiled, returning to her seat. Classmates from conservatory days now members of the Seattle Symphony looked up and smiled; I waved and smiled in return, grateful. My opera, *Amelia* had taken—from first sketches to the night of its staged premiere in Seattle in May 2010—nearly six years to compose. The culmination of my life to that point as a composer, *Amelia* was about to be launched with a 3.6-million-dollar production by the Seattle Opera, one of America's largest companies.

Alone, it had been part of my job to walk nearly every foot of McCaw during rehearsals, to ascertain what the audience would hear and see from every angle. I had "infiltrated" the theater just as I had the vast old Oriental Landmark Movie Theater of my youth. The dream of being a world-class opera composer that I had formulated there thirty-two years earlier, lying on the Oriental's stage on my back with a heap of musty safety curtain beneath my head, fingers interlaced at the nape of my neck, watching films from behind the screen, had become reality.

I glanced down at the opera's full score on the conductor's podium. *Amelia* was my sixth opera, so I performed a private ritual by discretely tapping the wood of the pit rail six times for luck. The jitters came. Turning back to the house, I let out a very long breath. My very sanity—the way I crafted it just behind my eyes—was on the line: the future, the present, the past, the living, the dead, the imaginary, all coexisted simultaneously in the opera, just as they did in my head. I was sharing not just my vision, but also my truth. The critics would slap me down in the morning, but, for now, it was my turn to sing.

I remembered the night before my first Juilliard audition in July 1979. I stood at the lip of the Uris Theater pit, desperate for someone to talk to, and poured out my anxiety about the audition to come and my excitement at standing right where I was during the intermission of *Sweeney Todd* to its surprised, amused keyboard player.

I turned back to the pit and made eye contact with David McDade, the opera company's chief accompanist, seated behind the piano. He smiled up at me in return, mouthed, "*In bocca al lupo"* silently. I smiled in return and mouthed, *"Crepi!"* Chuckling, he gave a little wave and looked back to his music. In a few seconds, the houselights would go "to half," and Gerard Schwarz would walk briskly to the podium. I looked back at the audience and tried to recall the instant that I became aware that music was always flowing through my mind.

Perhaps it was the night Father commanded me at age five to sing Friedrich-Wilhelm Möller's saccharine ditty *The Happy Wanderer* again and again for the only houseguests I recall our family ever having entertained. After the first half dozen times, I realized that Father was drunk, and that nobody was listening; in fact, people were embarrassed for me as, crimson with shame, terrified of what would happen to me if I stopped, I sang, and sang, and sang. Maybe it was when I was nine, bundled up in winter gear on the school bus, my warm breath as I quietly sang steaming up the window. I sang then because it made me feel better. Does it still? At what point did the melodies I sang become my own? Were they always?

I made for my seat. Catching my wife Gilda's eye, I nodded, noting with pure joy how dazzling she looked in her opera gown. I took my seat next to her on the aisle—a composer's privilege. My brother Kevin, my nephew Ryan, and Gilda's generous and loving family surrounded us. Am I crazy? I asked myself as the oboist gave the "A" and the aural primordial soup that a professional orchestra creates in response as they tune before the entrance of the conductor bubbled gently up from the pit. I thought of Monteverdi's *Orfeo*: *"...che tosto fugge, e spesso a gran salita il precipizio è presso."* I adjusted my bow tie and cummerbund. Both were tight. I had come to Seattle to attend rehearsals, revise as necessary, to learn as I always did, by observing the process of discovery and staging. Wife and son in New York, I had reverted to a quasi-feral state during the past six weeks—the drinking, debilitating insomnia, depression, and the dizzying mood swings, had all roared back.

I felt lost, alone, and agonizingly overexposed. I realized at that moment that I had far too much riding personally on this première than was psychologically and emotionally safe, let alone appropriate. I felt koi jumping in my stomach. *Do I simply suffer from a peculiar form of Lutheran Histrionic Personality Disorder?* I wondered, half-serious, the sweat beginning to pool under my collar. *Is it so important to me that this opera be a success that, even if it is not, I will make it one in my mind?* I had judged colleagues harshly over the years who I felt had "gone around the bend." Perhaps I had finally reached that point myself. I thought of my 20s, of how I was once jealous of others' self-absorption because I was certain it held—as I believed mine did—secrets of self-knowledge. I assumed that the self-absorbed held, so closely and tenderly, many brave secrets and thoughts that would heighten and illuminate my search for identity. The enormity of deception was due—like my current jitters—to my own arrogance. As it happened, either these people had checked out, gone benignly insane, or had closed-up for sanity—it was as simple as that. At the heart of the Sphinx, through the labyrinthine passages, was the rifled vault of a dead Pharaoh—no more. My frustration and anger were comical.

I twisted around and looked up into the balconies, checked my watch, and mastered myself. It was time to let go of my own concerns and to be the professional that I had labored to become. My responsibility was to gauge the effect as an author that the opera was having in real time on the audience around me and to make mental notes of changes I needed to make to improve the piece. The audience quieted. *Worrying once again my "barb of sorrow,"* I thought ruefully as the house lights dimmed. Whispering the most fleeting of prayers, I squeezed Gilda's hand and blinked hard as in silence *Amelia* was launched and the curtain glided upwards.

Rio Mar, Nicaragua, 1 January 2016

I squeezed Gilda's hand tightly as Harold Mojica, our friend who serves as caretaker of the little vacation house called *Rio Mar* that Gilda's parents maintain on Nicaragua's Pacific coast, threaded his way through Managua's New Year's Eve traffic. Harold had been working on his English by reading *Moby Dick* with my father-in-law, Bernie. "Did you know that Ishmael means 'God hears?' in Spanish?" he asked me. "Does He?" I wondered aloud as we made our way past the elaborate crèches erected by churches all over the city, the illuminated heroic images of Daniel Ortega and Hugo Chávez in the traffic circles, the Christmas trees a year-round reminder of Nicaraguan energy independence. "Indeed, he does," said Harold quietly. "Ishmael was the mid-ground between the Jews and the Muslims," I observed. *Just as I for so long considered myself caught between my living and my dead,* I thought. Harold rolled the window down and sniffed, "Eucalyptus," he observed, "and burnt leña." If Albuquerque's signature smell during the late fall is that of grilled peppers, then Managua's is the sweetly acrid odor of sugarcane ash.

We headed southwest to Diriamba, where we met Route 18, which used to consist entirely of potholes and is now a completely modern secondary highway. After we drove over the *policía acostado* ("sleeping policeman," or speed bump) at the traffic circle we turned south on Route 285 to Casares. When the town ended, so did the road. The Jeep crept along at about 10 kph in the dark as we zigzagged a path down the rutted track. We hugged the coast for the last few kilometers to the humble little house nestled on a narrow heel of *sonsiquite* (hardened mud) between Casares and Huehuete at the spot where the Rio Grande de Carazo pools before emptying into the Pacific Ocean. Harold's wife Iveth, carrying baby Hannah and accompanied by her daughter Nicole, emerged from their house and swung the gate open, smiling.

Parked safely behind the *rancho*, everyone piled out and embraced, slapping backs, kissing cheeks, tousling hair. Iveth and Gilda's mother put out freshly-brewed coffee, *picos, fresh tortillas, gallopinto,* ripe *sapote,* and everyone sat down and spoke lovingly and at cross purposes over the sound of the crashing waves until my sons began to freely-associate with fatigue, at which point I steered them to bed, threw my arms wide, pulled them into my armpits, and sang quietly to them before—halfway through their prayer, about 14 hours after beginning the day at our Big Victorian House in Upstate New York—their breathing became as deep and as steady as the sound of the waves.

Gilda turned in. I locked up the house. Harold let slip the dogs for the night. I heard their whimpers as they bolted from their pen, streamed over the rocks around the outside of the fence like the tide, and shot silently towards the beach. There was the muffled, fluttering rustle of hundreds of pelicans' wings like little conductors as they roosted in the trees directly across the brackish estuarial pool. Our neighbor Cuban Pete's horse nickered; then, inexplicably, *El Gallo* crowed—a strangled, adorably pathetic sort of second-rate fist-wringing sound that has always made me feel happy, and then—save for the crickets, the wind, and the surf—silence. I poured myself a cup of rich local coffee and, heavy mug in hand, slowly strolled the short distance to the ocean. The constellations above were crystalline and clear. In the few seconds that it took for me to reach the spot where the fresh and salt water mixed, everyone fell asleep.

Alone, looking out at the ocean during the first few moments of 2016, I thought about the boy whose fine, straight hair his mother used to trim by placing a soup bowl on his head and cutting around the rim; the boy who sat, trying so hard to be still for the light of his life as she sculpted him in clay; the boy whose dream of becoming an opera composer had been fulfilled; the boy whose path had led him here, to the Nicaraguan coast, his sons and wife asleep a few meters away; the boy who, like his brothers and Mother, had always harbored a deep, fatalistic conviction that he would, as the Other Daron had, die before his time.

◆◆ 1 ◆◆

The Other Daron
1887–1961

A biographer pursues his subject's truth by marching facts down the page after it like little soldiers, while an artist interlaces life's storylines and dreams, pleating and plaiting memory and associations until his personal truth emerges as a braid. My narrative's warp and woof start with the discovery of the birth of a little boy with congenital heart disease. He was born at the Evangelical Deaconess Hospital in Milwaukee, Wisconsin on 26 January 1960. He weighed six pounds and came into our world at 2:55 a.m.—almost the same time at which, 22 years later, his Mother died. He was baptized. He suffered from atresia (absence or closure of a natural passage or channel of the body) of the aortic orifice, hypoplasia (a condition of arrested development in which an organ or part remains below the normal size or in an immature state) of the left atrium (the main part of the left auricle) and the left ventricle (the chamber which receives blood from the left auricle and forces it into the arteries). He lived long enough to have begun to formulate some sort of impression of his parents and of the world, long enough for my parents to hold him, and to give to him—completely and without reservation—their love. The skein of his life's narrative ended as mine took flight, of course; since love alone was not enough to save him. After a four-day struggle, he died of a broken heart.

I am aware of these things because, the night that she died, Mother gave me the yellowed sheet of tissue used back then when generating carbon copies of the doctors' description of the baby's condition on a typewriter that Father had jotted notes on so that he could explain to her, recovering in another room in the hospital, what had happened. In pencil, he had written in the lower left corner of the document, "Cause? German measles. Unknown. Flu."

She gave the paper to me—along with his birth certificate, the "Isolette Baby Club" tag that had hung on his incubator, and his tiny footprint—because she feared (rightly, as it happened) that, after she died, Father would destroy it. I'd seen it before. In a drawer forbidden to me, in a pile of documents that mostly made no sense, I had found it with his death certificate. I'd read his name and wondered how it could be true. I'd already felt for the first time the specific sense of displacement that accompanies nascent self-awareness—the first inklings of adult woe, of the idea that my parents were not simply an extension of me, or me of them—the first intuitive understandings of why secrets are cloaked in enigmas. For a long time, I kept this embryonic awareness of self—the sweet sadness of it awakened by the discovery of my namesake, Daron Aric Hagen—secret.

"You were given Daron's name in his honor," Mother explained simply, the only time we ever discussed him. I had a responsibility, she said, to "transform sorrow into joy, and to live enough for two." She told me not to be sad, and that she missed him, but that she felt him with her always, always, and that I would come to feel that way, too. I did. I do.

The Other Daron was named after my great-grandfather Dorn, the son of Hans Hansen, who bought land in an area of Norway called Skjeggestad. Later generations of Hans and his wife Ellen Larsdatter took the name Skjeggestad. Dorn was twenty years old when his cousin Josefine Hem, who had already emigrated to Wisconsin from Norway, invited him: "So everyone who has travelled about says that this place is the best in America—especially for newcomers because here the climate is more like the Norwegian and the water is good to drink," she wrote. The passage from Christiana to Hull between decks, rail fare from Hull to Liverpool, passage aboard a Cunard steamer to New York, and rail fare to Wisconsin for the three of them cost 450 Norwegian *kroner*.

Dorn and his older siblings Lars and Lina arrived at Ellis Island in 1887 and, when asked their name, began spelling out "Skjegg…" and were interrupted by the registrar, who then asked them where they were from. "Hagen," replied Dorn, and Hagen (which means "garden" in Norwegian) is what they became. Once settled in Wisconsin, Dorn farmed and served as a Lutheran pastor. He married a young Swedish woman named Ada Pearson. Clinical depression goes way back in the males on both sides of my family—my grandfather and uncles on Mother's side; Father, my brothers and I all coped with it. After six years, succumbing to melancholia, Dorn was admitted to the Mendota Hospital for the Insane in Madison.

A century later, as an undergraduate at the University of Wisconsin–Madison crewing dinghies on Lake Mendota for my school chum Brian Anderson, whenever we sailed just beneath the cliffs that still plunge from the now-all-but-deserted compound's perimeter into the lake I'd mutter superstitiously, "Pride goeth before destruction," quoting Proverbs 16:18. I felt even then the place's sepulchral coldness, either because my childhood OCD (it hadn't yet been given a name) embraced magical and superstitious thinking, or simply because of the Irish-Norwegian fatalism shared by my entire family. Britt and I explored the grounds together in fall 1980. "Little brother," he said to me as we stood together in the ruins of the place, taking a deep drag on his Newport, "we both know that I'm gonna die young, just like Mom." I shrugged, looking down, hands in my pockets. "Probably Kevin will, too," he said, flicking the smoldering butt of his cigarette into the exposed foundation of one of the wards. I didn't respond. "But you," he continued, looking off, "you're a selfish little fucker. We think that maybe that, and your musical talent, will help you to survive this shit." I looked at him. Beefy linebacker material in high school, he had begun chipping heroin in college, and had grown very thin. He pulled another cigarette from the pack in his pocket, wadded it up, and dropped it on the ground at his feet. "Kevin and I worked hard to protect you from Dad. Don't let us down." Most of the place was deserted, but two years earlier the State had converted the Central State Hospital for the Criminally Insane in Waupun from a prison hospital into the Dodge Correctional Institution, transferring some of the patients, like Ed Gein, to Mendota. Michael Lesy's *Wisconsin Death Trip* (yes, much of our family hails from Black River Falls), published in 1973, doesn't even *begin* to scratch the surface of the incredible darkness made visible in that awful place.

Dorn was eventually paroled from Mendota and resumed farming and preaching. One Sunday he was wrongly accused of purloining an envelope filled with money from the offertory plate. Distraught, he couldn't cope with his congregation's censure; he threw a rope over a purlin in his barn and hung himself. The money was later found stuck to the underside of the drawer in which he had said that he put it. I think of Dorn every Sunday when I sing the Doxology and watch as my son Seamus, clad in red acolyte's vestments and already so spiritually insightful at the age of six that our priest Richard McKeon is slightly in awe of him, carries the collection plate up the aisle to him to be blessed.

When at the age of ten I was called by music, it *felt* like a call. Had I not become a composer, I would have, like Dorn, taken the chasuble. Once I accepted the call, all I ever wanted to be was Music. The rest, as they say, is Life. As for Death, since earliest childhood, the facts of Dorn's suicide and Daron's premature death have shaped not just my personal narrative but also determined the way that I've crafted my sanity. Although it may sound crazy (and maybe it is), I've always felt the presence of my dead, and one of the things that has been hardest for me to cope with as I get older is the fact that one's dead inevitably increase in number. One can honor them, sing for them, even ferry them, but, in the end, one can become surrounded by them. The truth is that I didn't wake them until I devised the end of my opera *Amelia*, in which the title character, while giving birth, suddenly realizes that all her departed loved ones surround her, and that they are all singing, "Anything is possible."

Mother's great-great grandfather Robert Rickaby served as a cabin boy on a British Naval ship; he was pressed by the Americans and served in the U.S. Navy during the Revolutionary War. He ultimately settled in New York State. His son, my great grandfather, made his way from New York to Wisconsin. When the Civil War broke out, Oscar F. Rickaby enlisted (Private, Company G; 14th Wisconsin Infantry) and was ultimately killed in action.

My grandfather, Howard Johnson, was born in Oconto County, Wisconsin to Ole Johnson and Emma Erickson. He came to Milwaukee from Green Bay, where he had worked in a greenhouse. He married Grandmother when they were both 22 years old, and moved to Milwaukee, where he found work at the Allis-Chalmers plant as a steelworker. I remember him as having had enormous knuckles, and hands like gnarled tree roots. Built like a draft horse, by the time I have memories of him he hobbled with obvious effort and great pain on artificial knees. Decades of hauling steel beams had ravaged his body.

Grandmother, the daughter of Bernard Berman and Annie Rickaby, was born in Symco, a little town in Waupaca County, Wisconsin. She took after her own blind mother, Annie Berman, who used to run away from home to live for a few days at a time with the Potawatomi Indians. Grandmother left a job as a schoolteacher to marry Grandfather on 6 May 1926. She was imperious, proud, and had—especially as she aged—a hyperactive imagination. Her cursive was exquisite. After a tumble in her 60s, she developed severe rheumatism in both hands that made her knuckles look like rhizomes. Fearful of losing use of them, she sat for hours in her living room wringing them as she watched television. And how she gardened! She specialized, like her daughter, in Irises, and was particularly proud of her huge White Cemetery Irises, which bloomed larger than a man's clasped hands, with orange furry tongues lolling out of their cupped palms. She believed in the literal resurrection of the flesh, and had relatives disinterred and reburied—moved around in the family plot before her death—so that when the Rapture happened the first people she would see were those she liked. For reasons that will become obvious, she insisted that Father be buried behind her.

I adored my uncles, Keith and Garth. Their sons and I were born within days of each other. Keith's son Jace K. Seavers (his mother remarried) grew up to be a successful jazz composer, lyricist, and bass player in Nashville; Garth's son Garret rose through the ranks in the United States Air Force to Chief Master Sergeant.

Mother was born on 6 January 1929 in Milwaukee. As a girl, she played the violin, and was a promising writer. Although in later years (especially after her brothers' deaths) she and her mother grew close, their temperaments were so alike that they fought continually. To me, she was smart, proud, funny, strong, tender, and good at everything to which she turned her hand. She starred in a 1948 production by the Milwaukee Theater Guild as Ellen in Mark Reed's play *Yes, My Darling Daughter*. She also worked as a radio actress in Milwaukee and Chicago before enrolling at the University of Wisconsin in Madison, where she majored in creative writing. Her prose came to the attention of Pulitzer prize-winning prairie author Mari Sandoz, of whom she became a protégé.

Father was born on 16 February 1928 in the tiny town of Boscobel, Wisconsin, to Jenny Thelma Taft, a housewife, and Joseph Hagen, a mechanic. Growing up in Viroqua, he was second oldest of fourteen children: Beryl, Earl, Ester, Donald, Louis, Clarice, Larry, Richard, Michael, Patrick, Caryl, Phyllis, Bryant, and Alan. He never spoke to my brothers or to me about his father, his mother, his siblings, or his Grandparents, the Tafts (we are somehow related to President William Howard Taft). I met several of them once or twice in passing as a boy, but never met my Grandparents on Father's side. He enlisted in the Navy in March 1946, received his boot training at San Diego, and went overseas that May. He stopped in Guam, Saipan, Pagan Island, China, Japan, New Zealand, and Samoa. Admiral Richard Evelyn Byrd led an expedition called Operation Highjump in 1946 to Antarctica; Father was a talented radioman with the rank of communications specialist.

"They didn't know," Father told me as a child, "what problems the ionospheric

Left: **My mother, advertising executive, visual artist, and writer, Gwen Leone Johnson in 1948, a few years before she married my father.** *Right:* **My father, attorney Earl Arthur Hagen, photographed by my mother in fall 1952 on Lake Mendota, in Madison, Wisconsin, while he was finishing law school and she was studying creative writing with Mari Sandoz.**

conditions there would cause for the communications gadgetry. Back then, it was as close as my generation could get to something like walking on the moon." The ship on which he served, the icebreaker Burton Island, and a supply ship ferried Byrd, his dogs, his men, and his equipment South. "I got to know Byrd," Father said. "He was very much of a gentleman, a very handsome fellow. He was one of the Byrds of Virginia. It was special because he was kind of a childhood hero of mine. I had read all about him." They journeyed as far south as they could, crashing through sheets of ice. "As far as you could see, it was white ice. There was a sort of pristine cleanness about it. Sound seemed to carry forever." The Burton Island left Byrd and his men to set up their base camp, Little America IV. The icebreaker then headed out into McMurdo Sound in the Ross Sea. They found Captain Robert Scott's base camp there, just as it had been left 42 years earlier, when it was abandoned. "Everything was pretty much intact. There was even canned food and newspapers." On 28 February 1947, the icebreaker returned to Little America IV to evacuate Byrd, his men, and their 47 dogs. Shortly after returning to San Pedro, his ship was ordered to the Arctic Sea, at the opposite end of the world. On its way North, it picked up an LST, a type of landing craft, in Seattle. "It was loaded with electronic gear," Father told me. "We towed it behind us, but we didn't know why we were doing it." They towed the craft as far north into the Arctic Sea as they could and beached it on an uninhabited island, electrical gear, and all. He said that they later learned it was part of an early warning system to alert the U.S. of an attack from the Soviet Union. I am told that as a little boy I loved to fondle the spot where his earlobe would have been had he not snapped it off by accident one morning somewhere in the Ross Sea while serving watch on deck. "I tossed it overboard," he laughed. "What did I need it for?"

Following his discharge, Father joined the young men who gained access to college through the GI Bill: he enrolled in the law school at the University of Wisconsin at Madison, where at a poetry reading he met my mother. He courted her with what she described in her journal as "flattering, furious, frightening determination. He was tall, slender, darkly handsome, athletic, articulate, emotionally volcanic, alternately smoldering with anger and ebullient. His love of the Law was fiery and pure." She said that, at least at first, his mood swings frightened her, but that she never knew a man with whom she felt safer or more loved. He spoke easily, well, and passionately. They were members of a close-knit knot of friends who called themselves "the Cave Dwellers" who met weekly in the Memorial Union *Rathskeller* to argue aesthetics, politics, and social justice. He presented her with volumes of his favorite poetry—Byron, Keats, and Shelley. She showed him her short stories, which, he told her in a letter, "coruscated talent."

I am loved, she wrote in her journal in July 1951. *There's a fundamental consistency in his love for me. There are many times when he's not actively there for me, but I feel a strong undercurrent of sincere faith even at those times. He can move away from me so that I can become detached from his identity, but he's true for me always in an inexplicable tie. I can love him with a great rush of tenderness or only disinterestedly. But there's the essential knowledge that what we have is good and growing. Isn't it strange!*

They were married in December 1951. On the marriage certificate, his occupation is listed as "student," Mother's as "advertising" as she had put her aspirations as a writer on hold to take a job to help him pay for law school. When he passed the bar, they made a pact: he would support the family as a lawyer; she would make Art. Together they would raise their children.

My grandparents owned a two-story duplex nearly identical to thousands of other homes set cheek by jowl in the long, deep green tunnels formed by the Dutch Elm trees whose limbs met and interlocked above the numbered side streets of South Milwaukee. After marrying, my parents rented the upstairs flat from them. Father was hired by the American Bar Association in Chicago to travel around the Midwest lecturing young attorneys on legal ethics—the rules governing the conduct of lawyers and judges.

Continuing a family tradition, they chose for their sons Celtic middle names beginning with the letter "A" like our father's, whose middle name was Arthur—Kevin *Alansson*, Britt *Arvid*, and Daron *Aric*. (Gilda and I continued the tradition—our sons' middle names are *Alejándro* and *Alemán*, together the first and last names of Gilda's Nicaraguan grandfather.) Aric is a variant of Alaric, the king who led the Goths in the conquest of Rome. In Old Norse, it means, "Rule with mercy." Hagen is a royal boy's name of Irish and Gaelic origin. The Irish pronounce it, as Father did, *hay-gen*. However, it is also a variant of the Old Norse *Hakon*, derived from the elements *ha* (high, chosen) and *konr* (son, descendant). The Norwegians pronounce it *hah-gen*. The German variant is pronounced *hah-gen* as well.

My brother Kevin wore metal braces on his legs for most of his childhood that did not correct the contour of his legs; they did succeed in causing him excruciating pain, about which he never complained. This stoicism developed into an uncomplaining endurance of psychic pain. My brother Britt also wore leg braces, about which he complained bitterly and which he kicked off in his sleep. Mother described the prospect of a lifetime of bowleggedness, to which he, throwing his braces down the stairs, shouted "Fine!" I cheered him on. She rounded on me and asked, "You, too?" I nodded. She placed her hands on her hips, looked down at the floor, shook her head, smiled ruefully, and said, "My boys." So much for braces.

I arrived less than a year after the Other Daron's death. I, the second Daron Aric Hagen, was delivered of Gwen Leone Johnson (aged thirty-two years) and Earl Arthur Hagen (aged thirty-three) on 4 November 1961 at 9:50 p.m. at Mount Sinai Hospital in downtown Milwaukee. "Previous pregnancies" listed on my birth certificate included two "children now living" (my brothers Britt and Kevin), one "abortion prior to twenty weeks," no "children born dead—20 weeks or more gestation," and one (the first Daron) "child born alive—now dead." I weighed six pounds and eleven ounces. And, like my elder son 47 years later, when I was born I did not cry.

◆◆ 2 ◆◆

The Big Cedar House
1961–1967

Some streets in the near north suburbs of Milwaukee are still flanked by tall stately American and Dutch Elms. During the first part of the 20th century, this was the street tree of choice for many mid-western cities. Its tall vase shaped form with the leaves touching mid street created a cool, cathedral-like feeling on city streets. During my childhood, all but a very few of them were felled by disease. The house at 2018 South 28th Street looked pretty much like all the other houses in the neighborhood, except that a single magnificent Elm tree—the only one left on the block—survived in front of it.

My first clear memory is of looking up, ecstatically happy, from within my stroller at sunshine filtering greenly through the canopy of leaves formed by the trees on the street in front of the duplex. (When my son Atticus was three, as we picnicked beneath a Sycamore tree in Riverside Park, he asked what kind of trees there were in Heaven. "Sycamores, or elms," I replied, with certitude. He shook his head gravely, making a mental note.) My second memory is of sleeping with my toy vacuum cleaner and Tao, the sister of Pra (one of Mother's Seal Point Siamese cats who, because she kept weaving between her legs when she was carrying me, was given away to relatives shortly after I was born), contented.

The only room that was off-limits to me at my grandparents' house as a child was their bedroom. Naturally, I spent as much time in there as I could. Both single mattresses were very, very hard, and covered with textured white spreads of indeterminate age that smelled of lye soap. Grandfather's bed was closest to the window. Grandmother's sheets smelled of lavender; his smelled like Bengay and Copenhagen chewing tobacco. To my delight, he snuck me sugar wafer cookies from the bottom drawer of his bedside table, in which he also kept a pocketknife, a bottle of Bay Rum aftershave, and a fingernail clipper. I once checked her bedside table for treasures and found nothing but a King James Bible.

In the front closet, there was a large canvas blue bag filled with well-worn Froebel blocks. Next to it sat Grandfather's enormous galoshes, their tops broad enough that I could wear them as hats, and a pile of thick telephone books. On a high shelf, resting in tissue inside a hatbox, was Grandmother's mink stole shawl collar, which both attracted and repelled me. As was traditional, it was circular: a little preserved mink's face, black glass eyes on either side of its snout, its teeth lodged into its own tail, formed the clasp. Every time I stayed overnight, I drew the box down from the shelf, buried my face in the supremely sleek fur, and carried on long conversations with the mink. When I was in high school, long after she had ceased caring about her appearance, I bought her a very expensive wide brim hat made of blue wool felt and velvet by André of Montreal which, when I gave it to her, made her smile more broadly than I had ever seen before. She wore it one Easter, put it in another hatbox, which she stacked atop the mink, and never wore either again.

In fall 1962, our family moved west of Milwaukee to the northeastern corner of New Berlin, a lightly developed area consisting mainly of farmland south of Brookfield and the Village of Elm Grove, and between West Allis and the affluent town of Waukesha. We lived at the end of a cul-de-sac named after Enoch Gardner Needham, the farmer whose 1868 Italianate cut-stone house still stands nearby and whose farm was purchased in 1912 by a West Allis businessman named Otto Conrad and developed by him as New Berlin's first subdivision. The first area residents were blue collar workers at the (now defunct) Allis Chalmers manufacturing plant just to the east, which could be reached by the Milwaukee Electric Light and Streetcar Company's inter-urban light rail line (now a bike path) built for that purpose.

The densely-wooded slice of the original farmstead, Needham's Woods, was subdivided during the 50s. 13014 West Needham Drive consisted of a low-lying, triangular lot bounded on three sides by a stream called Underwood Creek. In 1957, a German couple named Feichtmeier designed and built on it a Frank Lloyd Wright–style cedar house banded by tall picture windows and topped with sweeping slabs of sloped roof.

When they sold it to my parents, the asking price for the house was surprisingly low. It took a few rainstorms for them to understand why. As the suburbs to the north in Brookfield developed, the volume of rain water flowing downwards into Needham's Woods gradually increased, until, by the early 70s, every time it rained, the placid, trickling, six-inch-deep Underwood Creek in which I spent entire summer days building dams, became a roiling, surging, six-foot-deep river and our backyard a lake. (Forty years later, the current owners are in the middle of a lawsuit with the City of New Berlin. Remediation is likely to cost over ten million dollars.)

All of that was in the future when we settled there in the early 60s. At the beginning, Father was our family's breadwinner. He boarded the train to Chicago on Monday mornings where he worked for the American Bar Association, and returned home on Friday nights, each week slightly more unraveled from the fabric of our family's life than the last. In 1954, seven years before my birth, Mother, writing about Father, observed in her journal:

> *I knew he was acting again and the knowledge irritated and embarrassed me—for him. However, as I watched him I knew none of these things could touch him. There was something just magnificent about him. He was completely absorbed in his pose. He moved his long thin hands in an awkward pantomime as he talked. But, his eyes glistened, trembling over with a light that took him away from and above his adolescent posturing, and made him instead a figure taut with life, eloquent with intensity. These were the moments I adored him: despising his affectations, but breathless before the drama of the emotion he was capable of evoking from within himself. For all his debaucheries, Earl was a young god. A satyr, perhaps, but slim and so graceful, compelling even in his vulgarity. But now he's becoming fat, and there's something obscene about a fat satyr. And once his lips may have tasted of a secret and forbidden wild honey—now the complacent flavor of pot-roast.*

One summer she trimmed her long auburn hair short like a boy's. Sundresses gave way to Capri pants and men's dress shirts cinched at the waist. Pulling off her gardening gloves, she'd laugh at how rough her hands had grown laying out sprawling, verdant flowerbeds filled with Irises, Tulips, Phlox, Poppies, Roses, Jacob's Ladder, Columbine, Forget-Me-Nots; as well as more tender Annuals like Impatience and Prince William, Marigolds and Firecrackers. She happily destroyed the shocks in the beat-up Ford station wagon we called "Thunder-'n-Lightning" by hauling home Lannon stone from a nearby quarry and huge bags of cocoa bean shells from the Ambrosia chocolate factory. She'd spread the shells on the gardens as the sun rose, wet them with a fine mist from the hose, then sit back and wait for the noonday sun to unlock the combined aromas of chocolate and flower blossoms, good earth, and newly-mown grass. We listened to the birds back then. She disliked blue jays—"Nasty, bossy birds," she'd say, stubbing out her cigarette—and crows; but she loved the wren's call, and managed to entice at least one to move in each summer.

The Ford sailed over the smooth, sun-soft asphalt-paved country roads bounded by cornfields, lumbered up over hills in heavy *jetés* through mirages on the way to Lake Denoon, all of us contented, kittenish with heat, like characters in a Paul Bowles novel. Once there, my brothers would disappear for the rest of the afternoon with the other big boys. Naked, I collected stones in the shallows and arrayed them on the dock in tribute to my dazzling Mama, dispenser of sandwiches, quick embraces, and suntan lotion, working the *Saturday Review* acrostic under an umbrella on the beach.

How comforting and cool the Big Cedar House felt during the long evenings that followed those days—Father far off in Chicago, Kevin sprawled on his bed reading Tolkien and Heinlein, Britt building model airplanes in the basement, the sound of Mother's typewriter breaking through the chirping of the crickets in short, chaotic bursts. The stories that rolled off the old Royal's platen were submitted to the big east coast magazines—*The New Yorker, Dial, Saturday Review*, and *Ladies' Home Journal*.

Father and my brothers Britt (*left*) and Kevin in the flat above my grandparents' home in South Milwaukee a few months before I was born, in 1961.

Mother's cheekbones capped a radiant, intelligent smile like serifs on the letter U. Her nearly translucent skin was the result of her three-pack-a-day smoking habit. She had the same ropy hands her mother did. Until I saw Natalie Wood in *West Side Story*, I thought her the prettiest woman in the world.

On the weekends, Father set us to work manicuring the yard. He designed, and we erected, retaining walls from truckloads of broken asphalt and concrete, built traffic bond pathways, cleared underbrush, and felled trees. Father built for us a sandbox nestled into a bend of Underwood Creek that was as big as a tennis court in which I—playing hooky—constructed elaborate, labyrinthine sand cities. What began as a request for permission to nail a few boards together in the crotch of a tree turned into Father's multi-year project to construct a scale version of our own home perched on fifteen-foot-high telephone poles, replete with running electricity, a cantilevered porch, and cased windows. In his mind, he built it for us; but in serving as his terrified atelier, we became pencils in his hand.

We'd pile into the station wagon and drive around dusk to the "Bluemound Drive-In." At the foot of the giant screens were playgrounds for us kids. We'd play until nightfall, and then scurry to our parents' cars for the first feature. The metal speaker hung over the lip of the window carried the jingle as four story tall cartoons of smiling hotdogs in buns, boxes of popcorn, and giant plastic cups filled with soda marched across the screen singing, "Let's all go to the snack-bar, to get some 7-Up!" Mother doled out bologna, liverwurst, and salami sandwiches on white Wonder Bread, lavishly spread with mayonnaise and iceberg lettuce from a large green wicker basket. There was Dad's Root Beer and Graf's 50–50 for us, steaming black coffee from a thermos for them.

Swept up in the drama of a showing of *The Ten Commandments* at the Drive-in one Saturday evening, I reenacted—hockey-stick staff in one hand, phone book commandments in the other—Moses' parting of the Red Sea on the back patio when we got home while a "ringy-ding-ding" party tootled away in our neighbor's backyard. "GO TO GOD!" I roared into the darkness at the top of my prepubescent voice. Frank Sinatra's voice (Bert Kämpfert's *Strangers in the Night*) stopped abruptly, the record player's needle scratched to a halt, and a lone glass shattered in the ensuing silence.

Over the years, we kept a dozen dogs and cats, rabbits and guinea pigs, snakes and turtles. Dusk brought a parade across the back lawn of raccoon mamas and papas, strings of babies trailing behind. At least a dozen lived under the garage. My beloved beagle Cinnamon was an agreeable bitch—so agreeable that she had three litters of puppies in two years. We washed the afterbirth off the pups with tepid water and fed them with medicine droppers warmed milk and honey. I delivered a few of them, reaching into her womb and easing them out as she looked over her shoulder at me, too spent to push them out.

In August 1965, I was four: the sound that stirred my heart most was the dog day burr of summer cicadas. I'd run into the middle of the lawn, close my eyes, lean my head as far back as it would go, feel the sun on my face, spin around, and imagine I was swimming in the hot, lively air above me, awakened after a seventeen-year-long subterranean slumber. A man from the school district came by to administer a test. "What is Mars?" he asked me as we sat on the back porch drinking lemonade. "A candy bar," I replied sensibly. "But what else might it be?" he asked. "We haven't discussed that yet," I answered gravely. A week later, I began kindergarten two years early.

Left at my grandparents' home overnight, Grandfather took me with him to the tavern at the corner of 35th Street and Rogers for Sons of Norway meetings. These consisted (in my memory, at least) of a dozen old men with snowy white hair built like oil drums wearing flannel shirts and green work bibs speaking Norwegian and eating steamed cod and lutefisk with big mugs of Pabst Blue Ribbon beer—the beer was fresh: the Pabst brewery was less than a mile away. Enormous rough hands tousled my long, straight hair as I sat, perched atop a bar stool, drinking Orange Nesbit soda pop from the bottle. As their voices grew louder, the tousling got rougher, until I'd retreat to a booth in the back, where I'd feed the fistful of nickels (the cost rose to a dime at some point) I'd been given into the jukebox. I'd sing along with Frankie Valli (*Can't Take My Eyes Off You*), Tom Jones (*I'll Never Fall in Love Again*), Oliver (*Jean*), Blood, Sweat & Tears (*God Bless the Child*), and the Beatles (*Something*), my orange moustache growing darker with each bottle of pop until I fell asleep. At the end of the night, Grandfather would scoop me up, loft me easily over his shoulder, and ferry me home through the quiet Milwaukee night, my face buried into the deeply comforting crease between his shoulder and neck, where I'd breathe in the safety of his immensity.

In August 1966, I was five: the "59 Outdoor" showed the film *Born Free*—the adorable lion cubs, the stunning shots of the African veldt, John Barry's intoxicating score. Heaven. Falling asleep in the back of the Ford in my pajamas with the Main Title of the grown-up second feature as my lullaby, feeling safe, and contented, I dozed until I was slung over Father's shoulder like a sack full of potatoes, heat lightning flashing in the distance and gravel crunching beneath his feet. The drowsy bliss of being carried in from the car to the house afterwards; he smelled *good* then, like *safety*—like Mennen aftershave and Borkum Riff pipe tobacco, healthy sweat, and Ivory soap. During the humid summer months, the aroma of the Western Red cedar exterior of the Big Cedar House and the Atlantic cedar paneling inside combined with tobacco (Father's pipe tobacco; Mother's Pall Mall cigarettes) made the house smell like a humidor. Waking slightly as he'd place me gently in my bed, I could make out the smell of mown grass, pot roast, our pets, and my own skin.

That was the summer that I modeled for Mother's statue of the boy holding a frog behind his back. When not modeling for her, or I swam with my friends Derek Wittowski, David Eyrise, David Burns, and Mark Medved for ten-hour stretches at the Greenfield Park pool, turned as brown as a filbert, became drunk with sunshine, and enjoyed the healthy silkiness of my own skin. I spent afternoons building dams across Underwood Creek, drawing treasure maps, catching and releasing bugs, or making believe I was *La Longue Carabine* in the woods. My brothers and I trespassed, burgled, smoked cigarettes, and vandalized. I got concussions, impetigo, poison ivy, ringworm, broken bones, crushed toes, and stitches. We fought a lot, but we were also fiercely protective of one another. I was the Baby, and I knew it; Kevin was the Responsible One and accepted the role; Britt was the One Who Fought Back. Whether we grew to dislike Father because he was absent during the week when we were small, or because he was an angry, abusive, authoritarian on the weekends when he was home, I don't know. Despite being roused at 5 a.m. on the weekends for service in what my brothers and I referred to amongst ourselves as "Dad's Backyard Boot camp," they were certainly the happiest of my childhood.

In August 1967, I was six: I received my first piece of mail—a creamy envelope with "The American Bar Association, Chicago, Illinois" embossed in the corner reserved for the return address. "Master Daron Aric Hagen, Esquire" marched across the middle in heavy, serifed Times Roman—clearly typed on a manual like Mother's Royal. The letter sat all summer, much caressed and deeply treasured, propped against the lamp on my bedside table as, before bedtime each night, Father read to me from Harper Lee's *To Kill a Mockingbird*. As summer deepened, so did my love for Scout, Atticus, and Jem. Father's voice halted frequently for emphasis and to give me a chance to digest what was happening as he read the trial scene. I sometimes drifted off to sleep during the pauses, jerking awake when he resumed. Finally, he read, "He would be there all night, and he would be there when Jem waked up in the morning." Confused, anguished, I made believe I had fallen asleep. After he withdrew, I opened the envelope, drew out the single sheet of paper on which he had typed, "I love you, son," and thought, *If I ever have a son, I'll name him Atticus.* Those were the hours that I loved Father best.

◆◆ 3 ◆◆

We're Little. He's Big
1968

Watching the beatings in Chicago during the Democratic National Convention on television, aware of the growing unrest on college campuses, furious with each new revelation that our government had been lying to us about the course of the war, Kevin announced that he planned to campaign for Nixon because "he said he'll get us out of Vietnam." News of the Tet offensive in January had radicalized him: he began taking the bus downtown to volunteer for the Hunger Hike on weekends; and took me with him on the Badger Bus to Madison to march in anti-war demonstrations. "What do you know about *anything*?" Father hissed, grounding us, when he found out. In April, when the Reverend King was assassinated, we joined a demonstration in front of the Milwaukee County Courthouse. With icy certitude, Father promised us that if we protested again, he'd beat us to within an inch of our lives. We believed him, because we never knew which man would step through the front door—a jovially stoned Falstaff, or a nastily drunk Richard III. Drunk, he'd yank us out of bed in the middle of the night and command us to scrub the kitchen floor. "This place looks like a pig sty," he'd bellow. "Clean it up!" Again, and again, he'd hiss, "You all think you're smarter than me," as we, small, terrified, groggy, in our pajamas, faces inches from the linoleum, scrubbed on, buttocks raised as though in prayer.

I was drawn to the piano because Kevin, whom I idolized, was a gifted pianist. At the beginning of my first lesson, Adam Klescewski, our piano teacher, a Holocaust survivor, sat me down on the piano bench backwards and commanded me to sing an A, which I did. I possessed absolute pitch, grasped immediately the concept of sharps and flats, and demanded to know what was between the notes. I now retain excellent relative pitch—where did the "perfection" go? I wonder. He taught me the names of the lines and spaces in the treble and bass clefs: "Every Good Boy Does Fine; FACE; Good Boys Do Fine Always; All Cows Eat Grass." I hated practicing. (I *still* do) and soon began paying Britt—who ratted me out anyway—a dollar to tell Mother that I had practiced. He'd tell her anyway. Then, he'd say, "No-no-no, this time I *promise* I won't tell her you didn't practice!" So, what began as a bribe transformed smoothly into extortion. (Even early on, Britt had skills.) After a few months, the little spinet with the feather-light action lost its appeal. During my final lesson, I noticed digits tattooed on Klescewski's forearm. That afternoon, by chance, I discovered on a very high shelf, along with a lot of other books about the Holocaust, an oversized book of tenebrous, horrifying concentration camp photographs called *Despotism*. Secretly, obsessively, returning to the book, I associated from that point on practicing the piano with Klescewski's tattoo.

I was taken to a Milwaukee Symphony Orchestra concert that included the Largo of the Ninth Symphony of Antonín Dvořák. Nixon had won the '68 election and my favorite toy was a plastic Apollo 7 model. The weather was warm, and raining pitchforks. Small and awestruck in a plush red velvet seat in Uiehlein Concert Hall, I was mesmerized by the conductor, Kenneth Schermerhorn. He was strikingly handsome, and athletic. Charismatic, when he raised his arms it was easy to imagine that he was celebrating the Eucharist. In fact, he radiated the authority of a priest, but his back was to us, and there was sensuality in his movements when he cued the glittering array of brass instruments, sumptuous strings, and bird-like woodwinds that stirred me. He was more than a shepherd guiding a flock; he was the orchestra's supreme sovereign—he was the only one who literally knew the score, and the congregation read only their assigned lines. I didn't possess then the language to put words to what I was thinking and feeling, but I understand now that what I was experiencing was the intersection of aesthetic, political, psychological, and spiritual forces that constitute performance at the highest level. It blew my mind. The concert hall was like a cathedral, the audience like a congregation, and the communion—for me, at least—entirely spiritual. As Stephen Colburn played the ravishing English horn solo in the Largo of the Dvořák, I felt a lump in my throat, a profound sense of longing, the feeling of being tugged out of myself and suspended in midair. That was the moment, at the age of seven, that I knew that, no matter what, I intended to *be* Music.

In retrospect, I'm not surprised that—sitting in Uiehlein Hall trying to decide which of the many instruments on stage I would most like to play—I decided to become a composer first and a performer second. It was because Father had unintentionally taught me that although Power can compel, it does not last; Mother had by example taught me that Authority can inspire, and therefore last forever. Like Love, Authority must be earned. Every time a new piece of music is read for the first time the composer starts with all the Power and no Authority. If the music inspires and moves the performers, then the composer's Authority grows. If it does not, well, as Virgil Thomson once told me, "Don't worry about withdrawing pieces, baby; they have a way of withdrawing themselves."

During winter—the Big Cedar House was minimally insulated—beautiful sheets of ice formed over the picture windows, so that they looked like frosted Depression glass. Glittering, dangerous icicles—some as long as ten feet and too heavy to lift—hung down from the eaves like enormous fangs. My brothers and I used to knock them down with shovels. Much of the roof was flat and required shoveling after a heavy snow. It leaked steadily in every season, sort of like a grand upside-down ark, or—as I fantasized as a child lying on my back on the floor and looking up into the front room's lofty rafters—a capsized Viking Longship.

My brothers and I never determined whether Father had been fired by the American Bar Association for drunkenness, or whether Mother's explanation that he had tired of teaching theory and decided to go into private practice was true. Maybe both were. In any event, some sort of adult discussion about it had taken place. "Your dad will be happier with us. This is going to be a fresh start; you'll see," she told us as we watched Neil Armstrong take "one small step." We were genuinely frightened by the prospect of having Father around all the time. The immediate effect was economic: Father's income dropped to that of a freelance newly hanging his shingle. Consequently, every few months, the power and the telephone were disconnected for non-payment; the furnace would be shut off for wont of fuel oil; several times, the bank sent someone over to inspect the house prior to foreclosure.

At least for a few years, I think that Father worked as hard to moderate his drinking as he did to build his practice with his law partners, John J. Valenti (later Milwaukee County

Court Commissioner and County Supervisor) and James Koconis (also a Milwaukee County Board Supervisor). Private practice should have suited him. He had partners, yes; but he was his own boss. He had to show up for court, of course; otherwise, his schedule was his own. Britt worked for him briefly as a paralegal and speculated that Father was a fox who could be beaten by the superior research of hedgehogs in jury trials because he felt that charisma trumped preparation. He practiced a fair amount of criminal law early on, but Mother made him stop when, during a case involving local heavies, we began receiving threatening telephone calls at home. He had a weakness for *pro bono* clients. Like Atticus Finch accepting vegetables from farmers during the Depression, he accepted as payment broken stereos, appliances, even a truckload of gravel once. It appeared, from what I could piece together from the handful of files that were still in his office downtown in the Plankinton Building after he died when I closed it, that, after our family dissolved, he settled into uninspired probate work for the balance of his career. Possibly he was just better at talking *about* the law than *practicing* it.

Perhaps Father told himself, as I used to, that the people with whom he drank were friends and allies with whom he was "networking." Every couple of weeks—usually after a night out carousing—with his buddies Peter Kafkas (later an Office of Disability Adjudication and Review Judge) and Louise Tesmer (then an assistant district attorney for Milwaukee County, later a Wisconsin Circuit Court Judge and a member of the Wisconsin State Assembly)—Father's frustration would boil over, and bad things happened.

Now that he lived at home, he stopped eating dinner with us and spent his time exclusively in the den on the bottom floor of the house. That was fine with us. The trips to the drive-in as a family stopped. The idea that we as a family shall have ever done such a thing became laughable. My brothers and I joined every after-school activity that we could to avoid running into him. Father's nickname for me was "Fats." (I was an overweight kid until well into high school.) He probably didn't mean anything by it; but the negative self-image, once established, stuck. My weight has gone up and down over the years, but nobody, not even my lovers, would ever, *ever* accuse me of thinking that I was attractive. Deeming oneself unattractive was one thing; but it was obvious to me even then that he had instilled in my brothers a sense of self-loathing long before they got to high school. Although I had learned to keep my head down and benefited from their efforts to shield me, my brothers were beginning to receive the harshest bullying, and the hardest blows of our childhoods.

A big summer rainstorm was forecast. The perennially leaky roof on which we stood requiring repairs, my brothers and I stood atop the Big Cedar House with Father. Our feet sank into the tar and gravel as we watched him pour molten glop over what he guessed was the offending spot. Kevin, now twelve, ventured, "Dad, it's going to slide off the roof. I don't think we're doing this the right way." It was obvious even to our Father that he had made a mistake. The rain began as we silently watched the tar slither into the flowerbeds below. Father's fist shot out and connected with Kevin hard enough that he fell to his knees. "I'm your father, you little shit," he snarled as Kevin, expressionless, unwilling to give him the satisfaction of appearing to have had an effect, looked right through him. "That means I'm always right. Never forget that." Years later, Britt recounted the scene that unfolded later that evening to me in a letter:

> *I can remember to the minute when Kevin chose his strategy for coping: it was one of those rainy spring midnights when we were in the basement sweeping the flood water toward the drain. Dad was angry with himself again for having bought a house in an obvious floodplain. Kevin was active in the Hunger Hike and was passionately involving himself in the perhaps flawed but well-intentioned effort to feed the hungry. Kevin was quite a passionate idealist as a teen, as you may remember. Dad hit Kevin on*

the shoulder and head, hard, and said, "By the way, there's not going to be any more of this Peace March save the world shit, either." I watched the doors to Kevin's heart slam shut.

A teacher at Linfield School described me on my report card as an "anxious gifted child" and recommended to Mother an article in the *Journal of Child Psychology and Psychiatry* entitled "The Autistic Process and Its Treatment." I was accident-prone, moody, and prey to nervous tics. I don't remember whether my brothers had them, but my repertoire included eye blinking, throat clearing, the compulsion to touch tree trunks, an inability to stop when singing circular melodies, and the silent repeating of everything I said after I said it aloud. I manifested stress by obsessively licking my lips, which grew livid and chapped, covered with cold sores. Throughout grade school, I felt like a leper because of them. Carmex—a waxy paste imbued with camphor and menthol—at least gave some relief, but it stank. The blisters split my lips so badly that Doctor Stoklas (his yellow barn also served as the headquarters for his thriving veterinary practice) put stitches in them to hold them together. That June, watching television as the news broke of Robert F. Kennedy's assassination, I worried the sutures with my fingers until they came out. Hand covered with blood, I showed it to Mother, who was weeping in front of the television. She rounded on me and slapped me, hard, for the first and only time: "Honey," she cried afterwards, hugging me, sobbing, "now you'll have a scar there for the rest of your life." Unlike the grandfatherly smells of Bengay and Bay Rum, which I still love, the smell of Carmex, like the smell of Borkum Riff tobacco, now revolt me. Although I could conceal nearly all my tics, the repetition of words was noticeable because I moved my lips when I did it. Mother was concerned enough that she made an appointment for me with a child psychologist. I have no recollection of what I said to her, but, as a result, Mother sent me to live for the summer on my cousin Clifford Duffeck's dairy farm.

Clifford's farm was far to the north, close to the Upper Peninsula, outside of a small town named Lena. He worked my cousin Gary and me hard. I knew how to work and loved it. We baled hay all day, pulling new bales from the baler as it pushed them on to the wagon, shoveled the amazing amount of shit that cows generate, and learned how to operate the scary-looking milking apparatus. Clifford was a decent, fair, gentle man for whom it was easy to work. He also functioned as a person within what I now understand to have been a dignified, non-abusive emotional range. I expect that, besides simply giving me a break from our Father, the hope was that I would have an example in my life of an older authority figure who didn't resort to physical or emotional violence. I loved living Upstate with Clifford and his family. When the summer ended, having had a break from Father's extreme mood swings, I returned to New Berlin with a better-developed sense of myself physically. I also shed the silent mouthing of words and the lip-licking. To my parents' relief, over the next few years I shed most of the symptoms that might be associated nowadays with either an autism spectrum or obsessive-compulsive disorder. As an adult, a few harmless eccentricities persist: under extraordinary emotional stress I cannot seem to resist scratching wounds until they bleed; I reflexively touch tree trunks; and I superstitiously rap my knuckles on the wooden rails of orchestra pits in theaters and opera houses.

The night I returned home, Britt and I feigned sleep when Father arrived home from work. Rain slashed down in the woods surrounding the Big Cedar House like a thousand machetes whacking at the branches—rain so intense that it made that scary tropical 20,000 frequencies at once end-of-the-universe-white-noise sound that televisions used to make after sign-off. Through the picture windows, I could see the trees flailing wildly in the wind, black and white except for when the lightning turned them a lurid, verdant green. I realized that the basement would flood again—if it hadn't already. The waspish, angry buzzing sound of voices came up to us from the kitchen—Father brutally dressing Kevin down for some infraction, Mother furious with Father for coming home drunk. Something shattered; pots and pans hit the floor; the rain slapped in sheets against the windows with a sound that I now associate with someone slapping change down on a bar. Suddenly, silence. Neither of us had the faintest idea what Kevin had done wrong. Britt whispered in the dark, "When he gets here, stand behind me." Beat. Cinnamon, my beagle, curled between my ankles, poked her head up, and cocked her ears. The door flew open. Cinnamon's claws scratched on the wooden floor as she scampered under the bed. "Get up, Goddammit," Father roared, a silhouette against the bright light. Britt pulled his knees up to his chest and curled into fetal position. I froze. Father grabbed Britt and pulled him out of bed. There was a thud as his buttocks hit the floor. Tiny fists balled, he sprang suddenly to his feet, glaring his defiance at Father. I pulled myself to my feet and stood next to him. I looked from Britt to Father: his small, yellow teeth clenched the stem of his pipe so hard that it seemed to vibrate. His eyes were wild. His face was distorted, livid. My heart exploded. There was nobody around to call out to, no time to react. My legs were useless. The sheer amplitude of Father's emotion hit me head on like a wave and brought me to my knees as though in prayer. I began trembling uncontrollably, ears ringing with the roar of the rain. He raised his hand horse head high, as if encountering enormous resistance. I looked up and saw the magnificent innocence of my big brother's indignation, his chin thrust up towards Our Father, every inch a brave little buck, his eyes blazing. Britt's shining, unbroken spirit gave me courage. I pushed up from the floor with my fingertips like a newborn fawn and reached my feet unsteadily as Britt threw his arm around my shoulder. *We're Little. He's Big*, I thought, biting the inside of my cheek, drawing blood to keep myself from crying. Tasting the blood, I wailed, "Stop it!" It was as though Father had only just noticed that we were there, so swept up was he by the intensity of his own drama. "Stop it. Stop it. Stop it," he yelled back at me, snapping his pipe in two. The word fuck twisted out of his mouth. We looked up at him, watching as emotions fled across his face like panicked soldiers. Not for the first time or the last, I saw his hand, with all the force of a 200-pound, 40-year-old man, swing as though in slow motion toward the side of my head. Britt yanked me back at the last moment. The palm curled into a knot as it passed me by. Beat. Father looked at his clenched fist and collapsed in on himself like an umbrella. My flannel pajamas were wet. I shivered. I realized that I had peed myself. Suddenly, he was gone, and the only sound in the dark was of me sobbing. "Stop it," Britt whispered. "You don't want him to come back." *It was his fault*, I remember thinking. *It wasn't our fault, it was his.* And then, like throwing a switch, I realized that it didn't matter whether I respected Father or not; it only mattered that he thought that I did. I could think and do whatever I pleased, if I kept it to myself. *He doesn't know that he doesn't know me*, I realized. *And I don't have to set him straight.* As Britt stripped off my wet pajamas, pulled out a tee shirt and some underwear, and tossed them on my bed, I realized that he was still vibrating in the moment that had just passed. I could see that there were tears of rage rolling down his cheeks, but I knew that to acknowledge them would be to compromise his dignity. As I put my clothes on, I watched as my ten-year-old brother walked to the door and locked it. "We're not supposed to do that," I said. "He'll be mad." "Fuck him," Britt replied. The rain had slowed to a drizzle, but we both knew that the basement was flooded and that it was going to be a very long night. I tried to give him a hug, but he shrugged me off. He didn't want to be thanked. In the near-silence, we heard Mother's footsteps as she climbed the stairs, heard her pause in front of our bedroom door, and then continue into her room. We listened as she shut and locked its door. The next morning, my brothers and I would band together for the first (and only) time to ask her to intervene with Father. "What kind of men would you grow up to be if I came between you and your father?" she would reply with cold pity. "You'll have to work it out yourselves," she would say, dismissing us. "Go." But that night, in that moment, Britt was perfect. The doors of his heart thrown wide, he did what a big brother could do: he asked, "Do you want to see my booger museum?" "Really?" I replied, breathless with excitement. "It's right here, on the wall, just behind my bed," he whispered. As together we marveled over the disgusting little rufous knots of dried mucilaginous glop he had stuck to the cedar paneling behind the headboard, he was my hero, and his collection the coolest thing I had ever seen.

◆◆ 4 ◆◆

Just Let It Go
1969–1976

One of the most comforting sounds I knew at the age of eight was the sound of Mother's manual Royal typewriter. The telegraphic patter, a rush of keystrokes followed by the thud of the space bar; the zestful (or pensive, or trepidatious) winding sound followed by a sharp click as she pulled on the return lever and hauled the carriage back to begin a new line. The whirr (or whine, or snarl) as a sheet of paper was pulled out; the stuttering sound as a new sheet was fed to the beast. I could tell how her work was going just by the sound of her typing. Even when it was going badly (longer pauses, more cigarettes, the sound of her chair as it screeched when she got up to look out the window) it made me feel safe. She nearly always cooked at the same time. For some reason, I remember the smells mostly of cabbage, roast beef, baking bread, and stews. She listened to violin concerti, one after the next, or the local classical radio station, WFMR, or Frank Sinatra singing Cole Porter.

I worked hard not to disturb her, but I was young, and, if it was summer, I'd inevitably ask her one too many questions, derail her train of thought, and pull her out into the sunshine, where she'd set me a task pulling weeds as she tended her magnificent irises. The hotter the sun beat down, the more intense the smell of the cocoa bean shells that we used to pick up in great sacks for free at the Ambrosia Chocolate Company in the Menominee River Valley and spread on the gardens like mulch. Massive broods of cicadas sang, their husks mixing in with the cocoa bean shells when the nymphs burrowed up out of the ground, molted, and reached maturity.

She was beautiful, and she knew everything. I was her smart son, and I wanted to learn everything. I was adored. I could read just well enough to make my way through a few paragraphs of her manuscripts now and then. The language was grown up: adult dialogue about being unfaithful, or desperate, or simply puzzled. I still recall fragments of stories about handsome young men standing at the screen door, restive wives left on their own with their children and a copy of *A Room of One's Own*, moths throwing themselves at flames, and the folly of parenthood. I remember how the stack of manuscript pages grew and disappeared into large manila envelopes, which she sent to magazines in Philadelphia, New York, Los Angeles, or Chicago.

That otherwise uneventful summer climaxed with a series of increasingly dire telephone-calls from her beloved brother Keith. A sensitive fine artist and chronic alcoholic, Keith had taken commercial work as an art director at the *Chicago Tribune* to support his family. During the last, he confessed that he intended to kill himself.

I don't remember where my brothers were, but I was still just a peanut, and there had been no time to get a babysitter. My parents took me with them as they proceeded from one bar to the next, one hotel to the next, in downtown Milwaukee, looking for him. In the end, they found him in a room at the Ambassador Hotel on Wisconsin Avenue, where he had washed down a lethal dose of chloral hydrate with vodka.

The streetlights came on as we drove westwards toward the suburbs. The javelin-like flares of light hurtled across the hood of the car as, from under a blanket in the back seat, I watched them fly by overhead. Wearing Kevin's coonskin hat (*Daniel Boone* was our favorite television show) and footie pajamas, I observed through the car window as they talked with the police, intuiting that tragedy had, for the moment at least, made me superfluous. I curled up tightly, hugging my knees, into the tiniest ball that I could. Cold. Mother, seated in the back bay of the ambulance next to the gurney, holding her dead brother's hand. The blood-clot-red rotating lights of the police car. The wondering why an ambulance was required to convey a dead person.

As we drove home, my parents spoke in subdued, strained voices, their indistinct conversation a jumble of abstract sounds, the music of them like a transmission heard from far off in space—little vocal jabs, dying falls, murmurs, sudden popped consonants, and graceful-sounding upward queries. Pauses, followed by a tumble of syllables met with another silence. "Let it go," I heard Father say to Mother. I listened to the "kuddah-*chunk*, kuddah-*chunk*" tattoo the tires made as they passed over seams in the concrete. "Just let it go."

Crackle of gravel in the driveway. The ticks and sighs of the hot engine as it cooled. The slam of the screen door as Father heaved my uncle's suitcase into the foyer. He went to the kitchen, sat heavily at the table, and poured himself the first of the only three drinks I ever saw him pour in our home. (Our second and third were the night Mother died.) I played with the horse track betting stubs that fell out as Mother, tears running down her cheeks, silently unpacked her brother's clothes for the last time, throwing away, one by one, his suits, still smelling acridly of booze, aftershave, cigarettes, and stale sweat.

The summer ended with Uncle Keith's funeral, which seemed to inspire a sea change among the adults; I could sense it as Father reached into the open casket and placed coins to pay Charon on his brother-in-law's eyes. Had his suicide induced Father to cut back on his own drinking? For whatever reason, that fall things were lighter around the Big Cedar House. School began. I was excited for two reasons: first, it meant that I would see Jean, the pretty girl who lived on Alfred Street that I had loved since the age of eight; second, because it meant that I was finally old enough to play in the band.

Jesus Christ Superstar dropped in the States in summer 1973. That fall, Kevin bought the LP's. Mr. Germanson allowed me to play them for the class. When I followed that up by playing the "God Said" trope from Bernstein's *MASS*, though, letters from angry parents prompted a telephone call from the principal, Mr. Buege (pronounced "biggy") to Mother, whom family lore holds told him that the Sixties were over and that he had better get hip. Dashing, floridly over-qualified Harry Shoplas taught band. He played a shiny trumpet, which he often carried tucked under his arm as he strutted down the hallways of Linfield Elementary School like Tony Manero in *Saturday Night Fever* prowling the streets of Bay Ridge, leaving in his wake the smell of Aqua Velva and valve oil. Shoplas flew to the barricades, proclaimed Bernstein and Lloyd Webber "modern day Beethovens" and handed me a euphonium I think because I was overweight and looked like I could lug it back and forth to school. He switched me to alto saxophone—Britt played the baritone saxophone in Harry's dance band and I aspired to playing with him. I loved the smell of wet reeds, and the taste of the cane, but I could never get the thing to play softly. Our fifth-grade band concert closed with a Bert Kämpfert tune called *Spanish Eyes*, which I recall vividly because it was the last thing I played on the saxophone.

Between classes, Shoplas smoked cigarettes in a basement lair that he shared with Norman Cummings, the second-coolest teacher at the school. My sixth grade teacher, Cummings submitted a tape recording of my radio play *Silo 14* (featuring myself, Mark Schaefer, Keith Sams, Derek Wittowski, and Mark Sorenson) to a nationwide competition. "By far the most professionally done among all the entries, it would have been the grand prize winner had it been available." The play concerned two guided missile technicians who mistakenly believe they have launched armed atomic missiles. Already a fan of Rod Serling, I had the men commit suicide out of remorse—after their deaths, the entire thing is revealed to have been a "readiness exercise." Next, I was allowed to write, direct, and star in a play that was performed in an assembly before the school body, and then a live recreation over the public-address system of Orson Welles' 1938 Mercury Theater production of *War of the Worlds*. My fascination with Welles—particularly his work during the 30s—continues to this day.

Our family was picnicking in a glen surrounded by long rows of cedar trees that were, per Father, planted by the Civilian Conservation Corps during the Depression in the Scuppernong area of Wisconsin's Kettle Moraine State Park. Feigning sleep on a blanket nearby, I heard my parents say *I love you* for the only time while tapping Dixie cups filled with pallid Mateus Rose together and watching Britt and Kevin play amongst the towering, apse-like rows of trees. Soon afterwards, inspired by what I'd witnessed, I summoned at last the nerve to declare to my first serious crush Jean Wilson my love for her: I poured my heart into my first love letter and passed it to her. The anticipation of a reply, heart pounding; exactly like sitting in the audience waiting for the curtain to rise—the chanceful-ness. And then, holding her reply in my fist, turning the note over on its back, peeling it open, reading it, experiencing for the first time how four words, written in the loopy handwriting of an eleven-year-old, can transform one's entire universe: "I love you, too." Thereafter, I walked her home from school nearly every day for two years, but never mustered the courage to kiss her, or even to hold her hand. Dan Quakkelaar set us up on a date years later, after our paths had separated—I think that we held hands during a movie, but what was the film? Where was it? Did we kiss? I think she'd been saved; I evidently, had not been. Her "personal relationship with Jesus Christ" proved an insurmountable obstacle. I still regret having lost touch with her. 40 years later, I can remember absolutely everything about her face—every detail, every single one.

Other adolescent Lutheran boys were getting their first *frisson* from the King James Bible; Nicolai Rimsky-Korsakov's *Principles of Orchestration* called out to me at the Brookfield Square Mall Walden Books. I carried it around everywhere the way a gunslinger packs his pistols. Just as my light was beginning to flare, Mother described the dimming of hers:

> I know that the dark specter lies much closer to the surface than I thought and that it is an integral part of the same great sea. I know it is not brave, dead sailors who learn to sail it, or prophets in magical coats who plumb it, because even the best of us are no more than fitfully inspired and successful fishermen and that most of us are, thanks to a compassionate God, contented shrimp reapers in isolated tide pools.

Like Mother, I loved crafting prose, but I intuited even then that for me words are too falsely specific, too easily (and willfully) trivialized or misapprehended. By contrast, music is abstract, meaningless and, simultaneously, capable of conveying the ambiguity and subtlety of the finest emotions. As Franz Liszt wrote, "Music embodies feeling without forcing it to contend and combine with thought, as it is forced in most arts and especially in the art of words." Whereas feelings can be evoked in prose, music can—if it is good—speak directly to the lizard brain.

During the Christmas holidays in 1973, Britt took me to see *The Sting*. Scott Joplin's music captivated me. *The Entertainer* was lovely, of course; but it was *Solace*, a haunting, sad tango, that affected me as deeply as the Dvořák had. I wanted desperately to be able to play it on the piano. Having forgotten pretty much everything that the fearsome Adam Klescewski had taught me, and in any event, not being able to afford lessons, I re-taught myself how to read music. I sent away to Belwyn Mills in New York for Vera Brodsky Lawrence's just-released Scott Joplin *Complete Piano Works,* the preface of which contained a lengthy biography of Joplin. Joplin's personal story moved me deeply: the fact that his ambitions as a serious composer of opera and symphonic works were thwarted by his race, his being self-taught, and even by his own publisher, captured my imagination. He had had the score of his surviving opera *Treemonisha* published at his own expense, and—though happily married—had died of syphilis contracted years earlier, while working as a pianist in a bordello. Inspired by his music and his story, I taught myself *Maple Leaf Rag, The Entertainer*, and *Solace* by writing the letter names of the notes next to the dots on the lines and spaces.

If in Rimsky-Korsakov's orchestration manual I had found my sacred text, then I had still to find a celebrant. Wallace Tomchek was the first person I met with the requisite charisma. Wally taught chorus and drama at Pilgrim Park Junior High School. A short Jewish homosexual who closely resembled Norman Mailer with curly auburn hair and a slight potbelly, the ferocity of Wally's passion for—and absolute commitment to—musical excellence was terrifying and irresistible. I loved him for it. In 1972, He taught me, and accompanied me in performing, the first art song I learned and sang—Norman Dello Joio's 1948 *There Is a Lady Sweet and Kind*. Wally introduced me to the world in which poetry and music inextricably intertwine. When James Chute, who was writing my entry in *The New Grove* in 2000, telephoned to ask what I thought the core of my output was, I told him art song because I began setting poetry to music, grafting my tunes with the poetry I have most loved before having written a single instrumental piece, inspired by Tomchek and Dello Joio's song. My first settings were of poetry by Poe, Whitman, Rossetti, Frost, and Joyce from a Harcourt anthology of British and American poets edited by Louis Untermeyer that I turn to for poems to this day. I have since set over 350 poems short and long, written dozens of works for chorus and multiple voices, and set libretti by Edward Albee, Barbara Grecki, Rob Handel, J.D. McClatchy, Gardner McFall, Paul Muldoon, and myself.

One afternoon, Wally called me into his office and commanded me to recite my (then) favorite poem. I launched into James Weldon Johnson's great narrative poem *The Creation*. After I had declaimed about ten lines, he cut me off. "Really?" he asked, incredulous. "That's your favorite poem?" I shrugged. "Well. Okay," he said. "Now set it to music." Over the next few months, I made of it an ambitious piece of juvenilia—a 25-minute-long cantata for four soloists, mixed choir, five violins, piano, and large symphonic band.

The challenging, college-level choral repertoire Wally taught us was both sophisticated and eclectic—Gesualdo madrigals, slick "swing choir" arrangements of tunes like Johnny Mercer's *Dream* in nine-part close harmony, and a yearly fully staged musical with orchestra which he designed, directed, rehearsed, and conducted. He also encouraged me to direct: I recall with particular fondness directing, among other things, a production of Thornton Wilder's *The Happy Journey to Trenton and Camden* for him.

In November 1974, Wally took our class on a field trip to a screening of the movie version of the musical *1776*. William Daniels' portrayal of John Adams—part Orson Welles, part William Shatner—enthralled me. I adopted as my credo an actual Adams quotation: "There are only two creatures of value on the face of the earth: those with the commitment, and those who require the commitment of others." I solemnly swore to myself that for the rest of my life whatever I lacked in musical talent I would make up for in hard work and commitment. I still tell every young composer worth their salt that this is a worthwhile stance.

When I moved from singing and playing other peoples' music to composing, I needed help hearing contrapuntal textures. Back then, I recorded myself playing half of the orchestra on the piano on an open reel tape recorder and played the other half with the playback—a variation on what garage bands fooling around with early 8 channel sound mixers did during the 80s and what anybody who owns a computer running the software program called "Garage Band" can do today. I realized after a while that, if I continued working that way, I'd never develop the sort of technique I imagined that a real composer ought to have. I made a conscious effort to overcome the need for it, and—with steady application over the next couple of years—did. This was a breakthrough for me. Being able to "hear" what is written on the page allowed me to begin imagining textures and gestures that couldn't be played at the piano. Nowadays, there's no stigma attached to not being able to imagine in one's head the sound of a full orchestra. That is neither good nor bad, though I tell my students, "If you can't imagine it, then don't write it." I do admit to feeling disappointed, though, when it is clear from their music that a composer didn't hear it all in her or his head, because the human brain's the best computer, and I'm old school enough to believe that that's where all the best editing takes place.

During summer 1976, inspired by *Jesus Christ Superstar*, I wrote the book, lyrics, and music for a full-length rock musical love story called *Together*. Since singing in chorus and playing piano for musical theater productions provided my primary performance outlet, it seems inevitable to me now that my first theatrical project was a musical show. The pit-players were all friends, who generously taught me how to score for their instruments as I crafted the arrangements. The process of composing, orchestrating, and staging *Together* entirely fulfilled me as a person interested in music, words, and drama; it confirmed once and for all that I was born to compose for the theater.

Good (amateurs call them "inspired") ideas, even when they seem fragmentary or pointless at the time, are too precious to destroy. I've spun entire pieces out of fragments packed away in my teens, when I intuited that I didn't yet have the experience to make them fly but hoped that someday I would. For example, 20 years after writing the score for *Together*, the verses from the title song became the choruses of the go-for-broke 70s-folk-rock aria that serves as the centerpiece of my opera *Vera of Las Vegas*. It runs even deeper than that, though: 37 years later, I returned to Wisconsin to direct the premiere of my first commercial musical, *I Hear America Singing*, at the Skylight Music Theatre, and the ballad *I Believe in Song* unfolded from the refrain of another *Together* song. I never throw anything out. Never.

Once I had decided that I was a *composer*, I committed to it entirely. I took my work and myself very, very seriously. Precociously "professional," I began keeping a "Work Log," I keep it still, and in the same dog-eared notebook. Diaries are largely self-exculpatory exercises, letters are geared toward either the recipient or history, and memory is fickle. If it seems at times in this narrative as though I draw the exact date that I finished a piece like a gun, it is because that bit of information can be found in that book and relied upon as true. It represents my life's only entirely factual record.

If I took myself seriously, Britt certainly did not. He regularly stole my "Work Log," stuffed the piano with rags, stuck tacks in the heads of the hammers, or took my manuscripts and drew pictures of pimply, cucumber-like penises or women with enormous R. Crumb-style breasts in their underwear on them. He had a thing for the actress Linda Evans. I'd launch into the umpteenth rendition of *Solace* and he'd hurtle out of Mother's armchair, pull me off the piano bench, noogie me, and say, "Play something new or shut the fuck up, asshole. I'm trying to watch *The Big Valley!*"

It being the bicentennial year, Tomchek mounted a patriotic pageant called *Spirit of '76*, "a rock celebration for young Americans," with music by gospel songwriter Paul Johnson. Our troupe toured around the southern half of Wisconsin, performing it in American Legion halls, high schools, and nursing homes—even the Milwaukee County Mental Health complex. I recall a performance there, gazing out over the audience of six hundred psychiatric patients, gripping my microphone in as close an approximation of Mick Jagger as I was able, and squealing "let freedom ring" in my white polyester pants and bicentennial logo tee shirt. Halfway through my number, careening up the center aisle, arms flapping like the wings of a pelican, a lone patient joined me—delirious, rapturous—in song. He was exquisite, florid, a soaring golden bird in his own universe. I couldn't take my eyes off him. As I launched into the chorus, I glanced at Wally, whose arms flapped also like a pelican's wings in front of the little pit orchestra. At that instant, as two orderlies converged on the patient, every eye onstage and in the audience followed him as he was frog-marched out of the auditorium, ecstatic.

Afterward, Wally drew me aside. "Did you see that?" he exulted, eyes glittering, slightly mad. "Did you?" He was ecstatic. "How could I miss it?" I answered. Wally continued, ignoring me, "Remember that moment! Look at what he achieved! Think about what you just witnessed, what you—what we all—just went through ... *together* we made that moment! Sure, the stakes change, but the hands don't! Now *that's* live performance!" Whether seated in a Greenwich Village piano bar covering show tunes while coping with "handsy" patrons, putting my own operas over from the piano for wealthy commissioners, being admonished to keep better time by ballet teachers, playing at villas in France and Italy for diplomats and scholars, performing onstage at Curtis or countless other concert halls, accepting the condescension of famous singers with big egos while coaching them, accompanying Gilda in Nicaraguan folk songs on a frail German spinet for a *tombola* in Nicaragua, or guiding my sons' small fingers through "Twinkle, Twinkle" at the family piano, Wally's exhortation has never been far from my mind.

I rarely saw Mother write anymore. Her typewriter sat for weeks with a single page in it from a story she was working on called *The Season the Moths Descended*. One paragraph, which I read again and again, turned out to be the last bit of fiction she ever wrote—

On the inside—they were sitting at the table, by candlelight—shadows pressing against the window-glass, fluttering as the flame gutted the tallow. And all around was darkness—a cave of warmth. Outside, against the windows, the moths were fluttering and beating like spasmodic pulses—or nervous, gasping breaths.

The cover letters for the stories that rolled off the old Royal's platen to the big east coast magazines were written on letterhead inscribed with our home's name, Brightwood, and our rural Wisconsin return address. Had the address alone caused the interns and junior editors to send them back unopened? Had they pursed their lips with amusement? Not a single manuscript was accepted—in fifteen years, not one. By 1974 she had stopped saving the rejection slips. The rejections (from the same magazines that I have friends and colleagues published in and working at today) that she used to read, standing in our Midwestern kitchen, surrounded by children, the smell of pot-roast, and a self-medicating bipolar husband running to fat, must have been devastating.

One summer day in 1976 I stood in the rain in my swim trunks and watched as Mother dumped everything—her manuscripts, the rejection slips, the pretty letterhead, and the Royal typewriter—into a garbage can at the head of our gravel driveway. Last went the clay and the tubes of paint. I stood there, watching the rain make the ink on the pages run, and then turn the paper into mucous-colored pulp.

I think about that rainy day when I sit on a committee judging applications for a prize or commission. How easy it was to dismiss her work, unread; I see it done sometimes by some of the people with whom I serve on composition juries and grant panels. I think about it every time I give a composition lesson or coach singers in a Masterclass. I think about that day when, on occasion, I sit across the table from a smug, careerist, entitled punk with money, a degree, and connections. With fury, undiminished by the passage of forty years, I think about Mother walking slowly back into the house and stopping when she saw me moving toward the garbage can, intending I suppose to fish some of the things out. She was a good writer. And her work with Mari Sandoz helped her to become an excellent one. I can't prove that she was, of course; she destroyed the evidence. I suppose that makes her either a victim or a heroine. But the deeper truth is that that fact may not have been the deciding factor in the end. "Leave it," she commanded, her voice tired, and remote. "Let it go." Rain fell straight down. "Just let it go."

◆◆ 5 ◆◆

Waking Slow
1976–1978

A few weeks after throwing out all her manuscripts and art supplies, Mother began working as a maid at a Ramada Sands hotel managed by her brother Garth. In time, she left that job for one doing paste-up at a local advertising agency, and then copy-writing, layout, and so on. Once Mother began working full time, it fell to my brothers and me to make dinners and to keep the house. We were very glad to help because we adored her as much as we feared Father. She moved up quickly, and, by the time I left for college, she was employed as the creative director of a glossy regional advertising-driven magazine called *Exclusively Yours* and had supplanted Father (whose private practice had never thrived) as the family's principal breadwinner.

Kevin organized a professional theater troupe called Act One Productions, then directed and starred in (with Britt) a production of Frederick Rolfe's *Hadrian VII* that played to an audience of about fifty people scattered like fishing boats across a sea of 2600 empty seats. I found my brothers' idealism breathtaking; the folly of their project was a thing of beauty. Kevin's next production was Weill and Brecht's *The Threepenny Opera*, in which I was delighted when Kevin cast me in a non-speaking role as one of Macheath's henchmen. Kevin was a fine director, already displaying as a teenager the talents that would later serve him so well in his thirty-year-plus career in orchestra management.

When Kevin moved to Madison to attend college, I began staying with him on weekends. I would take the Badger Bus from Milwaukee, drop my backpack at Kevin's apartment, and, pulse purring with anticipation, run to the cool, silent, stacks where I would spend the entire weekend alternating between flirting with college girls and paging contentedly through scores. I recall opening for the first time Sir Peter Maxwell Davies' *Eight Songs for a Mad King*. There, forming a cage, were the bars of music of the composition itself. A bracing flood of associations ran through my mind. I thought of Ilse Aichinger's *The Bound Man*, whose bonds served him as a source of inspiration and strength. I recognized for the first time the irony of music being composed that seemed so free—especially aleatoric pieces like *Music of Changes*—by John Cage.

As a composer, in flashes over the years, some lasting longer than others, I've been consciously aware of being "on," or "there," or coming from the "right place." Music emerges from a lonely, unmapped part of the consciousness. The moments I've been aware that I'm accessing that place have been my most pleasurable as a composer. The rest is the lifelong relationship between oneself, the music's evolving form, and the compromises essential to bringing something new into the world. My romance with printed music, begun during those blissful days of musical spelunking in the Mills Music Library, has never ended. After I die, my papers will reside there.

Britt grew more remote. He got a job as chef at a local steak joint and joined in the food-service ritual of drinking with the rest of the staff after closing. Deep down, he was still sentimental and tenderhearted, but Father had succeeded in breaking something inside him; the emptiness that I filled with Music he began to fill with alcohol. He was as cynical and self-loathing as a 19-year-old can be. Still, the final summer before he moved out, we spent dusk each day sitting on the curb in Greenfield Park, smoking cigarettes, and flirting with the enticing, sexually aware (and therefore theoretically available) teenage girls who hung out there. He graduated high school and followed Kevin to Madison, leaving me alone in the Big Cedar House with our parents.

Like my brothers, I spoke to Father only when Mother insisted. He ate dinner in diners. Mother arranged for us all to meet on Friday nights at a restaurant. His attendance was sporadic. One night he didn't show up at all and Mother stopped trying. Since he drove drunk it would not have surprised us to come home to a police car parked in the driveway bearing a cop with bad news. When we arrived, Father greeted Mother at the door, falsely cheerful: "Can you believe I actually ran into a tow truck?" That night, Father threatened to move out. Hurling his suits into a cardboard suitcase in the den of the Big Cedar House, he, flung the change from his pockets onto the floor and ordered me to pick it up. "Money's all you want from me; so, take it!" he snarled. I begged him to stop. "I'm moving downtown." Why did I ask him to stay when I wanted him to leave? "Why shouldn't I?" he asked. "Because … we won't be a family anymore," I sobbed. He stayed. I still bitterly regret my weakness and selfishness in having said that. Could I at that moment have given him the push that would have enabled Mother to leave him at last and to get on with her life?

Along with his driver's record, Father had ruined his credit. Back then in Wisconsin a woman's credit was linked to her husband's. When she needed to buy a car, the Wauwatosa Savings Bank in Elm Grove told her that she was a bad risk. So, she started from scratch to build her own credit there. The smug bank officer (with whose daughter I went to school) made her beg for a personal loan, which she paid back over the next six months. On Saturday mornings, she demanded that the eye-rolling teller give her cash for her paycheck before she handed most of it back to repay the bank. Next, they gave her a small car loan. Father's aggravation was palpable when, his latest car a fused jumble of metal, he was forced to hitch a ride to work with her.

At the beginning of my senior year, Mother bought me my first suit, which was to be worn for the first time during our long-planned trip to New York City. The smarmy, balding salesman at the Marshall Fields department store looked her up and down and led her to a rack of cheap polyester suits. "No, I'm here to buy something good," she told him. "Well, ma'am, what do think that might be?" I recall the patronizing salesman asking, looking at his watch. Her jaw tightened. I knew that she was deciding whether to destroy him. She dropped her Pall Mall on the beige carpet as she looked brightly into his watery eyes. "I think you can figure out exactly what I mean," she said sweetly, watching him watch her foot tick-tock back and forth on the butt like a metronome.

It was decided that Kevin and I would go. Kevin, who aspired to be an opera singer, wanted desperately to see Lincoln Center. Kevin trembled with excitement as we stood together in the middle of Lincoln Center Plaza. I wanted to see the places John Cheever had written about. It was the first time we'd ever been further away from Milwaukee than Indiana. Father, who bitterly resented the expense, refused to make the trip, so Mother paid for it. She took us to see John Cullum at his gravelly, purling best in *Shenandoah*. Raul

Julia's terrifying turn as Macheath in *Threepenny Opera* at the Mitzi Newhouse enthralled me, but I felt betrayed by the new translation—I was already a Marc Blitzstein partisan. We walked in Central Park. We ate vichyssoise (Mother taught us to articulate the "s" in "niçoise" and "vichyssoise," so that we wouldn't sound like other Americans) in an overpriced sidewalk café in Midtown (I now walk past the spot and think of her every time I visit the Century on 43rd Street) and rode the Staten Island Ferry. I recall Mother's satisfaction when, viewing a picture at the Metropolitan Museum of Art together, I noted how "beautiful" the man in it was. "Yes, men can be beautiful," she said, wistfully. She hugged Kevin and me around the shoulders and told us that we could accomplish anything in life; that if we did our best, then nobody could ever think badly of us.

It never occurred to me, passing the flocks of ballet students and the knots of instrumentalists streaming in and out of the Modernist, grandly imposing, granite-clad Juilliard School, that I'd soon audition there. Kevin made it to Manhattan for work now and then, but his road led elsewhere. For me, however, that was the day, standing on

My beloved brother Kevin Alansson Hagen's first professional headshot, taken sometime during the late seventies. He was a gifted pianist, singer and director who enjoyed a 35-year career in symphony orchestra management.

the steps of the MET, that I decided that I would someday live in Gotham. It took me another seven years, but I got there, and loved being a Manhattanite for three decades.

The trip gave me something to dream on when school rolled around again. I began putting together a music curriculum myself to run in tandem with my high school classes, enrolling in advanced music theory instruction at the Wisconsin Conservatory of Music. I was the youngest "adult student" division pupil of Judy Kramer, a no-nonsense, practical musician of great gifts and determination. When she found out that I was having no success in interesting my choir teacher Kay Hartzell, a dedicated and sensitive musician, in trying out my music, she wrote a letter to my high school guidance counselor. It read, in part, "I feel that Daron is receiving negative input, as far as his talents go, at school which is a shame…. It is to the advantage of most musicians to read through different styles of music, in addition to material being prepared for performance, and what could be better than the music of one of their peers?" A few months later, Kay relented, and permitted me to conduct in concert the chorus in one of my early compositions.

The instruction I had been receiving from Judy, coupled with the obsessiveness with which I was composing—typically five or six hours a day—vaulted my composing skills way beyond my keyboard skills. To mend that, I began piano lessons with Duane Dishaw, a sweet-natured young man at the Wisconsin Conservatory of Music. Father ferried me to them, forty minutes in each direction. During my lesson, Father warmed a bar stool. Duane, like all my piano teachers, was impressed by how comfortable I was at the keyboard. What he didn't know was that this was because, the previous winter, Mother had caused Father to agree that, if I were seated at the little spinet in the front room, I could not be disturbed. I began not just composing and practicing at the piano but eating and doing my homework there.

Because of my love of voices, words, and drama I was drawn to musical theater and opera. Then, as now, I sang my vocal music, accompanying myself at the piano. Then, I did it because I sensed that the singer and the song must be one. Now, I do it because I know that melody (and by extension all music, arising as it does from the act of singing) must be created acknowledging the physical effort required to produce it. How a singer feels physically when performing a phrase is a crucial manifestation of how he feels. I considered and failed to adapt Cheever's short story *O City of Broken Dreams* as a one-act opera, then began sketching a dramatization of Edgar Lee Masters' *Spoon River Anthology*. I abandoned that in favor of *Through the Glass*, into which I poured everything I was absorbing by listening obsessively to Kevin's LP's of Benjamin Britten's *Billy Budd*, and *Peter Grimes*, Giacamo Puccini's *Turandot*, and Kurt Weill's *Aufstieg und Fall der Stadt Mahagonny*.

I was also composing for orchestra, but I'd never played in one. It was time to change that. Harry Sturm, assistant principal cellist of the Chicago Symphony under Fritz Reiner, was hired by the City of Milwaukee to run something called the Park Promenade Youth Orchestra. I played piano in it that year. He must have liked the rake of my sails, for he took me under his bow, devised for me an introduction to the ways of the orchestra. First, I was to play piano in the ensemble for a concert. Second, I was to station myself in various parts of the ensemble and listen to how they interacted as he conducted rehearsals for another concert. Third, I was to take lessons in the rudiments of conducting from his assistant, Michael Kamenski. Fourth, I was to compose, rehearse, and conduct the premiere of a new composition. The result was *Suite for a Lonely City*—the piece that Mother sent to Leonard Bernstein that inspired a letter from him that changed my life. In his review of the concert, Jay Joslyn, the *Milwaukee Journal* critic then, wrote that I must have felt like Moses atop Mount Pisgah, looking down from the podium into an orchestral Promised Land as I led the other boys and girls through the premiere. I did.

I began composing during classes. (I still dream that I haven't graduated high school for lack of attendance.) How peculiar I must

My conducting debut at age 16 with the Park Promenade Youth Orchestra in the première of *Suite for a Lonely City* on August 10, 1978, at the Humboldt Park bandshell in Milwaukee, Wisconsin.

have seemed, corralling friends after school and asking them to show me how their instruments worked, telling my best-intentioned math teacher (a fascinating man, really, who had taught in Nigeria, Indonesia, and Brazil) Max Hilmer, that "math is an art; trigonometry is just a technique!" when he wondered how someone who could craft algorithms that aped music composition, teach himself FORTRAN and COBOL over the weekend in order to ace a computer science exam, and hack into the UW-Madison mainframe with his buddies David Merkel and Dan Quakkelaar in order to play *Star Trek* via teletype, could exhibit no interest in (or talent for) calculus.

Whether I became an insomniac as an adolescent because I loved the quiet of the early morning, or because Father made me one by rousing us at odd hours to clean up the house, I don't know. I didn't master the ability to get to sleep, once lost, until I married Gilda, and then we had children, and there was no time for sleep. In any event, the early morning was an excellent time to compose; and I did most of it then, after coming home from the movies, a date, or work. I wrote a *lot* of music—symphonies, string quartets, tone poems, art songs, piano pieces. I wrote pieces that I no longer remember having written. I would compose until I was so tired that I would literally begin walking into walls. "Honey, what sort of music can *possibly* come out of your brain if it's fried?" she would ask, directing me to bed. "And, when you wake up, can you kindly take a shower before you go to school?"

The gardens that once sprawled luxuriantly behind the Big Cedar House ran back. Successive floods smeared the gravel paths and spread mud across the lawns. The house was only about thirty years old; but because corners had been cut in its construction, it aged poorly. It was hard not to think of what the place had been and what it had become as a metaphor for the condition of our family.

Mother had become a high-powered, chain-smoking advertising executive, an artistic director with a staff, turning out a new issue of an ad-driven glossy regional magazine every few weeks. I threw myself into my nascent loves—the theatre, the yearbook, symphony concerts, old movies at the Oriental Landmark Theater. I got a job as a pinsetter, bottle boy, and occasional (under age) bartender at a local bowling alley. Learning how to tend bar required that I learn how to drink. That I did. I would, with considerable application, and despite Father's negative example, become very, very good at it. As my world began to provide a way out of Wisconsin, Mother's began to consist more and more of days at the office followed by evenings stoned on prescription Valium, her estranged alcoholic husband prowling around "his" part of the Big Cedar House feeling misunderstood, unappreciated, righteous and wronged. If I realized that, by taking her car every night to go on my escapades I was trapping her in the suburbs with her husband, I was too self-involved, too selfish, too desperate to escape, to pay any serious attention to what I callously viewed as their sadistic quadrille. I only knew that I desperately wanted OUT.

I was self-aware enough to realize that the hours each Saturday morning that I ferried Mother around in her car doing errands were precious. She loved it when I recited poems, so I took to memorizing long swatches of verse for her. We always lunched at Grandmother's house on 28th Street. The corned beef and cabbage she served every weekend melted in our mouths. I knew I was leaving Milwaukee forever, and it made me precociously sentimental. Mother always ate a chocolate bar while she shopped because, she said, "it keeps me from impulse buying." On the way to the bank, the nursery, or the post office, we drove past the manicured lawns and gracious homes in the Village of Elm Grove where most of my friends lived. We chatted happily about art, music, and literature. "What's the poem this week?" Mother asked. "I wake to sleep," I began Theodore Roethke's *The Waking* from behind the wheel. "Uh huh," she said, blowing a cloud of smoke out of the side of her mouth towards the open window, "I know: 'and take my waking slow.'" "I learn by going," I continued. "Where I have to go," she concluded. I grinned happily. "It's a poem about death," I said. She tossed her cigarette out the window, unwrapped a stick of Dentyne gum, and pressed it into her mouth. After a few beats, she turned and flashed me a sunny, lopsided smile. "Oh, honey," she said at that moment, more glamorous to me than Rita Hayworth doing the hair-flip in the movie *Gilda,* "isn't it obvious? It's a poem about rebirth!"

✦✦ 6 ✦✦

Cathedral of Dreams
1978–1979

Father was plastered. Around seven, he had called, slurring, from the Clock, a cocktail lounge downtown, and demanded a ride home. Mother had taken too much Valium to drive. Learner's Permit in hand, I headed downtown to pick him up. Double parked on Wisconsin Avenue, I waved him down. He sloped to the driver's side, in no condition to take the wheel. "Slide over," he commanded, pounding heavily on the window. Oh, he was mightily pissed. His face was flushed; his mouth was twisted into a snarl. He'd jeopardize both our lives if he got in. For the first time, I had the nerve to refuse him the keys. I drove us home. I was sixteen. It was as though Father, who we had been surrendering as a family to drinking and depression by dribs and drabs over the course of my childhood, had finally made himself into the Man Who Lived Downstairs.

Music alone couldn't yet fill the emptiness I felt, and I was too sheltered a suburban adolescent to adequately come to terms with the wild, impractical, somewhat lurid thoughts and desires my brain was generating. That night, without asking, I simply took the keys, and drove my friends Brian Anderson and David Merkel to the Oriental Landmark Theater, a Grand Prewar Temple to Cinema in downtown Milwaukee. It was only a 25-minute drive from 13014 West Needham Drive to 2230 North Farwell Avenue. For the next two years, I practically lived there. I have had a profound attachment to the place since the first moment that I entered it.

I'll never forget how it smelled. Freshly popped corn and stale cigarette smoke filled the lobby with its fragrance. Onstage, the wet dog musk of moldy fire curtains combined with the ancient aroma of long-settled dust. The air, high up in the huge balcony that yawed heavily over the orchestra like a sumo wrestler's ceremonial sash, had the arid taste of steam-heat in the winter, and the slight tang of refrigerated moisture on sultry late summer evenings.

The Oriental provided us with a refuge, a chance to see grown up movies, of which many our parents would never approve, a place to dream, to share Communion in the Dark, to play. It was the crucible in which I first began ginning up what Gore Vidal called one's "sacred story." Hormones and an unshakeable belief that in some specific way I had something unique to offer the world provided the cocktail of raw material. Our English teacher, Diane C. Doerfler provided the catalyst. Doerf, as we called her, was an inspirational teacher, a planter of seeds. I recall her now as I saw her then—tomboyish, a lovely combination of Katharine Hepburn and Jeanne Moreau, seemingly something of a Transcendentalist, personally elusive. She began the year by etching in a quick rat-a-tat-tat of chalk on the board LIFE = ART. Then, she paused, turned back to us grinning like a Siamese cat, scanned the room, purred, "Well, what do you make of that?" Thanks to the movies I saw at the Oriental and the books that Doerf gave me, my world was enlarged at the expense of myself, enabling me to grow into and desire access to, the world at large.

Designed by Gustave A. Dick and Alex Bauer, the themes of the Oriental's decor are in fact East Indian, with no traces of Chinese or Japanese artwork. It is said to be the only standard movie palace ever built to incorporate East Indian decor. Opened to the public on 27 July 1927 on the site of Farwell Station, a horse and streetcar barn as the flagship of a chain of 47 movie theaters operated by John and Thomas Saxe, Irish brothers who began as sign painters at the turn of the century, the 1800-seat Oriental incorporated elements of East Indian, Moorish, Islamic, and Byzantine design. It included three eight-foot-high chandeliers adorned with images of the Buddha, eight gleaming black porcelain lions flanking a massive tiled ceremonial staircase to the balcony, hand-painted frescoes of Turkish scenes, dozens of custom draperies, and literally hundreds of elephants—elephants everywhere, from the bathrooms to the 1920s smoking lounges to the remotest corners of the balcony.

Failing, after fifty years of continuous operation as a traditional movie palace, it came into the hands of Robert and Melvyn Pritchett, Milwaukee brothers and electricians who acquired it in 1972. They chose the films that they showed themselves until 1976, when they agreed to a proposal by the Landmark Theater (then Parallax) chain to take over programming.

There were six enormous Buddha statues—three on each side of the broad orchestra—adorned with glowing "rubies" in their foreheads, smoldering green eyes, and dim orange pools of light that warmed their ample tummies from below that remained on until the marquee was shut off, the work lights extinguished, and the lonesome ghost light turned on. The Pritchetts clearly loved the palace, and tolerated my adoration to the point where, on several occasions just before locking up for the night, they allowed me to perform the ritual.

The Oriental also boasted a shallow orchestra pit suitable for a vaudeville-circuit-sized ensemble of about 25 players, access tunnels, storage rooms, dressing rooms (with smeared autographs of now forgotten, once nearly-famous performers still on the walls), and a spacious stage with the original rigging still in place, and an organ's pipe loft. During my day, the organ was in disrepair. Now restored, every Friday and Saturday before the 7 p.m. show, the plush sounds of the Kimball Theatre Pipe Organ—the largest of its kind in a theater in America and the third largest in the world—introduce the film before the instrument sinks into the pit.

For a while, after its vaudeville years had long passed, the Oriental occasionally served as a live performance venue. I saw Laurie Anderson there. The Violent Femmes got their start by standing in one night as the opening act for the Pretenders. When I knew it best, the Oriental was still a calendar house, a place where adult things happened. It had danger implicit in its darkness, its genteel shabbiness, in the avant-garde and erotic films on its monthly bill of fare. In 1978 a double feature set you back $2.50—well within the budget of a teenage refugee from the suburbs in possession of a probationary driver's license and his mother's '75 Ford Granada.

Communion in the Dark, the sitting around a campfire telling stories to explore the unknowable, remains one of the chief reasons I compose operas. François Truffaut's *La nuit américaine* explores the theme of whether making art is more important than life for the people who make it. First seen at the Oriental, this film led me to a comprehensive engagement with Truffaut's films over the years, which climaxed in meeting him at the end of a retrospective of his work at the Regency Cinema, a second-run house on Broadway near Juilliard, in 1986. When I began composing my opera *Shining Brow*, which explores this, I asked Paul Muldoon to make this one of Frank Lloyd Wright's foremost concerns: "Can a man be a faithful husband and father," asks Wright, "and still remain true to his art?"

Suspending the audience's disbelief being the first step in making art, I made conscious note of the strategies filmmakers used to do it. During those years, I assembled the psychological and emotional skill set required for coping with life as a creative person. I couldn't help watching films critically; I was keenly aware of the artifice, and loved it. The venue was a refuge, but the films were not an escape.

The August 1978 evening that I fell in love forever with the Oriental the double bill was *Casablanca* and *To Have and Have Not*. Although it would be years before I understood that is only a single step from Max Steiner to Richard Strauss, from the moment Steiner's grand *Warner Brothers Fanfare* began, I was enthralled—more by the music than the images and narratives. Steiner's godfather had been no less a musical force than Richard Strauss; his piano teacher was Johannes Brahms, and he took composition lessons from Gustav Mahler. These men took their work seriously: as the saying goes, "there was also a movie going on."

The large and appreciative audience knew the film, hissed the villains, and cheered the great lines. It was the first time I ever felt surrounded by an audience so in tune with the rhythm of a script and set of actors that they literally sighed in unison. A few folks mouthed the dialogue along with the actors. Men wept openly during Rick's breakdown scene; people stood up when partisans at Rick's began singing *La Marseillaise* to drown out the Nazis singing *Die Wacht am Rhein*; couples consoled one another when Rick and Ilse parted.

It transported me. During the intermission, I began prowling around the theater, which already felt like home. (The only other place that has affected me in exactly this way is the artist colony Yaddo—more about that later.) My parents were on their own *Revolutionary Road* in the suburbs, their lives together unspooling. Mine was rapidly expanding here, in the semi-darkness, among the threadbare velvet seats, the mildew-perfumed draperies, the dicey wiring, illuminated only by "emeralds," "rubies," and a shaft of light slicing down from the projection booth to the broad, off-white screen with a blemish in the upper left hand quadrant.

The second feature began: Ernest Hemingway's story, adapted by William Faulkner, directed by Howard Hawks, with Humphrey Bogart and … Lauren Bacall. "You know how to whistle, don't you, Steve? Just put your lips together and … blow." The frisson I experienced was real. Seeing the film thirty-five years after it was made, I could not in my wildest dreams have imagined that I would one day meet Bacall—well, fall at her feet, anyway—on a stairway at the Dakota.

Twenty-six days later, I brought friends to see Toshirō Mifune in Hiroshi Inagaki's great *Samurai Trilogy*. There were only about thirty people scattered around the theater. The first of countless games of hide-and-seek was played out in the soaring balcony; the illusion that we were alone in the vast screening chamber became, during the third hour, a reality. No doors were locked and we got into everything: the dressing rooms, the tunnels, and the service closets. I watched Musashi's duel from behind the screen, lying onstage on my back with a sand bag beneath my head, my fingers interlaced at the nape of my neck.

That October, I was given a tour of the projection booth during the screening of Federico Fellini's *Juliet of the Spirits* and *8 ½*. I realized, watching the screen through the same hole (the "fourth wall") that the powerful projector was throwing the image through, that all the settings in Fellini were intentionally artificial so that they would appear on film as hyper-real. Opera.

The next week *West Side Story* continued to counterpoint my evolving young thoughts. I'd seen the film on television, of course, and had spent fifth grade walking to and from Linfield Elementary School singing the tune of *Maria*, substituting Jean's name. However, I had never seen the Jets swoop across a three-story tall movie screen. The boys leapt; so did my heart. The hair on my arms stood up. We were being invited not to buy into the idea of a bunch of tough street kids dancing but to witness their spirits fly through the air.

The Oriental provided my first introduction to serious camp. The double bill was *Humoresque* and *Johnny Guitar*. (Truffaut famously referred to it as a "phony Western.") The film was to me like *Weißbier* with a slab of lemon in it: all the roles, from Joan Crawford to Sterling Hayden, were clearly gender-swapped. Paired with an even higher-camp classic starring a beautiful young prizefighter of a James Garfield, a leonine Crawford, an exquisitely rumpled Oscar Levant, and Isaac Stern's hands, it made for a swampy, soupy, delightfully sentimental evening at the movies—an impossible film to forget, and one I've seen a hundred times.

Lower camp was also on the bill. The Oriental is the world record holder for a current and continuing film engagement. *The Rocky Horror Picture Show* has played as a midnight film since January 1978. I was one of the original regulars. I dressed the part for a dozens of showings, danced the *Time Warp*, brought bags of rice, toast, squirt guns, newspapers, and so forth, knew my lines ("Dammnit, Janet!") and delighted in the lovely community of genuinely joyful people that has made the Oriental the U.S. record holder for a continuing engagement of the film.

On 8 December 1978, during a double bill (*East of Eden* and *Rebel Without a Cause*), I held hands with a date for the first time. Leonard Rosenman's sophisticated modernist scores (he studied with Arnold Schoenberg, Luigi Dallapiccola, and Roger Sessions) for these back-to-back knockouts moved me more, I'm afraid, than the crisscrossing of young fingers in the dark. Eleven days later, more *film noir*—I saw *The Third Man* for the first time and immediately determined someday to turn it into an opera. In fact, I pitched an updated adaptation of the Graham Greene screenplay in 2006 to Speight Jenkins, Intendant of Seattle Opera, who nearly went for it.

I didn't just visit or even inhabit the Oriental, I infiltrated it, climbing into the organ loft, sleeping on the stage, haunting the projection booth, canoodling in the balcony, and spelunking the tunnels. Any movie would do in my Cathedral of Dreams, because, if the media can be the message, sometimes the venue is the vision.

♦♦ 7 ♦♦

Ars Longa Vita Brevis
1979–1981

Of course, I was in love. Kristie Foell had piercing, bird-like eyes, and exquisitely pale, almost diaphanous skin, like that of the child at the keyboard in Renoir's *Piano Lesson*. Her fragile, pure, airy, but very accurate soprano inspired my first published art songs, including *Thou Wouldst be Loved*, and *Dream Within a Dream*, and my first opera, a (withdrawn) monodrama called *Through the Glass*. (Ironically, these remain, over 40 years later, my most frequently performed songs. It feels quite odd to coach them as a man in my late 50s.) She was willful, exceptionally intelligent, and—unlike me—took grades very seriously. We discussed marriage. I had a ring made. On Saturday nights, we kissed in the car; on Sunday mornings, we prayed with her devout parents in church. Although my family attended the Lutheran church a handful of times when Father was trying to build his law practice, the only thing that stuck was the Lord's Prayer. The "born again" evangelical movement hit Wisconsin in '79, and most of the nicer, brighter kids at school adopted the lingo and call to witness. I don't recall whether it was Kristie or her parents who insisted upon it, but I was a steady churchgoer while we dated. I courted her with sweet sincerity and dogged persistence. Despite my wildly impractical musical ambitions, I had every intention, at 17, of marrying her. It seems to me now that, when I knew her, she was fighting her parents' exaggerated protestant asceticism. I challenged her to embrace the aesthetic and offered her a perspective of an art-centered and secular outside world that led away from Wisconsin.

Father was robbed and beaten that fall in an alley downtown while drunk. He refused to remain in the hospital, so we set up a bed for him in the kitchen. He recuperated there for a week. Mother took only two vacations during her life—one to Estoril, Portugal, for a few days; the other was to Jamaica for a week. Mother at this point took the extraordinary step of flying to Kingston. Something had happened between them. Had the drinking gotten so bad that she couldn't take it anymore? Had a jealous husband meted out the beating? A creditor? A prostitute's pimp? Had he been unfaithful for the last time? Had she taken a lover? Had she, seeing the light at the end of the tunnel in the shape of her last son leaving the house, decided to finally leave him? They spoke twice on the telephone. From the side of the conversations I heard ("You slut. You whore. What are you doing down there?") I got the impression that Mother was deciding whether to leave him.

When Mother returned from Jamaica, she retained a well-known Chicago-based divorce lawyer. (Father, when she informed him, was genuinely rattled: "You *are* serious," he said, shaking his head in wonderment.) In the event, Wisconsin marital finance laws

44

enabled Father to tie Mother's hands financially so that, if she left him (she planned to move to Paris and recommence pursuing her dream of being a writer once I graduated high school and was out of the house for good), she would be saddled with his debts and possess no equity in the family home. She had to admit that he had her trapped. Divorce plans were scrapped; Paris was probably shelved for good. Her Valium use increased.

I appreciate now—and am intensely grateful for—the disbelief with which my parents received the well-meaning but misguided advice of the high school guidance counselor who, with a sad sigh and a glance at my peculiar grades, told them that I'd be lucky to get in to the local technical college. When it became apparent that I, so focused on music, hadn't given college a thought, they didn't raise an eyebrow. They saw that I had a passion, and that I was pursuing it. That was good enough for them. As it happens, on a connecting flight to Memphis, she sat next to composer John Beall, who was then in the middle of a long and fruitful career on the faculty of West Virginia University. Needing advice about how to help her son, she struck up a conversation with John. Without his generous, thoughtful counsel, his description of what "being a composer" would likely entail, Mother would have had a much harder time blessing my otherwise clueless leap into the music world.

It seemed far-fetched, a sort of Hail Mary pass, but when Mother asked me what I thought we ought to do, I suggested that we send a score and cassette recording of my *Suite for a Lonely City* to Helen Coates. (I had read a biography of Bernstein that described how his childhood piano teacher, Ms. Coates, had become his personal secretary.) My hope was that she might forward the materials to the maestro, who, if moved to do so, might be willing to lend a few words of either encouragement or discouragement. Mother must have written quite a letter, because Miss Coates passed the materials on to her boss, who (in an example of his extraordinary generosity of spirit) replied enthusiastically.

Mother, looking slightly stunned, allowed me to read the letter once she had finished. "LEONARD BERNSTEIN," read the raised serifed letters marching grandly across the top of a half page of letterhead. "Yes," I read, astonished and trembling in our rural Wisconsin kitchen, "your son is the Real Thing, a born composer. I think he should come to New York and study at Juilliard with my friend David Diamond."

Mother sent this man Diamond, of whom we had never heard, a letter. He wrote back to her, "Helen Coates did deliver your son's score to Mr. Bernstein and Mr. Bernstein sent it on to me here with his reactions which were enthusiastic. He clearly feels your son should study with me here [at Juilliard].... Above all, though, the composition jury will need much more music to consider." I also wrote to Lukas Foss, John Harbison, and Dominick Argento and asked each for guidance. All three wrote kindly letters advising me to enroll in Madison for a year. A letter from Krzysztof Penderecki, who was teaching at Yale, urged me to apply there, but I was too intimidated to accept the challenge. I wrote to Diamond that I had decided on Wisconsin for a year, at least, before coming to the coast. After admonishing me for not putting my return address on the envelope of the letter, he concluded, "If you have been accepted into the Wisconsin school by all means go there and see how you fare.... Make your application next year."

A few months after graduating high school, I proudly accepted my first professional fee as an orchestrator from John-David Anello, the founding conductor of the Milwaukee Pops and the Florentine Opera Company. Anello was one of Father's clients. I recall vividly his conspicuously large, majestically chiseled head. He had deeply-set eye sockets, thrusting cheek bones, a noble nose, and a very high, broad forehead atop which flowed backwards a leonine mane of hair. His hands were enormous—bony, gnarled joints bulged like rings from his very long fingers. Father took me to his gracious home on Milwaukee's lakefront one evening after one of our rare joint-appearances at a Mensa meeting. A true *basso profundo*, his velvety voice rolled out of him like muted thunder. Really, he was quite grand. He led Father and me into his study and then turned and ordered Father to wait in the next room, which I liked. "My boy, I conduct the Milwaukee Symphony in some outdoor concerts each summer for the county—something I call 'Music Under the Stars'—and I need somebody to arrange a Burt Bacharach tune for one of them. Your dad says that you can do it." His heavily lidded eyes met mine: "Can you?" I was thrilled. I still have the municipal pay stub. The same summer Anello also gave me my first music-copying gig—extracting by hand the solo piano part for the *Yellow River Concerto*.

I moved out of the Big Cedar House and in with Britt in Madison during late summer when the smell—we lived down wind—generated by the Oscar Mayer Company's meat processing plant there was at its most revolting. A last-minute applicant, I was nevertheless entitled, as a resident of the State, to enroll in the University. It was the fall that James Mallon and Leon Varjian and the (student government) Pail & Shovel Party blanketed Bascom Hill with 1008 plastic pink flamingos. What a glorious, quixotic, rebellious, and ultimately rather sweet prank it was—a stunt so delicious that, 30 years later, in tribute, the City Council made the Flamingo Madison's official bird.

I landed a work-study job sorting mail for the university. The free postage enabled me to send one, sometimes two letters a day to Kristie. Britt and I fought constantly. His hedonism and drug use frightened me. He considered me—quite rightly—a prig and at Kristie's disposal. I practiced on a borrowed electric piano, observed as my cat Rimsky learned to pee in the toilet by spread-eagling himself across the round opening of the seat, and spent hours on the telephone with Kristie. In love, I hied back to Milwaukee every weekend to date her, though I admit that our long-distance relationship made it easier for me to idealize her, to pursue my music without having to accommodate her needs as a person.

My conducting teacher at UW, Catherine Comet, was a prodigy. She had studied privately with Nadia Boulanger for three years as a pre-teen, graduated from Juilliard. "Nadia never told me that I couldn't be a conductor," Comet told me. "She never charged me for a lesson, saying that when I began making money as a conductor, I could pay her back. I did." A drop-dead beautiful Parisian with impeccable technique, she terrified me. I idolized her. "How did you learn the instruments of the orchestra?" I asked her. "I dated them," she deadpanned. I left Madison before taking an orchestration class, but not before her disquisitions about instrumental combinations and the proper notation of string harmonics during my lessons had left me both edified and traumatized. I am still proud of the five measures of an orchestra piece I composed at the time that Comet singled out as "deliciously scored."

Balmy summer evenings, after a day of boating Lake Mendota with Brian Anderson, we'd saunter into the *Rathskeller* at the student union where my parents used to meet their friends, snare a pitcher of beer for a buck, and slowly get high while watching the sun set, talking. I sincerely loved living in Madison; I still feel that the twenty or so months that I was fortunate enough to live there, and the warm, humane relationships that were forged, constituted a safe place (at least in memory) to which I frequently returned during the next decade. At one of the very lowest points in my life, deeply depressed, tending bar and drinking heavily in summer 1996, just before a lifesaver of a commission from Paul Sperry and the sage counsel of treasured childhood friend Margaret Bergamini provided the impetus for pulling myself together, I got very close to quitting music and moving back to Madison for good.

My composition teacher was tall, handsome, bearded virtuoso jazz saxophonist Les Thimmig. Les grew up in Joliet, Illinois, began playing the clarinet at 6, and by 13 was subbing in Chicago jazz bands and the pits of bus-and-truck productions of Broadway shows. By 16 he had his union card; he went on to spend his formative years playing for Woody Herman, Lionel Hampton, and Duke Ellington, among others. He received his undergraduate degree from the Eastman School of Music and his master's and doctorate from Yale, all in composition. He studied with Donald Martino—whose stylistic influence can be heard in the first two-thirds of many Thimmig works, which then blossom into punchy Third-Stream bebop charts—and had been "out there" where I wanted to go—the coast, the "scene," the Larger World. Les was big—physically intimidating and coolly aloof in that gigging jazz musician way. I grew to admire him.

I had applied late, and Les made it clear to me that he was doing me a favor by adding me to an already-full studio. It could not possibly have ingratiated me to him when, by way of explanation, I described Bernstein's letter to Mother; and I doubt that the advice I'd subsequently received from Argento, Foss, and Harbison to attend Madison "until I was ready to reapply to a school on the coast" inspired him to restrain himself from busting my chops. In turn, I reflexively responded poorly to being patronized—whether deserved (it was) or not. During my lessons, Les' eyes drifted periodically to the clock over his desk. "Sorry, man," he explained early on, "I've got a busy schedule. I'll have to eat my lunch during your lesson." Bits of it fell on my music. As he paged through it, his large hand swept the crumbs away, and then came to rest on the desktop, where his fingers drummed accompaniments to the music (not mine) running through his head.

Les conducted a reading session of *Kamala at the Riverbank*, a tone poem I'd spent the fall writing. Diamond's response, when I sent it to him, was dismissive:

Certainly, I hope you will make a good impression in all the entrance exams required. After all, Mr. Bernstein's recommendation to me matters, but it will not matter that much to the jury unless they agree. I say your potential is large. But you are very young and art is very long, and it takes many years, even decades to develop a strong technique, an individual style. As of now I sense enormous facility, no interesting thematic ideas, and little self-criticism. So, you see, there is the goal to set for real achievement in a very difficult art form. And I am willing to help you reach that goal. So, let us hope for good results from the jury, the exams, the Deans.

Demoralized, I nevertheless applied to Juilliard as I'd been instructed. My parents argued bitterly about whether to spend the money on the airplane ticket; Father agreed to contribute his share only when Mother said, "If he is turned down, then maybe it will convince him to go to law school the way you want him to." I'd impressed Les with my basic skills enough that he had felt comfortable hiring me to copy the parts to his latest orchestra piece, *Amethyst Remembrance*, but he made it clear that he thought Juilliard was the longest of shots. His letter of recommendation, which I steamed open, reflected his misgivings: "Daron's music operates within a narrow and highly derivative framework excused perhaps by his inexperience and youth."

I flew to New York, spent a day taking theory, music history, and ear training exams, attended that evening a performance of Sondheim's *Sweeney Todd* (Len Cariou was about to be replaced by George Hearn, Angela Lansbury—who, as a light grace note to this memory, displayed elegant generosity by sending to Gilda a beautiful letter when, in 2002, we married—was still playing Mrs. Lovett) at the Uris Theater, and the next morning presented myself at the appointed hour for my audition interview. It was evident to me the moment I entered the room that I was to be sent packing. The men who were to determine my future—Diamond, Elliott Carter, Milton Babbitt, and Vincent Persichetti—sat at a long table on one side of the room. I seated myself in a straight-backed chair on the other side, facing them. The scores I had submitted sat in a neat pile in front of Diamond.

"Lenny wrote to me about this young man," began Diamond. A flicker of interest—or annoyance—flitted across Babbitt's face. "Why do you want to be a composer?" asked Persichetti. "Because," I replied, "it is the only thing I have ever done that I know I will never be as good at as I want to be." My bravado met with cool disapproval. Diamond moved to the piano and, moving from low to high, stabbed at six or seven pitches. "Kindly sing the pitches back and name them," he said. I started to sweat as I sang the first three or four and then trailed off. "Your ear is not your strong suit," he clucked. Next, Persichetti moved to the piano. "I am going to play a little medley for you of various themes. Just call out the name of each, if you can, as I play, and I'll move on to another." I recognized the unmistakable pungency of the *Tristan* progression.

"Good," he smiled warmly. I was dazzled as he *seguéd* directly into a Gershwin tune whose name I didn't recall, "That's fine," he said, continuing. Then I missed two, and he played something that was clearly Mozart, but what I didn't know. I tittered nervously. "What's that?" asked Persichetti. "I've never seen someone do that before," I effused. "That was wonderful!"

"Yes, well," said Diamond. "Evidently the repertoire is not your strong suit either." Carter looked out the window. Babbitt looked at the table in front of him. Neither made eye contact with me or said a word. Diamond reached for one of my scores and flipped it open. After paging through it idly, he pushed it over to Babbitt, who didn't look at it. "Mr. Hagen," said Diamond funereally, "it is felt that you should … return to Wisconsin and … develop your technique."

Clammy with cold sweat in my Kermit-green leisure suit with a round-trip airplane ticket in the pocket, I thanked the men who had just passed judgment on me, excused myself, went to the nearest bathroom, and vomited. Seated on the toilet, I wept with humiliation, fury, and frustration. They had been clear: I was not good enough. I flew home a day early. My parents, who didn't know that I'd be arriving that night, were asleep when I arrived.

Around 4 a.m. Father woke up, still drunk, mounted the stairs to the third floor, and began pounding on Mother's locked bedroom door, braying, "Let me in. Let me in." "Oh, Earl," she pleaded in a voice reserved for him alone. "For God's sake, please leave me alone." Presently, he stopped pounding, and did. I gathered my things and slipped out of the house, took the next bus to Madison, and never revealed to them that I had witnessed their sad moon play.

I moved home for the summer and took a job working the graveyard shift in a White Hen Pantry convenience store to be closer to Kristie, who had been accepted to Yale. Ron Cuzner, the velvet-voiced jazz aficionado who then hosted "The Dark Side," an overnight program on the local classical station, WFMR, was my company, along with the occasional stoner, pair of cops, prostitute, or insomniac. I read philosophy, analyzed Beatles tunes, and wrote poetry when not stocking the shelves, making sandwiches, and selling porno magazines.

That summer Kristie sang a 45-minute monodrama on my own libretto called *Through the Glass* that I wrote for her. Matthew and David Eyrise lit it; I staged it in the round and conducted the little chamber orchestra. Riffing on tropes from Lewis Carroll's *Alice in Wonderland* crossed with Samuel Beckett's *Krapp's Last Tape,* my libretto was a hot mess. The through-story, such as it was, concerned the moment at which a woman suffers some sort of nervous collapse, recovers, and decides to get on with her life. This is essentially the same story I chose to tell in *Amelia,* for the Seattle Opera, over thirty years later.

The opera began *in medias res,* with Alice, the protagonist, performing a solo vocal improvisation as the audience took their seats. The ending, of which I was very, very proud, was meant to mirror the beginning—Alice was to improvise a cappella on the last few bars of the opera as the lights faded to black. The audience was supposed, somehow, to understand that the piece had ended. Well. The lights went down. The orchestra players turned off their stand lights. I ceremoniously put down my baton. Matt brought the houselights up. All the while, heroic Kristie sang and sang, the moment increasingly overextended. Into this awkwardness I gravely announced, "It is finished." I looked out around surreptitiously at the bewildered faces of the audience and waited for them to erupt into applause. Instead, there was a sort of sound exactly like when the last four or five kernels pop when you're making popcorn, and people sort of slunk off.

I returned to Madison determined to develop my musical skills. One piece of good news: I was awarded the ASCAP-Raymond Hubbel Scholarship, which allowed me to rent, for $160 a month, a room in a flophouse on Gorham Street, across from the first Rocky Rococo's pizza parlor. Without the distraction of brawls with Britt, I spent nearly every waking moment studying theory, practicing the piano, and writing music. I had the good fortune then to study music theory with Bruce Benward, a gentle, sage, supportive, and intellectually ravenous Yoda figure. During his career, Benward published several widely used, seminal textbooks, including *Music in Theory and Practice.* (I was taught his system of singing scale degrees instead of pitch names or *solfège,* as well as his idiosyncratic—pop music-based—method of assigning roman numerals to chords—as personal as Vincent Persichetti's, in his textbook.) Benward was one of the first theorists anywhere to explore computer-assisted music instruction—in 1980(!) I used his computer software to practice ear training.

I continued mailing one or two letters a day to Kristie, who had begun her studies at Yale. In time, she became so idealized a figure to me that I no longer knew her. Twenty years later, a tenured professor of German at Bowling Green State University, she sent all my letters back to me. I was touched that she had kept them; appalled that she had returned them. I've never opened the box, and probably never will; but they are safely stowed among my papers. A few months before he died, Father sent me the two decades' worth of letters I had written to him and to Mother. I meant never to open that box either, but, just before sealing it for good, I did; peered in, drew out at random four or five. Of course, we scarcely see ourselves as others see us, or as we portray ourselves to our loved ones in prose, but the cringe worthy, painful shock of recognition when I caught a whiff of the plucky, I'm-gonna-make-it tone, the staccato enumeration of fleeting achievements, the attitudinizing, the "insider" airs, was still as unexpected as it was acute. I quickly re-sealed the box and, shuddering, put it away.

Karlos Moser, the head of the university's opera program, and I were working one rainy November 1980 day on some songs that I had contributed to a revue called *House to Half.* Karlos, who had cast Kevin as Ben Hubbard in his production of Marc Blitzstein's *Regina* during the late 70s, observed in passing that the State Historical Society possessed Blitzstein's papers. Thrilled, I sprinted across the street to the archives, filled out a request to see them, and was astonished to be granted immediate access. Within thirty minutes, I held in my hands a Photostat of the manuscript of Blitzstein's fair copy of the first page of *The Cradle Will Rock.*

Marc Blitzstein's music is not exactly an obsession of mine, but I do find the musical DNA of which it is composed indispensable. Strands of that DNA—strict adherence to economy of means, a passion for combining words and music, the belief that music can promote social justice, an abhorrence of pretension—are woven contrapuntally, inextricably, into the music that I compose, and have been, nearly from the start. Blitzstein's music is powered by the ironic marriage of opposites. A fierce advocate of the poor and disenfranchised, he was born in Philadelphia in 1905 to affluent parents. Determined to write music popular with Regular Joes, he studied composition and piano at the Curtis Institute of Music. Then he went on to Berlin to study with Arnold Schoenberg and to Paris where he worked with Nadia Boulanger. He began as a modernist, but he turned populist in the '30s, shortly before he (an openly gay communist) married novelist Eva Goldbeck. Three Portuguese sailors in Martinique beat him to death in 1964 after a sexual encounter. In 1937, he entered Broadway history when the Works Progress Administration shut down *The Cradle Will Rock*—an opera presented as a musical. As the story goes, director Orson Welles and producer John Houseman walked the musicians, cast and audience from the Maxine Elliott Theater to the nearby Venice Theater, where—in order to evade union restrictions—they performed the piece from the audience, with Blitzstein (not a union member) accompanying from an upright piano onstage. To some, Blitzstein's signature gambit of destabilizing tonality by throwing a suspended fourth in the bass was crude. But, like a beat cop's billy to the ribs, it got things moving.

In spring 1980 composer Homer Lambrecht gave a presentation at UW not about his own work but about "emerging digital technologies and how they relate to music." He had studied computer music at M.I.T. and earned a doctorate at UW-Madison. "His favorite philosophers, Henri Bergson and Gilles Deleuze," read his biography, "have been essential to his tentative understanding of the indeterminate elasticity of that which is nameless and contingent on the dynamics of Now." I didn't even know who these men were, let alone understand what the sentence meant. I puzzled over it, and him, as he spoke. Karen Fox and Jeff Bitzer—my two closest friends and classmates—and I took him out for coffee and cheesecake after his seminar and learned that he would be our teacher the next year. Leaning back in his chair, drawing on his pipe and describing, with quiet fervor, that music was "far, far more than pitches and rhythms," I thought him the quintessential Midwestern intellectual. Unlike Les, he didn't respond to my ambitious naïveté with annoyance; instead, he treated me with what seemed like compassionate rue. "Have you spent any time with the 'cascading canonic writing' of Witold Lutosławski and György Ligeti?" he asked me. "Um, no," I admitted. He listed some of the already-famous east-bloc works that I needed to get to know. "Karl Husa, Karlheinz Stockhausen, Iannis Xenakis," he ticked off on his fingers. "Oh, I've looked at their scores," I said, eagerly. "Yes, but you probably haven't really *listened* to them and learned to *hear* them, yet," he said, rubbing his hands together. "We're going to read philosophy. And we're going to have some great musical adventures, my friends," he said. "I'm going to explode your worlds."

Around the same time, I learned that the Curtis Institute of Music had hired composer and author Ned Rorem to teach composition. I had sung and accompanied his most famous art song, *Early in the Morning,* a setting of Robert Hillyer's poem, in a state music competition. I had read in high school his *Paris Diaries* and I had watched him sally forth (and stand on his head) as a celebrity guest on the 10 November episode of *The Dick Cavett Show.* Whereas Homer's humble, *innig* brilliance appealed deeply to my core values as a person and nascent artist, Rorem's vividly self-described personal connections to the famous composers whose work I admired, his frank presentation of himself as a "public intellectual" along the lines of Gore Vidal and Norman Mailer, suave writing style, and shameless narcissism impressed and intrigued me.

For his part, Homer counseled against Curtis: "Your musical world is just beginning to expand," he said. "Are you sure you want to limit yourself that way? I mean, you could use technology, explore mixed-media, and write film scores...." Homer accomplished exactly what he said he would; he transformed through analysis and discussion the passing acquaintance that I'd acquired during the many afternoons spent prowling the Mills Music Library stacks looking at scores into a more comprehensive *Weltanschauung* and a delight in intellectual and musical eclecticism. I have often thought since that my dream composer dinner would include Lukas Foss, Homer, Luciano Berio, and myself. Two of the four are dead, now, so that's out. But a fellow can dream. And I did still dream of making it to the coast and "getting on with things." How, I asked him, could I resist a chance to be included in a continuum of artists larger than me, feel as though my work was part of a tradition, a "school?"

Rorem was born in Indiana in 1923, studied at the American Conservatory, then Northwestern, then Curtis and finally Juilliard. His teachers included Leo Sowerby, David Diamond, and Virgil Thomson. From 1949 to 1958 he was based in Paris, though he spent two of those years in Morocco: his published diaries of this and later periods are, if not always exactly factual, always inspiring in their intellectual vigor, and bracing in their openness about his sexuality and amorous exploits.

I knew that Curtis was a conservatory in Philadelphia, that all the pupils attended on full scholarship, that it had the lowest acceptance rate of any institution of higher education in the United States, and that it had a student body of approximately 150—enough to fill the orchestra, voice, conducting, and composition studios. I also knew that George Rochberg, Lukas Foss, Bernstein and Blitzstein had been students there, and that Samuel Barber and Gian Carlo Menotti had met there, fallen in love, been nurtured as talents, and ultimately joined the faculty.

Expecting nothing at all, I applied. Lessons with Homer, and our quest of sampling the cheesecake at every restaurant and café in Madison, had been a privilege. Under his guidance I wrote a sprawling orchestral blowout called *Triptych* into which I threw absolutely everything I had learned from him, from swooning Debussy-ian strings to Lutosławski-esque "event boxes"; from tender chorales to slashing climaxes. I secretly subtitled it "Everything I've Learned About Every Kind of Music in One Piece So Please Get Me Outta Here." Thanks to Homer's guidance and my redoubled dedication to hard work, the piece was a big leap forward from *Kamala at the Riverbank*. It won the university's composition contest, was rehearsed, and premièred in concert by the university orchestra.

Seated at one of the brightly-colored metal tables next to Lake Mendota behind the Memorial Union, reading the July 3rd *New York Times* with my feet up, a hoddle of coffee cooling at my elbow, I read the headline "Rare Cancer Seen in 41 Homosexuals" and leaned forward to read the sub-headline: "Outbreak Occurs Among Men in New York and California—8 Dead Inside 2 Years." I put down my coffee cup and smoothed the newspaper on the table. "Holy shit," I whispered to myself. *I wonder what that's about?* Beside my coffee lay a letter that I'd had a few days earlier from the registrar at Curtis telling me that Rorem had accepted me as a student.

Brian Anderson approached the table, hands clasped before him, bursting with energy. "Are you ready to set sail?" he asked. We had a date to take one of the for-hire skiffs out on the lake for the day. I was a Brooks Brothers shirt and blue jeans sort of guy. I grooved to Stockhausen more than Sondheim, Berio more than Barber, and the Beatles more even than Bartók. I didn't know why lightning had struck, only that it had; I wasn't going to wait for it to strike again. I stole a glance across the lake at the Mendota Hospital for the Insane for luck and rose to embrace Brian. "Call me Ishmael," I told him, stuffing the letter in my pocket. "Okay, okay, you're Ishmael," he said. "Let's find our boat."

◆◆ 8 ◆◆

Icarus
1981–1982

When I reached the coast, it was the smell of the air that first struck me. *You Can't Go Home Again, Moby Dick,* and *Christopher and His Kind*, music paper, some pencils, and a sandwich, in an army-surplus rucksack slung over my shoulder, I stood in the middle of Philadelphia's Thirtieth Street Station, contemplating my future in the wee hours of a late August morning, air streaming up the escalators into the glorious 30s Art Deco celebration of rail travel at its height, having just disembarked the Owl. The place was so big that single-engine airplanes could land on the roof. To me, its cavernous interior was the belly of the whale, site of my final separation from known world and self. I had accomplished nothing and ached with potential; I was ripe for transformation, and eager for the "road of trials" to unfurl before me. When I looked up into the sad, empty eyes of Walker Hancock's ebony statue of the archangel Michael cradling a dead soldier for the first time, a *frisson* of dread-laced excitement caused me to drop the backpack. Out of it tumbled the Melville, the Wolfe, the Isherwood, the sandwich, and the pencils; music paper slid out and splayed like a fan on the polished floor. As I dropped to my knees to gather up my things, the unique combination of smells—the very nature of the air—that is Philadelphia's, hit me. I treasure Managua's tropical combination of burnt cane, dust, and ocean; Venice's brisk, Adriatic brininess interlaced with the somniferous, insinuating reek of dead and dying things; Milwaukee's honeyed compendium of summertime smells—chocolate, yeast, and hops. None of these smells move me as deeply as Philly's edgy brimstone and ozone train yard smell mixed with the rancid-butter-reek of autumn Ginkgos and the clingy, low-tide-tang of the Schuylkill River.

Philadelphia was smaller then: by law, buildings could not exceed in height the statue of William Penn atop City Hall. One could sense the deep veins of Quaker restraint, Pennsylvania Dutch otherness, and Amish stillness even in the architecture. After one put aside the Corinthian columns of Depression-era edifices like 30th Street station and the art museum, older buildings still reflected a bourgeois second-city desire for comfort and commercial continuity. The narrow, cobbled, colonial side streets, just wide enough for a horse and buggy, reinforced the human scale of things; Penn's five greens decorated the downtown like emeralds. I walked.

After a few hours, I ended up at an all-night greasy spoon across the street from the Warwick Hotel, a block from the Curtis Institute of Music, called Little Pete's. The refrigerated air that poured out as I opened the door smelt of burnt toast and grease—I learned later that what I smelled was scrapple. The coffee I ordered as dawn broke was just terrible;

the eggs weren't much better. I loved them. Two old men drank tea and argued about Goethe. I read Isherwood as the sun rose, and then wrote a letter to Kristie until 9 a.m. My 60-something server had a broad south Philly accent and called me "honey." When I told her that this qualified (no kidding) as the first day of the rest of my life she smiled wistfully and brought me a free slice of pie. As I walked down Locust Street from Little Pete's to the Institute, I thought about the effect my acceptance to Curtis would have on my relationship with Kristie. It was clear that everything in my life had just changed, but I was still taken by surprise when, trembling the way that Kevin had a few years earlier at Lincoln Center, it struck me as inevitable that, to survive in this place, in this new city, I would need to eliminate all distractions.

From the sidewalk, the mansion at 1726 Locust Street had the same genteel robber baron vibe as the Red Galesburg brick and Michigan brownstone Neo-Classical Revival style McIntosh-Goodrich Mansion in Milwaukee, where Father had driven me for my theory and piano lessons at the Wisconsin Conservatory of Music, but Philadelphia's Drexel Mansion was creamy-white, Renaissance and Romanesque-style, and emotionally cooler. The heavily serifed bronze letters with the faint green patina ghosts around them to the right of the stairs leading up to the exquisitely-decorated wrought-iron doors read: THE CURTIS INSTITUTE OF MUSIC. I gulped hard, mounted the stairs, pulled open the heavy door, tumbled into the owl light of the common room, and stopped suddenly. To be honest, I could scarcely breathe. But what I could make out as the most powerful scent that sweltering morning was furniture polish. The second was of dust; the third was the booze on the breath of Clarence, the burly African American security guard, as he drawled, "Now who might you be?" Back then the stairway was not yet enclosed, so the odor of the chunks of camphor that were placed in the pianos in the studios upstairs drifted faintly down.

On one wall hung a Norman Rockwell portrait of a woman who looked to me as though she may have been an angel. Whoever she was, I knew that I loved her. I walked straight over and stood before it, feeling suddenly loved in return. Shirley Schachtel, the elegant, gently formal, and kindly receptionist, joined me, touched my arm and said, "Yes, that's she." I looked at her questioningly. Shirley explained. The extraordinary only child of the magazine and newspaper magnate Cyrus Curtis, founder of *Ladies' Home Journal*, at age thirteen in 1890, Mary Louise Curtis writing under her mother's maiden name (Mary L. Knapp) joined a staff of fifteen people at *Ladies' Home Journal*, the first year of Edward W. Bok's long tenure as editor. Bok, fourteen years her senior, took her for his wife when she was nineteen. After consulting Leopold Stokowski and Josef Hoffmann on how best to train talented youngsters in 1924, she established the Curtis Institute of Music.

Mrs. Bok purchased three mansions on Rittenhouse Square, joined and renovated them, and invited a faculty of prominent musicians to teach there. In 1943, thirteen years after Edward Bok's death, she married the director of the Institute, violinist Efrem Zimbalist, becoming Mary Louise Curtis Bok Zimbalist. (I grew up watching Efrem Zimbalist's son, the actor Efrem Zimbalist, Jr., portray Inspector Lewis Erskine on the television series *The F.B.I.*, and his granddaughter, actor Stephanie Zimbalist, play Laura Holt on *Remington Steele*. Philadelphia Orchestra principal oboist John de Lancie, a later director of the Institute, was the father of actor John de Lancie, known to Trekkers everywhere as Q on *Star Trek: The Next Generation*.)

By some unfathomable, unforeseen stroke of luck, Ned Rorem had plucked me from the minors and placed me in the majors. Influential people would hear my music; great players would perform it. I began trembling and forgot to breathe. Cold sweat slid down my temple. Noting my distress, Ms. Schachtel guided me quickly to a chair near the fireplace.

The smell of her delicate perfume as she placed her hand on my shoulder made me nauseous. I sat down and looked down at my hands to steady myself. "So, you are brand new," she observed. "Did you come to compose?" she asked. "Yes. Oh, yes," I answered fiercely, looking up. I was Orpheus, and I was on fire.

I grew confident enough after a few weeks to not either mumble unintelligibly or chatter over-enthusiastically when I met someone. However, to the insecure, hyper-sensitive young man that I was then, every smirk directed at me stung; every exquisite childhood humiliation (from kid stuff like being laughed at in ear training class when I messed up, to being told that I ought to read the books being written about instead of the reviews of them when I was seen carrying an issue of the *New York Review of Books*) stuck. Over time, I grew enough scar tissue around my heart so that I could at least function. I developed my own brand of cool arrogance. I recall feeling overexposed and all too aware that there were things going on in the room to which I'd never be made privy.

The school found me a cozy apartment at Eleventh and Spruce. One early September night, sitting on the marble front step of my place around 10, I watched as a convertible full of drunken thugs cruised slowly down Spruce shouting about "beating up fags." One waved a baseball bat. A guy in black leather pants and chains walking down the street bounded suddenly up on the trunk of the car and tore the bat out of the first guy's hands. Suddenly the car took off, and leather pants tumbled as neatly as a cat off the trunk and onto his feet in the middle of the street. I couldn't help giving him the thumbs up. He sat down next to me, welcomed me to the neighborhood, and asked me why, if I wasn't gay, I had moved into the heart of the gay community. I laughed and told him. "Well," he said, giving me his card, "welcome to the neighborhood. If you ever need anything, give me a call." He was a surgeon at Thomas Jefferson University Hospital.

In due course a notecard was tacked to the bulletin board outside the registrar's office with "Mr. Rorem" typed at the top. Beneath, in a neat column, were the names "Robert Convery—2 p.m. Norman Stumpf—3 p.m. Daron Hagen—4 p.m." and, at the bottom, "Room 235J." I was terrified. One's major teacher could, if he desired, rescind one's scholarship and have one sent home. It gave our teachers a tremendous psychological advantage. At precisely 4 p.m. I climbed the narrow steps to the mansion's top floor classroom and knocked. Norman came to the door and winked at me, scooting out as he let me in. Within sat Ned Rorem with a pink scarf around his neck, draped against the piano as though awaiting his close-up. 15 September 1981, the day we met; the day of my first lesson. Before him on the rack sat the vocal score of my little monodrama *Through the Glass*, and the full score of *Triptych*, which had evidently achieved its goal of "getting me outta here."

Per Ned's *Nantucket Diary*, I was "the new one from Madison, bearded, bright, and seething with a desire to please." Ned motioned me to sit down. I watched in silence as he paged slowly through my orchestra piece—minute followed minute, page-followed page. (Years later Diamond told me that Roger Sessions had done the same thing to him at his first lesson.) Finally, he jabbed his finger at the same fistful of measures that Catherine Comet had liked and said, "This. This is good. I don't know what to make of the rest."

He turned to my little opera, stretching like a cat. "Do you read?" he asked. "What do you mean?" I asked in return. He motioned towards the score. "You've written your own libretto. Don't do that. Yours is pretty good—what I can make of it. You understand words. And I am extremely impressed that you conducted it and stage directed it yourself." "Thank you," I said. "No. I meant: do you read" he continued, ignoring me. "Fiction, history, biography ... memoirs?" For the next fifteen minutes, we talked about literature. "Read my diaries if you haven't already," he commanded. "That will be a good starting place."

James Holmes snapped this picture of Ned Rorem (*left*) and me at their home on Nantucket Island, Massachusetts, during the summer of 1984.

Ned may have had in mind a character out of Simenon or Proust, but he seemed to me more like a character out of Balzac or Zola. His lisp surprised me; the brutality of his criticism did not. Like most intellectuals, he stated his opinions as fact—I had been brought up to expect that. There was something magnificent about him; he was completely absorbed in his pose. His affectations embarrassed me; his commitment to carrying them off impressed me. I had just read Philip Roth's *Anatomy Lesson* in which a character observes: "I know writers. Beautiful feelings. They sweep you away with their beautiful feelings. But the feelings quickly disappear once you are no longer posing for them. Once they've got you figured out and written down, you go. All they give is their attention."

Ned seemed to me to be the sort of man who thought he had you figured out within minutes. He obviously wasn't teaching because he enjoyed it; so, I intuited right away that I would have to perform, to be extraordinary, to get the best from him. He handed me a sheet of paper on which he had typed Robert Browning's *Love in a Life*. "Set this to music this week. And set another of your own choosing. Keep the piano part simple. Use an ostinato." He turned his back to me by way of dismissal. "I am coming back to Philadelphia in a week. We'll see one another then. Be a good boy."

Excited, relieved, and inspired, I thanked Ned and let myself out. I hope that nobody heard me miss the first step and slide on my rear end halfway down the first flight of stairs. Norman, bless him, was waiting for me in the Common Room. Norm was profoundly gentle—lanky, bearded, and extremely bright. He'd come to Curtis after graduating from Yale, so he was a few years older than me. He wrote music of delicate beauty and intellectual suavity that did not aspire to "hand of author" moments any more than he did. He became my best friend, frequent tennis and jogging partner, fellow music-copyist, and co-diviner of the moods of our mentor. That evening, he and David Loeb's student David Powell took me to a little bar called "RN's" next to the medical college. It became, because nurses drank there, and because the cheese fries were particularly gloppy, our favorite watering hole.

On 29 November, Norman and I stood together in front of the Academy of Music where we had just heard Bernstein conduct the Orchestre National de France. "C'mon, that's gotta be him," said Norman, pointing to a pair of figures sharing a smoke on the front steps. The taller of the two was an usher. We recognized him because he admitted us to Philadelphia Orchestra concerts without tickets. The shorter of the two was clearly the maestro. "No way," I said. "Way," said Norman. "Should we say 'hi' do you think?" he asked. "No," I said, "let's not spoil their moment."

We had attended the concert to meet him. I had memorized the thirty-second speech I would deliver backstage when finally given a chance to meet the maestro. The line was long. I rehearsed under my breath as I waited. The Green Room smelled of minks, drinks, stale Chanel No. 5, cigarette smoke, and sweat. I reached the front of the line, looked down, and saw a small man with a hairy chest cradling a tumbler of scotch on his belly with one hand, a cigarette in a holder dangling from the other, dressed in a silk smoking jacket, smiling a crooked, toothy smile. Out tumbled my speech: "You wrote my mother a letter," I began. "I'm here in Philly now, studying with Ned. Thank you for helping to make that possible."

"Of course, I know who you are," he said, shocking me. I wondered at that moment if he were lying to be kind; his next words proved that he was not: "You're the boy from Wisconsin who wrote *Suite for a Lonely City*." He looked me over, "How's Ned?" "Fine," I stammered, "just fine." "Good. Good. Work hard. Write a lot of music. Music needs you," he said. I blushed. "We need you. Come and see me in New York." Big Hug, two beats too long. I looked around the Green Room, giddy, altered. The minks swept in.

I promised myself as Norman and I left that I would not ask to meet with the Maestro until I felt ready. "The Letter" had served as such a *deus ex machina* in my life that I consciously feared that I would be too much a disappointment to him, that the man himself would be a disappointment to me, if I entered his orbit prematurely. I waited—except for a summer at Tanglewood—six years.

Michaela Paetsch, a violin pupil of Szymon Goldberg who, like Norman, had come to Curtis from Yale, was a beautiful Colorado horsewoman from a large, musical family. The night I fell in love with her she was practicing the Bartók Solo Sonata with the lights off at Curtis in the Horszowski Room. I laid on my back, listening, fingers knitted behind my head, stretched out on the wine-dark, rufous plushness of the carpet, staring at the ceiling. Pale amber light glowed dimly in the windows, shed from a streetlamp out in Rittenhouse Square. Otherwise, it was the sort of dark that sharpened the senses and stopped time. The next day, she allowed me to carry her violin when I walked her to her train. I knew then that I had won as much of her heart as I ever would. She lived I knew not where and never learned—only that it appeared to be a train-ride off, by way of Suburban Station. With what I now realize was extreme selfishness I courted her tenaciously for months. I did have a vague idea at the time that by pursuing her I was toying with my future; I was somewhat aware that the fact of a relationship might compromise us both (by making us appear less committed to our studies) in the eyes of our teachers, our friends, and the school; I was even dimly aware of my own hypocrisy in splitting with one lover and then taking up with another. After each walk, a little giddy, downcast, yet hopeful—the way you can be when you are in your early twenties and in love and have time and health and just enough money, I bought the *Daily News* and the *New York Times* and worked my way through them at Little Pete's diner until I felt the urge to compose percolate up within me like a welcome fever.

… To compose! Do you remember what it was like to taste your first kiss, to take your first sip of your favorite wine, to smell your baby's breath, to hear the surrendering sigh and the slight catch of breath accompanying your first completely mutually satisfactory orgasm? Combine them all and you'll begin to understand how composing felt to me then. It was a sexy, grown up feeling. It wasn't the nascent anima of a sheltered teenager embracing the aesthetic by watching old movies at the Oriental; it was the euphoria of a young man entirely aware that this was his time, and that his music was coming from the right place.

Like most of the major faculty, Ned only came to the school to teach when his schedule permitted. Most of the time, we went to him. "Good luck, boys," Michael Carrigan, the school's Registrar, would say as he handed us each a small envelope with thirty dollars in it. Stamped on each in the heavily serifed typeface that seemed to evoke the Ages was THE CURTIS INSTITUTE OF MUSIC. Below that was scrawled in loopy letters our name and the date—something-something-nineteen-eighty-something. Our train-fare and lunch money: we were Ned's first generation of composition students at Curtis; we were on our way from Philadelphia to New York for our lessons.

We were scrupulous about ringing Ned's buzzer at precisely the appointed hour. To be early or late was to begin our lessons with explanations. Not good. I remember that I nearly always wore a suit and tie, because I understood that respect was due, and because I also understood that a lesson with Ned wasn't just a lesson, it was a performance. Lessons began with lunch laid out on the red dining room table. There was always a quiche from Soutine's (the now-closed patisserie just down the street), Godiva chocolates, and sometimes berries. Always, there was a pitcher filled with liquid of indeterminate color that we dubbed Mystery Juice. Years later, Ned's partner James Holmes revealed to me that it consisted of a *mélange* of whatever unfinished juices there were to be found in the refrigerator on the morning of our lessons.

There were books everywhere; paintings of Ned on the living room walls. On the piano were "carelessly" placed copies of whatever his music publisher, the august Boosey and Hawkes had just published. Jim might pass through on his way to an engagement. Wallace the cat, fat, foul-tempered, and plagued by seizures set off by rhythmic sounds, would flit in from the bedroom, rub on our legs, and then hiss at us imperiously before stalking out.

Over lunch, Norman, Robert Convery, and I were quizzed on the concerts we had attended, the music we had listened to, the books we had read, and whatever gossip had manifested itself at Curtis since our previous lessons. Ned didn't talk about himself. Although we were never explicitly instructed to do so, it was clear that we were expected to express ourselves as concisely and as articulately as possible. I was good at this, so I relished it.

Talking Part finished, Ned would move into the living room and seat himself at the piano, followed by whoever had volunteered to go first. The rest of us would sit in the dining room at the table and talk quietly or peruse Ned's library. (It was considered an honor to be entrusted with a book for the week.) One squirmed (or not) on a little, uncomfortable cane-seated chair next to Ned as he played through whatever one had brought. Bringing sketches to a lesson could be disastrous—we had learned through bitter experience that an entire lesson could be devoted to cleaning up our notation if we didn't bring our work in as immaculately notated as possible.

Listening to somebody else's lesson was as illuminating as one's own; eavesdropping when Ned periodically took a phone call to talk business was equally enlightening. It took me a couple of weeks to realize that I was fortunate to have read all his books before joining his studio, because he occasionally vamped—or was he testing us? We never could tell—

by making points that he had already made in his published writings. We called this "playing tapes" and it seemed to please Ned when we caught him at it. "Instruction is not offered, it is seized," He would explain, pulling a pencil from the juice glass on the piano.

I had a habit back then which annoyed Ned enormously. If he asked me whether I had read something that I had not, I would say that I had, and then read the book the following week. I ended up reading a lot. I was eager to impress, and too eager for him to get to the point, to (I thought at the time) risk having my lesson derailed by my lack of erudition. It took me a few too many rather nasty, embarrassing moments (thanks to Ned) to be cured of this character flaw. Decades later, it irritates me when my students do it to me with virulence only possible in one once guilty of the same thing.

Ned was at his best with me when he was the most brutal, and the better my music was, the more merciless his critique. He never pretended to be an academic; he was a mid-career professional. Consequently, his reactions were like dispatches from the creative and intellectual front lines, uninflected, and deadly serious. I often disagreed with Ned, but I never for a moment doubted that he was speaking from vast experience and from the gut.

Afterwards, Norman and I usually walked down Broadway to Times Square together, talking about our lessons. I remember that we did enjoy being Young and we talked about it, as well as our excitement at feeling as though we were on a meaningful journey. Brew and Burger restaurants were everywhere then; we would step into one and spend our lunch allowance on a pitcher of beer and burgers, wrangle like pups over the Big Issues, Music, Tonality, Modernism, Minimalism,—isms, isms, isms. We laughed a lot, and the Big City on those evenings opened for us like Pandora's box. Resilience and Hope always sustained us.

Little Pete's was the setting for countless post-lesson symposiæ on the casually dropped *aperçu* and dry, acerbic criticisms Ned made while slashing through my compositions, his pencil waving this way and that like a rapier. "Did he tell you that you succeeded in being boring?" I asked Norman, over Pete's wretched, perennially burnt Joe, one afternoon. "Not this time," Norman replied. "But he told me that William Flanagan wrote my song better in the late 50s." "Who was he?" I asked. "That's what I said," replied Norman. I already knew what Ned's answer had been: find out.

The school invited Gian Carlo Menotti to come for a few weeks that winter. During his time in Philadelphia, he coached performances of his music, attended a concert of his orchestral works (including the hauntingly beautiful ballet score *Sebastian*), and gave lessons to the composition students. His operas had been awarded two Pulitzer Prizes—one for *The Consul* and one for *The Saint of Bleecker Street*—in the 50s, when the award meant different things than it does today. An Italian by birth who, despite retaining his Italian citizenship, proudly referred to himself as an American composer, he wrote for NBC the infectious Christmas opera *Amahl and the Night Visitors*, along with two-dozen other operas. *The Medium* was the first opera I saw live. Milwaukee's Florentine Opera sent its young artists out in a touring production to junior high schools. It was evident to me even at the age of fifteen that the money had been drummed up to bring them by my fearsome chorus teacher and guru, Wally Tomchek. The performance, on the school stage before the entire student body, was riveting. To this day I remember the haunting refrain, and the music to which it is pinned: "Toby, Toby, are you there?" A composer who can manage *that* feat deserves complete respect.

Norman and I took Gian Carlo to lunch at the once magnificent, still dustily opulent Barclay Hotel, home to Eugene Ormandy and his wife. The almond-mauve, curtained dining room was appointed like an interior from Visconti's film of *Death in Venice* crossed with the funeral parlor in Tony Richardson's film of *The Loved One*. "So, what would you like to know?" Menotti asked, taking a seat and wiping his lips delicately with a napkin. "Opera," Norman said, "we've got to talk about opera." "Right," I agreed. "Why don't we talk about *la parola scenica*?" I asked. "Ah," Gian Carlo smoothed the tablecloth with his long fingers as though creating a space, "you are referring to Verdi's phrase—well, let me tell you…." He began with Verdi, pinpointing the key phrase of music in his favorite scenes; then he moved on to Richard Strauss. His description of collaboration was trenchant: "A stage director looks at a scene one way," he began. "The composer looks at the scene in another way. The librettist sees it a third way. The composer must craft a scene so clear in intent that all three are compelled to agree." He looked at me, hard: "You *get* this," he said. "You'll direct your own operas someday and learn this firsthand."

Dessert demolished, coffee drunk, Gian Carlo called for fruit. Eyes twinkling, he said, "Boys, I know that you invited me to lunch. But this is my hotel, and I have already told them to charge it to my room." He raised his hand peremptorily. "Don't spend your money on an old man; spend it on something fun." After making us promise to remain in touch, he rose gracefully from his chair and glided out of the dining room. Deprived of his gravity and glamour, we felt like men in a lingerie shop, surrounded by elderly Ladies Who Lunch poking at their salads and stout executives tucking into their steaks. I slipped a pear into my jacket pocket on our way out. Walking down Locust Street, Norman and I were pleased to have unanticipated mad money in our pockets. Literally skipping down the sidewalk, I began, "I feel…" and Norman continued, "…As though the world…" patting first his tummy and then his wallet. "…Is our Oistrakh," I completed.

Fueled by the rapt pleasure of composing, those first months in Philadelphia were the happiest of my youth. The wild knowledge that my dreams were in fact coming true, that the sky was the limit; the dawning understanding that, with unstinting hard work and commitment, any door might open, anything was possible. Norm and I stretched out head-to-head on benches in Rittenhouse Square one night around three, picking out stars between the sycamore leaves, and feeling our oats. "This is where we began," he sang, from *Merrily We Roll Along*. "Being what we can," I sang back. It was an incredible, Icarus-like high that we enjoyed even more for knowing that it couldn't last. For, in the center of the moment dwelled a cherophobic dread—the conviction that the state of being happy was somehow shallow, that the bottom was going to fall out, and that everything would inevitably turn to shit: "…*Che tosto fugge, e spesso a gran salita il precipizio è presso*."

It was snowing lightly—little feathery, inhibited flakes that seemed shamed at having arrived as too-early guests, when Mother met me at the airport. I'd returned to Milwaukee for the Christmas Holidays. "Here," she said, handing me the keys, "you drive. I have some news for you." Once in the car, she broke into a fit of deep coughs that drained her. "That's a bad cold," I observed. "Yeah," she agreed, "bad." I turned the key in the ignition, and guessed, "You're finally going to leave Dad and move to Paris?" She twisted her head toward the passenger window and looked out. The window was steamed up. "No.," she said, and turned back to me, giving me that sudden, dazzling smile. It always killed me. "There's a Hitchcock double feature at the Oriental tonight," she said, brightly. "Let's go."

That night, during intermission, Bernard Herrmann's music for the final few minutes of Truffaut's *Fahrenheit 451* played. Mother reached for my hand and, as we both stared at the blank screen, she told me that she had been diagnosed with a particularly nasty form of inoperable lung cancer. First, there would be chemotherapy. There would be a rally. Then she would "get bored of dying," she predicted, "get on with life, and die."

"I'll come home to take care of you," I said. "Christ, no," she said. "Do. Not. Come.

Home. I want you to get on with your life. Get. Out. Of. Here." The music stopped. The lights dimmed. We held hands as the Main Title for *The 39 Steps* began. We watched the entire thing, holding hands like high school kids. She'd obviously chosen the Oriental, of all places, to share her news because she knew that I felt safe here; she'd timed her news to coincide with intermission so that I'd have the entirety of the second film to begin digesting it. By the time the lights went up after the second feature, I had recovered enough to ask, "What's next?" Pulling on her coat and arranging her scarf around her neck, she looked pensively into the middle distance. "Ice cream, I'd say," she said.

When we got home, Mother handed me her private diary, which consisted of blank pages bound in a hard cover that had been stamped *Britannica Book of the Year 1944*. She said, "Here, take this. Take it back to Philadelphia with you. Keep it for yourself and for your brothers. If you don't, your father will destroy it after I'm gone." Then she commanded me to return to school and concentrate on my studies.

I returned by train to a Philadelphia all but paralyzed by sixteen inches of snow. The first night, unable to sleep, I sat at a table in a little diner at Eleventh and Spruce Streets alone by a plate glass window, looking out at the enormous snowflakes falling straight down, holding open in my left hand a copy of *Le Père Goriot* and nursing a mug of hot coffee in my right. At midnight, a pre-war electric trolley skimmed soundlessly by on its tracks, windows steamed up by the passengers, giving them the color and texture of Hopper's *Nighthawks*. A spray of sparks erupted from the point at which the wires above met the contact arm. I put down the Balzac and opened her diary and read—

I write this out because I've long had a prophetic, unequivocal, almost resigned feeling that I shall not see our children grow to become young adults....

The high-flying, lusty Icarus of autumn had gotten just what he deserved. I shut Mother's diary and opened my own. The waitress came by, placed her hand on my shoulder, and whispered, "We need to close for the night. The snow is getting heavy. Can you settle?" I pulled a five-dollar bill out of my pocket and handed it to her. "Keep the change," I smiled. I wrote in my diary:

It's like Britt said that day at Mendota, we've all known from the start that we are going to die early. So, where does that leave me? What have I got? Drive I've got. Who knows what talent is? Inspiration? I know I've got my portion. Fuck it. I can't even imagine being alive at 30. Whatever I lack in talent, I'll make up in hard work.

Mother's illness stood like a sheet of heavy glass between myself and everyone else. I told nobody at Curtis about it—the last thing I wanted from my schoolmates was pity. I threw myself into my studies—counterpoint, harmony, ear-training, piano lessons. These last took place in the "Barber-Menotti" Room with Marion Zarzeczna, a protégé of Mieczysław Horszowski who joined the faculty there the year after my birth and served as a "secondary" teacher. "Why do you play your own music with such carelessness?" she asked me when I brought my *Echo's Songs* in for a lesson. She listened to me perform every song in the cycle and then had me go back and relearn them all with a pianist's voicing, fingerings, and ears. "When we're through you'll not play your music like a composer anymore," she promised. Before I made my first appearance as a collaborative pianist in Curtis Hall, she arranged for me to play first for formidable Eleanor Sokoloff, who complimented me on the colors I was able to draw from the piano "with such a limited technique," and then for her husband Vladimir, who was more generous: "You're a fine collaborative pianist," he said. "Soloist not so much."

One of my work-study jobs was to copy parts for the school's orchestra when required. Clint Nieweg—the Philadelphia Orchestra's librarian—would send over the Philadelphia Orchestra's string parts. My job was to transfer those bowings into the school's set. Edwin Heilakka, the affable, courtly gentleman who ran the Institute's orchestra library, asked me to help him organize Leopold Stokowski's scores—the maestro had just died and his widow had bestowed them upon the school. I remember opening some scores and having bread and butter letters from Roy Harris, Howard Hanson, Darius Milhaud, Copland, Bernard Herrmann, Barber, Ned, others slip out from where he had left them. My fingers practically tingled as I drew out of one of the boxes Stokowski's full score of *The Rite of Spring*, which contained not just his clever orchestration changes in one color, but Stravinsky's own modifications for performance specifically in the Academy of Music in another.

In 1929, Philadelphia philanthropist Edwin A. Fleisher—founder, a half century before Venezuela's famed *El Sistema*, of the Little Symphony, the first training orchestra in the United States—donated his personal collection of performance parts for over three thousand works to the Free Library of Philadelphia, thereby founding the Fleisher Collection of Orchestral Music. During the Depression, he co-sponsored a WPA Copying Project dedicated to creating performance sets from unpublished manuscripts by Pan-American composers collected by Nicolas Slonimsky. Upon his death in 1959, Fleisher endowed the collection. It remains the largest circulating collection of orchestral performance sets in the world. To this day, the Orchestra Society of Philadelphia, the reading orchestra with which I have had so many musical adventures since our first concert in 1982, plays almost exclusively from Fleisher materials.

Norman, who had won a job copying there, knew that I needed to make some money, so he introduced me to Kile Smith, who had also just been hired as a copyist, and Sam Dennison, the collection's curator, as "the new kid at Curtis." Gruff Sam asked me if I had any work samples. I hadn't thought to bring any. "But I copied the solo part to the *Yellow River Concerto* for John-David Anello and the Milwaukee Symphony last summer," I offered. "We have that," said Sam, dispatching Romulus Franchescini to the stacks for the part. A few moments later, I held in my hands the ridiculous thing, copied in blue ballpoint pen— a travesty, really, and not at all good. Sam looked at me and smiled. "This is *terrible!*" he laughed. I looked down. "Oh," he explained, "your copying's not very good. Yet. But you've got potential. You'll get better. *This piece* won't," he laughed. "There's a desk here for you if you want it. You'll learn by doing." I was hired, and, to my astonishment, became a part time employee of the Free Library. I was set to work not just as a hand copyist but also as a printer's assistant to Frank Deodato, in whose lair in the stacks hulked an ancient, ammonia fume-spewing Ozalid printing machine. Following an afternoon assisting Frank, the smell of his cigars, the ammonia, the stale sweat, and the dust, combined to produce a sort of weird, toxic high that left my eyes burning and my head spinning.

I learned more by prowling through the Fleisher stacks than I did even in the Mills Music Library's. How ennobling and humbling it was to be surrounded by thousands of forgotten works by forgotten composers, all hand-copied by forgotten Music Monks, all striving toward a sort of immortality conferred upon them by dint of having been catalogued and shelved. It was quite the sobering counterbalance to the high blown euphoria of being an arriviste hotshot at Curtis where I enjoyed each Saturday morning what I felt was the catbird's seat, perched behind a grand piano on the stage of Curtis Hall, stationed slightly above and behind William Smith—treasured mentor and friend—as he rehearsed the orchestra in whatever repertoire the Philadelphians were playing that week. Bill collected facsimile scores, and would bring a copy of the work at hand, if he had it, for me to look at; Clint would send over their full score, which contained all the bowings that helped make the Philadelphia Sound; and I would bring my own score. As I listened to rehearsal and Bill dispensed his profoundly useful, unpretentious brand of wisdom to my classmates, I would array before me for comparison all three scores, taking notes, listening, and learning.

The school didn't offer a class in orchestration when I was there. In any event, I was by this point developing my technique by composing as much orchestral music as I possibly could. De Lancie had miraculously (and with what now seems Olympian generosity) decreed that I was to be allowed (nay, required, since he told me that he cordially detested the idea of composers "sitting on their hands" while conductors and performers tried to make sense of their scores) to conduct the premieres of whichever orchestral works I could complete. True to his word, he authorized me to compose and conduct the premieres of about six hours' worth of orchestral music—concertos for violin and cello, an orchestral song cycle, a suite, an overture, a symphony, and *Prayer for Peace* for string orchestra—while a student.

Eleven months after breaking the news to me that she was ill, Mother in a final supreme effort, had Father drive her out from Wisconsin to attend my November 1982 Curtis debut, conducting my classmates in a program of my orchestral works. The afternoon that Mother arrived, Michaela performed a Bach solo suite for her in the living room of the apartment that I shared with Robert La Rue and David McGill. Exhausted by the trip, Mother slipped in and out of consciousness as she listened. Afterwards, Michaela having left for a rehearsal, Mother excused herself, went to the bathroom, and threw up. "She was lovely," mother said, emerging. "It wasn't her playing; it was the chemo." Her wry grin. "She can sure play the violin," she said. I nodded. "You love her?" I shrugged. "Madly." Her sunny smile. "Honey, she's wonderful. But you'll never marry her. She's already married." I frowned. "And so are you." I guided her to the couch.

"I need to take a nap before your concert tonight," she said. I left the room to get a blanket. From the other room, I heard her say, with effort, "All your doors are opening up for you right now. Let them. Let her let them." I came back in the room. "Don't be sad," she said, reaching for my hand, "I can't tell you that everything's going to be alright, but I can tell you that it is going to be interesting." I left her for work in the lobby of the Barclay Hotel, where I covered show tunes for tips as Ned, according to his diary, "dine[d] … with the de Lancies at the Art Alliance." A few hours after that, under my baton, Michaela performed the violin concerto I had written for her, and Karen Hale an orchestral song cycle on words of Anne Sexton. Following the concert, Mother presented me with a copy of Bernstein's *Findings*, with this hand-written inscription:

> *"To Daron—*
> *On his recital debut at Curtis. When the whole world was opening for him. My fondest hopes are*
> *that your 'findings' result in your being a humane and mostly happy man."*

Ned had made a date to meet my parents just after the concert in the Barclay bar. I'd been describing my lessons to Mother on the telephone, and she had read Ned's books. Mother was keen to meet him. "I still see the transparent skin, the eager eyes like candles as she leaned across the table at the Barclay bar, pride subduing fever," he wrote of her. Ned tactfully made no mention of the fact that Father, knowing that he was an alcoholic, repeatedly asked him why he didn't want a drink.

A couple of nights later, I pushed my last key in the Barclay lobby. Mr. Ormandy knew me by sight because I attended Philadelphia Orchestra rehearsals; he also knew that I was a composition student. He had not known, until that moment, that I had also been seated periodically at the Steinway in his lobby noodling my way through the great American songbook. I was playing the Gershwin brothers' *Someone Who'll Watch over Me* the moment that he caught my eye, stopped, smiled sadly, and shook his head. I never had the nerve to ask whether it was because he disapproved of the song, my playing, or my moonlighting.

After a few hours at the Barclay, my custom was to stroll over to Little Pete's for coffee and the papers. I'd call home from the pay phone there and spin colorful stories for Mother about how well I was doing at school. (I was, in fact, feeling increasingly socially isolated.) She would in her turn give me sanitized descriptions of what chemotherapy was like, her handsome oncologist, and her slow-motion demise. I composed from four to five hours per day, practiced piano and ear training for about 90 minutes, copied parts at Fleisher for three to four hours, and then drank. Drinking dampened my hyperarousal, and the din of music in my brain—insistent, repetitive, overflowing like water from a bathtub. I was drowning in it. The noise made it impossible to think, let alone sleep. Many mornings, as dawn broke, my body still young enough to absorb the alcohol, I did my counterpoint exercises seated at Little Pete's lime green counter, "scrambled eggs and" a few inches away, untouched, the dread of disappointing Ford Lallerstedt by presenting mediocre work pulling me back from the edge.

Father, we all admitted, was emotionally disturbed, probably bi-polar—certainly alcoholic. Although I'd barely begun to piece together what that might mean to me in the end, I did begin seeing a therapist to whom I was referred by the surgeon who'd given me his card a few months earlier. After the taverns closed, Norman—whose nervous state was even more febrile than my own—and I would walk Philadelphia's streets, sometimes together, sometimes alone, our paths unchanging, from one square to the next, until together we would watch the sunrise, drinking coffee, bare feet dangling in the icy water of Calder's Swann Memorial Fountain. By now, of necessity, my therapist, Michaela, Norman and his siblings, Kile, Ned, and my roommates knew about Mother's declining health. As far as I know, though, very few others were in on my secret. The report from home was that as soon as the semester ended, I should come home to say goodbye.

Mother was asleep when I arrived. I left my suitcase, packed, by the front door, and donned clothes from childhood. Father moved from room to room like a storm crow, performing strange, purposeless tasks. I pulled vellum, India ink, my Osmiroid fountain pens, and the manuscript of the copying job I was doing from my elephant portfolio and, seeing no point in doing anything else, passed the time by working.

She woke up around midnight and asked for water. "Honey, you made it," she observed, a wry look on her face. "Kevin and Judy are coming tomorrow with the baby," I said. She looked away. Her body was sparrow-small. She swam in the white silk shirt and plaid pants she wore. "You could use a change of clothes," I offered. I picked her up and bathed her gently with warm water, changed the linens, and placed her in the middle of the enormous bed, clean and gaunt. I left the room for a moment to carry the soiled sheets to the basement. When I returned, she was unconscious.

The next morning, Grandmother and Britt arrived. Father refused to speak with them. Kevin and Judith arrived, with their son Ryan in arms. I sat down next to Mother, who had clearly drawn up her last bit of strength for the visit. She put her arm behind my back. Kevin placed Ryan in my lap, and I gave him my finger to wrap his tiny ones around. Mother looked at him as he clucked and whimpered, smiling that "*quel* day" smile she had on particularly crappy days, but also glowing slightly, as though she was winning a contest with someone unseen. Father flapped around the periphery, baffled, bereft and impotent.

After they left, and Father had carried Mother, who had passed out, to her bed, the Big Cedar House was completely still. "Your mother wants to be taken outside to look at the house one last time tomorrow," he said. "And?" I asked. "Well, there's a sapling growing out of the roof just over there," he said, pointing towards the corner of the living room. "She'll be horrified by that." I couldn't help but drop my chin to my chest and look at him over my glasses. "You think, dad?" "Climb up there and pull it out for me, will you?" Later, it was hard not to think of the task as a metaphor when, standing in six inches of snow on the roof, I tugged the sapling out, along with a sizable chunk of rotted eave, and tossed it to the ground below.

A few hours later, I heard her cry out, and discovered her writhing on the floor at the foot of the bed, where she had collapsed on her way to the bathroom to throw up. A bottle of Chanel No. 5—the only perfume she ever wore—lay on its side, half under the bed, open. Over the years she had often fallen asleep in bed, a cigarette burning in an ashtray beside her. The perfume smell mingled with that of the carpet, which was dotted with cigarette burns. She had sent my brothers away. Why was I, her twenty-year-old son, sitting on the floor, cradling his mother's head as her husband, my father—downstairs in the den—played Solitaire? It seemed to me a cringeworthy little suburban *pietà* in reverse.

"I love you more than I can say," she said, stroking my face. Her eyes rolled. I gently wiped the crusts of sputum from the corners of her mouth. "Oh, Lord," she sighed through her pain, "the dosage wasn't high enough." She looked at me with pity as I held her. "I was hoping to die tonight, Sweetheart," she explained, looking up at me like an infant seeking the breast. "Please..." she begged. It was her choice to make. In making it, she made Death a thief, a cheater, a punk. She had been saving up the pain pills so that she could overdose. In deciding to end things on her terms, she beat the insinuating fucker at his own game. I gave her all the pills that were left, enough to stop her heart. I was proud of her when, in my arms, a little while later, after murmuring, "Well, honey, I was never bored," she died.

♦♦ 9 ♦♦

Subjectivity Is Boring
1982–1984

Father's feet crunched on the driveway's gravel ahead of me. I carried her sparrow-light, lifeless body to the car and propped it up in the front seat. I thought of him carrying me in from the car, drowsy and happy, after a night at the drive-in, slung over his shoulder like a sack of potatoes, when I was as easy to lift as she was now. He used to smell like aftershave and pipe tobacco, I remembered; how comforting that combination of smells had once been, and how intensely I had grown to detest the cloying odor of Borkum Riff, his acrid, shabby suits, and cheap shoes.

My hands shot out from my position in the back seat to cradle Mother's head when Father throwing the car into reverse caused it to loll crazily to the side.

Three letters were burnt out over the entrance: N, C, and Y. Mercurochrome-red neon letters, luridly smudged like badly applied lipstick by what I suppose to have been tears, though I can't remember, read EMERGE. It seemed absurd to pile her into a wheelchair to present her to the triage nurse, but there you have it: even Charon must abide by the rules. I do not cry when I am unhappy. I *never* cry when I feel that I am being manipulated, and I didn't cry then. I simply did my job. A bored resident pronounced her no longer quick. The last time I saw her she was covered loosely with a sheet, her arm hanging out over the edge of the gurney, her husband twisting her wedding ring off, explaining, "These things tend to disappear in morgues, trust me."

Father dealt with death's legalities. I walked out into the parking lot, where an empty ambulance and a cop car were parked. An exhausted paramedic and an orderly sat on the curb, sharing a cigarette, blowing the smoke out into the cold night air. I looked up at the Milky Way, stuffed my hands in my pockets, wondered what was going on inside, walked back in, found a pay phone, dropped some change in, and called Michaela in Colorado. No answer.

Victims of a car wreck were wheeled in. Blood. I've got to get out of here, I thought. "But where can I go? Where is my life? Back to Philadelphia? No. To Colorado, to stay with Michaela and her family? Why not? School's on break; it is as good a place to go as any." I returned to the pay phone and booked a ticket for the first flight out. Father emerged through the crash doors. "Let's go home," he said, throwing me the car keys. "You drive."

Home. Home? Sighing, upon returning from ferrying together her corpse to the hospital, Father poured each of us an amaretto and stretched out behind his desk. At that moment, I thought him ugly. I could tell that he wanted to talk man to man for the first time. The liquor smelled like death. I didn't want to. Mother had told him in front of me the day before that, if he didn't find a way to communicate with his sons, then we would turn our backs on him. He talked.

Father could be a captivating, charming man; he was capable of real eloquence, but I couldn't keep myself from feeling that on some level he still thought that the past few days—my mother's, his wife's slow-motion quadrille with death—had been about him. He loved the law and could conjure beauty when talking about it. He had the sort of mind that remembered all sorts of things; he was skilled at recalling trivia and injecting it into conversations both to delight his friends and to disarm his opponents. I don't know whether he was a good lawyer or not, but he adored Mother; she loved him for that. He loved her and the law with a white-hot purity that I can't help but admire. When we played chess, even when we both knew a dozen moves in advance that I was going to lose, he never permitted me to resign. He quoted Atticus Finch to me: "Courage is when you're licked before you begin but you begin anyway and you see it through no matter what." He liked to work with his hands and taught his sons countless practical skills. I often disliked him, but I always loved him; I never doubted that he loved me. His friends and clients seemed to love him and to respect him. He was often and for long periods profoundly depressed.

We were in his den. "All your good qualities," he began, the evening she died, the evening before the morning I left, never to return during his lifetime, making a steeple of his fingers, "you got from your mother; all the bad ones come from me." We stayed up for the rest of the night. This was not unusual. Growing up, we often ran into one another after everyone else was asleep. I don't know what he did for the rest of the night, but I knew I was never coming back, so I moved from room to room, trying to fix each one in memory. I took several favorite books, some pictures, and two small statues she had sculpted—of Icarus hanging, a chance-ful thing, at the instant before he began his fall, and of Lear with his Fool. I wrapped them in dirty shirts and socks, zipped them into my cheap luggage, and set them beside the front door.

The sun rose. Birds sang. The cab came. I felt as though I watched myself fly to Colorado Springs where I was to spend a week with Michaela, her disapproving mother, and her talented siblings. Ten hours later, I was astride a horse. A gifted horsewoman, Michaela had patiently instructed me how to sit on a placid mare and had herself gracefully mounted her gorgeous ebony stallion Nakiro. Shell-shocked, I scrambled to stay in my saddle as we threaded our way up the McNeil Trail toward the summit of Cheyenne Mountain. Michaela shifted in her saddle, looked back at me, and shook her long blond hair out of her cowboy hat. "'NORAD' is beneath us," she said, smiling broadly. "My name backwards," I mused, recalling that I had read somewhere that there were three huge underground reservoirs down there, so large that workers sometimes crossed them in rowboats. "Like Justinian," I said aloud. "Who?" "It doesn't matter," I said to the horse.

I flew from Colorado to Chicago and boarded the Broadway Limited for Philadelphia. School, when I got there, was the furthest thing from my mind. I checked the "A-H" student mailbox and found a note from the Director commanding me to report at 9 a.m. sharp for the first rehearsal at the Academy of Music of my *Prayer for Peace* by William Smith and the Philadelphia Orchestra.

I had conducted the first (student) performance of it in Curtis Hall the previous April. Smith, associate conductor of the Philadelphia Orchestra, had been in the audience. I loved and respected Bill. The cool kids rolled their eyes and whispered, smirking behind his back, that he smelled like booze, but he treated me like a son, and was—as one of the few faculty members who knew about Mother's health—unfailingly supportive. Bill decided to premiere my piece with the orchestra—the first such debut of a Curtis composer by the orchestra since Samuel Barber's *Overture to the School for Scandal*. Halfway through the first rehearsal, I felt the tide of opinion among the players turn in my piece's favor when violinist William dePasquale turned to his violist brother Joe and said, "I know he's young, but c'mon, let's give the kid a break." Concertmaster Norman Carol then shot me a look that said, "you're in" and from then on everything unfolded smoothly.

Kevin, who had flown out for the performance, and I sat together, a few seats away from the *Philadelphia Inquirer* music critic Daniel Webster, who, a few days earlier, had taken me to lunch and admonished me, "Daron, all you think you can be is one of those orchestrators or film composers out in Hollywood. Don't you understand that once you've graduated Curtis those guys shall have wanted to be *you*?" After the performance, as we stood together in the wings between bows, Bill said, "Daron my boy, you're like Villa-Lobos: you're prolific. When you're great, you're off the charts; the rest of the time, you're still worth playing. So, write a lot. A *lot*."

That winter, some scenes from the film *Trading Places* were shot at Curtis. I was hanging out in the Common Room, hoping to catch a glimpse of Eddie Murphy, of whom I was a big fan, when I overheard this breathless exchange between two young female violinists: "Dan Aykroyd is downstairs in the percussion studio getting stoned!" said one, to which the other replied, "Oh, how I *wish* I played the drums!"

I loved Philadelphia's sycamores because the specific nature of the sunlight through their leaves reminded me of my first, purest, and most contented poetic memory—watching from my stroller as the sun filtered through the leaves overhead. Rittenhouse Square was filled with them. It remains the only one of the five large greens in central Philadelphia to survive as William Penn envisioned it. The park was named in 1825 for a Revolutionary patriot and instrument maker, David Rittenhouse. In 1913, Paul Phillipe Cret redesigned it in the Parisian style in which it has remained to the present. Directly in front of Curtis, facing the park at the corner of Locust and 18th Streets, the tender sycamore leaves opened in the watery spring sunshine. Henry McIllhenny owned the brownstone at the southwest corner of the park. Ned brought Henry (he of the Tabasco sauce fortune, and my benefactor during those days) to a concert of my songs in a church on Walnut Street. Later that April evening, Ned, Norman, Robert Convery, and David Powell came over for a dinner consisting of chicken pilaf, cold lentil salad, heavy red wine, and (at Ned's request) my Grandmother's killer banana cream pie. Satie *Gnossiennes* tinkled away in the background as Ned told us about the "hate mail" he had received in response to an article he had just written about Richard Strauss for *Opera News*. It was the last time that I saw Norman truly happy. "Dogs are German," laughed Norman. "And cats are French," replied Ned. "Baldness is German," I said. Norman replied, "And *toupées* are French."

The school's orchestra was scheduled to spend the summer in France in the mountain town of Evian. I was permitted to tag along not as a composer but as the fellow beating a triangle at the end of Ravel's *Daphnis et Chloé*. To my schoolmates' amusement, before the trip, Robert Fitzpatrick, the affectionately sepulchral Dean of Students, described to the orchestra the tour's manifest as "seventy-two musicians and a composer." While at the festival I was introduced by John de Lancie to Witold Lutosławski, who invited me to leave some of my scores for him at his hotel. A few days later, I was honored to receive the first of several lessons from him. I was 21; he was 69. "Your talent is obvious," he said, paging through my Violin Concerto. "Wieniawski," he murmured. Smiling, he continued, "and Berg." He gently turned several more pages. His eyebrows rose. He looked at me and asked, "Britten?" "Don't know it," I replied. He shrugged. "Ah," he stopped. I followed his finger to a passage for the soloist with solo timpani. "Weill!" I chuckled. "Is there anything original in the piece, do you think?" I asked, respectfully. He looked at me from across what felt like an abyss of history. Echoing Adorno's maxim that to write poetry after Auschwitz is barbaric, he asked, "It isn't just you," he began. "How can anyone compose … this kind of music after World War II?" I replied that I only knew of those horrors of war by way of books. "Yes," he replied, without inflection. I had never met someone who could be so still. "Maestro?" I asked. After a moment, he closed the score. It was clear that, from his perspective, the piece was meretricious. "It's all you, of course; it's all you. How could it not be? Be young. Write like this. Write. Create. Or the Bad Guys Win."

I had composed the concerto into full score in about two weeks in 1983 for Michaela, who premièred it under my baton with the Curtis Orchestra. When it received a BMI Prize, Milton Babbitt told me that he had voted for it because it reminded him of "Max Bruch on Mushrooms." (A quarter century later, I revised it and turned it into *Masquerade*, a double concerto, which Jaime Laredo and Sharon Robinson premièred with the Sacramento Philharmonic conducted by Laura Jackson in 2008, on the day that Atticus was born.) Several days later I sat beside Lutostawski as a then relatively unknown violinist named Anne-Sophie Mutter played the Brahms Violin Concerto with my schoolmates and was astonished when, during the applause that followed, he tapped my arm and said quietly: "I am going to write something for that girl, watch and see." He wrote her *Chain 2*.

I was at loose ends when the flight landed at JFK. Between apartments, Michaela at the Marlborough Festival in Vermont or somewhere else, I explored Manhattan. To my delight, John Houseman's production of *The Cradle Will Rock* had just gone up at the Fairbanks. Before the performance, Houseman took the stage to tell the story of the night the show opened—Blitzstein at the piano, Orson Welles dashing around the theater, playing multiple characters, everyone afire with the moment. Ordinarily too abashed to importune, I threw myself at Houseman afterwards. "You captured lightning in a bottle, didn't you?" I enthused. "Yes, my boy," he drawled in his Professor Kingsfield voice, "I'm acutely aware of that." I laughed. He was disarmed. "You look like Blitzstein," he remarked. I flushed with pleasure. He frowned. "He ended badly." I waited. Beat. "Yes, I know," I said, "I'm a composer." He thrust his chin upwards theatrically as though searching for answers among the klieg lights: "Dear God," he said, exploding the G, extending the O into a melisma, and plucking the final D like a pizzicato. "What does one *do* with a composer?" I laughed again, shook his hand vigorously, and thanked him for his time. "Not at all," he said. "Good luck." He stared at me, hard, for three long beats. "You'll need it." Perfect.

I spent the rest of the summer in Philadelphia copying music at the Fleisher Collection to make money. Every day, on our way to the Free Library, Norman and I stopped at Rindelaub's bakery for coffee and a donut. Norman was unraveling, and he knew it. I could see it, and was trying everything I could to help him keep it together. One morning, by carefully alternating pressure with two fingers of his hand, Norman succeeded in cramming an entire jelly donut into his mouth. "I can't watch movies anymore, Daron," he said. "Why is that?" I asked, dipping my napkin in my coffee and using it to wipe raspberry filling off his beard. "I've always seen my life as a play." We had discussed this frequently. "So?" I prompted. "Well," he said, looking away, "now that it's a tragedy I don't know how to get out."

I shadowed Norman as closely as I could until that August, cross-legged on the floor, I sat before a pile of mail and the telephone in the shotgun apartment on Spruce Street, unable to summon the courage either to open the letters or to answer the phone. He had been calling frequently to be, as he described it, "reminded of reality." When the phone began ringing, I was powerless to move my hands to answer it. A wave of nausea began at my knees and began working its way up towards my head. I felt certain that, if it reached my head, I was going to flip out. Sweat literally streamed from my pores like the woman's gag tears in Chaplin's *A Dog's Life*. When the phone stopped ringing, Clara (my tortoise-shell kitten—a gift from Kile Smith who named her brother Hendrix) climbed into my lap. I found that I could move my hands to pet her. Presently, able to wipe the sweat off my face, I looked at the rotary dial on the phone and had the presence of mind to find it quaint as I dialed my therapist's number. *Sounds like you're having an anxiety attack, buddy; come and see me this afternoon.* It felt like a betrayal (it still does) but I followed his advice and began to see less of Norman. When he returned home to his parent's house, I felt relieved: he'd be in their care—he'd get on with his life; he'd be free of Curtis. Then the news came that he had hung himself.

Although I can now imagine just how difficult (and dangerous) disclosing the news of Norman's death to Curtis' highly-strung, mostly very-young student body would be, I was furious then about how it was handled, bitter about the fact that the administration had not been immediately forthcoming. To keep a grip on myself, I had poured all my energy and feelings into composing a memorial symphony—based on Norman's musical setting of our favorite poem, Roethke's *The Waking*—for him. One night in November fury overcame fear and I confronted the Director, John de Lancie on the way to his car. "Sir," I began, "I want to write a symphony in memory of Norman. Will you sign off on the orchestra performing it?" I was out of line, and I knew it. "I've supported you this far," de Lancie seethed. "But this is too much music for the orchestra to learn. We teach composition at Curtis, not orchestration." "What does that even *mean*?" I blurted. "Norman *killed* himself. The school doesn't even officially acknowledge that it happened. I want to do this thing. Music is Communion. I want to give us as a student body an opportunity for catharsis. I want to make things better." I felt like sobbing but was too angry to generate tears. "For Norman. *Please.*" I stopped. I want to remember what he said, and how he looked at me, but I don't. He relented; the piece was added to the concert, and, a few days later, I led the orchestra in its single performance. Ned wrote of that night in his diary, "Last night ... Daron's affecting memorial symphony ... for Norman. Poor Norman's parents were present, amiable but lost, like Bill Flanagan's parents at his memorial long ago."

Much of what happened that spring is obscured in my memory behind a sort of psychic scar tissue. At some point, my therapist, citing "clinical depression," prescribed drugs to alleviate the symptoms. Disgusted by what I perceived as weakness, frightened by the prospect of taking mood-altering medication, and embarrassed by the idea that someone might find out and either make fun of me or deem me an "unviable candidate" for a professional career, I balled the prescription in my fist on the way out of his office and tossed it into the nearest garbage can. I drank a lot; I ate little; I sometimes went for days without sleep. I know that I composed; I copied music; I pursued my studies. I *always worked*. Always. My "Work Log" says that I composed 40 minutes of music, most of which is still in print.

I'd been living with—and recall having been hell to live *with*—bassoonist David McGill and cellist Robert La Rue on Spruce Street about a block from school. Somehow, Michaela and I had continued our relationship, although not exactly openly. Henry James scholar Sheldon Novick was renting rooms in his brownstone at 2214 Delancey Place. When Ned was a student at Curtis, his parents rented for him a room in the house directly across the street owned by the parents of Shirley (née Gabis) Perle. Michaela and I roomed together on the top floor. Robert La Rue lived downstairs; violist Lisa Ponton took a room down the hall from him. I constructed on Delancey Place a simulacrum of family life that worked for a while—at least for a while.

"The Green" has long been the traditional actors' term for the stage. Shakespeare, in *Midsummer Night's Dream*, has Quince refer to the "green plot" at one point. One story holds that the Blackfriars Theatre in London as far back as five hundred years ago had a green room backstage where the actors waited to go on. In the concert music world, during the concert, Green Rooms are either empty or used as resting places for performers. During intermission, they are usually reserved for friends of the soloist, and people in the business. Socially fraught and politically complex places, after the concert, all at once, they serve as an estuarial vessel in which audience meets performer, management estimates artist appeal, younger artists supplicate themselves before older ones, donors are cultivated, and artists trawl their competitors' connections. Certainly, important performances take place in them—as the saying goes, "the opera is rarely kept on the stage." Now, isn't it odd that they are rarely green?

The Director's wife, Madam de Lancie, served tea one afternoon each week in the Institute's Common Room. My understanding was that the ritual was meant to prepare us for how to behave in Green Rooms. Madam de Lancie sat behind one enormous samovar; her guest host was stationed behind the other. It was always a courtly, if somewhat ramshackle minuet. "Str-r-r-ong ... or-r-r ... weak?" she gurgled when one reached the head of the line, teacup balanced delicately between thumb and index finger. She always chuckled when I would aver "Not so strong." This meant that she would fill my cup halfway and then hand it to her guest (back then it was usually the spouse of whomever was conducting the Philadelphia Orchestra that week), who would complete the pour. With tea one had a cookie. Living on a pin, Norman and I (and generations of other Curtis students) filled the pockets of our blazers with cookies from the large table in the Bok Room. Fifteen years later, checking the pockets of one long-unworn jacket before donating it to the Salvation Army, I found Zuzu's petals-like crumbs.

Another function of the weekly tea was to provide students the opportunity to interact socially with the teachers whom they admired, feared, and were inspired by. I found Ford Mylius Lallerstedt III the most intimidating, and I loved him for it. My awe of Ford's astonishing intellect and facility at score reading and counterpoint solutions made me insecure and precluded immediate performance success for me; but it also kindled a lifelong passion for the teaching and study of counterpoint. Speaking to him at tea was the closest I could come at the time to getting to know him. Edward Aldwell, as he did with generations of Curtis students, stole my heart. By sitting down at the piano at the beginning of his lectures and performing for us the Bach fugue that we would study that day (and then performing it for us again at the end of the lecture), he gracefully fused artistic authority with intellectual power. He changed my life and has epitomized for me ever since the idea of what it is to be a "thinking musician." Ed came often to tea and was exceptionally kind to me. He was one of the few people at Curtis who knew what I was going through. Thirty years after it happened, classmate Hugh Sung, who had gone on to serve on the Curtis faculty, and was interviewing Gilda and me for a podcast, recalled Norman, jacket-less on a cold winter day shortly before his suicide, standing in the middle of the Common Room during Tea Time with his hands pressed to his temples, screaming.

One afternoon at tea composer, pianist, and conductor Lukas Foss and I struck up a conversation about Stockhausen. Lukas *was* music—being around his natural gift and magical, positive personality made my heart sing. Born in 1922 in Berlin, Lukas began his education there before moving to Paris to study piano, composition, and flute. He moved with his family to Philadelphia in 1937 and enrolled at Curtis. A protégé of Serge Koussevitzky's, he studied composition with Hindemith as a special student at Yale until 1940. The youngest composer ever to receive a Guggenheim, he taught at UCLA (where he succeeded Arnold Schoenberg) until 1970. He conducted the Brooklyn Philharmonic until 1990 and taught at Boston University from 1991 until his death in 2009. His compositional catalogue consists of three periods: first, a Neo-classic, second, an avant-garde phase that combined elements of Neo-classicism with improvisation, serial techniques, and chance operations, and finally a deliciously eclectic final period in which he fused elements of idioms and styles spanning most of western music history.

In January 1984, a few months after meeting Lukas, Kevin arranged for me to serve as his driver during a visit to Milwaukee. We heard the squeal of tires, the blare of a car horn, and considered oncoming traffic on a one-way street. A man waved us over to the side of the road with his arm as he drove towards us. "The melting major to minor chord at the very end," he enthused, hands massaging the air between his chest and the dashboard, "is original here. Some say that this is where Mahler got the idea for the same effect in his sixth." We were riffing on Beethoven's third, the great *Eroica*, the score of which sat on his lap. "At the end of the second movement, I'm going to try something interesting: as the theme disintegrates—the part marked *sotto voce*—I'm going to remove players one by one from the tune." "Like Beethoven's hearing leaving him. Cool. How do the players feel about the idea?" "Oh, they are not too happy. They are a little upset about the scherzo, too." "How come?" "I'm making a little Rossini-style accelerando through the theme so that it sounds like nervous laughter." "Beethoven's nervous breakdown?" "Night fears following the loss of his hearing…." "Chattering teeth in a death skull…?" "Worse. The effects of lead poisoning." "Wow," I said, turning the wrong direction on to a one-way street. Horns honked, cars swerved. "What's that?" asked Lukas, abruptly conscious of his surroundings. "We're driving the wrong way down a one-way street," I answered, as mildly as I could. "Oh," he replied, completely disinterested. "Then, when the finale begins, the variations are a triumph of the…" I pulled over. We were now five minutes late to the rehearsal and I was hopelessly lost, even though I had grown up in Milwaukee. "…A triumph," I attempted to complete his thought, "of the rational, conscious mind, expressed through the exercise of craft that composing variations requires, over the irrational fears of the subconscious?" "That's interesting you should say that," he smiled. "I've always thought that fugue, so rational, was, in the end—take the *Grosse Fuge*—his avenue for exploring madness." Somehow, we made it to the rehearsal.

Taking lessons from "outside" teachers while enrolled at Curtis was forbidden, so I told nobody. I'm astonished now by the fact that it never occurred to me to offer to pay for the occasional lessons that Lukas generously gave me, and touched by the fact that he never asked me to. Lukas' friendship with Kevin also deepened during this time from a professional one to a close personal one. He was family, I rationalized, and so what could be wrong with his looking at my music? I was exactly as comfortable talking about music with Lukas as I was uncomfortable discussing it with Ned. (As far as I know, Ned didn't find out about the lessons until after Lukas died in 2009.) They were friends, but also competitors: "I don't have a problem with Lukas jumping on every new stylistic bandwagon that comes along," quipped Ned to me around this time. "I just can't stand that he always wants to be the driver."

For his part, Ned had mastered the "musical transatlantic accent"—just pretty-enough, just ugly-enough, texturally rich, colorfully orchestrated. He alternated between plush "felt" melodies and emotionally cool "abstract" ones in his work, just as Samuel Barber had. Conflating matters of "class" and "taste," this vacillation is still the ticket if a composer wants to be judged highbrow but also "accessible." Take one step too far in one direction and those in the club snidely decree that you should go west and write film scores because your ideas are too derivative; one step too far in the other direction and you're a heartless modernist who should give up composition and teach counterpoint somewhere.

The older I get, the more I look to Lukas as having been the teacher who had the most influence on my music. Why? Lukas was only interested in music. He wasn't interested in what style something was in, or whether it was "academically respectable" or not; he only cared about whether it connected with people emotionally. "If it connects," he would say, "then it is the good stuff. If it doesn't, then it is the other."

Over the past three years, the ebullience and high flying "chancefulness" of composing had given way to a less sensually pleasing, but more emotionally nourishing interplay between head and heart. At Curtis, a teacher and his pupil decide together when their work is done. I had earned a bachelor's degree, but neither Ned nor I cared about that. I felt strongly that it was time to get on with my life, and Ned felt I was "ready, as far as these things go." I loved Philadelphia and the school deeply. I didn't *have* to graduate, and abandon the school's comforting *prétentieux*, its proud stance of *Ars super omnia*. A certain splendid, complacent egoism had begun to frame my relationship with making art that made me uncomfortable. I sat down at my portable Royal typewriter, wrote to Diamond, and told him exactly what I reckoned he'd want to hear—

> *I am writing to you because I feel I'm finally ready to come to Juilliard. Studying with Mr. Rorem has been a revelation, but I realize that my facility can still get ahead of my self-criticism and honestly feel that you are the single best man to help me with that.*

Did I sincerely believe that David was the right teacher for me? I don't think that I cared. I intended to move to New York, and I needed a place to hang my hat. When I told Ned, he looked alarmed, "Are you sure? What makes you think you're not ready to just go out and *start?*" I told myself then that learning from David's command of large-scale forms (symphonies, string quartets) would perfectly compliment the grounding I had received from Ned by way of his virtuosity in small ones (song cycles, suites). It turned out to be true.

March is the month during which most conservatories hold auditions. On the way to my Juilliard interview, I passed the bathroom in which five years earlier I had vomited. The door opened, and David Diamond, in a zippy blue pin stripe suit, poked his head out. Rain fell straight down. I straightened my tie, shot my cuffs, and sidled past him, into the room. I scanned the table set up before the windows, through which the Hudson could be seen like a gray stain, and recognized Milton Babbitt, Elliot Carter, and Vincent Persichetti.

"Mr. Hagen," Diamond drawled. His thin lips and pale face were dour, but his eyes shone. "You may sit down." So serious! I stripped off my raincoat and dropped *The New Yorker* magazines I'd brought to catch up on during the train ride from Philly. They slid to the floor. I flapped my arms. "Oh, for the love-a Mike!" I hissed. I looked up into Vincent Persichetti's kind eyes. He had been trying to see what I was reading. "Hello, Mr. Car—," I said, lunging at him. "No, he's Roger Sessions," piped Babbitt. "That's not funny, Milton," scolded Diamond. My head swiveled to respond. I opened my mouth like a koi. "We all remember you from four years ago, Mr. Hagen. And, looking at the number of scores you've sent us … well … it seems as though you have been working very … hard." Diamond offered the observation as a question, his eyebrows rising. "You've been very … prolific … haven't you?"

I returned his gaze steadily as he fingered the American Academy of Arts and Letters pin in his lapel. Was it a trick question? This time, telephone conversations had been had, arrangements been made: Ned had spoken with Bernstein, and with Diamond. I had made hay at Curtis, had acquired some connections, and managed a couple of minor achievements. Was Diamond inferring that I had been too prolific? Shrugging, I looked out over the roof of LaGuardia High School. Through the gauze of rain, I could see the sun setting. What looked at first glance like a murder of crows over the Hudson River turned out to be a colony of gulls.

"Let's see," Diamond continued. "Vincent, will you do the honors?" Persichetti stubbed out his cigarette, scrunched his eyes up behind his glasses, and slid onto the piano bench. He winked at me. This time when he launched into his mad medley, I was ready for him: "Coronation Scene from *Boris Godunov!*" I said. An insane modulation and he was playing a Chopin Mazurka. "Chopin: don't remember which one," I said. He began the *Tristan* progression, and I said quickly, "*Tristan*, of course." "Nope," he said. "Trick question." He continued. "Of course, it's *Golliwog's Cakewalk*." "Uh huh," he smiled. He played one, unmistakable crunchy chord. "*Rite of Spring!*" I laughed. Something pointillist, lovely, but stylistically diffuse. "Pretty," I mused. "I don't recognize it." He stopped. "Something of my own," he smiled. "Neat!" I said.

"Mr. Hagen," Diamond began, "I have no doubt whatsoever that you will be, or plan to be, as prolific as ever. I would say that is a blessing which must be haloed by the development of more severe self-criticism and a larger awareness of structural invention." I looked from one face to the next. "Okay!" I said. "When do I start?" Laughter. "Well," said Carter, looking at me and speaking for the first time. "David will work out the details of your scholarship. That's that."

A few months later, at my final lesson with Ned, I presented him with the manuscript of a diary that I had written covering the time we had worked together. Taken aback, he flipped through it, and placed it carefully on a pile of papers on his red dining room table. "I'll read it, Daron," he promised. I thought myself rather brave. "But I haven't much hope for it." I deflated. "Why?" I asked, sincere. He had evidently formulated a summing up of me for my character prior to our final meeting, and now, he delivered it, suavely wrought, an opinion stated with all the simple conviction of fact: "You tell people what you think they want to hear. Since you're bright, you're usually right. But sometimes you're not." It occurred to me then that I felt psychically the way that I had felt physically the night that I sliced off a knuckle into some corned beef. There was blood everywhere, of course; but the blade was so sharp that I never felt it. In fact, it was the single cruelest thing that Ned ever said to me—and probably the most therapeutic. A few days later I had Ned's letter—

I read your whole diary in almost one fell swoop and was quite impressed. Diaries are dangerous, being the most subjective of literary forms (and subjectivity is boring), but yours makes it, and is the real thing.... When we are next together we can talk more. Meanwhile, know that I was truly moved by much of it.

I no longer had an address. Sheldon allowed me to store my belongings in the basement of his townhouse on Delancey Place as I had not yet found a place to live in Manhattan. Seated on a box on which I had scrawled, "These musical sketches belong to Daron Hagen: Someday I will return for them," I observed the ancient Russian pagan ritual of sitting in silence on my luggage for a few moments, collecting my thoughts. I wrote in my journal—

Two nights ago, in Wisconsin—gin-coffee-gin-coffee at the hotel bar as Kristie's wedding reception unfolded nearby. To my heart: slow down; to my life: speed up. Self-flagellation & self-pity; puke in the parking lot. Shostakovich string quartets in Kevin's living room 'til dawn. A pass by the Big Cedar

House on our way to the airport. "Should we see dad?" Kevin: "Hell, no, he's made his bed." Ties severed. On the plane, thoughts of serving as Mom's Charon a few months ago. Packing, today, ritualistically tearing up pictures of Michaela. Train to Yaddo (rhymes with shadow) this afternoon.

Already I had spirits enough travelling with me, I needed no more tail-wind for the journey to come.

◆◆ 10 ◆◆

Yaddo
1984–2015

Like mine, Yaddo's story is about the presence that absence makes. Spencer and Katrina Trask created Yaddo for the same reason that my parents created me. They were trying to transform sorrow into joy. Yaddo serves as both a memorial to the Trask's dead children and a testament to their parent's determination to transubstantiate loss into art. To me, Yaddo, the artist's retreat in Saratoga Springs, New York, is not just a hallowed place, but also my home.

I knew of the place only what I had read in Ned's dairies when he telephoned its President, Curtis Harnack (that wonderfully humane man), and his brilliant, wise wife, Hortense Calisher to arrange for my first visit. "Yaddo," wrote Ned, "is necessary for you now. Don't try so hard to be Rastignac. Perhaps a little less need to get ahead, to be a 'professional'; a little more introspection and, indeed, egotism, will do you good. But who knows? One man's meat, etc.…" He advised me to ask Diamond what books I should read before beginning my studies with him at Juilliard the following September. Along with decreeing that I spend the summer studying "Beethoven Quartets op. 59, No. 1, Opus 131, Haydn's Opus 33, No. 1, Mozart, Brahms, Bruckner, and Berg," he had commanded me to read Thomas Mann's *Doktor Faustus* and Romain Rolland's *Jean-Christophe*.

I arrived at Yaddo with the need not to be Rastignac, but Orpheus; I desired nothing more than to sing Mother's spirit out of the Underworld, bring her back to life. Expecting nothing, knowing nothing, and having been told nothing by Ned except "You might not like it; these places are not for everyone," I disembarked at the Saratoga Springs train station. I had with me the clothes on my back, Mann and Roland in my backpack, four shirts, three pair of underwear, two pair of jeans, four pair of socks, mechanical pencils and erasers, thirty dollars, and lots and lots of King Brand manuscript paper.

James Mahon, a courtly, red-bearded Charon with a mild voice and probing, intense eyes who gravely addressed me as "sir" long before I had any claim to it, placed my backpack gently in the beat up old company station wagon. We drove slowly through town, past Town Hall and the Post Office, and the Adirondack Trust bank. We passed the Parting Glass, where mingled during August the jockeys from the Saratoga Race Track and their tall, glossy girlfriends, the Yaddo artists, the City Ballet dancers, the Philadelphia Orchestra players, the townies, and the bettors.

James turned on to broad, tree-lined Union Avenue—one of the Hudson Valley's grandest boulevards. Flanked by over a dozen Queen Anne–style mansions built during the late 1800s, it begins at Congress Park and culminates a mile and a half later at the

Northway. In 1978, the entire area was listed in the National Register of Historic Places as the Union Avenue Historical District. As the car rolled by the racetrack, with its bevy of Victorian structures, I felt as though we were going back in time. We passed the National Museum of Racing. I thought aloud: "Seabiscuit." "Ah, yes sir," James drawled, glancing at me curiously in the rearview mirror, "that was a brave little pony now, wasn't it?"

"Whitney," I said, "Jerome, Vanderbilt…." "Ah, yes sir," James drawled, "those would be some other names associated with the race track, that's for certain." On our right, at the far end of Union Avenue, adjacent to the track, began a dense, shadowy forest. "This would be Yaddo, sir," James said, turning on to the grounds.

Spencer Trask, founder of the well-known Wall Street firm, and his wife Katrina had the mansion built in 1892 by architect William Halsey Wood, who did little but execute the designs provided by his clients. 55 rooms, a medieval dining hall and tower, barns, outbuildings, four man-made ponds bearing the children's

Enjoying a thermos full of coffee, the *New York Times* read from front to back, and conversation after breakfast in the Linoleum Room during my first visit to Yaddo, in Saratoga Springs, New York, in summer 1984. Once my mother died, Yaddo became my de facto home-base for three decades until I married Gilda (photograph by Lynn Freed).

names, a rock garden, and a large formal rose garden, all laid out to Spencer's specifications.

James slowed the car as we passed between the lakes. We veered left, and then right, then climbed the drive, and to our left the mansion blossomed into view atop the hill. I gasped. Embarrassed, I looked toward the rearview mirror and saw that James' eyes were warm. "Yes sir," he smiled, "that's the Main House. We'll be driving past West House, Pine Garde, and East House so that I can drop you at the Office." We shook hands and he handed me my backpack after I got out.

Tears spontaneously flowed as beloved, infinitely capable program director Rosemary Misurelli (who I had never met) bundled me up in her Rabelaisian Earth Mother arms at the front door of the office. "I feel as though I have come home," I burbled. Weeping, she covered my face with kisses, and then took me in to meet Curt, who asked me why I was crying. "I have no idea," I said. "Are you okay?" he asked. "I think so," I said. "I don't understand why I'm crying." "Oh, I do," he said, with a kind, open mid-western smile.

Upon arrival, a Special Assistant to the President escorts every artist to his or her studio and bedroom. That summer, Doug Martin and Nancy Brett served. I was given a tour of the grounds, and then shown into the mansion's grand hall. Hanging there were two life-sized full portraits. Before being told her identity, I was as irresistibly drawn to Eastman Johnson's painting as I had been to the Norman Rockwell portrait of Mary Louise Curtis Bok Zimbalist. We hadn't met, but my heart instinctively moved out to her. I felt safe here. "Yes, that's her," Nancy said, gently pulling me away and leading me up the sweeping stairs. "Katrina Trask?" I asked. "Yes," she said, pointing up at the two-story tall Tiffany window atop the stairs. "That's her, too."

We turned left at the foot of the window, passed a large brass spittoon, and reached the sliding door leading to Oratory (a place of prayer), the room next to what had been Spencer's den that would serve as my bedroom.

Everyone who has lived and worked at Yaddo over the past century has heard stories about the ghosts. There's the Puritanical one that keeps watch in the bedroom on the second floor of the mansion opposite the stairs that opens the windows when something naughty is happening in the room. There's the Testy one that slams the closet door in Katrina's bedroom when the current occupant spends a little too much time on the fainting couch.

In May 2007, I sat before the upright piano in the Acosta Nichols Tower studio, writing with trepidation the title *Amelia* over what would become the first page of over four hundred pages of piano sketch of my opera about flight and rebirth. A bird flew in through the open door and flew frightened circles high above me in the white cone of the ceiling. I got up and spoke quietly to t he bird, "You'll be okay, friend. Everything will be fine. The door is open. Fly through it." As though on cue, the bird swooped down and glided back out through the door to safety in the surrounding forest. It was the plainest sort of blessing, and a perfect example of the sort of thing that happens at Yaddo.

Yaddo is about the work, first. My work book lists the following pieces composed all, or in part, there between 1984 and the present: four major operas: *Amelia, Bandanna, Little Nemo in Slumberland*, and *Shining Brow*; two cantatas: *A Walt Whitman Requiem* and *Light Fantastic*; my Symphony No. 3; and nearly a hundred art songs and chamber works, large and small.

Much of Yaddo's magic derives from the effect that it has on one's fellow artists. For example, I had learned about the extravagance, the power, and the beauty of raw talent at Curtis, that talent is like a natural resource—amoral and unearned. It can be cultivated and strengthened by its possessor, and it can be misused, of course. But I had never (and have never, since) met anyone quite as joyously talented as David Del Tredici, who I befriended during my first residency. He was—and remains—a nova.

I first met Joel Conarroe that summer. Joel, the author of books and articles about American literature and anthologies of poetry, president of the Guggenheim Foundation from 1985–2002 (and a trustee until his retirement in 2016); former chair of the English Department, Ombudsman, and Dean of the Faculty of Arts and Sciences at the University of Pennsylvania, and former president of the PEN American center, was deeply gentle, erudite, decent, and agreeable company over dinner during the weeks that our visits overlapped. In 1994, Joel and David Del Tredici reached out to Donald S. Rice, then Chairman of Yaddo's Board of Directors, and together nominated me for membership in the Corporation. Subsequently elected by the Directors and Members that year, I was further elected by our brothers and sisters fifteen years later to continue beyond the restriction of a term limit as a "Lifetime Member"—an honor bestowed on only one other Member: Susan Brynteson, Yaddo's beloved Librarian, and (now retired) Vice provost and head of the University of

Delaware Library. In his letter commending me to Don, Joel described me as "represent[ing] the best of what Yaddo is all about." I treasure Joel's approbation and this honor above any other I've received in my life.

I was taught a briskly affectionate character lesson of immense value one evening at West House during the early 80s by novelist Lynn Freed. She'd been in residence long enough to observe our small society in action, but it was our first real conversation. "What do you make of so-and-so?" she asked. "And him? And her?" We compared notes. Presently, she asked, "Darling boy, why are you such a Rabbit with people in public, and so Dead-Spot-On-Brutal in your assessment of them in private? Surely there's a balance, no?"

When at 16 I told my English teacher Diane Doerfler that I intended to move to the east coast, she presented me with the volume of John Cheever's short stories I possess to this day: "Read these," she said, throwing me a rope. "He and Updike seem to get it right." Only a few years later Susan Cheever and I became friends at Yaddo. I imagine Doerf would be pleased to know that I told Susan about her gift. Years later, playwright / actor Ayad Akhtar was made a member of the Corporation. He charmed me, when we met for the first time during the annual fall meeting, by regaling me during dinner with fulsome reminiscences of Doerf, whom he credited as "an essential guiding force in his early development."

It was at Yaddo—reading the Trask family's exquisite 1901 Little, Brown and Company *Works of Honoré de Balzac* shelved in West House—that, over the course of fifteen years, I savored every word of Balzac's monumental *La Comedie Humaine*, in English, and then in French. He remains to me as precious as Georges Simenon is to Ned. Rastignac—he, whose name is an insult in France, has served all my life both as a warning and as a negative example, as surely as Romain Rolland's Jean-Christophe has constituted a blessing and an imprecation. In other words, on the one hand, "*La vie humaine se compose de deux parties: on tue le temps, le temps vous tue,*" and, on the other, "There are some dead who are more alive than the living."

Katrina Trask's was one of what Rick Moody calls the "momentous and astonishing and beautiful deaths" that have taken place at Yaddo. During my first visit—summer 1984— I spent several weeks composing a requiem, what poet and memoirist Richard McCann might call a "ghost letter" to Katrina. Richard wrote, in one of his poems, "Quiet! Don't you know that the dead go on hearing for hours?" I believe that they continue hearing forever if they are of a mind to. I believe that Katrina Trask continues to hear what goes on at Yaddo to this day.

Near the end of my first visit, novelist Doug Unger was sitting on the second-floor landing, around eleven-thirty in the evening, reading *The New Yorker*. Across from him sat a third person, whose name escapes me. That reassuring, late-night quietude (the plashing of water in the little fountain next to the front door, the soughing and whispering of the pines, underpinned by the steady thrum of automobile wheels on the Northway) unique to this house surrounded us. I didn't know at the time that Doug was up there. I was reading in the Great Hall, next to the fireplace with the phoenix on it.

At that instant, I less "saw" than "felt" Katrina Trask's presence. In the same way that one might glimpse a child streaking out of a suburban front yard and into the street, and with the same terrible wave of heart-in-the-mouth dread, perceived peripherally, intuited while focusing elsewhere, a woman descending the main staircase in what John Cheever mischievously described as "poor Katrina's shower curtain" came before my mind's eye. It was unquestionably Katrina's ghost. Her right hand was slightly raised, as it is in the portrait, and in it was a telegram, a poem, or a letter. Allan Gurganus suavely describes what I saw as "some essence quorum of our souls' intensities." At the instant that I noticed the apparition, I heard a cry from the second floor. I leapt to the foot of the stairs to see what the matter was. Looking up, I saw ashen-faced Doug.

"What did you see?" I asked. "A woman in a white dress, so help me God," he said.

From behind him in the darkness the third person—who couldn't possibly have seen the staircase—said, softly, "It was Katrina." We coughed, laughed, looked at our feet. I have seen an angel, I thought. I used to describe the feeling I took away from the moment as being exactly like the way I used to feel when I heard the crunch of gravel in the driveway that meant Mother was home. Now, as a father, I recognize that the feeling was more like the way I feel when my children are sleeping in the next room, yet I am in every way but physically with them.

That afternoon, a little drunk, during a playful "recite your favorite line of poetry" challenge on the patio, my recitation—with what must have been deemed excessive gravity—of Roethke's line from the last tercet of *The Waking*, "This shaking keeps me steady. I should know," had been greeted with derision. "See, I *am* that 'lowly worm' climbing 'the winding stair,'" I protested, stubbornly, pointing to the staircase on which I would, hours later, see Katrina. "The 'shaking' is our fear of death *and* the embracing of the ecstasy of being wide open to life all at once. It's Katrina on the stairs reading the telegram relaying the new that Spencer has died. At Yaddo the great victory is that there is happiness without dread."

How, I wondered as a boy, would it feel to experience happiness without dread, and, if I did, how long would it last before the inevitable happened and I ended up, at two in the morning, my ass is in the air, scrubbing again and again the same square foot of asphalt tile until I had forgotten what the question was? Now I wonder, when I'm telling my sons a bedtime story about the animals at Yaddo (who have names, and speak, and have adventures, and inhabit a Hundred Acre Wood that is entirely real to my boys, as real as Yaddo is to me, and as precious), I wonder how it is possible that there is no dread in our home; how is it possible that this happy story won't end for my sons the way that it ended for my brothers?

After much discussion, and many Yaddo bedtime stories, and Elaina Richardson's permission, I agreed to take Atticus with me to attend the 24 July 2015 ceremony at Yaddo at which the mansion and grounds would be proclaimed a National Historic Landmark.

The water in the "Sleepy Naiads" fountain was cold and clear. "Brr," said Atticus, now aged 6, pulling his small, perfect feet out. It was his first visit to Yaddo. To look our best, we had dressed in matching starched white shirts and shorts. But a child's a child, and we'd decided that, before touring the mansion together, we ought to dip our feet in the fountain. I passed him his stockings. We sat in the grass. I handed him his shoes. "You make the ears," he explained. "Then you jump through the hole, right?" I asked. "Uh huh. And then you pull the ears tight," he said, pulling on his shoelaces with a look of satisfaction.

Atticus' attention shifted from his shoelaces to follow my gaze up the hill as I took in the mansion. "Papa?" "Yes, honey." "How did the children die?" I looked back down at the grass, deciding how much to say. "There were four of them. They all died before they were teenagers," I said. His eyes widened. "Do you really want to hear this?" He nodded gravely. "One lived only 12 days."

Atticus shook his head in wonder: "Like the 'Other Daron,' Papa?" "Yeah," I answered. "No wonder you love this place so much," he said. "More than you know, baby," I said. "So, tell me," he said, placing his hand on my beard the way that I sometimes stroke his cheek. "The oldest child had Uncle Kevin's middle name, Alansson," I began. Atticus looked up at the house as I spoke. "He died of some childhood disease. The middle children were

Christina and Spencer Jr. At some point when they were children, they caught Diphtheria kissing their Mama goodbye." He turned suddenly, and asked, "Did their Mama die, too?" "No," I answered, "their mama Katrina was okay." He threw his arms around me, and began to cry. "It's okay, baby," I said, stroking his hair. He looked up at me, and asked, "What happened to the last one?" I pulled him close. He buried his head in my chest. "The last child was named Katrina," I told him, stroking his hair. "She lived only nine days."

Presently, we gathered up our things and walked to the car. "Can we come back, Papa?" "Not only *can* we return, we *must*," I told him firmly, digging my chin into the top of his head as I held him, tears falling into his hair's golden ringlets. "Why, Papa?" I looked at him—his tender, small frame just beginning to flesh out with the wiry strength of the man into whom he'd grow, and I thought to myself that Life is fragile, that Art is fragile, too; I thought that the Loud drown out the Rest most of the time, but that Art, so simultaneously ephemeral and eternal, like Love, can do more than prompt a tyrant's tears; it can give strength and hope to those fighting for a better world for our kids, a safer place to bring them up, a more tolerant mindset, more open hearts. I had to look away from him. and up the hill towards the mansion as I formulated a simpler answer, an answer that, hopefully, even a child might understand. "Because Yaddo," I whispered, "is a place where sorrow is transformed into joy."

◆◆ 11 ◆◆

Copland's Tears
1984–1985

When I moved to New York City in autumn 1984, it still felt more like a "culmination of an era" sort of place than a New Beginning. Aaron Copland was still alive, his struggle with Alzheimer's not yet commonly known. Philip Glass was the most influential minimalist; Jacob Druckman and Elliott Carter were the most influential modernists. Darmstadt composers, like Morton Feldman, Lucian Berio, and—particularly—Heinz Werner Henze excited me, but "Internationalism" already seemed *passé* to me—now, in the 2010's, it seems to be back with a vengeance. In '86, Pierre Boulez brought his Ensemble InterContemporain to Columbia University where he conducted *Répons*. *Times* critic Donal Henahan poo-pooed it, but I recall every serious composer in New York was there and we were electrified. At the other extreme (or not), David Del Tredici succeeded Druckman as composer in residence with the New York Philharmonic, and Ned was fulfilling the biggest commissions of his career—from the Chicago Symphony, and several from the Philharmonic (all of which I copied for him), signaling the heavy musical establishment's tectonic shift towards neo-romanticism. These composers were all still at the top of their game; they were the stars in their courses, and I remember caring about, and arguing with colleagues about, their music as something vital and important. Tim Page's "New Old, and Unexpected" radio show on WNYC was influential and discussed.

When young composers talked music, there was a lot of talk about "Uptown," "Midtown," and "Downtown" music. "Uptown" consisted of complex, modernist, academic, and internationalist pieces composed by graduate students at Columbia University and performed on college campuses. The composers of this sort of music drank mainly at the Marlin, a terrific old watering hole near Columbia that catered to punk rockers, career drinkers, musicians, and students. "Midtown" consisted of Americana composed by the pupils of David Diamond and Vincent Persichetti; modernist scores by Milton Babbitt's and Elliott Carter's students at Juilliard and performed at Lincoln Center. Those of us writing this sort of music drank mainly at Paddy McGlade's, just around the corner from Juilliard. My first neighborhood bar, it stood at the southwest corner of 67th Street and Columbus Avenue for more than a century. "Downtown" consisted of west-coast style minimalism melded to east coast visual art by folks like Philip Glass and performed in Greenwich Village lofts and galleries. The NoName Bar on Hudson Street was the hangout for the purveyors of this stuff, and it put the others to shame with its mixture of musicians, artists, stockbrokers, and activists.

I drank everywhere. It seemed to me that the best Uptown modernists and spektralists at Columbia were also playing jazz in the Village at night, that the Downtown minimalists would eventually have to start putting decent tunes on top of their accompaniment patterns, and that the Midtown guys would stay the course, settling into an eclectic neo-romanticism once Boulez's influence had waned.

The bedroom in the fifteenth-floor apartment I shared with painter Charlotte Hastings and a succession of short-term lodgers at 467 Central Park West (then one of the Upper West Side's dodgier neighborhoods) overlooked what are now pricey condominiums but then looked like the ruins of a castle. (It was in fact the 1887 New York Cancer Hospital, located on the block front from 105th to 106th Streets. The beautiful red brick and brown-stone chateau was among the first cancer hospitals in the United States, with circular wards "to diminish hiding places for germs.") The apartment was two blocks from the Cathedral of Saint John the Divine, where, every morning, after too much coffee at the Hungarian Pastry Shop, I read the *Times* in the cool, half-light of the apse to the ghostly accompaniment of the cathedral organist practicing Messiaen.

My idealistic, even laughable stance was that a composer of art music should, without turning his work into a commodity, earn his living by accepting commissions. The schol-arship Juilliard awarded me (it was for some reason in Irving Berlin's name) covered tuition, plus a little extra. To earn money for living expenses, I was willing to fly without a net, and did: no steady job, no health insurance, certainly no savings. I lived financially in the moment, buying myself four weeks of freedom to compose by burying myself for ten days in a copying job. Several meaningful composition prizes were thrown in my direction, but I understood that they were awarded for my work's potential, and because it was clear that I needed the money. When there wasn't any copying work, I played the piano in pit orches-tras, dance classes, and in cocktail bars. My hope was that, at some point, I'd begin to be able to wean myself from copying work because commissions would support me. The first major commission I received was from Mark Gottschalk and the Loomis Chaffee Academy for *A Walt Whitman Requiem*, the second came from the International Chamber Artists Series for *Trio Concertante*, and the third was from the great organist Leonard Raver, for *Occasional Notes*.

When Leonard sent the piece along to Robert Schuneman, the president of E.C. Schirmer, a music-publishing house in Boston, Bob published it. Although I briefly con-sidered Arnold Broido's offer of an exclusive publishing agreement with Theodore Presser, I ultimately threw my lot in with Bob. His was one of the smaller houses; his steadfastly fine character, feisty underdog attitude, and essential goodness were clear to me from the moment we met. Over the next thirty years we remained friends and buckled many musical swashes. I loved Bob and his wife Cynthia, and they, in turn, tolerated with patience and wisdom my frequent periods of professional frustration and depression. They watched me grow up and helped me to grow up. Although I severed our exclusive publishing agreement in 1995, we continued to take on recording projects together, and he invested substantial sums in commercial recordings of my music.

A few months before he died of cancer in December 2015 Bob called to disclose the news that he was no longer playing soccer every weekend. "Are you sick?" I asked. "Dying," he answered in the matter-of-fact, so-what-of-it tone I'd come to appreciate from my busi-ness partner and friend. "What can I do for you?" I asked him. "It's what I'm going to do for you," he said. "I'm going to send you back a bunch of your early music before I sell the catalogue," he said. "I want you to have the copyrights back. The new company's a good one, but you have kids now, and you need to control your own music." I've known very few men whose essential goodness was unalloyed. Bob was one.

With what I imagined to be sangfroid, I informed Mary Anthony Cox, the famous (and rightly beloved) Boulanger-trained ear-training teacher, "Ma'am, I don't foresee having time to practice for your class." I customarily sat beside Martin Matalon—who went on to be recipient of the 2005 *Grand Prix des Lycéens* and 2001 *Prix de L'Institut de France Académie des Beaux Arts.* Martin was a charming Argentine composer who at the time seemed to have arrived at the same relationship with the study of ear training I had. Oh, ear training was exquisite torment. "Honey," Mary Anthony would purr, "sing me a half diminished seventh chord in third position starting on la." My mind would go utterly blank. Then she would make it worse by trying to help clear the air with a simple question. "Honey, you're at 66th and Broadway and you want to get to 92nd Street. Which train do you get on?" We all sat in a circle. The tension was incredible. Cruel snickers. "Uptown or downtown?" she would sweetly needle. "Ah … um," I'd begin, having lost the ability to speak, let alone sing, let alone find the pitch la. Worse, out of the corner of my eye I could see Martin, bright red, eyes squeezed tightly shut, writhing with the effort required to not lose it on the spot. When Mary Anthony called on Martin, his discomfort, which was every bit as acute as mine, had the exact same effect on me. Never defy an ear-training instructor; never play a trick on a psychiatrist; and never attempt to force potty-training on a toddler—you will lose and they will win. Wise Mary Anthony laughed last and long: I ended up having to continue practicing ear training for another nine years to teach it properly as one of my duties on the faculty of Bard College.

There was also a required music copying class, but more about that later. To my way of thinking then, I was attending Juilliard for one reason: my composition lessons with Diamond. I worked hard to please him.

My contemporaries—all a couple of years older than me—at Juilliard included Daniel Brewbaker, the brothers Sebastian and Nathan Currier, Richard Danielpour, Kenneth Fuchs, Laura Karpman, Lowell Liebermann, Martin Matalon, and Elena Ruehr, among others. I thought they were all dynamic, impressive composers, but I instinctively kept to myself—so much so that many of my classmates thought that I still lived in Philadelphia.

Every few weeks, the department held a composition seminar at which we either presented our new works, or a visiting composer presented theirs. The faculty attended, as well as all of one's colleagues. At the first seminar, I sat next to Persichetti and Babbitt protégé, composer-flautist Su Lian Tan. When she asked what kind of music I wrote I replied, "only masterpieces" and we became pals. I found the seminars desperately dry. After my first presentation, Diamond pulled me into the hallway and chewed me out: "Never, *ever* do that again. Your *piece* is brilliant. *You* are brilliant. *What* you said was brilliant. *How* you said it was *unacceptable.* You're a better composer than most of the people in that room. If you don't treat yourself with respect, how can you *possibly* expect your colleagues to?"

David studied at the Eastman School with Bernard Rogers, in New York with Roger Sessions and in France with Nadia Boulanger; while living in Paris, he also befriended André Gide, Albert Roussel, Maurice Ravel, and Igor Stravinsky. He was a superb artisan whose Neo-classic compositions grafted intense lyricism with a neurotic and deeply felt hyper-contrapuntal compositional style. He became a star in the compositional firmament quite young and spent the rest of his career beguiling and reviling performers and colleagues.

Like Witold Lutosławski, David wore excellently tailored suits. He occasionally rouged his cheeks. His shoes were always shined. He enjoyed sincere flattery. A serious drinker when he chose to be, he preferred very cold, very dry champagne and excellent vodka, if it was available, followed by brandy. David was fun to drink with. He enjoyed the fact that I could hold my liquor. He loved good food, arguments, and books. The pretentious infuriated him, though he seemed to appreciate people who could pull it off. It seemed to me that he felt that Society had short-changed him; it had contradicted his hopes. While his default mien was grave, he could be pixyish and ebullient. Posterity was important to him: he left behind meticulously crafted ballets, eleven symphonies, concertos, ten string quartets, numerous chamber works, and many admirable songs.

Bernstein famously referred to David as "a vital branch in the stream of American music," while Virgil (for whom—like Ned, like me—David briefly worked) wrote, "Composers, like pearls, are of three chief sorts, real, artificial and cultured. David Diamond is unquestionably of the first sort; his talent and his sincerity have never been doubted by his hearers, by his critics, or by his composer colleagues."

Our every conversation ultimately circled back to the three intertwined things we had most in common: anger, depression, and chronic insomnia. Were the causes chemical, or the result of pathological narcissism? Were they darker, more Nixonian? "When I was younger," David once told me, "I rarely slept, always worried about money. My anger and my hostility drove me to extremes of behavior that must have seemed theatrical to some. Sessions, for example, when I confessed to him in a lesson that I intended to kill myself by jumping out of the balcony at Carnegie Hall, admonished me to jump from the second tier, as jumping from the first would leave me with broken legs, while the latter would guarantee a split skull, or at least a broken neck."

A superb raconteur, David's reminiscences of the 30s and 40s were peppered with vivid character sketches of Greta Garbo, Clifford Odets, Carson and Reeves McCullers, Copland, and Blitzstein, among others. A compulsive diarist, the shelves in his Rochester home contained dozens of books filled with his graceful, athletic handwriting. He confided to me over the years—usually in dark asides after some perceived slight—that he was writing an autobiography that would settle this or that person's hash.

After David's death, Gerard Schwarz, who genuinely loved him and continues to champion his music, loaned me a copy of an unpublished manuscript, which I read. I understand now why he chose never to complete it: the first fifty pages ring with his feisty voice and promise a memoir as pleasurable and captivating as an evening spent drinking champagne with him, listening to him tilt at windmills, and lacerate colleagues. Sadly, the document loses its way, tells rather than shows, never progresses far beyond the 60s, and becomes a circular argument, exactly the sort of self-justifying document that David, as an avid and careful reader, disliked. Perhaps another, more polished, manuscript is out there somewhere, awaiting the hand of an experienced editor. I hope so: the world deserves to hear his version—whatever that may have been—of things.

David could transform in a heartbeat from needy to imperious. This made him numerous enemies. Not just his enemies questioned the accuracy of his memory. I believe that he tried hard to be truthful, but that he was more the Don than de Passamonte, more Pierrot than Pedrolino—in other words, the extraordinary intensity of his feelings (he was as ruthless with himself as he was with others) sometimes distorted the way he perceived not the truth, but the world.

Lessons could be grueling, especially if he had gotten it into his head that you had somehow betrayed him. I used to write music reviews for *EAR*, a downtown new music magazine. For a (rave) review of David's Symphony No. 10 (premièred a few weeks earlier by Bernstein with the American Composers Orchestra), I had created what I thought was a pretty spicy lede: "Diamond's Tenth looms over the audience like an enormous tombstone." Someone had gotten a copy into David's hands.

"You have a deep-seated subconscious desire to destroy me," he bellowed. "Get out of my sight!" It was my first taste of his legendary temper. In my case, at least, it was always as fleet as it was quick. His apologies, when they did come, were always sincere. I admired him, and I always accepted them.

For Ned I composed three art songs each week for three years—one on a poem of my choice; one on a poem of his choice; one of a poem he had set. At David's behest, I constructed two fugues (each more elaborate than the last) a week for two years—one on a fugue subject of his choice, one on a subject of my own devising. Ned's regimen helped me to learn how to access my emotions and express them fluently with musical notes. David's regimen helped me to learn how to explore the relationship that those notes have with one another on the abstract, purely musical level.

David's obsession with fugue as a compositional procedure mirrored his lifelong effort as an intellect to make sense of the world in which he lived. When Bernard Rands without malice wondered aloud during a composition seminar what the point of writing fugues was at the end of the twentieth century, David was apoplectic. Bernard was calling into question the very method by which David fashioned his sanity.

Inspired by the Copland-Sessions Concerts, I produced during those years several dozen recitals in Philadelphia and New York featuring my own, and colleagues' music. I called them *Perpetuum Mobile* concerts because, at the time, constant movement was my way of life. My intentions were good, but I see now how naïve I was to have mounted them—particularly at my own expense. I wanted colleagues to like me, yes; and I thought that working together, we might all benefit professionally. I was genuinely surprised and hurt when several of the Juilliard composers whose music I featured treated me as though I was hitching my star to theirs. Diamond explained to me that I didn't care about other people; I just wanted to look as though I did:

> *Daron,* the letter from David began, continuing a conversation begun a few days earlier on the telephone, *You are confused by my use of the word selfish. I refer to self-absorption, pre-occupation with self, self-advertisement, a certain exhibitionism and charm at the same time being generous in your Perpetuum Mobile concerts for young composers is not the inner you, it's the outer man saying, "look gang, I'm for the other young'uns." Giving in this way is not altruism of the spirit.*

I did manage to get some music played by good friends (who also happened to be fine composers): John Beall, the soulful West Virginian Mother had met once on a plane, Jeffrey Bitzer, who had landed at Columbia University; William Coble, a Del Tredici protégé from Boston; Eric Sawyer, Kathryn Harris, Bright Sheng, Robert Savage, Louis Karchin, Debra Fernandez, Robert Convery, and a host of others. I was touched that, after I'd pretty much mothballed the series, Troy Peters and Jennifer Higdon (then both still students at Curtis) breathed life into it for a few final months before concluding (far more quickly than I ever did) that it was a lot more trouble than it was worth.

One of the composers I'd featured on the series, fellow Milwaukeean Michael Torke, and I had recently met at a BMI Young Composers Awards ceremony. After graduating from high school, he had gone straight to Eastman, and then to Yale, where he had worked briefly with Martin Bresnick and Jacob Druckman. He was planning to drop out of Yale and move to New York; and he had contacted me to ask whether he could sublet my apartment for the summer. We hit it off, and, as young composers used to do, I pitched in to help hand-copy the parts to the orchestra piece that launched his career, *Ecstatic Orange.*

Edward Albee agreed to allow some limited rights to me for his one act play *The Sandbox* when Houston Grand Opera's (then) touring / outreach program Texas Opera Theater asked for something to include in their "One Aria Opera Project" in June 1985. The chamber version of *The Sandbox* was premiered in Houston. Three years earlier, as an exercise, I had set to music without changing a word Edward's play *The Sandbox.* The idea had begun as an aria for Karen Hale, who needed a contemporary piece for auditions. I never meant to do anything with it, so I hadn't bothered to clear the rights with Edward. In March 1984, I'm reasonably certain that I became the only composer who has ever staged and conducted the premiere (I made a little chamber orchestra arrangement) of one of his operas in Curtis (now Field) Hall at the Curtis Institute. The orchestra was set up on the floor; the action took place on the stage. The (rather surprised) audience surrounded us. The performance featured the school's registrar Michael Carrigan, who sang Daddy; Mitch Newman played the violin (in the original it is a clarinet); Karen Hale sang Grandmother; and fellow composition student (the award-winning composer of the scores for the highly-successful *Might and Magic* computer games) Paul Romero portrayed—oiled up in a tiny Speedo—the mute role of the Angel of Death. I asked Ned for Edward's address and sent an audio recording of my little "musicalization" (I can't call it an opera, as the music was simply "piggy-backed" on to his play) to him. Director Michael Kahn took me aside during production and asked me why I had not changed any of Albee's words. "I wanted to see if it could be viable as a musical play," I answered. "Well," he sighed, "you have your answer: it is. But ask yourself this: does the music need to be there? What does it add?" He had me there. "Very little," I admitted. "Then I think you need to think about that," he smiled. I withdrew the piece.

The bill also featured new "one aria" operas by Stewart Wallace, Michael Ching, and James Legg. Legg's one act opera, *The Informer*, was the finest example of progressive American opera composing I had and have ever heard. The repertoire lost that could have been written because of Legg's premature death is one of the great tragedies, like Blitzstein's, of American opera. Legg fluidly integrated the stylistic traits of the Broadway musical tradition, the progressive European opera tradition, and the first-rate American opera canon. At the time of his death on 20 November 2000, he was working on an opera based on Arthur Miller's *All My Sons* and the score for a Broadway-bound version of *The Full Monty*.

Karen and I rented a tiny third floor walk-up at 931 Amsterdam. It was in the middle of a dicey barrio that ran like a spine up the middle of the Upper West Side. I paid our rent each month in cash to a "lawyer" in the lobby of the post office. At night, I could trace the progress of the rats in the paper-thin walls by listening to the sound of their scurrying feet. I didn't need an alarm clock, as the bells of the West End Presbyterian Church were probably fifteen feet away from my window and pealed promptly each day at 7 a.m. Back from Houston, on my way out of the building, our upstairs neighbor produced a knife as I passed him in the hallway. "Who do you think you are, living in this neighborhood? Give me your money, asshole," he said. Stupidly, I said, "If I had any money, would I be living here?" and walked on. He was I think either too stoned or too surprised to follow me. Shortly thereafter, Karen, and I moved to an apartment that I hated at 148th and Broadway, in Washington Heights.

Gunther Schuller accepted me as a composer fellow at Tanglewood. The Gelin Prize covered my expenses. Accordingly, I was supposed to take some lessons with that year's composer in residence, Leon Kirchner. Leon was a massive presence whose fierce, eagle-blue eyes dominated his handsome, craggy face. He and Gilbert Kalish had heard La Rue and the Lehner Trio perform my *Trio Concertante* in Boston and wanted to program it. But I wanted to hear my new string quartet.

That summer, over the course of three afternoons, armed with colored pencils, Louis Krasner and I analyzed my string quartet; he told me stories about working with Berg and Schoenberg while premiering their concertos, about being coached by Bartók as a member of the Kolisch Quartet. Louis coached my quartet "like Brahms," he explained, "because, even though your language is harmonically dissonant, your melodies ache to sing." "You'll go much, much further than this," Kirchner predicted to me after my quartet's premiere. "It's a very good piece—more Korngold than Berg, and all you. You've got a great future ahead." I was thrilled. "No buts?" I asked. "Well, if I have to point it out, I'd say that I wish that you would concentrate more on those beautiful melodies you seem to be able to spin," he said. "This quartet is not the direction I think you are going to go."

One evening at Seranak ("SERgeAndNAtaliaKoussevitzky"), Serge Koussevitzky's home overlooking the Berkshires across the highway from the Tanglewood grounds, after hearing me improvise at the piano in the style of Marc Blitzstein and a discussion about Blitzstein's music, Bernstein asked me to have a go at completing Blitzstein's unfinished opera *Sacco and Vanzetti*. I told him I'd be happy to have a try but couldn't afford to do it for free. At Bernstein's behest, Jacob Druckman approached me on the back patio several days later and put a little money on the table for the project on behalf of the New York Philharmonic, for whom he was then serving as composer in residence. My instinct was that I should refuse it. I told Druckman that I felt that if I wanted to establish myself as a composer, then I needed to be known for my own music, not for what I had done for others.' He said that I had a point and was impressed enough by the professionalism with which I handled the situation to speak to his wife Muriel about a ballet commission. But examining Blitzstein's sketches was just too inviting an invitation to refuse. After spending a few days with them, I concluded that the most responsible thing for me to do was to leave the thing alone—they were just too fragmentary, too raw. The finished score would require the creation of too much original material to flesh it out.

A few days later, as Bernstein conducted the Copland Third, my Tanglewood summer ended in the Shed, seated next to Mr. Copland. Every few minutes he turned his head slightly, smiled sweetly, and asked me gently, quietly, "What is the year? What summer is this?" Copland's tears.

Leonard Bernstein and I listening to my Piano Trio No. 1: *Trio Concertante* in the living room at Seranak during an August 1985 evening LB spent listening to fellowship composers' music at Tanglewood.

◆◆ 12 ◆◆

Other Men's Music
1985–1987

Whether producing the *Perpetuum Mobile* concerts constituted "altruism of the spirit" or not, presenting rarely performed pieces gave me a lot of pleasure. I facilitated the first performances of the Blitzstein Piano Sonata since the 20s, for example. The series brought me to Sylvia Goldstein's attention. Sylvia was, along with David Huntley, the compassionate, human face of Boosey and Hawkes back then. Whenever a new piece by a Boosey composer then making waves was premiered, a bunch of us would gather at David's apartment to listen to a cassette recording with the score and debate its merits. Sylvia managed Aaron Copland's affairs. She thought of me when Mr. Copland needed a new assistant and put me in touch with Ellis Freedman. I was granted an interview at his Park Avenue office during which I suggested splitting it up between myself and another composer so that neither of us would have to give up touch with the New York scene. The job would entail commuting to Peekskill and staying there overnight once a week. Take home salary offered was $300 per week—enough to cease living hand-to-mouth. It pained Ellis that I turned down the job working for Mr. Copland, but we remained good friends. (Composer Ronald Caltabiano, then mentored by Carter and Persichetti, now dean of the Jordan College of Fine Arts at Butler University, took the job, which lasted for five years, until Copland's death.) I would call him once a month just to visit. When it came time to negotiate the commissioning agreement for *Shining Brow*, he refused to accept payment. He continued to represent me *gratis* until his death in 2003 at the age of 82, at which point I became, as did so many others, a client of Jim Kendrick's. An extraordinary intellect, he was also profoundly attuned to his composer clients' needs and aspirations. With me he was invariably fatherly, concerned that I should "eat, sleep, and find a nice girl to center me."

A few months later, I could see snowflakes whirling outside through a tall sliver of one of Juilliard's slit-like windows over Diamond's shoulder as he declared, "Fugue subjects," briskly sketching one on the sheet of music paper on the piano rack in front of us, "are like snakes. Every one of them has a head, a body, and a tail." Chop, he slashed a line between the head and the body. Chop, he slashed another between the body and the tail. "Or like people," I replied, "with a head, a body, and a tale." He laughed pleasantly. The Regency Theater just around the corner was in the middle of its three-week Truffaut retrospective; Marc Blitzstein's Piano Concerto had just been performed at Carnegie Hall for the first time in fifty years.

"Or a Life," he frowned, leaning over the keyboard, "with a memorable Beginning, Middle ripe for development, and an End…." He stopped writing and straightened up.

"Now sketch a counter-subject." I took the pencil from him and began adding my squiggles to the line above his. He pursed his lips. A sharp intake of breath: "Something memorable," he said, "not … mechanical." I tried again, but all I could think was that Life, like "a Pretty Girl, is like a Melody."

I looked at the oil of Pierrot he had painted that hung over the piano. It wasn't very good. Clowns frighten me. I giggled nervously. "What's so funny?" he asked. "If Life is a Melody, then Energy must be the human compulsion to organize sound into Song," I rallied, half-serious. "And Force is the application of creative energy," he smiled encouragingly. "And composition is Birth?" I asked. "And pulse is Gravity," he answered. "Which makes entropy, or the lack of pulse, Death," he said, taking the pencil. "Look," he circled the head of my counter-subject, "this is memorable, so why not just take the tail of the subject, invert it, and use that as the head of the counter-subject?" Chop, I thought: the snake devouring its tail. Chop. "In my beginning is my end. Eliot," I risked. He chuckled. "Right. The Ouroboros. My end is my beginning. Mary, Queen of the Scots. Earlier. Better," he replied with finality as through the door the three light knocks of his next student indicated that my lesson was nearly up. I carefully placed the enormous pages of my manuscript into the elephant portfolio in which I had brought it. It took me twenty-six years to understand what David said next: "Mr. Hagen—," he admonished gravely as I reached for the doorknob. I turned around, and his voice softened. "Dear One," he began again, "Don't let gravity win."

I copied the parts for David's Flute Concerto, commissioned by the New Haven Symphony for Jean Pierre Rampal. Rampal, while in every other way professional, urbane, and musically sublime, had been too busy to learn his part before the first rehearsal. As copyist, I was compelled to attend rehearsals and to correct any errors that might need fixing. It was snowy and nasty that week, and I disliked intensely the train ride from New York to New Haven. (I did manage to compose the Suite for Viola during them—so at least I have *that* to show for the commute.) Murry Sidlin, the conductor, vented his frustration when three or four errors that had eluded my proofreader's eye became known piecemeal because the orchestra, to save money, had excused certain players until the last minute.

I recall standing at the lip of the stage score in hand. David sat in the audience. Wheeling around and pointing at me from the podium, Sidlin shrieked, "Copyist! I thought you corrected these parts!" It was the copyist's and the composer's worst nightmare. Humiliated, I answered, "I'll correct them during the break, Maestro." Beat. "What's that?" bellowed Sidlin. "The break," I called out. "During the break." Sidlin writhed with frustration. I looked at Rampal. Holding his flute like a scepter, he stared out into the empty hall. Not long after, at my final lesson, David said, after observing that I had never brought him a vocal piece to look at, "I was speaking to Lenny the other night about you. He says that it's a shame that you never showed me your vocal music, because I could have cleaned up your prosody problems." I was astonished. A year later, at my first meeting at the Dakota with Bernstein, I was saddened but not surprised when he told me that he had never said that.

David had given me the impression that student composers at Juilliard were forbidden to take lessons with anyone except their principal teacher. I had not told him that I had been meeting periodically with Lukas Foss to show him my work. Meeting with Vincent Persichetti also felt illicit, dangerous—especially because of the way he leaned forward over the desk that separated us on which the full score of my first symphony was spread. It was near the end of what had been a delightfully instructive lesson. His bird-like eyes shone as he spoke; his sentences came out in staccato, conspiratorial bursts. His cigarette smoldered, forgotten, between his fingers; the long, drooping ash hanging from the business end was on the verge of falling off.

"Golly, you've got a handsome hand there," Vincent said, paging through my score. He got to the point. "Arnie tells me you won't take his class."

Arnold Arnstein, appreciated and respected by an entire generation of American composers, including Bernstein, Harris, Schuman, Barber, Piston, Persichetti, and Diamond, among others, was generally believed to be the finest living American music copyist. He really was. Years of the work had destroyed his eyes, which were reamed in red and watery, hugely enlarged by the thick glasses he wore. Arnie taught a class in music copying at Juilliard that all of us composers were required to take. I had been working already for five years as a professional copyist, and had some pretty heavy clients, including Diamond, George Perle, Ned (an excellent, patient employer who—without telling me—customarily paid other copyists more than me), and others, and so I had figured, with casual ignorance, that I should be exempted from attendance.

"We've got to figure out some sort of way to work this out, Daron," said Vincent. "Arnie's a great copyist, y'know; he could teach you a lot." He shot me a quick, inquiring look. "But, but," he not so much stuttered as drew quick gulps of air, "y'know, if you weren't so talented, I'd say, uh, sure, y'know, go ahead, take these copying jobs. But, I think you've gotta not do that. Um, do anything, uh, be a garbage man; just stop copying other people's music for them."

"But I need the money," I replied. The cigarette ash fell on my score, as I had feared it would. "Yeah, I know. Oops," he said, brushing off the ash, "Sorry." A quick, sweet smile, "Plus, you get half the money up front and all that; then you have to work it off," he sighed, looked at the floor. "Well. Maybe I could ask Arnie to put you on his crew for this Menotti opera he's copying right now. I hear it's wildly behind schedule and he needs extra guys. Then you could learn from him, y'see, get paid at the same time, and not have to take his class. How about that?"

I never took Arnie's class, but I know that I should have. Despite Vincent's advice, I went on to serve as a copyist, proofreader, or editor on hundreds of projects over the next fifteen years. Sometimes I hear a piece of music on the radio I've never "heard" before and realize that I copied the original set of parts for it during my salad days. It is even stranger to attend a rehearsal of one of my pieces and see yellowed, dog-eared, old rental library parts on the players' stands next to mine for someone else's piece that I don't even remember having copied.

The money was good; the work was always interesting; and there is absolutely no substitute for learning a piece by another composer from the inside out by extracting all the parts by hand. Every musician should do it once. It is possible to copy music mechanically, without engaging intellectually—sort of like driving while having a conversation. Sometimes I did marathon jobs during which I would listen to every Mahler symphony in order, go back, and begin again. But, if one is engaged during the process of copying another composer's parts, one is actually "playing" the composer's process the way a pianist "plays" a composer pianist's piece—your brain and fingers are going through the same motions that the composer's did when he wrote it. Several composers' styles and methods grew so familiar to me during those years that I blush to admit that I could still probably compose something in their style that would be hard to identify as a forgery.

Computer software "engraving programs" like Score, Finale, and Sibelius have rendered mine the last generation of American concert music and opera composers who shall have had the opportunity to serve our musical apprenticeships in the ancient, traditional, and I think honorable manner of extracting, by hand, using quills, India ink, and vellum, the individual parts from whence the musicians play. We professional music copyists during the 80s were like Local 802 Teamster Monks, running into one another at Associated Music just south of Columbus Circle when we stuck our heads out to pick up supplies, meet with our clients, share with our colleagues "secret saves" and anecdotes from the trenches of our drawing boards.

I find the transaction between composer, performer and audience that musical notation hopes to enable enormously puzzling. It is the ceaseless reaching for the elusive note just barely heard in one's imagination and just beyond the grasp of one's conscious mind, what Schreker called *Der Ferne Klang*, Mahler *Das Lied von der Erde*, that is to me endlessly enthralling. Printed music serves as an imperfect mirror through which the performer steps to enter the world of the piece itself; the performer turns around and faces outwards, from whence he came, and performs what he has discovered for those of us listening on the other side of the bars, the other side of the mirror. I am amazed that anything comprehensible, let alone moving, results.

The school year ended, and with it my time as a student of David's. Lowell Liebermann threw a party at his stylish Lincoln Center apartment. Lowell was handsome, ambitious, highly-intelligent, elitist, and accomplished. Diamond adored him, and called him, as he called me, "Genius Boy." I admired his craftsmanship and work ethic. Lowell's bookshelves were stocked with well-thumbed volumes—good literature, in good editions. One wall was covered floor-to-ceiling with orchestral scores. A gifted pianist, his grand piano dominated the living room. Tasteful *objets d'art* were carefully placed here and there. An inscribed portrait of Diamond hung between the bedroom and bathroom. The liquor was expensive. The conversation was elevated. The fond farewells to David were sincere. He'd be stepping off the Juilliard faculty in a few weeks, and this party was both a birthday celebration and a sendoff. Supine on the couch, vodka martini cradled on his chest, David held forth about Ravel's *L'Enfant et les sortilèges* to a ring of attentive upturned faces. I poured a scotch. Seen through the heavy tumbler, the tableaux looked like a Caravaggio. Uneasy, I put the glass down without drinking from it.

Virgil Thomson called what I did as a copyist to make money "working on other men's music," and fiercely disapproved—except when I worked for him. Brilliant polymath composer and conductor-pal Glen Roven used to grit his teeth in a fierce rictus of contempt when we'd swap stories about the "second class" status of "jobbing composers." Vincent had only recently told me to do anything but. Scholarship notwithstanding, I was self-supporting, and I needed the dough. I fingered the frayed cuff of my Brooks Brothers shirt, knew the lining of my jacket had long since begun to sag, took note of my scuffed, cheap shoes, and remembered that I was broke.

I had been taught at the back of Father's hand to never, ever, *ever* give the impression that I thought highly of myself. Indeed, I thought of myself with my ass in the air in my pajamas at the age of seven along with my brothers, scrubbing the kitchen floor in the middle of the night, Father hissing, "You all think you're smarter than me."

I gave Diamond the letter I'd written earlier and slipped away. A few days later, I put my books and papers into storage, gave away the furniture, and hit the road again, my knapsack on my back. First stop, Philadelphia, to drop Clara off at Kile and Jackie's for the summer. The coffee into which I ladled teaspoons full of sugar at Little Pete's diner as dawn broke was just as terrible as it had been that first night in Philadelphia, only I no longer loved it. A few tables away, two drunks sobering up slouched over scrapple, eggs, and the *Philadelphia Inquirer*.

Earlier in the day, on my way out of New York, I'd checked the mail one last time and found two letters. On one, David's familiar graceful handwriting; on the other, a blue airmail envelope, Michaela's even more familiar, somewhat cramped scrawl. I took a sip of coffee, picked up a butter knife, and gutted David's letter:

> *I have read the very touching letter you gave me on leaving Lowell's party several times and treasure the feelings expressed in it. It is good to know that I have contributed something of value to you as a teacher during your Juilliard years.*

I was relieved to have left David's studio gracefully; I was eager now to put some actual distance between us. I dropped his letter and reached for the frail airmail envelope. I hadn't asked Michaela to write. "We're no longer physically or emotionally together," she had said on the phone. "So, what's the point?" She had moved on. It was over. I knew that. I may as well be slitting my wrist, I felt, picking the butter knife back up and slitting open the tissue paper flap. I shivered involuntarily as I read. "So that was that," I thought bitterly, pushing the cup of burnt coffee, now cold, away. Gide: "Nothing thwarts happiness as much as the memory of happiness." The loneliest are those who cling to useless things and, knowing their uselessness, cannot let go.

I made a lean, white fist out of both letters and stuffed them into my army-surplus backpack with the books (I was struggling through the last volume of Sartre's *Les chemins de la liberté*), music paper, diary, some pencils, and a fifth of Ballantine's scotch I'd packed for my residency in Virginia. (I planned to buy some secondhand clothes at the Dollar Store in Amherst.) Presently, I found myself in the middle of Thirtieth Street Station almost exactly five years since first arriving there, but no longer "seething" with quite the same potential or "desire to please," waiting for a train. Amtrak's Owl brought me to Philadelphia; the Crescent took me away.

Half a day later, past midnight, I stood alone in the misty darkness of the Monroe, Virginia whistle stop, watching the train slope off towards Louisiana. Robert Johnson picked me up. He handed me a beer as I slid into the front seat. "Good to see you, Daron," he said. "Shotgun still okay?" I asked. "Why, sure," he smiled, shaking my hand. Not talking, we drove through the ink-black countryside towards the Artist colony. I'd had some scotch on the train; the cold beer chased it agreeably. I popped a second open and rolled down the window, savored the hot, dry air rushing by. The Virginia Center for the Creative Arts was then a working dairy farm. Soon I smelled cows, rosemary and juniper bushes. "You up for poker this week?" Robert asked, his ebony face shining in the moonlight. "Usual stakes?" I asked. "Uh … yeah," he drawled, before chuckling gently. "Some players in this bunch," he observed. "Fine," I said, closing my eyes and sinking into the leatherette upholstery. I dozed. After about thirty minutes, I opened my eyes, tossed the can into the backseat of the car, handed Robert a ten-dollar bill ("Don't worry; you'll win it back," he chuckled), retrieved my backpack, and walked into the residence hall. There was the familiar smell of cooking, the muffled songs of crickets and frogs chirping, the tingling sound of the grandfather clock's action, disturbed by my footfalls. After picking up my key and welcome packet, I walked through the deep summer night to the studio I had been assigned—C2. I knew it well and loved it. June bugs as big and as juicy as ripe figs slapped against one another in their eagerness to immolate themselves on the light burning beside the door. I listened for a moment in the darkness to the familiar burring of the crickets, tree frogs, and the verdant wind. A Luna Moth plastered itself against the screen.

Once in, I tossed my backpack on the cot. There was a long, shit-brown stain running down the center of the Bolivian flag that served as a bedspread. I had to smile. Conductor friend JoAnn Falletta had commissioned a new piece in honor of Bernstein for the Denver Chamber Orchestra that was due by the end of the summer; she'd also had me engaged as soloist for Gershwin's *I Got Rhythm Variations* on the same concert, and to curate a chamber music concert, on which I'd perform my own music. Thanks to her, I had a lot to compose and practice. "Fuck it," I thought, sighing heavily, taking a seat on the piano bench, rolling up my sleeves, flattening a sheet of empty music paper on the piano rack and licking the tip of my lucky mechanical pencil as the digital clock on the bed stand clicked over to 3:00.

The next day I began alternating six hour stretches composing, practicing, socializing, and sleeping. I was on fire, finishing the Bernstein tribute in ten days, copying it, memorizing the Gershwin, and rushing into an attachment to effervescent, sure-hearted visual artist and painter Suzanne Chamlin. A few weeks later, the residency over, I crashed while waiting for the Crescent to return me to New York, performing the silent luggage ritual as I had the day I moved away from Philadelphia. The writing was purple, but the sentiment was sincere, when I wrote in my journal that—

> *a hand reached into my chest today and squeezed my heart when we kissed. I was left there with arms full of farm kittens, the crazy-good Ivory-soap-and-oil-paints smell of Suzanne's hair hanging about me like remembered happiness, thinking that I can barely tolerate me, so how could I ever expect* her *to?*

Hoping to stave off the depressive swoop that I'd learned to expect after manic episodes, I stopped drinking, and recommitted to composing and exercising. For a while at least, my mood stabilized. I began running each day around the Central Park Reservoir, and immediately began to feel the physical and psychological benefits of accomplishing 3.2 miles each day. I loved making periodic small talk with Albert Arroyo, the "Mayor of Central Park," while stretching. Plans and schemes and ideas and themes ran through my mind, my footfalls exactly at my preferred pace (I dislike running with others) as the chain link fence flowed by over my left shoulder and I reached the northeast corner where, as the track curved to the west, I'd tossed Mother's keys in the water (so I'd always know where to find them). My ritual was to say, out loud, "I love you, Mama," as I passed the spot, just as the orange afternoon sun setting over the Upper West Side revealed itself, bouncing, sparkling, off the surface of the water, dazzling, exhilarating.

A new school year began at Juilliard. I had a new teacher. Trained at the American Conservatory of Music and at Northwestern University, composer Joseph Schwantner began as a guitarist. One of the most successful composers of his generation (his exquisitely orchestrated *Aftertones of Infinity* received the Pulitzer Prize in 1979), he was forty-three and squarely in mid-career when I had the pleasure of studying with him. I admired Joe's down to earth, easy-going professionalism, and what seemed like an effortless ability to cope with life as it is, rather than the way he wished it to be. For example, before such information became readily available on the Internet, Joe had taken the time to compile a list of the exact standing instrumentation of every major American orchestra. "Bear in mind," he remarked sensibly, handing me a copy of the valuable hand-written document, "that an orchestra is likely to turn down a piece that is larger than their instrumentation without even considering it." We looked together through *Grand Line*, the dense, modernist orchestra piece I'd written in Virginia. "Optional guitar!" he mused, wryly. "Why 'optional?' You've already written something so challenging as to be unplayable by all but a few orchestras. Why not just require it?" He fingered the heavy ozalid-printed pages. "Beautiful copying. Your hand, I presume?" I was grateful to have the compliment from a man famous for creating graphically gorgeous scores. (A few weeks later, Joe gave me a small ruler with a handle on it of his own invention and construction that I treasured for many years before accidentally leaving it on a train in Italy.) "You should send this to Gerard Schwarz at the

New York Chamber Symphony," he suggested. I explained that David—who said that he had the maestro's ear—had told me that he would probably never program my music. Joe looked thoughtful. "I wouldn't be so certain," he answered. I cocked my head. "Go ahead and send it," he urged. "It can't hurt." In the end, with money sent by Britt, I had about twenty copies of *Grand Line* printed and sent them to all the composers in residence currently underwritten by what was then called Meet the Composer. I heard from four: Christopher Rouse in Baltimore, and Tobias Picker in Houston were complimentary, but noncommittal; John Harbison, in Los Angeles were warmer, and requested a recording, if one materialized. Years later, Schwarz told me that he never received the copy that I gave David to give to him.

In lieu of taking Arnie's music copying course, I agreed to join his team of union copyists that fall. They were preparing the performance parts for Gian Carlo Menotti's *Goya*—his final, *giovane scuola*-style opera and, in the event, a star vehicle for the great tenor Placido Domingo. It was a harried, hair-raising project: music was arriving from Gian Carlo on the day that a scene was scheduled for rehearsal. In November, I travelled to Washington to attend the world premiere.

New York Times music critic Donal Henahan, with astonishing cruelty, described *Goya* as "a rather stupefying exercise in banality ... a parody of a Menotti opera." At the time, I found the review (slipping the word "rather" in like a shiv before the word "stupefying," as though Menotti had failed even at being entirely stupefying) insolent. But I was still too young to understand how profoundly disrespectful he was being, and how wounded to the core—after two-dozen operas and a lifetime of service to his art—Gian Carlo was.

The pain in his voice on the telephone when I reached him at his hotel the morning it ran in the newspaper was heartbreaking. "He's just a critic. You're Gian Carlo Menotti," I sputtered uselessly, unable to believe that somebody who had accomplished so much could be so hurt by someone whose opinion mattered so little in the end. I realized during the next three or four beats of silence on the line that I had overstepped. What did I know about life at his age, his level of achievement? What did I know about his art, his soul, really? Nothing. I was twenty-five and had accomplished little; he was seventy-five, had founded two music festivals, written two-dozen operas, and won two Pulitzer prizes. "I'm sorry," I said. "I know that what I say doesn't matter." "Ah, *caro*, someday you'll understand," Gian Carlo sighed.

The next day, back in New York, I swung my feet over the side of the bed, put some food in a bowl for Clara, stuffed espresso into the mouth of the aluminum stove-top brewer, ran the shower (which delivered only tepid water) and noted my lamentable self in the mirror only for the briefest instant before throwing on jeans and a tee shirt. I returned to the bedroom and looked out the window and down at the playground of St. Joan of Arc High School. At night—during the hottest weeks of the summer—the plaintive cries of young couples having sex drifted up from a dark corner under my window. The sounds of their orgasms mingled with Clara's affectionate mewing. She yawned, climbed off the pile of vellum on which I was in the process of hand copying the parts to George Perle's new wind quintet, threaded herself between my ankles, and shot into the kitchen to eat her breakfast. Sitting down at the drawing board, I dipped my Osmiroid fountain pen first into alcohol to clean the nib, and then nipped it like a lover. Then I dipped it into a specially mixed batch of Higgins engrossing ink.

The phone rang. That, I thought to myself, would be Helen Carter. "Hello? Hello?" a high-pitched, frantic voice piped from the receiver. "You've been working on the parts to Elliott's *Pastoral* for Theodore Presser for an entire week now," she admonished. "When are you going to finish them?" "Ma'am," I asked, wearily, "Do you know what time it is?" Beat. "Well, I'm awake," she said. I sighed. "Where are my husband's parts!" she cried. I just let that one sit there for a beat. "I'm finishing a job for George Perle right now," I said. "They should be done in about a week." Another beat. "Well. Okay, then. Send them directly to Presser, will you?" "Yes, Ma'am," I said, writing a note to myself.

A few hours later, I headed to George's nearby spacious Central Park West apartment for a work session on another job that I was doing for him—the parts to his *Dance Overture*. Shirley met me at the door. "I assume you're gay," she said, amiably. "Afraid not," I replied. "Not even Bi." She crinkled her nose. "But then why does Lenny like you?" she asked, arch. There was no appropriate response, so I cocked my head, looked at my feet, and maintained what I imagined was respectful silence.

"George!" she sang, "Daron's here! Shall I send him in?" George sat in a corner of the living room, smiling broadly, wearing a blackjack dealer's visor. I spread the work before him on the table. We gossiped gently about mutual friends and colleagues. "You know," he said, "I don't try to be accessible. When I write a piece, I write what I want to hear, and what I think will be fun to listen to and fun to play." "This," I thought, "is the opposite of fun." The meter changed every bar, metric modulations abounded, ranges were extreme; the orchestration was hyper-kinetic, almost spastic.

George was a demanding client: "The lines are a little crowded, don't you think?" he said, nearly whispering. "Okay, I'll spread out the music more next time," I promised. He caught about three errors per part and carefully marked each in non-reproducing blue pencil. "Not bad," he sighed, sitting back in his chair. "These shouldn't take you too long to fix." I rubbed my eyes. "This was a hard job," I said. "Why is that?" he asked. I paused. George chose his words carefully; so would I: "All the metric modulations...." "Oh!" he clapped his hands and began to laugh, "They're taking a long time to copy! You're not making any money!" I blushed.

"I've been copying music for George Perle," I explained a few days later to Homer Lambrecht as we wrapped our hands around enormous Reubens at the Carnegie Deli. "And I've composed a great Matthew 7:6 limerick for you." "The Sermon on the *Mount*?" Homer asked dubiously. "Yeah. Here it is—*A serious fella named Perle / Got hitched to a girl named Shirl. / Though, to some of the species, / His pieces were feces, / To Shirley they surely were pearls.*" I waited. Homer smiled, but didn't laugh. I was manic, and knew it. "Um, sorry," I muttered. "It's okay," smiled Homer. We'd just come from Carnegie Hall, where Catherine Comet had conducted the American Composers Orchestra in a rehearsal of his sumptuous, resplendently orchestrated *From an Ark of Emerging Shadows*. "How's things going at Juilliard?" he asked, changing the subject. "Oh, I don't know," I said. "I'm supposed to work with Bernard Rands this semester. I like his music, and he's my first 'Post-Darmstadt School' colorist, but...." "Well, he's a little more than that," Homer gently corrected me. "Of course," I backpedaled. "What I meant was, I'm ready to stop going to school, and I don't know what we'll do together." "Oh, you'll learn a ton," said Homer. "Look at his music. Ask him questions. Enjoy his company." "I will," I promised. "Are you still with Michaela?" he asked. "I'm having a really hard time accepting that she's moved on," I admitted. "Well, Daron," he said, "nature also teaches us how to let things die."

I began lessons with Rands (now the spouse of composer Augusta Read Thomas) the same week. Bernard received the Pulitzer Prize in 1984. His lush compositional style appeals to internationalist intellectuals and sentimental Neo-romantics (like me) alike. Bernard had a keen ear for orchestrational touches—the sort of super-elegant, quasi-spectral, subtle affects that Ned, for all his Francophilia, eschewed as fussy. Although it was obvious to me that if he had not been assigned me as a student, he would not have taken me as one, I appreciated the fact that he treated me as cordially as he did and dedicated a fiendishly difficult solo cello etude in fourths (the hardest interval to play in tune on a stringed instrument) called *Higher, Louder, Faster!* to him. I wove together the tune of *Tea for Two* wicked passagework, open string left-handed pizzicatos, and "passively aggressive, purposefully unidiomatic writing" to portray Life at Juilliard. "The listener," wrote Robert La Rue about the etude, "may choose to enjoy the composer's gleeful, poker-faced subversiveness, or rejoice as the performer grows up a bit, casts off inhibitions, and learns to love rough edges and rawness again."

During my first lesson, after paging through the score of whatever I was working on at the time, Bernard looked up at me over the rims of his glasses and asked, "So what do you want from me?" It was a good question. I still returned to Lincoln Center for my composition lessons and ear training class, but, otherwise, the center of my activities had shifted away from school. In truth, I could think of nothing that I wanted except to graduate and be done with it.

Five months later, in between fulfilling commissions and working as a freelance pianist and copyist, I'd managed almost by accident to complete the coursework at Juilliard for the masters' degree. As it had become time to discuss whether I would remain at Juilliard to pursue my "terminal degree," I was summoned to the same room in which I had first auditioned. Diamond, Babbitt, and Persichetti were already there. They sat in a row on the other side of the room. It was hot for June, but a familiar icy remoteness gripped me. I became hyper-aware of my surroundings. When we met seven years previous, I was an annoyance to them, a fly that deserved to be swatted—no, flicked—back to Wisconsin. I remembered the ridiculous green leisure suit I'd worn to that audition. This time I wore a Juilliard sweatshirt and blue jeans. I had a clear idea of where I stood, professionally. Now I was competing with them for commissions.

During their lifetimes, composition programs had sprung up around the country; the doctorate (which had barely existed in composition) had become an exclusionary degree: if one wanted the financial safety net of a career in Academe, one now had to have one. I smiled at David. He gave me a schoolmarmish scowl in return, and began, "Despite my objections, Daron, you have continued to accept commissions while engaged in your studies here at Juilliard. You produce concerts, you accompany dance classes, you copy music, you conduct a chorus at NYU, and every time I talk to you, you have a new *amour*. I think that you should take a year or two off to consider your life choices before returning to complete your degree. Perhaps then you'll be prepared to concentrate on your composing in a more disciplined fashion."

"You need to *decide*," David decreed, "what is really *important* to you." At that moment, David reminded me of my high school trigonometry teacher Max Hilmer, sincerely baffled that I didn't want to be like him, of Diane Doerfler, who had taught me that "making art is more important than teaching about it," of Ned, who misinterpreted my fear of being thrown out of school as "a seething desire to please." At core, though, I felt as though I was being manipulated, and life with Father had taught me to become emotionless (that familiar icy remoteness), and capable of brutality when I felt that I was being subjected to it. Oh, I was seething now, all right, but not with a "desire to please." *You spend your time*, I thought, *or you are spent.*

"May I have some time to think about this?" I asked. David was suddenly magnanimous: "By all means, Daron. Take as much time as you need to decide." He clapped his hands together and then spread them before him like a blackjack dealer completing his shift. I smiled coolly in return, excused myself, and walked as slowly as possible to the door. Closing it with elaborate care behind me, I looked across the hallway at the door of the bathroom in which I had thrown up before retreating to Wisconsin. I walked briskly to the elevators. As I jabbed the call button, the remoteness dissipated, a film of cold perspiration slicked my forehead, and I began to feel again.

With a ping, the doors parted, revealing a flock of ballerinas in leotards clutching diet Pepsis and wadded-up packs of cigarettes. I took a deep breath, held it, and plunged into their midst. They unselfconsciously banged into one another and brushed up against me. I got an erection. Their voices piled atop one another like flamingos. I exhaled explosively. Their long pink necks and sweaty, gangling frames generated a miasma of musty leggings, baby powder, crotch, and cigarette-smoke. There was no air. I felt hot. Then I felt cold. I poked at the first-floor button, three, four, five times. My ears began buzzing; my reflection in the doors began to blur. I was going to pass out. I looked around at their rouged baby-faces and their hard eyes. My hands turned to ice. Another ping. Just in time. I tumbled out into the Juilliard lobby and down the stone-lined tunnel of the entranceway across from the (then) Chinese consulate on 67th Street.

I needed to sit. Looking for a bench, I saw Mary Anthony Cox. As I passed her, she noted my distress and indicated that I should join her. I admired and trusted Mary Anthony. She was one of the best teachers I had ever had. She asked what was wrong. I put my hands out before me, palms down, and watched them gradually cease trembling. Then, I described my meeting with the composition faculty.

"Honey," she sighed, "you are a round peg. Graduate school is a square hole. Of course, you can make yourself fit in here, but you don't belong. You're a composer. You write music. So, do it. Mozart didn't need a doctorate to write his operas. You don't need one to write yours." I fingered the bus ticket to Peterborough, New Hampshire in my pocket, thanked her, and left. Maybe I'm making this up, but I recall the sun hitting me flat on the face like a hot bed sheet when I emerged on to the 66th Street sidewalk. I looked up at what is now an extension of the Phillips Club, removed my glasses, swept my hand through my hair, and walked east. Within five minutes, considering the decadent amber of a glass of scotch, I was polishing a stool at Paddy McGlade's. My army-surplus backpack, already packed, sat at my feet. There was nowhere I had to be. I had three days of Owl Light to kill before arriving at the MacDowell Colony, where I planned to get cracking on *Heliotrope,* an orchestra piece commissioned by ASCAP to commemorate the 75th anniversary of its founding.

Dawn. The ticket receipts on the bedside table indicated that I had taken the Peter Pan Bus from the Port Authority to Peterborough, New Hampshire, but I couldn't remember the trip—I'd been drinking for the last few days. I sat up in bed, shaking violently. The sheets were soaked. A lurid dream of such vividness that I could remember every detail was in the front of my mind. I grabbed for my journal, and wrote out the first variant of what I came to call the "Green Room Dream":

I am living in the cockroach-infested back room of a sprawling apartment very high up in a once fashionable, now structurally unsound, building. All the walls are a grimy, mottled green. The floors are the same snot-yellow linoleum ones that were in the kitchen of the Big Cedar House. There are sheets of manuscript paper everywhere, swept into unordered piles by wind like leaves in the corners because, although it is midwinter, the windows have been left wide open. I go to the bathroom. When I look in the toilet, I see a leg and an arm. I pull it out, yelling—my voice muffled as though I am screaming inside a velvet-lined baritone saxophone case—'Help me, help me!' Somehow, I manage to pull her out of the toilet, and drag her down a long hallway to a door I haven't seen before. I open the door. I pull her through the entranceway and close the door behind me. My cat Clara is sitting in one corner, hair standing on end. I look to see why. One wall of the room has disappeared, and the Manhattan skyline can be seen, far below. I look at Mother. Her mouth is slack, laxly open, with brackish saliva puddle in the corner of her lip. I think to myself, "Christ, do I remember CPR?" and search the mouth with my finger. Bending down, I think, "But this is what she wanted because she wanted to die with some dignity." The floor begins to tilt downwards towards the missing wall. I begin sliding.

Dry heaves, tachycardia, shakes, and a splitting headache. I closed the book and rose from the bed, stumbled to the bathroom, and threw up, collapsing to the floor next to the toilet. I don't know how long I sat there, staring out the window at the trees swaying back and forth in the spring breeze. In time, I noticed that the sky was eggshell blue. After a while, I noticed that the towels smelled of lemon. I peeled off my tee shirt and briefs, climbed into the shower, turned the water on, leaned my forearms against the tiled wall, and placed my forehead against my wrist. As the water flowed over me, I replayed the "Green Room Dream" behind my closed eyes, not realizing that it would recur on and off with minor variations for the next fifteen years.

From across the fields I heard the breakfast bell sound. I pulled on a tee shirt, stumbled into the bright sunlight, and smelled the clean country air. That summer, whether alone or with California poet Kim Addonizio (we were for a time ineluctably drawn to one another), I ritualistically touched every tree trunk between my bedroom and Colony Hall, tenderly promising each, "I'll remember you. I'll remember you."

Virgil Thomson was looking for someone to do some "work for hire" arrangements. His secretary Lou Rispoli reached me at MacDowell by way of the pay phone and asked if I might be willing to come in for an interview. I arrived at the Chelsea Hotel a few days later hot and tired, broke and cocky. To the left of the front doors of the grand old joint hung a plaque on which were listed the names of former residents—giants of the 20s and 30s. At the bottom of the plaque, someone had used something sharp to scratch, "and Sid Vicious!"

Virgil looked like a crazy person, sitting in his wing chair, plucking alternately at the squealing hearing aids in his ears and squinting at me like a benignant swashbuckler as he quizzed me about my background. His belt wrapped around what had to be his chest; his chin seemed to stop where his tummy began. He was shaped like the illustrations of Tik-tok in L. Frank Baum's *Oz* books. When, a few weeks earlier, Ned had told me that Virgil was looking for someone to do some orchestrating for him, I had pounced on the opportunity. "But you'll have to submit to an interview," said Ned. "No promises."

Born in Missouri in 1896, Thomson attended Harvard before spending an extended period in Paris where he studied with Boulanger and became a professional and social associate of that group of composers referred to as *Les Six*. As the powerful music critic of the *New York Herald Tribune* after returning to the States, he used his position to promote his career as a composer. He could get it wildly wrong: panning Gershwin's *Porgy and Bess* did not constitute his finest moment. His legendary collaboration with Gertrude Stein produced *Four Saints in Three Acts*, a work I've always thought indebted to Satie's brief opera *Socrate*. Author of eight books, including an autobiography, he received the Pulitzer Prize and no less than twenty honorary doctorates during his long and fascinating career. Virgil's relationship with his pupil Ned was like Ned's with me—often rocky, but always affectionate. "I don't mind Ned stealing my moves," Virgil quipped to me once. "I mind it when he says that he didn't."

"So, what's it like being a young composer these days?" he shrieked. "Where do you get your money?" he continued, not waiting for me to answer. I leant forward in my chair, clasped my hands together in what I hoped was the picture of earnestness, and rolled out some sort of answer. I don't think he heard me. The earpieces started up again, this time on different pitches. He batted his ears. I winced. He turned his head just so and they were both silenced. "I know all about being a young composer," he shouted, triumphantly. "It's all about optimizing your leisure time!" "Yes, sir." "What's that? Call me Mr. Thomson, or Virgil. Or boss," he finished. Now his eyes were twinkling. "Okay, boss." "No, I don't like that. Stick to Mr. Thomson." "Okay!" I shouted. "What was it like studying with Ned?" he asked, suddenly in a normal tone of voice. "Wonderful," I shouted. "Great!" I gave a "thumbs up." "You don't have to shout!" he shouted. "I'm not deaf, you know! Okay. Right," he barreled on. "Look, I have some piano pieces I want you to orchestrate, and some orchestra pieces I want you to turn into piano pieces. Plus, I need you to do a piano reduction of *Louisiana Story*. Can you do that?" "Sure!" "What?" "Yes!" "Read my article *How Composers Eat*, baby," Virgil said. "I have," I shouted. "Good. Don't get stuck being a copyist! Or being a performer, a professor, a critic, or getting into the appreciation-racket. Marry rich, if you can. Remain affably pushy. Try not to succumb to a conducting career—the money's good, but it kills your music."

I was hired and worked for Virgil for the next nine months. I don't recall that Virgil ever actually asked to see any of the work I did—it was all sent directly to Boosey. Nevertheless, he wanted to supervise my work, he said; consequently, I was to bring my gear to the Chelsea and do all the work at the table in his living room. He was exceedingly kind to me, and treated me in a comradely fashion, like a younger colleague who, as he would say, was "on the make."

"Virgil is sort of your musical grandfather," Ned told me around that time. "There are exactly as many years between you and me as there are between myself and Virgil." Lineage means a lot to me, so I was proud that Ned had taken orchestration lessons from Virgil in the same room forty years earlier, had copied parts for him at the same table at which I was then working. I recall the exact date of the last day that I worked for Virgil (27 May) because it was the day I received the results of my last HIV test. I had been dating a ballerina from City Ballet.

"Thank you for being so patient with an old man," Virgil said in his high, shrewd simper as I arrived for my final day of work. "Old!" I scoffed. "Who's old?" He smiled, delighted. "Ned tells me you're writing a ballet." His interest was merely polite. "Uh huh," I said, knowing that he didn't hear me and that it didn't matter. "Honey, did you study strict counterpoint?" he asked. "The strictest, Virgil," I laughed. "Invertible, and so forth?" he asked. "Uh huh." "Eh?" "YES!" I shouted. "And you're still studying with Ned?" "No." I said, "That was a couple of years ago." "Sorry," he replied. I walked over to the Duchamp as he instructed me on how to proceed with the reduction of the suite from *Louisiana Story*. He looked up at me. "It's lovely, isn't it?" he asked, in a remote voice. "Mmm," I agreed.

Things between my ballerina and me had become strained, in part because she had informed me a few weeks earlier that her previous boyfriend had tested positive for HIV and that her doctor had advised her to tell her other sexual partners to be tested. I imagine that nearly anyone having sex in Manhattan during the 80s worried about AIDS. At the beginning, there were people afraid to kiss one another on the cheek. Aside from my doctor, my chief source of information about the epidemic during those years was the gifted pianist and composer Robert Savage, who I'd first met at the Atlantic Center for the Arts in Florida during winter 1984. James Holmes was also a compassionate counselor. Robert and Jim both died of AIDS in 1993. I took four AIDS tests during those years. (Although I never had sex with a man, heterosexual transmission of the virus was of course possible.) Even for a straight male, AIDS had turned sex in Manhattan amongst performing artists into a game of Russian roulette. What's more, emotional intimacy terrified me. I feared the crazy things I might say in unguarded moments. I was too selfish, too raw, and too resentful of time not spent composing to be of use to anyone else. *Ars super* goddamn *omnia*.

I called the health clinic from a pay phone at the corner of 14th and Fifth Avenue and asked for the results of my HIV test. I was put on hold. The first coin dropped as a new voice came on asking why I was put on hold. "I have no idea," I replied. "Listen. I want the results of my blood test, if they're in." Beat. "Oh," replied the nurse in a strained voice. "What's your code number?" I gave it. I was put on hold again. I thought about every woman I had dated for the past two years. I thought, "This is the way I feel before going onstage—a combination of anticipating the worst possible news and the potential for ecstasy." I thought of how well Mother had told me of her cancer, and then how well she had fought her battle with it. "Hello?" It was the voice of the clinic's AIDS specialist. Why was he on the line? "Your results are—," he began. At that moment, a bus whooshed by and the taped operator broke into the line, demanding another quarter. "—Normal," he said. "—Deposit twenty-five—." "What's that?" I asked. "—Please deposit twenty-five—." "Oh God, that's great—," I said. "—Next three minutes." "Good luck," he said, rushing to get the words in. "—Please deposit—." "Thanks," I said, and replaced the receiver. A bus passed. Another bus. A taxi. A couple of cars. A biker. The light changed, once, maybe twice. I don't recall. A woman walked by, pushing a baby in a stroller. In time, a school kid tugged apologetically at my sleeve. "That phone in your hand," he said. "Are you done with it? I need to use the phone."

Joe Schwantner encouraged me to send *Grand Line* to Joan Tower in her capacity as composer-in-residence of the St. Louis Symphony; Joan turned it down but wrote me a kindly letter in which she asked whether there was a recording. Thimmig, with whom I was then studying, had introduced me to Joan in autumn 1979, when she and her new music chamber group, the Da Capo Chamber Players, played a concert at UW-Madison. Naturally, Da Capo played one of Les' pieces; they also included something by Columbia faculty member Roger Reynolds, and something by Joan.

Born in 1938, Joan had amassed professional capital and moral authority in the concert music world by touring with Da Capo, which commissioned and played an enormous amount of new music. I genuinely admired her first orchestral composition *Sequoia*—a gorgeous, poetic exploration of the pitch G—when I heard it premiered in 1981 on an American Composers Orchestra concert. By the 90s, *The New Yorker* was describing her as "one of the most successful women composers of all time."

I didn't know Joan, so I didn't yet know whether to take her seriously when, unexpectedly, I received a telephone call from her. "Hi, this is Joan," she began. "Joe Schwantner tells me that you're a real fast composer. Is that true?" I laughed, not knowing whether she was teasing me or being blunt. On a hunch, I answered, "Yes. Like Shostakovich, I think slow and write fast." After several beats of silence, she replied, "Well … um, yeah … whatever." "I'm not comparing myself to Shostakovich," I back-pedaled. "Right," she continued, "Here's the deal: I scheduled a piece by Kathryn Harris [flautist and composer who I'd gotten to know at Tanglewood, and who now teaches at Yale], for a reading and recording session by Leonard [Slatkin] and the orchestra and she can't make the deadline, so I thought that if you could put together a six minute piece and get the parts to St. Louis in three weeks, I'd invite you to do it instead. Can you do it?" "Of course," I cried, eager for a chance to swing a bat in the majors. Three weeks wasn't a lot of time. The hand-copied orchestra parts alone would require half that time alone to be extracted. "You know, writing for orchestra is real hard; if you're not up to it, I certainly understand," she said.

In order to present work I knew to be well-made in the allotted time, I orchestrated the first movement of my second piano trio, *J'entends*. I hired Michael Torke and Aaron Jay Kernis to proofread the parts; Philadelphia composer Robert Maggio copied the wind parts, and I copied the rest. That's how, on 7 October 1987, Joan and I sat, along with several other composers, in an empty concert hall in Kirksville, Missouri, following along in my score as Leonard Slatkin rehearsed and recorded *Fresh Ayre,* a six-minute showpiece that eventually became the first movement of my Symphony No. 2. After Leonard and the orchestra sight-read the piece, Joan turned to me and said, "Someday you'll learn how not to have so much going on at once in your orchestra pieces." "Seriously?" I replied, surprised. "Do you really think so?" (A few weeks later, I played the recording for Bernstein, who enthused, "I love how you manage to keep so many things going on at once.") "Yeah," she said. "I learned that when I wrote *Sequoia* in '81—you know that piece, don't you?" "Yes, I was at the premiere," I said. "It's a great piece." She seemed pleased, and intrigued; perhaps annoyed, by my self-assurance.

A boost came from Columbia University, which awarded the Bearns Prize to *J'entends,* the trio from whence *Fresh Ayre* was extracted; another boost came from ASCAP, which awarded *Fresh Ayre* the ASCAP-Nissim Prize. Along with the award came an introduction by ASCAP's Vice President for Concert Music Frances Richard to conductor Michael Morgan, who performed it with the Chicago Civic Orchestra.

After the reading session, in the van ferrying us from Kirksville to St. Louis, Joan asked me how I felt about teaching composition and theory. When I ground to a halt, she asked how I would teach them if I could teach them in any way I pleased. I talked some more. Eventually, she asked, "How would you like to come to teach at Bard in the fall?" I had never heard of the place, but I needed the money, so I told her I would consider it.

◆◆ 13 ◆◆

Learning to Profess
1987–1988

There was during those years a fellow who entered subway cars on the Seventh Avenue Local wearing a colander on his head who, brandishing a broken saxophone like a spear, would announce, "I am the Saxophone Player from Outer Space. Money makes me go away!" I remember, too, the African American preacher who spent every day walking up and down Broadway shouting "Hosanna" to passersby, having achieved a delirious, semi-ecstatic state through exhaustion and hyperventilation. In retrospect, I think I was pretty much a combination of the two.

JoAnn Falletta premiered *Grand Line* in November with the Denver Chamber Orchestra. I performed my Piano Trio No. 2 with Robert La Rue and Michaela's sister, Brigitte, and made my professional debut as a soloist playing the Gershwin *I Got Rhythm Variations*. "Any advice for me?" I asked Rob just before going onstage. "Don't just 'do a good job,'" he replied. "They deserve more than that." I had been practicing for four hours a day for the past few months and felt good. About two-thirds of the way through the little showpiece, I heard for the first time a lovely bass clarinet doubling hitherto buried in the orchestration. *Hmmm, that's nice. No wonder the celli sound so plump there,* I thought, realizing that I'd heard it because I'd gone up, even though my fingers had continued to move to their appointed destinations. Zooming back in, I ended satisfactorily. *The connection with the audience,* I thought, bowing afterwards with JoAnn, *is too fleeting. Even if I had the technique, being a soloist's not for me.*

I spent another winter subletting actor Robert Lunny's apartment on 93rd Street, composing, copying music, and conducting the NYU Washington Square Chorus. Lou Karchin had hired me to be his assistant conductor for a few years and had kindly passed the gig on to me. The first year, I hired Eric Sawyer to accompany. Sawyer studied with Leon Kirchner's at Harvard, and now teaches at Amherst College. The second year, I hired Aaron Jay Kernis. Aaron had to freelance back then just like everyone else to make ends meet. Our Mozart C minor Mass that spring was certainly enthusiastic, if stylistically loopy.

Canadian choreographer William Douglas and I were introduced by Muriel Topaz who, favorably impressed with the progress of *Interior*, a ballet that Diane Coburn Bruning and I were developing for the Juilliard Dance Division, wanted to see what I would do with a structuralist. Muriel was director at the time of the Juilliard Dance Division, a Labanotation advocate, and the wife of Jacob Druckman. A sensitive, intelligent man, Bill crafted sensually appealing choreography that had a Cartesian formality to it that reflected his early training as an architect. I made an elaborate set of variations on words of Virginia Woolf from *The Waves*, and Isak Dinesen from *Out of Africa*. Eric Fischl's erotic, sexually ambiguous canvases inspired the lighting, costume, and set design. There was just enough of a music budget to hire Karen Hale, my longtime cellist pal Robert La Rue, and Eric Sawyer, who played the piano. *And the Air* was premiered and had a longish run at the Merce Cunningham Studio at Westbeth during December 1987. After the company closed in New York they danced to a recording of us for a ten-city Canadian tour. I put the forty-minute score in a box and forgot about it until 2008, when I pruned half an hour of music and published it as a diptych called *Rapture and Regret*.

Cheryl Kaplan tolerated my impulsiveness in 1988 when one of the first things I did when we met at VCCA was to scoop her up in my arms and quote Helen: "And though she be but little, she is fierce!" Fierce she is: thirty years later, we're still pals: her teeming, restless intellect ranges from poetry to prose, filmmaking to visual art. For years we've toyed with making an oratorio out of her book-length poem, *Money Keeps Talking*. During a stint at *House Beautiful*, she later arranged for Paul Kreider, Carolann Page—a fellow Curtis-grad married at the time to Paul Gemignani with whose voice I had fallen in love as Pat in Adams' *Nixon in China*, on the strength of which I had asked for her to be cast as Mamah in *Shining Brow*—and me to perform arias from *Brow* at the magazine's 1994 Gala at the Guggenheim Museum. Back then, Cheryl maintained a *pied-à-terre* at 18 St. Mark's Place in the East Village. Knowing that I was looking to move, she kindly called to let me know that the apartment next to hers was available. With the help of Paul Moravec, Aaron, and Jim Legg (to whom I passed along my Upper West Side sublet), I moved my gear from the 93rd Street sublet to the East Village.

It was the real deal—a bohemian garret out of Dickens or Balzac. I loved it. The front door was a riotous, many-layered post-apocalyptic collage of rust scabs, half-torn-down posters for broken-up bands, loopy red and yellow graffiti tags, a couple of bullet holes, and an enormous black "anarcho-punk circle-A" that had been spray-painted on it during the late 70s. To the right was a travel agency run by an enigmatic Pole named Richie who either owned the building at the time or served as its owner's agent. In all seasons, Wayne the Sock Man—a grumpy neighborhood fixture—stood in front of the building behind a card table on which he spread his wares. He served as a sort of freelance doorman, since the front door hung open most of the time. The mailboxes in the foyer had all been pried open at one point or another and lolled open like tongues; the doorbells were all busted, and the guts of their wiring hung down like crazy, stiff, multi-colored strands of spaghetti. A cracked plastic sheath filled with dead bugs half-encased a sputtering fluorescent light above. There were usually used syringes swept fastidiously into an oddly tidy pile in one corner; and a couple of trash bags filled with the Sock Man's socks in the other.

When friends came to visit, they called me from the payphone on the northeast corner of Third Avenue and St. Mark's Place to let me know that they were on their way. I'd put my keys in a sock, open the dormer window, climb out onto the fire escape, and drop them five stories into the hands of the Sock Man, who would then hand them to my guest—this service in exchange for the occasional purchase of tube socks. My rent—$500 per month, payable in cash—was due whenever I could scrape it together. I occasionally paid Richie my rent in the form of VHS tapes of old movies, which he loved. At one point, the power went out. Con Ed sent a couple of men over, but they couldn't figure out how the fifth floor was wired up, and left before fixing it, so I ran the refrigerator off an extension cord plugged into an outlet in the hallway—in which Cheryl customarily dried canvas, and Grazyna clothes—for the last nine months that I lived there. The bathroom had no sink; the tub no shower; and the toilet never stopped running. I shaved holding a mirror in one hand and a razor in the other standing at the little wet bar that doubled as a kitchenette. Once, when Ned and Jim came for dinner, Ned banged his head on the ceiling so hard rising from the table that he had to lay down for a half an hour to recover his wits. There was just enough room for my battered baby grand, bookcases, and a *chaise longue* loaned to me by Grazyna and her husband Julius, who lived across the hall and whose marriage dissolved in tears over beef stroganoff in my living room one night. An airshaft carried the cries and moans of male prostitutes up from the apartment several floors down. A steep flight of steps led up to a loft too small to kneel in that was just large enough to hold a futon and some crates of books. I owned nothing of any real value to anyone else, really, except for a stereo I'd been lugging around since high school and a small Sony Walkman Professional, on which I listened to cassette recordings of my music. My floor mates and I may as well have been Mimi, Rodolfo, Musetta, and Marcello.

It was the blood on the doorknob and not the apartment door hanging open that alerted me to the fact that something was wrong when I arrived at home the night my flute quintet for composer Bruce Wolosoff called *The Presence Absence Makes* was premièred at Alice Tully Hall. We all left our doors unlocked on the sixth floor, and we were accustomed to treating our apartments as a shared suite. At first, I thought that Cheryl had hurt herself stretching canvas, but, when I pushed open the door and looked inside, there was blood everywhere. A burglar had shattered the small skylight in the loft, wriggled in, and taken the stereo. Poor Clara, sitting on the piano, arched her back, poor thing, and hissed at me as I entered. Cleaning the blood up took so long that I started to feel sorry for the poor guy—after all, there hadn't been anything of value for him to steal.

The next day, I told Frances Richard the story over lunch-time vodka stingers. "Unacceptable," she said. "Let me make a call." Three minutes later, she had a Hells Angel on the line. "Listen, this is Fran Richard. I have a young composer who lives on Saint Mark's Place here. He writes symphonies … operas. Somebody in the neighborhood stole his stereo last night. He needs it for his work." Head down, she looked at me over her glasses as she waited, mildly amused. "So you think you can find it for him?" Another beat. "Great. I thought so. Thank you." She hung up, jotted the clubhouse's address on a piece of paper. "They're decent guys down there," she said. "Go now. They're on Third Street. They think they might have … found it last night … and they want you to have it back."

Nights careened by—the *Under the Volcano Dia de los Muertos* Goth atmosphere and the specter of HIV/AIDS saturated everything and made people Russian Roulette crazy. I drank compulsively, but I worked obsessively; I never trivialized my art or glorified addiction. I don't believe that Hemingway ever said, "Write drunk, and edit sober." I never did, and I can't believe that, if he did say it, he practiced what he preached. Even when I came home paralytic and stupefied, I *still* sobered up and worked that much harder the next day. I consciously struck outwards, away from my center, dilly-dallying with other struggling artists, actors, drag queens, and musicians at places like the Pyramid Club and Cave Canem, CBGB's and the Yaffa Café. I filled hundreds of journal pages at the time with minutely detailed examinations of my own feelings, manic disquisitions on intertextuality (I was getting ready to compose *Heliotrope*) and creative influences, and febrile think pieces about the struggle between innocence and decadence. Each night, I became a cog in the libertine hurly-burly of the East Village. On the sidewalk, the aphrodisiacal smells of leathers, dope, cheap perfume, beer, cigarette smoke, and the City itself mingled with that of lubricious skin. The baths disgorged sexed up men; the clubs overflowed with famous, beautiful, intoxicating and intoxicated women. *Rocky Horror* without humor—sudden violence, operatic emotional display, and Technicolor, VistaVision despair. Jonathan Larson was most likely thinking up *Rent* in the same bars in which I was having my ass grabbed.

Days flowed by accompanied by the reassuring, inspiring thrum of freelance-life during the concert season—concerts attended grudgingly that turned out to be life changing; the stress and challenge of substituting as a pianist in the pits of Broadway shows; the snarky pleasure of playing in piano bars; the long hours spent working as a music editor, proofreader, and copyist. Drinking may have stopped time, but working made me happy. I finished pieces—lots of them. I loved the high of finishing a composition even more than the high of being drunk. Work. Glorious work—constant, obsessive, daily, reassuring, inspiring, and exciting work. Some days I simply walked down Broadway from the Bronx to the Battery because I could, and rode the State Island Ferry just to tune up my passion for the City by taking in its skyline and harbor. My eyes were shining pictures of necessity; my every lover was a gifted poet. I read the Sunday *New York Times* on Saturday night, and argued passionately with friends about the prose of friends whose books were all being published and dissected in the *New York Review of Books*. God, did we ever care. It was *our time*, and we knew it.

At Yaddo I composed *Lyric Variations* (the second movement of Symphony No. 2). Two months after throwing down double bars, JoAnn Falletta premiered it with the Milwaukee Symphony, for whom she was then serving as associate conductor to Lukas, who was finishing a stint as music director. I am profoundly grateful to JoAnn for her over thirty years of unstinting, staunch support.

Over lunch with Kevin (then operations director for the orchestra) and Lukas, the following story: They were on tour somewhere in Europe and, the orchestra having tuned up, everyone, including the audience, was waiting for Lukas to come onstage and ascend the podium. No Lukas. Kevin was used to packing extra socks, batons, and even pants for his forgetful friend. Backstage, there were three doors: one led to Lukas' dressing room; one led out to an alley behind the theater; the third led below-stage. Looking for his socks, Lukas had chosen the wrong door. Kevin was unfazed. In short order, he found Lukas in the basement, happily looking up at the numbered traps of the stage above. "Isn't this fascinating?" Lukas mused. "Yes," Kevin calmly replied, handing Lukas his socks and guiding him upstairs. "You know it is time to conduct now, don't you?" Long beat. "I wasn't worried, Kevin. I knew you would take care of me."

I shared my work several times at the Dakota with Bernstein, to whom I wrote, from Yaddo, on 18 May:

> *... Of course I recall arriving for our first meeting last August. [I was] bound up in an over-weighted regard for Ned and David and you cleared the vast majority of that away; I still think you are the only person who could have done that for me. You did me an enormous favor by transforming yourself through your words from a pedestal-bound hero into a man I could like and trust, be proud of knowing, learn from, and with whom I could feel genuinely connected. It makes me think of that terribly demoralizing scene in Rolland's* Jean-Christophe *in which the young composer pays homage to the older one and is treated by him with indifference. Well, you treated me wonderfully....*

In response, he invited me for another lesson. Discussing psychotherapy, I suggested to him that I thought that I might be cleverer than my therapist. "Now, you be careful thinking that," he laughed. "Let me give you some advice by way of telling you a famous story: Two chaps are lunching at the Carnegie Deli. The first says, 'I've just come from my shrink. He's brilliant. I told him my dream and he gave me the most fascinating read on it.' The other says, 'Really? What's his name?' The first tells him and they realize that they are both being shrunk by the same doctor. 'Let's play a trick on him,' says the second. 'I'll make up a wild dream, and then phone you, tell you the dream, and then you tell him the same dream.' So, they do this. A week later, back at the deli, the first one says to the second, 'So, what did he say when you told him my dream?' After a moment, the second chap says, 'He told me that I was the third guy this week to tell him that same dream.'"

I wrote a Harp Trio commissioned by the National Federation of Music Clubs and the Debussy Trio (led by harp virtuoso Marcia Dickstein and at the time managed by her mother, Curtis-trained violinist Diana Steiner) that became my first commercially recorded work. My relationship with Ned evolved from being a purely student-pupil one to a deeper exchange that included more personal news than collegial banter. To Ned alone I admitted that my life in constant motion was, nevertheless, lonely and unhappy. In reply to a letter from Yaddo in which I had described, at his request, my love life, he replied:

> Lonely Daron—Well, it's the condition of man. Colette said, "No one asks you to be happy. Just get your work done." Of course, the current ravages of the Greenhouse Effect suggest we're all doomed anyway.

When Muriel Topaz commissioned a ballet for the Juilliard Dance Division's 1989 Spring Gala, I wrote *Interior*, collaborating with Junoesque choreographer Diane Coburn Bruning. As a youngster, I had returned obsessively to a painting by Edgar Degas in one of Mother's art books called *Interior (The Rape)*. (Degas evidently referred to his 1874 oil painting simply as "my genre painting." The story that it is based on a scene from Émile Zola's great study of temperaments *Thérèse Raquin* may be entirely spurious.) I was astonished, the first time I was taken to tea at Henry McIllhenny's townhouse on Rittenhouse Square in 1983, to see Degas' painting hanging above Henry's living room couch. Henry told me then that the painting, with its disturbing combination of decorative, narrative, and impressionist elements, was one of his favorites. My idea was to use Degas' painting and Zola's novel as the starting points for *Interior,* a three-act ballet that combined narrative and pure dance traditions. Diane hunched nearly double in the garret on Saint Mark's Place, negotiating the ceiling and repeatedly bumping her head as she demonstrated moves. (I finished *Interior* on a plane from Chicago to New York. It was performed a dozen times or so, both as a ballet score and as a concert work—several times under my baton. In January 2003, I withdrew it, used the first two movements as the basis of a Chamber Symphony (itself based on paintings by Hudson Valley painters Elihu Vedder, Thomas Cole, and Thom O'Connor) for the Albany Symphony Orchestra. David Alan Miller introduced the work at the Art Institute of Albany in March 2003.)

I mixed into this stew of freelance work the new job teaching composition and theory ("and whatever else you'd like") at Bard College. The place was named after John Bard, who, in 1860, donated a part of his estate, Annandale, as well as the charming Chapel of the Holy Innocents, to Saint Stephen's College. In 1934, the college was renamed Bard, after its founder. In 1944, when it became coeducational, Bard severed its relationship with Columbia University—it had been for young men what Barnard was for young women. Situated on the Hudson ninety minutes north of Manhattan, Bard College at the time I began my stint on the faculty, was a beguilingly funky assortment of manor houses, their outliers, and inexpensive temporary structures. There was something wonderfully experimental about it—the students were mostly well off, often eccentric, and nearly always highly creative, and their young professor was only just beginning to learn how to profess.

For a decade (1988–1997) I was paid to be something called a "six-thirteenth-time" associate professor at Bard. Just four years older than my oldest pupils when I began, I was convinced that I would not teach there long enough even to leave a spare shirt behind when I returned to New York, let alone see them graduate. On Wednesday mornings, I pounded up the Hudson from Grand Central Station to Rhinecliff, was ferried from there to campus down winding River Road by a student, dropped into my role as Professor; on Thursday nights, I hurtled back down, there to resume my life as a New York Composer. If you had told me then that, long after leaving the faculty, a quarter century later, I'd be living in Rhinebeck, commuting regularly—typically on the same train, and from the same station, in the opposite direction—I'd have told you that you were mad.

In time, I began set aside the autocratic, judgmental teaching style of my mentors in favor of a more nurturing, experimental, and gentle approach appropriate for undergraduates at a liberal arts college. I relished giving lessons in unorthodox settings—peripatetically, a self-styled Aristotle in blue jeans and Brooks Brothers shirts, during walks down to the Hudson River and back behind Blythewood. The woods behind the music building were my Lyceum. My pupils built from found objects their own instruments and then composed for them. I used Method Acting exercises to enhance their musical improvisation skills, taught music history in reverse chronological order, felt … *free.*

For the first few years things were loose enough that I was allowed to teach my counterpoint class from the bench of the Chapel of the Holy Innocents' three-manual Austin organ. I loved the visceral thrill of lashing together history, the imagination, the ear, and the music by crashing—with literally all the stops pulled out—through *L'Homme armé* for my clutch of terrified pupils. John Ashbery, in a rumpled tweed jacket and corduroys, legs stretched out in front of him in the sun that streamed in sideways through the stained-glass windows, listened one afternoon as a student sang, to my accompaniment, Ned's setting of John's *Fear of Death*: "What is it now with me / And is it as I have become?" Robert Kelly—also on the faculty—whose poetry I also set and whose company I cherished, was my other faculty pole star.

Of all the subjects that I taught, my favorite was Counterpoint. The Process of studying and teaching Counterpoint is a perfect, pure metaphor for the process that is living the examined life. It all begins with the cantus firmus—the *Song of the Earth*, the Life Song, the New Song, first taught us by example, then created on our own by grafting inspiration to memory, training and common sense. A composer intentionally chooses the agitation of dissonance over the consolation of consonance. The entire history of western music is replayed in courtly, stylized fashion each time one moves through the various "species" of solutions—the lines grow more florid, dissonance is prolonged, tonality itself may become tenuous. Studying Counterpoint develops the skills required to pursue the painfully exquisite, life-long process of linking ear, heart, and intellect together to compose melodic lines to join life's cantus firmus. As in life, one strives for the perfect solution—if it sounds easy, so much the better. One inevitably fails to find it, picks oneself up, and tries again. There are the sudden, unexpected flashes of grace and inspiration that reveal a way forward. There is acceptance of compromise, the search for climax, the cruciform elegance of the interplay between melody's horizontal demands and harmony's vertical demands. Over time, there is the acceptance that melody generates harmony and not the other way around. In the end, one accepts the inevitable, disappointing cliché of the final cadence.

When I first joined the faculty, composer / thinker Benjamin Boretz, whom I admired deeply—we had both studied with Lukas; he was co-founder with Arthur Berger, of *Perspectives of New Music* and, from 62–70, music critic for *The Nation*—chaired the music department. Under his stewardship, there was what I felt was a deeply agreeable, healthy tug to the left—towards improvisation, innovation, aesthetic diversity, and experimentation. His was an amazing intellect intriguingly untethered. Sometimes I couldn't figure out what he was talking about, but that was half the fun of working with and for him. Strikingly handsome cellist Luis García Renart, a protégé of Pablo Casals, Mstislav Rostropovich and Aram Khachaturian, coached chamber music at the highest level, along with lessons. He also taught the introductory theory courses. I was tasked with offering ear training and the more advanced theory classes, and with imbuing the composition students with the craft that Joan Tower seemed at the time philosophically opposed to requiring of them. When Joan became department chair, just as her career began taking off, things shifted to the right—towards the conservative. Ben left the department to form his own, more exper-imental, "music learning" program, "Music Program Zero," which flourished until 1995.

The summer after Joan became chair I was offered a long-term residency at the Camargo Foundation, in Cassis. It would begin, if I accepted it, right away. Joan and I met over a basket of tortilla chips in a Mexican restaurant full of townies and colleagues in Tivoli, New York, a short distance from Bard to discuss my departure. She was about to turn 51; I was about to turn 28. A student of ours at Bard (our waiter) approached. Joan circled her glass of merlot with her finger. He nodded and headed for the bar to bring another.

"So, Daron: Fran Richard told me on the phone that you're moving to Europe?" Joan asked. I tried to explain. Her head bobbed slightly as I spoke, and she squinted slightly, as though either she couldn't see or hear me clearly. When I stopped abruptly, she brightened. "When are you coming back?" she asked, fishing in the tortilla basket for a chip. I considered sharing my thoughts, shrugged, said, "I'm sorry, Joan, I just don't know." The 1989–90 school year was about to begin. "You aren't giving me much notice," she observed. "I'll need to find a replacement." I'd waited until the last moment to tell her that I was leaving, hoping on some level, I suppose, that she would fire me. I knew it would be easy to replace me, but she had a point. I tossed out a few names—Robert Maggio, Jennifer Higdon, and George Tsontakis—but stopped, knowing that my opinion was not welcome or needed. Changing the subject, I asked her how she was. Joan talked. After a while, she ordered another merlot. I nodded encouragingly now and then. Eventually she asked, "Why are you going?" I studied her face carefully, trying to gauge the depth of her interest. I didn't want to end up teaching composition at a liberal arts college for the security and composing on the side. "I feel trapped," I told her. "I need to read, to live, to compose, to live in Europe. I know how lucky I am to have this job but … it isn't … *enough*."

The school year ended. I was again free to roam. Diana Steiner's daughter asked me to arrange some Gershwin tunes for the Debussy Trio, and the Sundance Institute for Tel-evision and Film commissioned Diane Coburn Bruning and me to create a film ballet called *Prufrock*. I recall writing a very moody score for solo cello that Robert La Rue recorded in a studio after I'd already left for Europe. I do recall having seen Wim Wender's magnificent film *Wings of Desire* together with Alvin Singleton in the Village the summer before, and having stolen the *gestalt*, if not the actual notes, of the cello solo that underpins Damiel's brooding opening monologue. In a box in somewhere I have a VHS recording of the elegant three-camera film that resulted, but I haven't looked at it in over thirty years, and now even the recording format is obsolete. I wonder if it is any good.

By July I was back at the MacDowell Colony. I shared a reading with Paul Muldoon in the Savage Library on 1 August. "I guessed the letter / Must be yours," he read; then I sang and played the setting I'd made that afternoon of his poem, *Thrush*. It was the first of what would become many similar joint presentations (we called them "dog and pony shows") to fellow artists, students, and opera boards. "Making a lean, white fist / Out of my freckled hand," he concluded, and I launched immediately into the two bar accompaniment pattern skulking around e minor that I had devised to underpin the song. The poem's one forceful image is that of a fist, and the song climaxes downwards on that word, marked *agnosciato* and *sforzando*. The onanistic melancholy following the climax is marked "suddenly remote" and is given a little augmented 13-chord sting before collapsing into the whimpering two bar pattern again to close. The strophic form mirrors the singer's obsessive return to the same emotional starting point; the slippery harmonies highlight his emotional evasiveness and lack of character.

Born in County Armagh, Northern Ireland, in 1951, Paul Muldoon has been described by the *Times Literary Supplement* as "the most significant English-language poet born since the Second World War." From 1973 to 1986, he worked in Belfast as a radio and television producer for the BBC. Since 1987, he has lived in the States. Paul was brilliant, ambitious, quick to skewer pretension, and impatient with mediocrity. Already it was obvious that he had every intention of becoming a celebrity poet. His hair back then looked as though it were trying to escape. A few years ago, he began writing lyrics for a rock band. When we first met, and were close, he spoke with great, and moving intensity of his youth as the son of a mushroom farmer. Awarded the Pulitzer Prize in 2003, he served for a while as poetry editor of *The New Yorker* and is on the faculty of Princeton University. In 2017 he received the queen's gold medal for poetry.

I received a call on one of the pay phones in Colony Hall from conductor Roland Johnson asking whether I might consider composing an opera about the American architect Frank Lloyd Wright for Madison Opera. He even had a title: *Shining Brow*. He stipulated that it would be a year or more before the company would be in the position to offer a commissioning agreement—let alone an advance—so saying yes in a way didn't mean anything in practical terms. Paul was reading the newspaper a few feet away. Without thinking, I leaned out of the booth and quipped, "Say, Paul, do you want to write an opera?" I'm not sure how serious I was. A beat later, he replied, "Sure. Why not?" Since, within a week, I'd be an expat, and the offer was speculative, I didn't give it another thought.

◆◆ 14 ◆◆

Entre les Pays
1988–1990

Drunk, I stuffed what amounted to two fistfuls of francs into the metal box in a bar on the Quai de Rive Neuve in Marseilles, listened to them thud dully and thought that the sound was like that of a heavy metal gate banging shut. Came next the distant, hollow rattling ring of the acoustic exchange. A heavy click, the sound of things being pushed around on a bedside table, and then, after a few beats of silence, a far-off, questioning, "Yes?" "How are you, Gramma?" I asked—my voice insipid with wine—on the crackly transatlantic telephone line. When sober, I could muster enough touristy curiosity to keep my spirits up; when drunk, I sentimentalized my rootlessness and felt lonesome. "I live in a nursing home," Grandmother responded, sensibly. "I eat through a tube in my stomach. How do you think I am?" Beat. *Would I ever have had the nerve to drunk-dial Mother?* I thought. *Not in this life.* Ashamed, I tried to think of something that might please her. "I'm living in Europe now," I said, proudly. "Do you think Mama would have liked that?" There was a burst of spooky crackling on the line. "I never understood what the two of you saw in living abroad," she sniffed. I tried another tack. "You know," I said, *"Common Ground* is going to be played by the New York Philharmonic." Bewilderment, more likely impatience, followed by a rally of her own: "That's nice, honey," she replied. Another beat of silence. "When are you going to get a job?" I had to chuckle. As a girl, she had run away from home to the Menominee River Valley, where, for a few days at a time, she would live with the Indians. My cultural references were as far removed from hers as hers had been from the Potawatomi. "I love you, Gramma," I told her, noticing my call's time running out. "Be a good boy, sweetheart," she answered, hanging up. "00:25" blinked a few times and then the numbers disappeared. I hung up the receiver, downed the rest of the cheap red wine swirling in the bottom of the heavy tumbler I had forgotten was in my other hand, returned it to the bar, headed towards the north end of the Boulevard d'Athènes where at the Gare de Marseilles Saint Charles I boarded a train for Cassis, where I began my lost year of eccentric vagabondage.

The villa named *Le Leque* in which I lived was perched atop an outcropping of stone at the entrance to the Cassis harbor facing the Michelin estate, due west, itself perched atop Cap Canaille, a headland that juts out between Cassis and La Ciotat. Originally the home of filmmaker and artist Jerome Hill, the house and adjoining buildings had become the centerpiece of the Camargo Foundation, where I had been awarded a six-month long residency. Streaming ceaselessly northwards on the dust-laden sirocco from Africa through the studio's tall French doors, the rhythmic slapping of the Mediterranean Sea on the cliff below accompanied cooking, underscored sex, counterpointed composing, and lulled me to sleep.

The emotionally-erratic (I should talk) radical feminist scholar living across the courtyard liked it when I played and sang through Gershwin standards, so each afternoon at four I'd throw the doors open and play and sing through entire Gershwin shows from overture to bows. One afternoon, after playing and singing *The Man I Love*, I couldn't help but feel that the two-measure bridge alone was worth an entire song. So, I pulled out the Ecco Press edition of Paul Muldoon's *Collected Poems* that I'd thrown in my luggage back in New York and used the Gershwin as an accompaniment pattern to kick off my setting of *Holy Thursday*. It came out easily, and in a single swoop. I was so pleased with it that I played and sang it for the collected scholars and artists, including my friend, poet Henri Cole (also in residence), just before dinner a few hours later. Over the next few days I folded in the settings I had done a few months earlier at MacDowell and set some new ones, creating a sturdy little set with which I'm still happy. Three years later, on 2 December 1992, Paul Sperry and I gave them their world premiere on one of composer Tom Cipullo's "Friends and Enemies of New Music" concerts at the Greenwich Music House in New York City.

The shelves in the studio contained the complete Noël Coward and George Gershwin vocal scores, as well as nearly the entire major operatic canon, including Richard Strauss'. By playing repeatedly through Otto Singer's "arrangement'" of *Der Rosenkavalier* I earned the score-faking skills that admiration, fear and respect for Ford Lallerstedt had prevented me—while studying with him, at least—from developing. In time, my hands learned that every key has a geography to it on the keyboard, that, often, once one internalizes the fustian weave of counterpoint in Strauss vocal scores, they are easy to "put over." I became aware that the music played by the thumbs and index fingers: these fingers played the inner voices of the orchestra—the violas, for example. The tune nearly always fell in the third through fifth fingers of the right hand, the bass line in the same fingers of the left. Once I studied the full scores of Strauss operas, I observed that the roiling, complex, constantly evolving interior lives of the characters (expressed in evolving motives, subtle chromatic harmonic and melodic shifts, and countermelodies) were right there.

During those first few months abroad, my French still nearly nil, I followed my daily amble through the Great American Songbook with an hour or so reading for company those novels of Hemingway, Fitzgerald, and Wolfe that I hadn't already read as a teenager in Wisconsin. I was lucky; I read everything by all three authors before I grew too old and impatient. I'd then write in my journal for an hour or so while throwing together a huge salad of greens from the farmer's market. These vegetables and greens consisted of whatever I could scrounge each day from the unsold and now slightly spoiled produce that the vendors customarily threw out when the market closed.

Most days I spread the *International Herald Tribune* and *Le Monde* side by side on a table at a library to work on my French. I would board the train for Marseilles, and then compose for several hours at the conservatory there. When she was free, the violist I had moved from *vous* to *tu* with and I would meet for lunch somewhere near the train station, canoodle, and wait for my 25-minute train ride back to Cassis. Each afternoon I'd pick up at my regular table at the waterfront café in Cassis where I'd left off the day before the reading of Mother's nicotine-stained 1934 Random House edition of Marcel Proust's *À la recherche du temps perdu*, comparing it to the French language edition I'd just purchased, as the coolly amused waitress dropped ripped receipts, lifted franc notes from the little pile in front of me, stacked saucers, and kept the coffee flowing.

Since I had promised myself that I would never return to the States, when Michael Pretina, the Director of the Camargo Foundation, tracked me down in town (Once the residency had ended, in exchange for dinner and a place to sleep, I'd taken a job bussing tables and washing dishes in a quay-side family-owned restaurant.) and told me that someone named Fran Richard had called from New York, I honestly couldn't remember who she was. The woman worked for ASCAP, Michael explained, and she seemed annoyed because she had been unable to reach me. I was awakened as though from a dream. As commanded, I called Fran. "Get your ass back here to New York," she said, harsh but affectionate. "Lukas and the Brooklyn Philharmonic are going to premiere *Heliotrope* at Cooper Union, and I expect you to be there." I told her I was broke. "Joan tells me that you told her you didn't plan on coming back." I didn't answer. "Bullshit," she said. "ASCAP will send you a plane ticket. We'll talk after the performance." She hung up.

In due course, Fran sent a plane ticket for a flight from Orly to JFK. I hitchhiked from Cassis to Paris to meet it. When we entered U.S. airspace, the Parisian flight attendant noted my unwillingness to switch to English. *"Je suis désolé. Vous êtes un Américain. Il est de votre pays,"* she said, sadly. Anguished, *"Je suis entre les pays,"* I tried to joke, twisting my head away from her and looking out the window at the World Trade Center as we flew past. "Paris," I thought. "Berlin. Vienna. Rome." I picked at a scab on my arm. "New York," I sighed, ripping off the scab and watching blood bubble out of the wound.

Rain slapped against the taxi's roof. The twenty-dollar bill balled in my fist had been the only money in my wallet for the past six months. I pressed it into the Pakistani driver's hand and tumbled out of the taxi in front of 18 Saint Mark's Place. I jiggled the key in the broken lock of the door with the anarchist graffiti on it. That the key worked, and the door opened seemed neither a good nor a bad thing. I climbed the six flights to my apartment. My clothing smelled of airport, my luggage of aviation fuel. There was nothing for me here. I'd warned the girls to whom I'd sublet the place only a few days before that I'd need to crash overnight in the guest room before heading back to Europe. I thought of the night a decade earlier when I had returned home without warning my parents and had overheard their sad moon play. "Let me in. Let me in," Father had keened like an animal. "Oh, Earl," she pleaded in an exhausted, intimate voice. "For God's sake, please leave me alone."

I had saved up some francs working at the restaurant. When I had called Bob Schuneman collect from Marseilles at E.C. Schirmer to tell him that I was "never coming back" (and I had meant it) he didn't try to reason with me. Rather, after a brief pause, he asked, "What sort of advance on your royalties are we talking about?" "Just enough to help get me on my feet here—find a room in Venice, for a start," I answered. "This is crazy, you know, Daron," he said, "but, if this is what you have to do, I'll cut the check." I had a little cash in my pocket and had been bumming around Germany, Italy, France, Austria, and Belgium for the past few weeks. (I had also been paid for finishing *Common Ground*, an ode to the fall of the Berlin Wall commissioned by the Barlow Endowment for Music Composition and premiered by Zdenek Macal and the Milwaukee Symphony—it became the finale of my Symphony No. 2.) To stretch my resources, I had slept fitfully on trains, in train stations, eaten very little, and drunk far too much. What was the phrase—too little butter over too much toast? By the time I had finally found a room in Venice I was exhausted, and my health was shot.

It was past 3 a.m. in New York City. The girls were asleep upstairs in the loft. I threw my bags into a corner and collapsed on the futon. After a couple of hours of sleep—the most in a row I'd had since leaving Luxembourg the week before—I woke with a start to the sound of two men having sex a floor below, carried up to me in the airshaft, the sputter and wheeze of steam venting from the radiator inches from my head. The ticking like a bomb followed by the metallic whirr of the refrigerator's compressor kicking in. Then silence. I was there. But I wasn't there. Clara padded in and curled up in her usual spot in my armpit. After tenderly grooming the hair on my forearm for a while, purring, she placed her tiny chin exactly in the crook of my arm and shuddered gently before contentedly falling asleep. I heard the girls' sighs as they awoke; their gentle pillow-murmurings not entirely muffled trickling down from upstairs like handfuls of soft, warm rain mixing with the amniotic sound of autumn drizzle on the roof. It was as though I was inside the whale's belly of a perfect art song—a captured instant, an incredibly prolonged suspension, what the Germans call an *Augenblick*—literally within the blink of an eye, *entre les pays*. Infinity in the palm of my hand: perfection. The longing, the bliss, the "time being" of such a moment, the ardent desire to capture and extend it forever (if that were even possible) in music, not mourning, or nostalgia, had made me a composer. The alarm chimed. The moment ended as 24 October 1989 began. Bare feet padded down the steep flight of wooden steps from the loft. I smelled brewing coffee. They didn't know I was there. Caitlin returned to the loft. My books, scores, recordings, my cat, even the hundreds of treasured letters, may as well have belonged to someone else. I dressed silently, fed Clara, and let myself out, leaving my passport and backpack by the door to signal that I'd be back. The 5 a.m. air was crisp and lively. Stragglers in pairs stumbled down St. Mark's Place; men left the baths across the street arm-in-arm. "Round the Clock" was open. I settled in and ordered coffee, eggs, and rye toast. Five hours to kill before meeting with Lukas to talk through the score of *Heliotrope* prior to his first rehearsal of it with the Brooklyn Philharmonic at Cooper Union. I paged through the *Times*, the *Post,* and the *Village Voice*. The coffee sharpened my senses. The food disgusted me. I had not told anyone that I would be coming back, even for a day. No one was relying on me. I didn't exist. How self-indulgent and sentimental my life was. I went to the bathroom. Explosive diarrhea. I was dehydrated. I looked at myself in the graffiti-covered mirror. "I hate this place," I said to my reflection. I threw cold water on my face from the faucet and returned to my table. My breakfast had arrived. Nauseated, I shoved the plate away untouched, dropped some singles on the table, and began walking north. Times Square. Standing in front of the statue of George M. Cohan at 6 a.m. I watched a weary sex worker stumble by on the arm of a client. I asked a cop for the time. "Go home, kid," he said. "Get some sleep." I stuffed my hands in my pockets and surveyed the closed peep shows, the forlorn Jersey kids too drunk to catch the PATH train home, the exhausted chicken hawks heading to breakfast at Howard Johnson's. By 7 a.m. standing in front of the Lincoln Center fountain, I had worked up a sweat. Tearing off my shoes and socks, I plunged my feet into the icy water and waited for a cop to roust me. Instead, a teenage girl walked up, wordlessly placed a to-go cup of black coffee next to me, and walked away. It was white, with blue stenciling on it that read in faux Greek letters "We Are Happy To Serve You."

I sipped the coffee and stared at the Marc Chagall murals decorating the Metropolitan Opera House façade. The watery, brilliant autumn sun felt close enough to touch. Feverish, I heard myself say aloud, "I am only a 'fugitive pigment'—my appearance changes over time." Sweating coldly, I realized I was going to vomit. "I am washed out by the sun," I thought. I threw up in the fountain. Raising my head, I looked from side to side. The plaza was empty. "Sick again at Lincoln Center," I observed grimly. I used my shirt to dry my feet, replaced my socks and shoes. Too nauseated to feel embarrassed, I walked to a street cart in front of the Empire Hotel. Fishing in my pockets for change, all I could find was francs. "And for the penny in your purse," I recited, tittering weirdly. I recalled Father throwing change at me as a kid and decided to pour them all into the vendor's hands, "I'll ferry you!" I accepted in return a stale bagel and a bottle of water. "Get outta here, you ass-hole," I heard him mutter to my back as I headed west towards the Hudson River. By 9 a.m. I had made it back to the Village and settled into my favorite chair at Caffé Reggio on Mac-Dougal Street. I particularly loved the window nook just to the left of Reggio's front door. It was to me a safe, familiar place—in it, I had written a lot of music, savored Balzac, and Patrick O'Brian novels, argued aesthetics with colleagues, and courted women. "Here," said the server as she brought me a second espresso. "You're as white as a sheet. You need to put something in your stomach." She placed a sandwich before me. "It's on the house." I bolted it. Then I nodded off.

Two hours later Lukas awakened me. "Are you okay?" he asked. The server had let me sleep. I waved my thanks to her; she looked up from her book and smiled. "Better than I have been for a while," I admitted, stretching. He sat down across from me and pulled the score of *Heliotrope* out of his satchel. "I used to meet Lenny here when we were your age," he laughed, and ordered a cup of tea. Out came his "reddy-blue" pencil; he jotted in the score as we talked. When we had finished, he shut it with a sigh and pushed it aside. "What

Observing the crowd at a reception given by the American Society of Composers, Authors, and Publisher's Symphonic and Concert Music Department at its New York office in spring 1990. One of my pieces had received a third Morton Gould Young Composers Prize, and I had just returned from Europe for the premiere of *Heliotrope*.

I love about your voice is it's—for lack of a better word—joyful, seemingly effortless fluency," Lukas observed. "You can do anything. And in pieces like this, you do." I laughed. "Would you please write that down and sign it?" He looked up, serious. "People will call your fluency facile; they'll hold your eclecticism against you. They'll say you're eager to please. You're not. You're just as quick to say nay as yea. You know damned well what you're saying and why. But there isn't a lot of 'live and let live' among composers and critics," he said. I realized that he was talking as much about himself as he was about me. "Some will think you do the things you do because you haven't got talent, or good taste, or because you're self-indulgent, insufficiently self-critical, or because you aren't well-trained. If you are none of those things and you still insist on being yourself, then you are a threat to their aesthetic stance and ... they do their best to ... make you fail or ... at least to marginalize you."

It was my favorite season in the Village. Cool air, people bundled in sweaters reading the *Times* (then nice and fat, the paper of record, filled with indispensable opinion and taste makers' words—the must read for every serious Manhattanite) with their friends in sidewalk cafes, fresh-faced NYU coeds, newly-minted locals, bumping into things because they're looking up at the buildings instead of where they're heading. Lukas and I strolled through Washington Square Park and savored the light as it streamed through the sycamores trees. "Breathe deeply," quipped Lukas, as we passed a fistful of guys smoking dope.

The Brooklyn Philharmonic's oboist could be heard giving the "A" as we entered the hall where in 1860 Abraham Lincoln delivered his great address. I had memorized parts of it for forensics in high school: "Let us have faith," I declaimed to Lukas, "that right makes might, and in that faith, let us, to the end, dare to do our duty as we understand it." Lukas stopped, surprised. "Lincoln," he said. "That's nice." I reached for his hand; he gave me a hug instead. "Have fun," I said.

Afterwards, an aggrieved clarinet player stomped up. "Do you know what you did to me?" he demanded. "You've got me doubling clarinet and bass clarinet, and you put the bass in bass clef. Do you know how incredibly annoying that is?" I did. "Well, I wrote it in treble clef, an octave higher, but it seems my copyist took it upon himself to put it down an octave. I'm sorry." He was unsatisfied. "You mean that you didn't look at your own parts before we got them?" "No," I admitted, sheepish. I *hadn't* looked at the parts. I had not intended to even be here. I'd entrusted them to Leonard Graves, a copyist in Hollywood. He had farmed them out to a handful of colleagues there, some of whom had done a slap-dash job. To my relief, Allan Kozinn (in front of whom at the concert Ned had told me that he hated the piece) described it in the *Times* as "a set of variations in an array of orchestral, theater and jazz styles that showed how far a composer can run with a simple theme, given the right combination of imagination and skill." (*Heliotrope* remains my most often-performed orchestral piece. Morton Gould, during his stint serving as President of ASCAP, once astonished me at a reception there sometime during the early 90s by admonishing me puckishly, "Daron, my boy, your score says that measures 41–54 you are doing Bill Schuman but I think you're wrong; I think you're doing me there. You should change that!")

After the concert, Fran—who bore at that time a striking resemblance to Bea Arthur in *Threepenny Opera*—held her gimlet glass in the air and examined the light through it. She had bought me a finger of twelve-year-old Macallan. I rested my nose in the tumbler and inhaled slowly and deeply its musky exquisiteness. Fran smiled, set her glass down, and turned her attention to Michael Torke, who had just risen to prominence with the debut by Lukas and the Brooklyn Philharmonic of *Ecstatic Orange* in the same hall in which we had just heard *Heliotrope*. They discussed his career. Once or twice, I ventured a comment, but Fran's gently raised index finger silenced me, as though to indicate that I was out of my league. After a spell, she waved me over. Watching Michael depart, she sighed heavily. "Daron, what are you doing living in Europe?" she asked. I muttered a few things about selfishness, hating Yuppies, feeling trapped, and needing time to think. She stirred her Screwdriver. The smell of orange juice nauseated me. She was deciding what to say. "There's nothing for you there," she began. Fran wanted to help. I wanted her to feel as though she was helping. She had decided what I needed to do. Now she was telling me. To me it appeared that she was talking about someone else. Why had I moved to Europe? I heard myself talk about love, about "innocence and decadence," about "the presence absence makes," about how there was nothing for me in the States either, about being in love with my violist from Marseilles. She was listening, but she wasn't hearing me. I observed her as she sized me up: what was worse, I wondered, the evident pity on her face or the fact that she clearly found me rather … ridiculous? I began to feel the urge to flee.

"Honey," she said, sighing again, "Love just isn't enough." So, that was it, I thought, to her I'm just another pampered, self-indulgent child-man. I could see her point. There was nothing else to talk about. Clearly, my artistic and professional transit concluded by my being parked on the faculty of some liberal arts college so that I could continue counting angels on the heads of pins. I wanted more. I excused myself, grabbed my backpack, and climbed aboard a bus to JFK. Within six hours, I was aboard a jet bound for Paris. I made my way from Orly to Gare de Lyon—Lausanne—over the Alps—Milano—Mestre ... Venezia.

I arrived, entirely cut loose and personally untethered, on the first train of the day, descended the marble steps of the station and strolled slowly to the Piazza San Marco as though in a dream. I smelled the Adriatic in the wind; it crept inside my pink woolen sweater and chilled the sweat beneath. I felt a frisson. I quickly downed three shots of espresso from a paper cup. The wire chair bit into my haunches; the pain felt good, like worrying a hangnail with your fingernail. The carabinieri goose-stepped ceremonially up to the flagpole in front of the basilica and raised *Il Tricolore*. There were no lights on in Caffé Florian, which wouldn't open for hours. A pale, pretty woman in a red dress only partly concealed beneath a royal blue pea coat sped with her head down against the driving rain past the Campanile towards the cobalt-blue sea. A daytime moon burnt like a ghost light over the silent city; the rising sun looked like a blood clot suspended in olive oil beside the Chiesa di San Giorgio. A few hours after that, drunk with bedazzlement and cheap morning wine, knees skinned from toppling down the Santa Lucia Station steps, I swore to make Venice home. The Piazza San Marco then was the antithesis of St. Mark's Place, just as Venetian musical life was the opposite of New York's, where well-meaning, battle-hardened realists like Fran Richard called the shots.

I reckoned I would sink roots in a floating city. A simple job at a restaurant was mine if I wanted it. Venice is an old—*old* place, man, and being depressed there was redundant. It was no secret that I identified with Charon; like Charon, Venice was suspended between life and death. Venice—solipsistic by design, existing only as a manifestation of what I (and legions of tourists, though I was determined to stay) imagined it to be, an empty stage in a closed theater. Venice was dead, but fecund because of all the things that had died there. I was 28, and entirely susceptible to what Mann called Venice's "somniferous eroticism." I wanted nothing more than to spend my life sitting in a chair in the Piazza, a tumbler of cheap red before me, hands folded behind my head, looking up at life unfolding backwards as though from behind the screen at the Oriental Theater as a boy, a completely chance-ful thing.

I lodged for the first few weeks at the Casa Boccassini, a family-run pensione set on the Calle del Fumo in a traditional Cannaregio-style Venetian townhouse a hundred metres from the Fondamente Nuove. It had for years been a favorite of Fred Hammond's, whose gracious introduction had enabled me to befriend the family that owned it. Humble, small, inexpensive, and very clean, it was only a few minutes' walk from the Rialto. One entered through an unmarked door and emerged into a small, well-kept garden in whose blue-tiled fountain lived fat koi that were surveilled—though not seen—by Fellini, the imperious, blind, polydactyl mouser whose neighborhood perambulations depended entirely on his ability to hurtle out of the unmarked door during the brief moments when it opened to admit or discharge guests. An ancient flowering wisteria whose blossoms dangled impiously down like lolling, long purple Chowchow tongues, shielded several tables whose tea lamps appeared to hover over them, disembodied, in the owl light. It was one of those places, like Yaddo, that exist out of time, never changing, and to which people returned in order to confront their past selves. It remains my Venetian touchstone.

My lover arrived from Marseilles and found us a sublet. We decided to have a drink in every single restaurant, hotel, and café in Venice. This took a while. One afternoon, sitting in the single room that we shared, she read *Paris Match* and I cut my hair with a pair of pinking shears without a mirror by drawing lengths of it away from my skull and hacking at them. She asked me if I thought we'd stay together after we ran out of places to drink. Mustering my wretched French, I replied, "*Je flotte quelque part entre deux mondes. Je ne suis ni vivant ni mort*" which as an explanation seemed at the time sensible to me and to satisfy her. Unsentimental from the start about the nature of our relationship, one day we discovered that we had simply run out of places to drink. Broke, we vacated the sublet, and she returned to her orchestra job. Her father, a passionate Communist professor who considered me *divine et ridicule* for having the temerity to call myself a composer after the Holocaust, hugged me warmly and kissed me on both cheeks at the train station, gave me an envelope bulging with lire and said, with dry affection, "*Ne nous appelez pas, fils. Nous allons vous appeler.*"

Left to my own devices, I drifted around like a kited check, hoping for either a love letter or a commission. Entirely aware that I was nothing special, but aware of my good fortune, I loved the Bride of the Sea, my favorite city on the planet, the Island of No Regret, *La Serenissima*. I sobbed in *La Fenice*, filled journals with true lies about myself, returned faithfully to my favorite pensione and observed the innkeeper's children growing up; I welcomed the New Year by drinking too much champagne in Harry's. I fell asleep in more than one church after dancing all night during Carnival, and performed there over the years the real-life, unmasked roles of *inamorato, Pedrolino* and *vecchio.* In other words, when my first wife cuckolded me, for her own reasons she chose Venice, making my love of the place a punch line. I read Ruskin while tracing his steps, shrugged when I didn't "get" it at the Biennale, experienced Stendhal's syndrome when I thought that I did. I bought flowers for a mother with her little boy on the Fondamente Nuove one sunny summer Sunday morning, then spent the rest of the day with them in the cemetery on the Isola di San Michele—even surprised myself there by discovering tears on my cheeks while standing at the foot of the grave of Stravinsky. *Venice and Its Lagoon* in hand, I walked Lorenzetti's walks, and missed everything because I was reading about it. I spent a hundred days losing myself and being lost, lost and not caring; avoided the old tourist traps, discovered new ones. Most foolish of all, I even thought that I knew the place. The joke, of course, was on me.

I had never been to Vienna, and a stop there to visit the graves of Beethoven, Wolf, and Schubert, seemed just the thing. Kristie Foell and her husband Christopher Williams put me up for a few days. Kristie was writing her book *Blind Reflections: Gender in Elias Canetti's* Die Blendung, a feminist study of gender portrayal in Canetti's book that draws on early twentieth-century Viennese psychoanalytic and gender theorists. Chris was working on a dissertation about Mahler's impact on Arnold Schoenberg and teaching in the Piaristengymnasium near the Theater in der Josephstadt. Even though I, too, had moved on, I had found it difficult, a few years earlier, to attend their wedding. Now, seated a few feet away on the floor of their Viennese flat, I looked Chris over: we could be brothers, I thought, so similar were we in physical build and conversational style. I think it annoyed Kristie that we hit it off. I had just come from Nice, where a visit to the Marc Chagall Chapel there had filled my head with the intersection between aesthetic innocence and artistic decadence. Chagall's ability to summon both childlike rapture and the horrors of the Holocaust in the course of the same piece reminded me of Olivier Messiaen's *Quatuor pour la fin du Temps*, which I had heard for the first time only a few years earlier at

Curtis. "Perhaps a little more Chagall, Daron, and a little less Bernstein," observed Kristie, acidly.

Hung over, the next morning I found myself in Vienna's Zentralfriedhof, standing in the same spot that Holly did when he leaned against the cart and watched Anna walk away in *The Third Man*. I first saw the film with Kristie at the Oriental Theater. Sitting in the dark as the final credits rolled, I made myself two promises: first, that I would visit Vienna, and two, that I would one day turn Graham Greene's novella into an opera. Walking the same streets trod once by the west's greatest composers had not had the effect on me that I'd thought it would. I was prepared for the place's chiaroscuro of timelessness and decay. However, I hadn't experienced the sort of *ewigkeit* in Vienna that I had expected—the "eternal now." Instead, I had felt smothered by an eternal and never-to-be-forgotten yesterday. I spent the afternoon in the Musiker section. Beethoven's monument left me strangely unmoved; Brahms' impressed, but didn't warm me; I felt nothing as I admired Schoenberg's chilly modernist cube. Hugo Wolf's monument squeezed my heart. Slowly, as the afternoon wore on, everything became gray scale. What for most of the day had been an insidious sideways-falling mist became at last a heavy, wet snowfall, like the one at the end of Truffaut's film of *Fahrenheit 451*.

More snow as the night train barreled through the countryside from Vienna, through Linz—Salzburg—Villach—Udine—Treviso—Mestre. My brothers and I had always loved *Long Day's Journey into Night*. I fancied that, in Venice, I would be "alone with myself in another world where truth is untrue and life can hide from itself." The familiar consolation of crossing the Ponte degli Scalzi into another world; touching ritualistically the bumper post at the end of the line as I passed from the train platform into the Santa Lucia station. The smells of seawater, espresso, and metal, a sudden smell of cigarette smoke as I passed a smoker. Then, ahead of me, was the long row of low clear doors like Juilliard's modernist teeth-windows opening to the plaza and Venice beyond. I stopped for a stiff drink standing to warm me, shouldered my backpack, and headed out, expecting and receiving the blessing of San Simeon Piccolo. Beat. Down the long, low marble steps and a turn to the left for a walk through the Giudecca in the snow to pick up some clothes from the place I'd last stayed. I forgot where the place was, got turned around, tried again, got frustrated, then scared, then cold, and then found myself for some reason all the way over in the Castello. *What the hell*, I thought, *I know how to get to Casa Boccassini from here I think I remember and I'll say hi to the owner and ask him to stand me a drink*. I began walking in circles. I got lost. In a bad way. I drank in a bar. Another bar. Finally, I dropped lire into the mouth of a payphone. My lover from Marseilles and I were quits with no regrets on either side and so there was nobody to think about but me. Into the vacuum swept Michaela. She had left me long before, but she was still my heroin, and I needed to hear her voice. The snow had turned to rain and now my shoes sloshed in the icy *Aqua Alta*. The heavy lire fell. I heard a whirr, a click, and a connection. Someone answered in French. I threw the receiver at the phone as hard as I could and turned away. *Just another excuse to feel sorry for yourself*, I thought, bitterly. More soul-sick stumbling around in the darkness. More crossing my own path, bathed in cold sweat. In time, I reached the Fondamente Nuove, slipped on the stone pier and landed on my hands and knees in the water. The wind off the Adriatic slapped saltwater on my face. I shook my head and opened my eyes, wide. Rainbows suddenly haloed the harbor lights. I saw stars. Quickly, I closed my eyes and rubbed them, hands cold. When I opened them, I looked up, and again saw stars, but this time strewn across the sky. It felt as though someone had punched me in the stomach, hard. Then I heard nothing and couldn't breathe. Then my ears began to buzz. I looked down at the stones. *Breathe!* I thought. *Why not just crawl, right now, into the sea? Do I have the courage to pull it off? Hell, I already feel like I'm drowning.* A strange voice sang, "Step into my ferry boat, be they black or blue...." I blacked out for a moment, but my diaphragm bucked. I became aware of the wind, the waves, and the crazy sound of a harbor bell bouncing across the water. I exhaled, then dragged air in, and exploded in deep, wracking coughs. Climbing to my knees, I made a strangled sort of tearing sound as my body fought against my brain to breathe. Head splitting, I scrambled to my feet, fell back against a wall, and looked to the north: there was San Cristoforo. *Christ, it looks like the Canaletto, only with no lights on*, I thought. I tittered weirdly and realized that my teeth were chattering. "Let it go, you piece of shit, you," I said out loud, curling my fingers and observing them sort of vibrate in front of me, then balling them into fists again and wringing them in frustration, anger, sadness, futility, and loneliness. I thought, "*And for the penny in your purse....*" I was sick. Flu? Exhaustion? Hypothermia? Delirium tremens? How badly can you treat a healthy young body before even it cries *basta, you're killing yourself shut the fuck up, you self-indulgent little prick, and ... grow up?* I stuffed my hands in my pockets and found £7000— about five bucks—enough for two shots of bad rye at a 24-hour bar. Open to the sea, I walked to a stool, sat, and shoved some bread and olives in my mouth. The bartender filled two shot glasses. I drank them off, thinking: *addict.* Then I put my head down on the bar and slept. When I came to, the sputtering fluorescent lights on the floating dock outside the bar buzzed B-flat. I waved goodbye to the bartender, got up, walked the few meters to the quay, and boarded the first vaporetto of the day. I slept again, rode free, and was ferried around Venice for a couple of hours, unconscious. In time, after the sun had risen and the seats were needed, the Charon who had been watching over me awakened me at the Venezia Santa Lucia. *Back where I began and I'm not even here,* I mused, looking around. I leaned against one of the three-pronged lampposts only a few feet from the canal and let my eyes wander up the smooth, elegant steps leading to the station. You know that feeling when you know time is passing, but anything is possible—the moment is suspended in "chance-fulness?" This was like that, only sideways. It felt like the moment that I had "tamped down the crazy" a few weeks before Norman moved away from Philadelphia—the moment that we parted ways. That time I had said no. This time, I didn't see any reason not to just go with the flow. I had experienced manic and depressive episodes before, but this was different. I couldn't remember the last time I had not just passed out but also actually slept— let alone *dreamed.* I felt ... dead inside. To remain here would require giving up once and for all connection to everything that I had always thought that I cared about. There would be no more going back—in a hundred ways, no going home. I slid to the pavement, my back pressed against the lamppost, and looked across the canal at the Chiesa San Simeon Piccolo. Finally, I just felt nothing. Alone, I sat in an empty, rifled tomb of my own design without moving for a very long time.

◆◆ 15 ◆◆

The Beginning of Something
1990–1991

I looked up from the pavement where my eyes had come to rest as a woman in a blue pea coat with a red bandanna in her hair approached. She stopped, sized me up in a beat, reached into a green plastic shopping bag, pulled out a small, warm hard roll, placed it in my hand, closed my fingers around it, and went on her way. Luke 24:5 came, unbidden, to mind: *"And as they were afraid, and bowed down their faces to the earth, they said unto them, why seek ye the quick among the dead?"* Watching her recede, I put the bread to my nose and inhaled deeply. I burst into tears, suddenly ravenous, tore off a piece of the bun with my teeth, and stuffed the rest into the pocket of my leather flight jacket. Attempting to get up, I felt the stabbing pain of paresthesia in my legs and fell to my knees as though in prayer. My legs were useless. I pushed up from the ground with my fingertips as pins and needles exploded in my shins and began hobbling towards the broad white marble steps of the station like a newborn fawn until the numbness went away. I lurched to the first pay phone I saw inside the station, leaned against it, and placed a collect call. "Bill, have you got a spare bed?" I asked, head beginning to pound. William Smart, Director of the Virginia Center for the Creative Arts, answered. "I'm afraid not," he said. "We've got a full house right now." I counted to five before pleading, "I've sublet the apartment on Saint Mark's Place and have no place to go…." Beat. "Bill, I need to dry out…." Another beat. We had had this conversation before. "…And you're probably broke, right?" he asked. "Afraid so," I answered. I had left for Europe without any money in my pocket. And now I was even more deeply in debt. I had no telephone number, no address, and no commissions. The banks had confiscated my plastic. I had defaulted on my student loans. I had spent a lot of money I didn't have to buy myself more time in Europe to figure out whether I sincerely wanted to return. I couldn't just kick Caitlin and her friend out of my apartment on Saint Mark's Place. They needed time to find somewhere to live. I wasn't naïve enough to expect Manna to arrive with the dew during the night; but it had, in fact, come from the hand of a stranger in a blue pea coat. I needed somewhere safe to recover my health. I needed time to compose, and to take copy work to pay debts. Bill helped me. He told me to come to Virginia, and that he would work something out. A few days later, as the plane succumbed to gravity and sank through charcoal-colored rain clouds towards the tarmac at JFK, so did my heart.

I reached Mt. San Angelo in the middle of one of those Virginia winter storms when the air is warm, but the trees are sheathed in ice and look like glittering dowsing rods swaying in the wind. Bill and I cleared out a small storage room. Together, we moved a battered upright piano into it, a desk, found a cot, and roused out one of the Bolivian flags that were used back then as bedspreads. I launched into fifteen-hour workdays, finishing the full score of *Common Ground*. Ned had just finished a brass quintet—he threw the copying to me. I wrote to Diamond and described my situation. He astonished me by contacting the American Academy of Arts and Letters and arranging for me to receive an "emergency grant" with which I managed to pay the most aggressive creditors something on account. I'm still grateful to David for doing it; but I am ashamed to have accepted money that could (and should) have been given to someone in deeper trouble.

After a couple of months, I ventured back to New York. I helped Caitlin and her friend pack their things and reclaimed the apartment on St. Mark's Place. I had an address and a phone number again. Ann Stanke was one of the first to call. At the time, I honestly couldn't recall why she wanted to talk to me. After admonishing me for having disappeared for six months, she announced that she had good news and bad news: the good news was that Madison Opera had decided to move ahead with commissioning *Shining Brow*. The bad news was that they were going to have to push the project back a year to have time to raise sufficient money to mount the première. I phoned Paul. When he said that he was still interested in writing a libretto for me, I immediately asked Ellis Freedman to start contract negotiations with the company.

Stroking Clara, cradled in the crook of my arm, I scanned the bookshelves, the walls: these were my books, these were paintings I'd bought from my contemporaries, and these photos were of my lovers—they all felt as though they were someone else's. I put Clara down and slipped out for a walk around the neighborhood. Cars clotted the intersection of Seventh Street and Second Avenue. In Caffé Della Pace, Dexter Gordon's sax sailed over a wash of parallel eleventh chords and a skittering of drums. I drank a couple of espressos and dared to consider what a big regional opera commission might mean. If I nailed it, then it could be the beginning of an actual career. I looked out the window towards St. Mark's Place: it had changed dramatically during my absence. For starters, not everyone was wearing black. Yuppies wearing Dockers now outnumbered the clubbers, drag queens, and punks. But my life on St. Mark's Place had a lot in common with the life I'd been leading near the Piazza San Marco—too much. I instinctively feared falling back into the lifestyle I'd led here before fleeing the States.

The full force of my self-betrayal hit me. I hadn't been living a brave artist's "chanceful" examined life between the beats; I'd been playing at the libertine during a hyperextended anacrusis. I desperately wanted a fresh start—a clean, white box, steps away from the Central Park reservoir—where I could simplify my life and rededicate myself to Music.

I returned to teaching at Bard. Father wired money so that I could put down a security deposit on a smaller (and cheaper) one-room "white box" apartment at the corner of Amsterdam and 74th Street, just off Verdi Square. Paul was living with his wife, novelist and poet Jean Hanff Korelitz, in Amherst at the time, so I trekked up for the weekend; together, we hammered out a filmic treatment for our opera. Paul began writing the libretto for the first act at once. We accepted an invitation from Richard Carney, Wright protégé and managing trustee of the Frank Lloyd Wright Foundation, to stay at Taliesin West in Scottsdale, Arizona, for a few days that March. After lunch with members of the Fellowship (during which Wright's recorded lunchtime conversation from decades previous played on a boom box), Paul and I settled into the little house Wright built for his daughter. The sun set as we traded impressions and prepared for a formal dinner at which I sat beside architect and Wright pupil Wes Peters, with whom I had a long, intense conversation about Wright's relationship with Olgivanna. "Was Mamah Cheney the love of his life?" I asked Wes. "She must have been," he replied, "but I can only say that after her death, for the rest of his life, he never allowed her to be discussed in his presence."

After dinner, Dick and I took a long walk in the desert and discussed the sort of opera I intended to compose. A fatherly bear of a man, he gestured to me to sit down on a boulder with him. Sighing, he said, "Well, Daron, I don't think any of us here want you to compose a dishonest piece. Mr. Wright could be a bastard. Promise me you'll try to convey his essential 'greatness' along with the rest." I didn't tell Dick that anybody who sings is rendered sympathetic. Instead, I shook his hand. "A promise, Dick." He picked up some dirt and threw it. "Fine. Come and stay with us for a while. Soak up the feel of the place. Make Mister Wright sing. I promise you that we'll not stand in your way."

I'd shared bits and pieces of the first act of *Brow* with Bernstein since returning from Venice, but I didn't work with him seriously on anything until I brought in the second act. I remember trivial details about Bernstein's Dakota studio—the exquisite floor-to-ceiling score shelves, the pair of ballet shoes hanging from the ladder runner, the drinks cart with half empty bottle of Ballantine's at the ready, the smell of the couch cushions, the paperback copy of *Candide* on the side table.

I was shown in. The maestro entered. I was nervous. We began with a tall glass of Ballantine's and a couple of rounds of anagrams. As we made small talk (conversation dealt not in double but in multiple *entendre*) he executed the *Times of London* crossword—from left to right, in rows, in the time it took him to write the letters. Puzzle dispatched, he turned to music. I sat down at the piano and performed one of his *Anniversaries,* memorized for the occasion.

Next, I played and sang the scene from *Brow* that I was working on. He ambled over to the bench, pushed me to the side, and started playing off my manuscript, squinting, sort of wheeze-singing as he briskly double-checked parts he wanted to speak to. "Okay, baby," he began, "Try this." He "put over" a few bars of what I had written and veered off in a new direction, improvising an entirely different line reading. Then he stopped, sucked on his plastic cigarette holder, quickly paged to a different part of the sketch, found something, and said, "Or you could have used this from before, like this." He played a few bars. "No, that wouldn't work." I improvised a different line reading. "No, no, you can't do that!" he laughed, "Marc did that in *No for an Answer!* Do you know that one?" "No?" He noodled a few bars. "No, that was Aaron's *Tender Land.* Ugh. God." Laughter.

During Wright's Act 1, scene one pitch to his future mistress, I quoted the *New York, New York* rising fourths motive that he had first used in *Trouble in Tahiti,* and then in *On the Town,* on the word, "suburbia," "Nice lift," he said, "very Strauss-ian. But you followed it up with stuff that sounds like Ned's little Frank O'Hara opera. Did I steal that from him for *Tahiti* or did he steal that from me? I can't recall. I know you're talking about theft by putting stolen music in his mouth, but you should come up with something else there."

At some point, I pointed out that I had been modeling the character of Wright musically on him, and the relationship between Wright and Sullivan on him and Blitzstein. He got it: "That's *Maria.* No, it's the orchestral play-in to the first scene of Marc's *Regina,*" he mused aloud. "Well, yes, I stole it from Marc." Silence. Sudden grin: "But *he* stole it from Aaron!"

Afterwards I tried my best not to seem too thrilled as I tumbled down the little steps to the right of the Dakota's front gate, swung left, crossed Central Park West, and plunged into Central Park for a long walk, during which I ran through, again and again, the things we had discussed during the previous hour. Gradually, like a passage of descending chords—I associated the feeling with the ones in *Der Rosenkavalier*; it's the reason I quote them in *Brow*—my brain returned to a more normal state and life, as I usually perceived it, resumed.

I had a date to meet Augusta Read Thomas for a drink at a cozy pub on Amsterdam. I mastered myself, still slightly giddy. "So, how did it go?" Gusty asked, leaning forward and taking my hands into hers. "I'm Gobsmacked!" I said. "I've just run into Lauren Bacall!" "No way," said Gusty, releasing my hands. "Way!" I said. "I was climbing the set of stairs to the right of the front entrance. She was on her way down. I looked up at her as I rounded the corner, freaked out, and fell at her feet." Gusty laughed. "What in the world happened next?" I took a sip of my beer. "She looked down at me, sorta' amused, I suppose, and said, 'That's all right, baby,' in that 'put-your-lips-together-and-blow' voice," I said. "My vocal chords no longer worked. I wanted to say that I was on my way to my first lesson with the Maestro, but all that came out was a sort of strangled 'grkzdsl' sound."

Bacall's friend Oscar Levant once quipped that the only thing that a conductor can rely on is that the players will inevitably grow to despise him. I learned this for myself soon after literally running into Bacall. I was set to attend the Milwaukee Symphony's performance of *Common Ground*. Commissioned by the Barlow Endowment, it was conceived as the finale of the three-movement Symphony No. 2 I alienated conductor Zdenek Macal forever when, in response to his request for a few words, I mounted the podium and, in five minutes, rattled off all my notes to the orchestra. The players shuffled their feet, applauding me, but really, they were just enjoying the discomfiture of their sovereign.

"You look fat," observed Father to me in front of his friends in the Green Room (which was then red) of Uiehlein Hall the next day. My head, as the old Irish story goes, was sticking up higher than those around mine were; Father gave it a smack. "Please Dad," I said, low. "This is my place of business." A look of absolute, amused, somehow triumphant, contempt lit up his face. "You call this business?" he asked, showing me his small, even, yellowed teeth. Standing there awkwardly before him in my fifty-dollar blazer and mismatched slacks, my shoes in need of a shine, I may have been the composer of the day at a fancy concert hall, but I was thousands of dollars in debt, and scrambling for music copying jobs. Per every sane and practical measurement of success, I was a failure. He always did have a knack for hitting on the cruelest thing to say. Father awaited my reaction. I looked him over. First, I carefully took in the grease spot on his tie, then the cardboard belt, the twenty-year-old, threadbare jacket, and the sickly-sweet smell of drinkers' sweat and, finally, the acrid, fruity tang of Borkum Riff tobacco. He was flanked by two friends. I didn't *have* to engage. He wasn't evil, he just demanded a response, I told myself. If he can't generate positive attention, like a needy child, he'll satisfy himself with the other. I gave him nothing.

Lawrence Leighton Smith conducted (with undisguised dislike) the New York Philharmonic's premiere that summer as part of its Horizons Festival at Aaron Davis Hall in Harlem (the same theater in which, 22 years later, my son Atticus would make his debut as a bunny with Dance Theater of Harlem) of *Common Ground*.

The Madison Opera had asked me a few weeks earlier to suggest a stage director for *Shining Brow*. I asked Bernstein to suggest one. He suggested a young writer for *Opera News* named Stephen Wadsworth, who, he said, had called him with a pitch for a sequel to *Trouble in Tahiti*. (The opera that resulted was *A Quiet Place*.) "He can be extremely demanding ... but he's as smart and gifted as they come, and entirely committed." There was that word. I was intrigued, sensed a colleague on the rise. "I've written an opera about Frank Lloyd Wright," I told Stephen on the phone shortly thereafter. "I'm looking for someone to bring it to life on the stage. Lenny says that you're that person. Would you like to come over for coffee and talk about it?" I knew that would get his attention.

In April 1991, a few weeks after I finished the vocal score of *Shining Brow,* we sat cross-legged on the floor of my tiny studio on Amsterdam Avenue under the piano and in front of the six linear feet of opera scores on the bookshelves and began sounding one another out by pulling scores at random from the shelf and discussing them. It helped that we both had been compelled to figure out how to work with Bernstein—Stephen as collaborator, me as pupil. Stephen could survive (even enjoy) his intellectual death marches; I thrived on his musical pop quizzes. We shared an appetite for conversations that functioned on multiple levels.

I know now that our first meeting was typical of Stephen's way with everyone—warm, clever, completely at ease, and intellectually competitive. His probing eyes habitually sought out mine; his compassionate face was extraordinarily expressive. His long fingers moved restlessly when he spoke. I found charming his ability to italicize what he was saying by giving you a hard, quick stare, and then releasing you. He was fun.

At first, it was the confidence and maturity of his opinions as we stuck our thumbs into scores and played "what's the most important moment in this scene" that impressed me most. In time, as we grew to know one another better, I realized that what I had interpreted as competitiveness was instead an urgent desire to understand: if an idea intrigued him, he reflexively craved an explanation. The talents that have served him so well in his illustrious career were already in full play as, over the course of six very long work sessions at the apartment in the Village he shared with baritone Kurt Ollmann, I played and sang through *Brow's* score. I was defensive, and compelled Stephen to "sell" me on every one of the dozen or so alterations to words and music (I had to my mind "finished" the score months previously) that he suggested. I'm not certain now why I fought him so hard—especially since I knew even then that his criticisms were always spot on. Possibly, it was because I wanted to see just how right he thought he was. He had staged *Der Fliegende Holländer* for Seattle Opera and enjoyed a promising career as a music writer for *Opera News.* But the inspiring array of achievements and activities that have swept him forward since dazzles me as I try to recollect even a fraction of them. Stage directing several *Ring Cycles,* leading the Handel revival in the States during the 1980s, translating Marivaux's plays, and now heading the Metropolitan Opera's Lindemann Young Artist Program and the Juilliard Opera Center—honestly, I don't know how he does it all.

It was only while recounting the story of our meeting at a May 2010 panel discussion with Speight Jenkins and Peter Kazaras in Seattle that I realized that the conversation about hiring Stephen was my last with Bernstein. LB died on 14 October. Events had unspooled rapidly: the calls from Craig Urquhart alerting everyone to the fact that concerts had been cancelled, and that we should stop by to say goodbye if we were in town. It all sounded dramatic, but not final. A few days later, while shiva was being sat for him at the Dakota, Ned, Paul Moravec, one of my students, and I ate dinner together in my tiny studio apartment in silence. I couldn't bring myself to go.

Common Ground had been nominated for the Kennedy Center Friedheim Prize, so I went on 28 October to Washington to hear Michael Charry conduct the Mannes College's Orchestra perform the piece at the awards concert. Composer William Kraft, Kennedy Center chairman James D. Wolfenson, and I shifted from foot to foot in the anteroom of the presidential box, waiting to be seated. A steward invited us to enjoy a split of champagne (with the presidential seal on it) from the ice-filled metal bowl on a side table, and then showed us to our seats. I was seated between Bill and the other Kennedy Center Friedheim

Prize finalist Ralph Shapey, whose gorgeous, complex Modernist Concerto for Piano Trio and Orchestra was the favorite to win. I was in awe of Shapey: his music was uncompromising, and he resembled an Old Testament prophet. After I shook his hand, I turned to Bill and discovered, with warm pleasure, that we had a mutual friend, landscape painter Babette Martino. Babette was second generation—both of her folks were painters. Like Babette, her father, Giovanni Martino, was a noted realist.

Below us, the audience murmured as they settled themselves and the orchestra tuned up. Presently, the restrained, elegant Michael Charry, George Szell's biographer and protégé of Pierre Monteux, took the podium to conduct my *Common Ground*. Afterwards, I stood up and took my bow. Shapey's piece was next. When I sat down, as the applause subsided, he turned to me and said, "You're a fraud and your piece is shit." He was 69. I was 29. I opened my mouth, raised my finger, closed my mouth, and dropped my hand into my lap. "You don't belong here," he hissed as his piece began. I cocked my head. Beat. I turned to Bill. "Oh, don't mind Ralph," Bill said, patting me on the shoulder. "He was bound to hate your music."

When Paul and I began *Shining Brow*, we first read everything we could lay hands on about Frank Lloyd Wright. We reconvened a few months later to co-author at his home in Amherst, Massachusetts a filmic treatment consisting of a dozen pages describing what would happen in each scene. I then planned how long each scene (and each section of each scene) would last, and the sort of musical form I would use to underpin the action of that scene. Giving the outline to Paul, I asked him to create several core images and literary motifs that I could then graft to musical ideas, along with some "parallel" poems for related characters, so that when I shared their music, the words would be easier to adapt. At one point, I needed a straightforward hymn, and he responded by creating his beautiful Goethe gloss, *Hymn to Nature*.

Over the course of eight weeks that winter at VCCA, I fleshed out the sketches I'd made during the fall in the City, completing the music for the first act. I wrote the most important sections first, beginning with the last three minutes; then the music that would be associated with the four or five most important dramatic spots (what I call the "emotional nuclear reactors") in the act; after that, I wrote the connective sections, which could and should be the least musically interesting.

The most affecting, emotionally expressive tool in an opera composer's kit is the ability to modulate. Aside from being crucial to maintaining large formal structures, it unlocks "gateways" to new emotional states and signals emotional evolution. Each character in *Brow* "lived" in a "home" key: Wright in B-flat major; Mamah in E major; Edwin and Sullivan in A minor; Catherine in C major. The lovers' keys were associated, of course, by the tritone, the "forbidden" interval, and the harmonic fulcrum on which modulation depends. As they interacted, so did the keys in which they lived.

When composing opera, my compositional process has changed little since the early 80s. I retype and reformat the libretto to reflect the underlying musical form in which it will be carried, storyboard it on the wall, and illuminate it with various colored pens and pencils—say, red for one character, blue for another, orange for another; musical / poetic themes and motives that I want to "track" also get colors. Standing before the entire opera tacked up on the wall and dreaming on its entirety is as close as I'm likely ever get to understanding how a painter must feel working on a mural. A real sense of the pallet of ideas at hand is literally rendered in the colors arrayed on the storyboard. Once the entire opera is "on the wall" I decide what the most important dramatic moments (the "emotional nuclear reactors") are in each scene; I specify what the climactic moment of the opera is, work downwards in triage fashion to the least important moment. I do not compose "from left to right." I compose the music for the most important half dozen moments in the opera first. The music for the rest of the piece then spreads outwards from these key moments like concentric ripples.

"Just two hours ago," President Bush began, "allied air forces began an attack on military targets in Iraq and Kuwait. These attacks continue as I speak. Ground forces are not engaged." The United States had just invaded Iraq. It was 16 January. I was in Madison to present the first act of *Brow* to the opera company and members of the Taliesin Fellowship. Conductor Roland Johnson asked me to stop at 5:45 so that we could all gather around a portable radio to listen to our President address the nation. "Tonight, as our forces fight, they and their families are in our prayers."

"Shall we continue this another time?" I asked Ann Stanke. She looked to Richard Carney, who asked me, "Do *you* have a problem with moving ahead with this presentation?" It seemed absurd to me, under the circumstances, but I needed the money, and would not get paid unless, by pulling off this presentation, I fulfilled the terms of the commissioning contract. "No," I lied, resuming my seat at the piano and picking up where I had left off. When I concluded, Wes Peters commented that, in his opinion, Paul's libretto was "too 'literiffic'—Mr. Wright would never have spoken like that." I reminded him that Stravinsky had set Auden's libretto for *The Rake's Progress*, and that, in any event, "Paul is a great poet whose words inspire me. I wouldn't dream of changing a word without his blessing." Roland observed, "The words—not the music or the story—will be the stumbling block for this opera. Tone them down if you can, okay?" Dick then pledged that the Fellowship would support my creation of the opera, and Roland "green lit" my moving on to the second act. It was my first taste, at twenty-nine, of what the life of a viable opera composer might be like, and I loved it.

Ten days later I was again in Philly, where the desk clerk at the Warwick Hotel looked me up and down, noted my jeans, and sniffed. Bill Smith and the Philadelphia Orchestra were slated to premiere my Symphony No. 1 in a few days. I'd come to attend rehearsals. "The Orchestra is paying for the room," I announced grandly. "Sure," he said. "But I'll need a credit card for the incidentals." "I don't have one. May I write a check?" I asked. "Not without a credit card." Two beats. "Then I'll register and promise not to incur incidentals," I said. "That is against policy," he said loftily, looking away. I blushed, pride bruised.

I rallied: "Kindly call Bernard Jacobson at the Orchestra. I'm sure that they will guarantee my check." "Hmm!" he sniffed, made me wait as he took a call. "Give me the phone," I said. Dialing Bernard's line, I felt shame and embarrassment collecting behind my forehead. Soon it would congeal into a fiery crown, a migraine. Bernard's delightful voice boomed with laughter when I explained the situation. "Oh, do put the little man on, will you?" he chuckled. The astonished clerk accepted the receiver and held it as though it were unclean. How gratifying it was to see his face grow stiff, and then slide downwards like an omelet flung against a wall. Astonished, doubtful, he cradled the phone and accepted my check. "So, the orchestra is playing your music?" He was still shaking his head as I stepped into the elevator.

Bill Smith had insisted, despite his failing health, on conducting the premiere. Before the first rehearsal, Bill and I conferred in the semi-darkness of his backstage office at the Academy of Music. A stroke had left him quite frail, but his eyes still shone brightly. "You see, I've fulfilled the promise I made to you four years ago over pints at the Parting Glass in Saratoga," he smiled. I had walked over from Yaddo, and he had just come from a rehearsal of *Daphnis* at the Saratoga Performing Arts Center.

At the end of the rehearsal, concertmaster Norman Carol and principal violist Joseph dePasquale approached me. "I'm so glad to be playing something by a young composer that gives us melodies with soul in them," said Norman. Joe shook my hand, and said, "I don't know what will happen to this piece, but I'm happy for you, and happy to play it."

There had been no Green Room for me after the premiere of *Prayer for Peace,* but the premiere of a major symphony merited one. For the first time, I stood next to the subscription concert conductor in composer's pride of place, secure in the knowledge that I had every right to be there, and knew exactly how to behave, if not what to expect. I'd been taught at Curtis Tea Time how to behave, but nobody had ever counseled me on how to benefit professionally from my work's exposure. Bob Schuneman, and his wife Cynthia, flew in from Boston; Ned, and Fran Richard, came by train from New York. Musician and composer friends like Michael Morgan, and Michael Torke, the de Lancies, my Fleisher Collection pals, Sam Dennison and Kile Smith, came—it was like a wedding. I knew that it was the beginning of something, but not what, or how. Bill clasped my hands in his violently trembling hands and said, "Beautiful. Beautiful—there's your first symphony at last." With bravado, he vowed to premiere the next one too, but we both knew he was dying.

◆◆ 16 ◆◆

An Uncivil Union
1991–1996

The Oscar Mayer Foundation underwrote the renovation, in 1974, of Madison, Wisconsin's Capitol Theater, a 1928 Rapp & Rapp movie palace built during the silent era. It became the city's premium performance venue—a house whose broad balcony was quite like Milwaukee's Oriental Landmark Theater. Along with the Pillsbury family in Wisconsin and in Minnesota, the S.C. Johnson family in Racine, Pleasant Rowland's company in Middleton, and hotelier Terry Haller, who, in 1988, had conceived the idea in the first place, Oscar Mayer also underwrote the development and premiere there of *Shining Brow*. The Madison Symphony Orchestra's music director Roland Johnson and Madison Opera's executive director Ann Stanke determined to use a performance of *Heliotrope* as an opportunity to introduce me to Dane County's major donors. I attended with my beloved piano teacher Jeannette Ross. Along with lots of former classmates and teachers, the April 1991 audience included a Rubenesque blonde whom Bill Coble had mentioned in passing as having met a few weeks earlier at a BMI luncheon in Chicago. "I know you," she said, offering her hand. "Bill says that you're brilliant." Surprised, I asked her name. "Donna," she said, tossing the long, straight blonde hair that fell to her shoulders in the same sort of coltish way that Michaela once did. "I study conducting and trumpet here at the 'dub,'" she said. "With John Aley?" I asked. "Uh huh, and James Smith." "Love them both," I replied, taking her hands in mine and considering her eyes. Beat. "You've 'gotta go," she said. "Yeah," I agreed, dropping her hands and turning to look for Jeannette, who had continued to our seats. After my piece was performed, I headed to the stage for a bow, trotted stage left behind the cyclorama to return to the house and ran into her again. "Hello, again," I said, waving with what I thought was insouciance before walking through a fire door, setting off the theater's alarms just as John Browning was set to begin the Prokofiev Third Piano Concerto. In the movie of my life (scripted by Gore Vidal on a treatment by Orson Welles; directed by François Truffaut, and scored by Benjamin Britten) in which the young Tobey Maguire is cast as the young me, I correctly interpret the alarm as a *force majeure*, immediately leave town, and, without a hiccup, continue my meteoric professional ascent (forget that meteors fall), and—with astonishing ease—assume my position in the compositional firmament.

Instead, after the concert, in the Green Room, I placed my hand on the small of her back and cavalierly issued her a dare: "If I send you a ticket, will you fly to New York to visit me for a few days?" When she said yes, I impulsively upped the ante. "Well then, will you marry me?" Again, her response astonished me: "Sure," she said. It was, on its surface, a bit of harmless flirtation, I thought. So, when we met the next day and canoodled a bit I thought that would be the end of it—I was a visiting low-level celebrity who had been talked-up by a pal; she was a theoretically available coed who had amused herself by toying with me. I was content to leave it at that.

Kevin was always the responsible brother; Britt was the one who fought back; I was the one free to follow my star. Nobody tied me down, held me back, or told me that my pursuit of my dreams was costing them theirs. On the contrary, I'd been taught—the narrative I'd constructed for Mother was that she had sacrificed her Art for the sake of her children—that, if you love someone, then his or her needs take precedence. She had also taught me, however, that I was living for two—the Other Daron and myself, and that I had a responsibility to *both* of us to not just survive but to self-actuate. I wanted it both ways: I also wanted not to be alone any more. So, I told myself that I was selfish enough to subordinate others' needs—even those I thought I loved—to Music's demands. "Can a man be a faithful husband and father, and still be true to his Art?" wondered Wright in Muldoon's libretto for *Brow*. I justified getting married by telling myself that I could marry someone *and* withhold myself from her.

Donna and I spent some time at Taliesin, in Spring Green when Edgar Tafel, the best known of Wright's disciples, decided that he was going to see to it personally that I experienced what it was like to "really to live in a Wright House—to duck when you pass through doorways, discover your feet hanging over the bottom of the bed at night, feel the rooms flowing from one to the next in the dark." He conjured for me the poetry that Wright could spin for clients. His impersonations of Wright's speaking voice were—aside from being incredibly funny—crucial to shaping my vocal characterization—particularly Wright's stilted line readings, and what Diamond, in a letter to me described as "...the pontification, the affected dress-ugh-y, like Stieglitz." Photographer Pedro Guerrero's reminiscences of Wright's gentler moments also helped me to firm up the conviction that part of his appeal must have been the ability to project great vulnerability in private. Richard Carney's descriptions of the tenderness that Wright could display in private informed my decision to create the gentle music that underpins Wright's soliloquies. Dick was a humane and generous man. My treasured former pupil and copyist Christopher Hume suffered from a degenerative spinal condition that required his settling in a town with excellent medical facilities. I suggested Madison. I asked Dick to look out for Chris. He took him under his wing. They remained close for the rest of their lives.

I spent August at VCCA composing a new orchestral tone poem based on musical ideas from *Shining Brow* called *Fire Music,* afternoons typing up longhand diary entries from the 80s, and evenings copying out the fair score by hand. Michael Torke was there. An entirely Midwestern person, his mouth was generous—he smiled easily and well. When he did, deep dimples appeared in his cheeks. He had a strong chin, and a broad, high, intelligent forehead. His eyes dominated his face—intensely probing; they could be warm one moment, shark-dead the next. A gifted pianist, his hands were strong; his gestures when he spoke often stabbed or parried. We had taken to lunching together in my studio. Amazingly, although Michael and I had both grown up in the suburbs of Milwaukee and our birthdays were only a few weeks apart, our paths never crossed as kids. Although we had met in passing at the Warwick Hotel in New York at a BMI Prize ceremony at which we were both picking up checks in 1983, we did not get to know one another until May 1985, when Michael called to ask whether he could sublet my apartment in New York. For my part, I was conducting the Orchestra Society of Philadelphia and wanted to program his *Ecstatic Orange,* whose premiere by Lukas and the Brooklyn Philharmonic had blown me away.

In addition to piano practice, and other homework, during my teens, I composed 3–4 hours per day. During my first year in Madison, I composed for about an hour each day. The second year, I composed for 5. Curtis was total immersion; so was Juilliard. Once I left school, except for the time between dog and wolf in Venice, I adhered religiously to Michael Torke's work regime: I set a stopwatch to 8 hours, and stopped it each time I ate, went to the bathroom, or did something else; I'd turn it back on when I got back to work and did not go to sleep until I had composed for 8 hours out of every 24. A composer spends time composing. Two days each week I taught; on those days, I composed only for an hour. I kept this up steadily from 1986 until 1991 when I married Donna, who—in the end—would not, and should not have been expected to—tolerate it.

At the beginning of one of her visits to New York, Donna said yes when I proposed to her in a taxi crossing the Triborough Bridge. The night before we married, lodged at Union South in Madison, I wrote in my journal,

> *Well, we're going to do it. There's a sense of unreality about it. If—as she says that she can—she can tolerate the fact that the only way that I can justify to my* self *this union is to promise myself that music will come first, and that she will come second, then we'll survive.*

The next morning, we did it—in a civil ceremony in the rotunda of the State Capitol in Madison, witnessed by Ann Stanke and Margaret Bergamini. With that, I made the most selfish, most wrong-headed, most self-destructive decision of my life. The amount of pain that Donna and I caused one another can never be forgiven; the amount of time and effort that we spent trying to make it work can never be unspent. If I sensed then that *Shining Brow* was going to be my breakthrough, then I must have also understood the incredible risk I was taking by putting my life into a stranger's hands.

JoAnn Falletta, serving at the time as music director of the Long Beach Symphony Orchestra, invited me to serve for a season as composer-in-residence there; she also asked one of her supporters, philanthropist Dr. Frankie Grover, a genuinely unique woman who was, I think, the only person ever to serve as dean of both the USC and UCLA neurology departments, to commission me to write something new as part of the gig. The position required several trips to the coast. One highpoint was the 140 mph sprints up Route 1 as a passenger in Frankie's forest green Jaguar, tailbone grinding into the brushed leather of my seat as, grinning, she took tight, fast

With longtime friend and champion, conductor JoAnn Falletta backstage following the concert premiere and Naxos live recording sessions of *Shining Brow* on November 4–5, 2006, by the Buffalo Philharmonic under her direction at Kleinhans Hall in Buffalo, New York (photograph by Gilda Lyons).

turns like a Formula One driver, delighting in my unconcealed terror. Another highpoint was the high-pressure film-scoring sessions in Los Angeles I attended as the guest of orchestra members—every bit the composer's equivalent of being a passenger in Frankie's Jag.

In March 1992, I brought my bride with me to Long Beach for the première of *Fire Music*, the tone poem I wrote for JoAnn and Frankie. Although it was our first outing as a married couple, it was already apparent that she did not care for the role of "artist's wife." I was sympathetic to, and supportive of, her desire not to be deemed an appendage to me when, after our performance together in a Green Room, Donna explained that my introducing her as "my wife" was demeaning, and that, in the future, I should introduce her as "my partner." The piece proved to be one of my more viable efforts. Based on ideas from *Shining Brow*, thirteen years later *Fire Music* served as my orchestral debut (by the American Composers Orchestra, or ACO) at Carnegie Hall. Courtly, gentle-hearted, genuinely honorable composer Francis Thorne, a co-founder of the ACO with Dennis Russell Davies in 1977, and I had lunched every couple of months at an Italian joint in Hell's Kitchen since the early 80s. Franny had studied with Diamond in Florence during David's exile there, and was fond of him; he understood David, and several times smoothed things out between us when, during an intense argument, one of us said something to the other which couldn't be taken back. In 2004, one of his last acts—in a career in which he selflessly championed numerous composers' works—before retiring from the ACO as an advisor was to insist that they play *Fire Music* at Carnegie Hall.

Carpal Tunnel Syndrome having rendered him physically unable to do the work himself, David Diamond wrote to me in May to ask whether I would orchestrate his opera *The Noblest Game*, which Christopher Keene had green-lit at New York City Opera. Thinking *not for all the tea in China*, I called him to respectfully decline. He asked if I'd be willing to suggest someone who might do the work. I suggested that he call Lowell, or Anthony Strilkow. I doubted that Keene, who was known to be succumbing to AIDS, would live long enough to conduct the premiere, and told David so. "I know," he said. "He's doing this for history, and I'm taking him at his word."

Michael Morgan was scheduled to make his New York Philharmonic debut, his program to include the premiere of *Philharmonia*, commissioned in celebration of the orchestra's 150th anniversary. In the Green Room at Avery Fisher Hall, the Orchestra's trumpet players surrounded me. "Okay, Daron," said Phil Smith, "the first thing you've got to understand is that trumpet players are like fighter pilots. When a section violinist screws up, nobody can hear it. When we crash and burn, everyone hears it." I nodded respectfully. "So, do you want me to change the opening?" (All four trumpets were required to play antiphonal valve trills on high C's from four different spots in the balconies. It was the most brutal set of parts I've ever written, and I knew it.) Bill's brother George Coble, sitting in for the concert, said, "You did this to us because we're the best, right? You're trying to bust our chops?" "No, no," I insisted, but he was right. I blushed. "We'll play them where you wrote them, because we can." He looked at the other guys for support. "But you had better put them down an octave if you ever want to hear the piece again," admonished Donna's teacher, Vince Penzarella. They all laughed and slapped me on the back. The piece received great reviews, but it seemed clear to me that to these men I had abused the privilege, delivered an unnecessarily difficult piece, and squandered a great opportunity: *Philharmonia* fails since it will never be frequently performed.

The next evening, Donna and I sat next to Kurt Masur in the composer's box. "Fascinating," Masur said to me during the applause afterwards. "It is really five very short pieces, is it not?" "Yes, sir—it consists of five one-minute pieces and a cadenza for the trumpets." "Hmm," he said, and suddenly smiled mischievously. "You made them work, didn't you?" Although the Philharmonic had performed my music before, this night was my debut as a composer at Avery Fisher Hall. I was thirty. The piece got good reviews in all the papers. The audience liked it. The orchestra liked it. Michael premiered beautifully the complete Symphony No. 2 with the Oakland Symphony in April 1993.

The following week, the cast and company of *Brow* gathered at the Bernstein family's Dakota apartment to give for Madison Opera's donors and staff a workshop performance (piano and two dozen singers) of the complete score. Ann Stanke, Madison Opera's founder and the commission's driving force, worked the room as Roland powwowed with the singers. At my suggestion, the company had hired Andrew Porter's sister Sheila to publicize the workshop and premiere. I asked Stephen to ask Jamie for the use of the apartment to exploit people's interest in visiting it one more time to fill the room with press that might not otherwise have had any interest in a commission, however laudable, by a small Midwestern company, of an unknown composer.

It had been impossible, strolling around Taliesin with Dick Carney (like me, an insomniac) in the wee hours, not to feel Wright's presence. It had been impossible at Yaddo not to feel the Trasks.' It had impossible to walk through the Common Room at Curtis without feeling the benevolent spirit of Mary Louise Curtis Bok. And it still felt, at the Dakota, as though Bernstein was slouching in the chair in the den, sipping a scotch, pulling on his plastic cigarette holder, growling one of the last things he said to me: "Play and sing that part again, baby—the part that sounds like Marc."

Ramping up to the premiere of the opera, I hadn't noticed that the phone wasn't ringing. Nobody was commissioning me, and I wasn't performing the sort of social and professional functions that I should have been to keep my shingle shiny. I vacillated between Curtis-grad entitlement and pleas for help. Although scrupulous about drinking alcohol only on Wednesday nights at Bard, I feared taking the route that Kevin had taken—absenting myself from a marriage while remaining physically there. I was, however, unable to restrain myself from collapsing into a dark, emotionally remote, depression whenever criticized.

A few days after the run-through at the Dakota, Carolann Page, Michael Sokol, and I performed some arias from *Brow* at the east side townhouse of Tamara Gulden for a swanky dinner party hosted by Tony Randall. Me, to Tony, before performing: "Nice to meet you, Mr. Randall." "Yes," he replied, "I *know*." Tony, to me, after we performed: "Daron, if I had known that you were so talented, I'd have been nicer." "Yes, Tony," I replied, "I *know*."

Everyone involved with the April 1993 opening night of *Shining Brow* knew that it was going to be a success. Today I realize how extremely rare that is. That night, at "the rail" of the house, behind the audience, (where authors traditionally are allowed to pace, fret, enjoy, and suffer, performances of their work) with Stephen Wadsworth, as baritone Michael Sokol sang Wright's halting, tragic, final lines "some such ... *finch*" (which I associated with Atticus Finch—aptly or not—and therefore accessed emotions I associated with Father reading the Harper Lee novel to me as a child—such is the seductive allusiveness of Muldoon's poetry that, if you've a will, there's always a way to hook in to it) of Madison Opera's première production. Stephen said, "Look!" "Eh?" I said. "Look at them," he said, sweeping a hand over the audience, who were experiencing the last few minutes of the opera. "They're all weeping." I looked. They were. "Yes, that's where we want them," I said. "No," he said. "That's where they want to be. You did it. I did it. Paul did it. The performers did it. Communion. We all did it. Together."

The next morning a telegram from Ned arrived, saying, "I always said that you would arrive at thirty." The reviews were excellent, and the consensus was that my career had begun in earnest. Returning to New York, I resumed my teaching responsibilities at Bard; Donna pursued her studies at Mannes, dividing her time between trumpet practice and score study. We decided that, since the conservatories would not take her as a conducting student, she would pursue her career through the summer festivals. Over our customary Wednesday evening drinks, I described the success that the première of *Brow* represented to Joan Tower, who did not seem to believe me.

That summer, Donna was accepted in the conducting program at the Aspen Summer Music Festival. I rented us a condominium at the foot of Aspen Mountain. Donna participated in the festival; I completed the full score of *Joyful Music*. A fourteen-minute blowout for solo mezzo-soprano (Wisconsinite and Metropolitan Opera stalwart Kitt Reuter Foss), trumpet (John Aley, who played his creamy Monette), a huge mixed chorus, and the Madison Symphony, it was commissioned to honor Roland Johnson, the man who had commissioned *Brow*. (I have since withdrawn it.) Aspen's visual splendor and the fact that she was doing exactly as she wished notwithstanding, Donna seemed miserable. Unwilling, and now unable, to mollify her, I steeled myself emotionally, intensified my focus on work and moved on to the next commission. My faculty colleague and friend, urbane Frescobaldi scholar and harpsichordist (music director of the Clarion Society, and founder of the E. Nakamichi Festival of Baroque Music in Los Angeles) Frederick Hammond, Irma Brandeis Professor of Romance Cultures at Bard, commissioned a song cycle for baritone, oboe, cello, and harpsichord called *Lost in Translation*. For years, Fred had graciously shared his Wednesday evenings with me and allowed me to sleep in his guest room during the school year. I respected him immensely and was honored when he asked for a new piece. I asked him to choose the poems himself, and he collected an inspiring set that included verses in Greek (George Seferis), Italian (Dino Campana), German (Rainer Maria Rilke), and English (W.H. Auden and James Merrill). I asked "deep image" poet Robert Kelly (a fellow Bard faculty member) for a poem as well.

Chris Gekker, then a member of the American Brass Quintet and Juilliard faculty member, gave a knockout performance of the flügelhorn concerto with strings that I'd written for Donna, under her baton, to which Jim Holmes, passing through with Ned on the way to the Vail Music Festival, came. After the performance, I was dispatched to the Popcorn Wagon for wraps. On my way home, I bumped into Jim. We sat together on a bench on Cooper Street, across from the Red Onion while he smoked a cigarette.

"A congress of baboons," he said, continuing the collective noun game we had begun playing. "An ascension of larks," I shot back. "A kendle of kittens," he said. "No," I said. "Really?" "Uh huh," he replied. The sound of breeze through the Aspen trees made me chuckle. "An aspiration of Aspens," I quipped. "A *skein*—," he began. "No, a *flock*—," I continued. "—Of wild geese," he concluded. "We're *both* right." Beat. Jim frowned and stretched his legs out. "How is married life, really?" he asked. I didn't want to talk about it. "An unkindness of ravens," I answered. He looked down. "It's a *murder*," he corrected me. "How's that?" "A *murder* of ravens," he said. "No, crows come in *murders*; ravens come in *unkindnesses*," I said. "Ah. You're right. Listen: when Ned and I came to dinner last night, you and Donna seemed … barely civil," he observed. "An 'uncivil' union," I quipped lamely. After a beat, I burst out, "Oh, hell, Jim, I know that marital pain is like age and illness—too universal even to bother with." He didn't look at me. "Where did you read that?" he asked. "Yeah, I know its bullshit," I admitted. "But believe me," I continued, "I understand entirely that the sort of suffering married couples inflict upon one another is boring." He pulled a pack of cigarettes out of his windbreaker and lit one. "Ned's never been easy to live with," he said, exhaling smoke. "But we understand one another; that's more important than love, in the end."

I stared at him, suddenly aware of the gentle rill of water in the little manicured rivulet that ran down the middle of the street. It was beautiful. "Does she understand you?" he asked. The answer was obvious. "I thought that she did," I answered, scratching my chin. "But I'm probably a terrible husband," I confessed. "You stopped drinking for a while there," Jim observed. "Yeah. She asked me to." "Why are you drinking again?" "I don't want to be 'there' when I am there," I answered. "Nice line reading," he said, gently. "Yeah. I know," I said, uneasily. "You need to begin couples counseling, at the very least," he advised. "More to the point: you're self-destructing, and you need to pull yourself together." Came a mountain zephyr. I shivered involuntarily, turned up the collar of my tweed jacket, looked at my feet. "Jesus, Daron," my old friend said, dropping his cigarette on the ground and extinguishing it with his foot exactly as Mother once had at Marshall Fields when I was a kid. "What in the world makes you think that she deserves—or that you do, for that matter— to live like this?"

It took the two of us to get here, I thought. *But I was the one who asked her to marry me. It's on me.* I recalled the night when I was a kid when Father's rage had made me pee myself and I'd flipped a switch in my heart from "loving and liking" him to "loving and fearing," him. At this moment, I flipped another switch from being "in love and liking" to "loving and disliking" my wife. I'd long detested myself, so there was no change in the position of that switch. My marriage was falling apart, and, knowing that it was, I had gradually backed away from the promise I'd made myself to not put her needs first. *It's all too little, too late,* I thought fecklessly, *she's learned to hate me, and I hate being hated.*

"Fix it. Or get out," Jim snapped. He stood up, squeezed my shoulder, and turned to leave. "See you back in New York in a couple of weeks," he smiled. I watched his back recede. *A nettle of New Yorkers,* I mused, lamely. After a while, I got up, picked up my bag, and returned to the condominium where awaited my angry, dissatisfied wife.

Brow was a critical and popular hit. It gets revived in several versions, and there's a cast recording on Naxos by JoAnn and the Buffalo Philharmonic. It identified me from then on as a viable theater composer.

Returning to New York, I learned that the Rockefeller Foundation had granted me a semester-long residency in Italy at the Villa Serbelloni. Again, at the last moment, cavalierly hoping to be fired, I informed Joan, who was herself about to take a sabbatical. Who would take our places? This time, when she asked if I had any ideas about who might replace us I strongly encouraged her to invite Jennifer Higdon, a friend and colleague just graduated from David Loeb's studio at Curtis and the University of Pennsylvania.

The breathtaking Villa Serbelloni should have served as the backdrop for a second honeymoon for us. Instead, we both frittered away the time by quarreling. I did manage to finish a Concerto for Horn With Winds and Strings, commissioned by Swedish French Horn virtuoso Sören Hermansson. After dinner one night with Mark Strand, I set a stanza of his *A Suite of Appearances.* The next day I played and sang it for him, elbow to elbow on the piano bench, his breathing with every phrase and sighing softly when the song was ended. "Where is endlessness Born / where does it go?" Over the years, I've done this for about a dozen poets. It remains my favorite way of honoring them. *A Suite of Appearances* ended up serving as the opening song of *Letting Go,* a song cycle completed in 2000 and premiered at the Auditório do Departamento de Comunicação e Arte da Universidade de Aveiro, in Portugal by soprano Claire Vangelisti and pianist Alfredo Carerra.

One November morning, I left my studio on the steep hill behind the villa facing Lake

Como for a walk. Nimbus slid down the mountainsides. The bells began first to the northwest. I pocketed the key and turned towards the ringing in Cadenabbia. Seconds later, more distinct, a few steps higher, the bells of Menaggio and Varenna began to peal; their composite rhythm that of a galloping horse's hoof beats. The call to vespers—brittle, harsh, at least a major second lower, louder than the rest, rolled from the belfry of Bellagio's church across the surface of the lake and up the Alps—returned as a softer, mellower echo. My ears rang in sympathy. Presently, the ringing stopped. I heard my nervous system's whine. As I looked up, a zephyr, like the sweet breath of a sleeping infant, caressed my cheek. "Aloft," I remembered the Longfellow I had set only that day, "through the intricate arches / Of its aerial roof, arose the chant of their vespers…." As though on cue, the wind tousled the surrounding pine trees and tore away their shrouds of mist. I shivered involuntarily, recalling the stanza's conclusion: "Mingling its notes with the soft susurrus and sighs of the branches." (Years later, the sensory trigger of this moment served as the inspiration for *Susurrus*, commissioned by the National Symphony Orchestra.)

We left Bellagio and began a tour of Italy that took us as far as Sicily. As the weather turned cold, we headed to off-season Venice—cold, shuttered, and nearly empty. Tired and quarrelsome after a long walk from the train station to the Cannaregio, we arrived after the Casa Boccassini had already been buttoned up tight for the night. Storm crows cackled in the branches of the leafless winter wisteria, which loomed over the garden like the exposed ribs of a skeleton. After much pounding on doors and frustration, the owner himself let us in, led us to the little counter where he took down our passport numbers, and gave me a hard, questioning look as he placed in my outstretched palm the skeleton key to our room. "It's sort of a dump, isn't it?" Donna observed as I carried our bags up the spiral staircase. "Well, it's not Bellagio. But then, what is?" I smiled, opening the door to our room. The bathroom was shared; there was a sink next to the bed. I spun the spigot. Nothing came out. "Crap," I muttered. "I'll go downstairs and ask him to turn on the water." I slipped out, descended the steps two at a time, and took a seat in the moonlight on one of the metal café chairs in the garden. The garden was barren. Fellini, I'd heard, had gone AWOL. He'd forsaken his duties and somehow made it to the Giudecca, where he had been spotted carousing with one of the brazen, semi-feral hussies that shadow the fishing boats. The fountain was dry, the koi were gone, and the blue Murano-tile-lined basin was filled with dead leaves that spun restlessly around in the wind like lees in the bottom of a glass. I closed my eyes for a second and breathed in the salty Adriatic air. As Samuel Clemens wrote, "To get the full value of joy, you must have someone to divide it with." The next night, after a day of sightseeing, despite sharing a *panettone* and bottle of insipid yellow dessert wine, I found it impossible to find attractive someone who so obviously disapproved of me. Christmas Eve at the Vatican devolved into a spat about where we would stand to get the best view of the Pope. I took no pleasure in the *Côte d'Azur*. A December sojourn in Florence became a joyless nightmare. The more we fought, the less I slept. I didn't much like her anymore; she certainly seemed to dislike me. We returned to the States together, if not exactly a couple.

As a sort of audition that spring, Ned and Gary asked me to travel to Curtis every few weeks to teach Ned's pupils—Daniel Ott, Eli Marshall, and Jonathan Holland. After each set of lessons, I'd jot Ned a note:

Ned—was delighted with your students' seriousness and technical facility when I taught them for you last week; they adore you and are good young men. I think I offered them a lot and felt both fulfilled and invigorated by the experience. I think that A. is the most gifted, B. the most ambitious, and C. the most sweet-natured. But they're all first-rate, aren't they?

Bob Schuneman offered me a "lifetime exclusive" publishing agreement. We were both planning on being in Washington during the winter—he for a convention, me for a stint serving the National Endowment for the Arts as a panelist—so we agreed to decide then about whether to seal the deal. In the end, I turned down Bob's generous offer.

"What about *me*?" cried Donna bitterly, when I returned to New York from Washington. "You get to go interesting places, do cool things. What about *me*? There's a letter in your desk drawer," she said. "I'm going out." Alone, I opened the drawer, withdrew the letter, and read it. In heartbreaking terms, she described that our relationship made her feel "dead inside." She couldn't understand, for example, why we didn't have sex anymore, and that I needed to fix that or our marriage would fall apart. I set the letter down and wept. Instead of ending things immediately as I ought to have, I wrote to Ned for advice. He replied:

> *I do feel that two people who engage in a mutual commitment, and who invest year after year in that commitment, do produce something that's singularly theirs. Short of being physically repelled by each other, it's too bad for them to throw the investment overboard. I should talk. Still, concessions and accommodations have to be made every day. You & Donna seem nice together. Keep working. (But I understand your* cri du coeur.)

My wife wanted to study conducting with Gunther Schuller at the Sandpoint Music Festival in Idaho that summer, so I rented a place there for us. Donna met with Gunther; I hunkered down for a summer of composing. There were two projects on my plate—a work for the King's Singers, and a violin concerto.

The Kings Singers had attended a performance of *Brow* whilst on tour in Wisconsin and, per Bob Chilcott, the men wanted "something dramatic, tuneful, fun, light, and accessible" for their fall tour. First I wrote a thirty-minute children's opera for unaccompanied voices based on Rudyard's Kipling's *Just So* story *The Elephant's Child*. I sent it off to England. Chilcott was blunt: they hated it. For the second time in six months, I struck out with the recipient of a new work. Scott Foss gallantly published it under the Lorenz imprint, and then it passed to Carl Fisher for a time. After it passed to me, I resolved to revise it someday, add piano, and make of it a chamber opera for young people. Rebounding, I wrote for them in three weeks *The Waking Father*, a cycle of Muldoon settings that they ultimately premiered to a standing ovation 27 July 1995 at Ozawa Hall at Tanglewood. Of *The Waking Father* at this time, forgetting that I had neither served as copyist for the piece or heard it, Ned wrote in his diary *Lies* that it "might as well have been composed by me, so much does it resemble, in technique and device and impact, my own *Pilgrim Strangers*, written for the Kings Singers eleven years ago, and for which Daron, as was the custom then, acted as my copyist."

My writing mentor and friend, Pulitzer prize-winning writer Tim Page, former *New York Times* music critic, and WNYC radio host of the program *New, Old, and Unexpected*, which explored the musical *zeitgeist* and served as a sort of soundtrack for the lives of many Manhattan composers of the 80s, was, at the time, producing projects for Catalyst Records. I had taken Tim's critical writing class at Juilliard. An avid fan of his radio program, I admired not just his superb prose and critical acumen, but his professional and personal ethics. Tim asked me to compose a concerto "on spec" for Maria Bachman, a superb young violinist who I had known very slightly when we were both students in Philadelphia. Unbeknownst to me at the time, while I was studying composition with Ned and bumbling around trying to find myself on the east coast, she was apparently already studying composition privately with George Rochberg while continuing her violin studies with Szymon

Goldberg. "If she likes it," Tim said, "we'll include it on the disc." Wary as I was of writing on spec, the opportunity of working with two people for whom I had such admiration was just too exciting to resist, so I said yes. I spent the rest of the summer on the violin concerto.

I resumed my duties at Bard that fall, and finished a sprawling piano piece called *Built Up Dark* commissioned by pianist / writer Bruce Brubaker, who premiered it the following March at the National Gallery of Art in Washington, D.C. The balance of the fall I spent revising the violin concerto. A somber, *innig* exploration of the insomniac's emotional landscape; in place of glittering passagework, dolorous, slithering chromatic runs created an atmosphere of dread-filled, emotional claustrophobia. In other words, there was almost nothing about the thing that would properly show off the gifts of a beautiful young soloist. Bruce was kind enough to allow Maria and me to read through the concerto at his apartment. She was polite, but it was obvious that she didn't like it, or me, particularly; she certainly wasn't going to record it for Catalyst. I'd been leaning more and more on music to hold myself together, with the result that Maria's disinterest was genuinely devastating to me. (During fall 1995, I turned it into a cello concerto, which Robert La Rue—whose temperament suited the thing—premiered with Leon Botstein and the American Symphony Chamber Orchestra. In 1997, I made a version for wind orchestra, which Rob recorded for Bob Schuneman's record label with Michael Haithcock and the Baylor Winds.)

One of my best faculty friends at Bard was William Weaver, the eminent translator of works by Umberto Eco, Primo Levi, and Italo Calvino, among others, Bill also worked as a commentator on the Metropolitan Opera Broadcasts, and made exquisite libretto translations. His monographs on Puccini and Verdi (*The Puccini Companion*, and *The Verdi Companion*) continue to serve as irreplaceable resources for me as an opera composer. Wednesday evenings when I wasn't drinking and discussing students with Joan, I either spent with Fred Hammond, or over pasta and champagne with Bill and his emotionally mercurial Japanese partner Kazuo Nakajima at the house they shared on campus in which Mary McCarthy used to live. I learned more about dramaturgy from Bill over dinner during those years than from anyone else. To dine with him was, in a way, to dine with Callas and the rest; only two other men I've known could match his operatic erudition: Speight Jenkins and Frank McCourt. He also taught me how to make an exquisite *Pasta Puttanesca* in less than five minutes.

Bill also maintained a villa called Monte San Sevino (on to which he had built an addition with royalties derived from his translation of *The Name of the Rose* that he called his Eco Chamber) and an apartment close by St. Vincent's Hospital in Greenwich Village. Over dinner in his Village pad, Bill asked me, "Do you know any poetry by Jimmy Merrill?" I did. Merrill, one of my favorite poets, had succumbed to AIDS only the previous February. I had read *The Changing Light at Sandover* in high school, and it was my good fortune to have from memory his *Kite Poem*. I closed my eyes and recited it, concluding:

> *Waiting in the sweet night by the raspberry bed,*
> *And kissed and kissed, as though to escape on a kite.*

When I opened my eyes, I saw that Bill was weeping. "Did you know him?" he asked. "No," I said. "I never met him." Beat. "Well," Bill sighed, looking down. "I have a proposition for you: I'd like to commission some songs in Jimmy's memory. I also have a young protégé named Charles Maxwell—a countertenor—who I'd like you to hear. If you like his voice, then I'd like you to premiere them with him." Flattered, honored, I agreed immediately. "But the rights—," I began. "Oh, just ask Sandy McClatchy to release them," he said. "He's

Jimmy's executor." I waited. "How much will you need for the work?" he asked. Uncomfortable, I looked down. "Let's do this," he said, smiling. He reached in his jacket pocket and drew out a little notepad. Ripping off a blank page and sliding it across the table to me, he said, "Why don't you write down on this piece of paper how much you need?" I did as I was told, wrote down a number that I thought was reasonable, folded the paper, and slid it back to him. Smiling, he opened it, read the number, put the paper down, drew his checkbook from another jacket pocket, and wrote a check. Still smiling, he ripped the check from the book, folded it carefully in half, took a sip of his chianti, and slid it back to me. I put it in my breast pocket without opening it. "Now!" he clapped his hands. "Let's have some dessert!" An hour later, walking to the subway, I thought to draw the check from my pocket: he'd given me exactly twice the amount for which I'd asked.

I thought at the time that composing for a male soprano was pretty much like writing for any other singer, but I was wrong. Writing for Charles Maxwell, I learned just how much physical strength and stamina is required to sustain singing for any length of time an octave higher than men customarily do. An African-American born in North Carolina, he projected the intelligent, elegant, self-contained dignity of one who had endured and overcome bigotry at home before emigrating to Italy, where he completed his studies at the Instituto Musicale "P. Mascagni" in Livorno. We debuted my *Merrill Songs* together at the Danny Kaye Playhouse in Manhattan the following November on a Clarion Concert, thanks to Fred Hammond—Fred had taken over as director of them as a favor to his mentor, Ralph Kirkpatrick. I was so intrigued by the otherworldly appeal of Charles' voice—it retained its brilliance and clarity even in the extremely high register without ever losing its volume—that I subsequently suggested to Muldoon that we make the character of Vera in our new opera *Vera of Las Vegas* a female impersonator—personal reinvention was to be the core theme, and playing *The Crying Game's* trope seemed an apt starting point—so that I could craft it especially for him.

In January 1995 Otto Luening and I kicked around ideas for a concert that I was presenting featuring some of the songs that he and his wife Catherine had premiered (I had set *Ah! Sunflower* and had a good sketch for *Sun of the Sleepless*, which both he and Ned had set) together over the years alongside settings if the same texts by Argento, and Jack Beeson. Catherine put lunch on the table in the dining room of the Columbia University faculty apartment at 460 Riverside Drive as we spoke. Otto, born in Milwaukee in 1900 and formerly on the faculty of Bennington College, had taught composition seemingly since the Pleistocene Age at Columbia; Ferruccio Busoni had encouraged him early on, and he had served as stage manager for James Joyce's English Players Company, knew Strauss and Freud in Vienna, and was an early pioneer in tape and electronic music.

I reminded Otto how, back in 1985, Kevin had organized an American Music Festival for the Milwaukee Symphony; how Kevin had flown to New York to visit Otto to discuss what pieces, if any, Otto might have on hand that could be programmed on it. Kevin and I had arrived for a similar lunch, and stayed until close to midnight as Otto shared stories about his childhood in Milwaukee, what it was like to walk the Margaretengürtel in Vienna with Mahler, what New York City was like during the early years of the 20th century. At the very end of the day, Kevin had asked Otto what of his he wanted the symphony to play and he said, "Oh, it doesn't matter, dear boy. It's only my music. Let's talk about something interesting." We visited awhile longer and departed. Outside, on the street, Kevin turned to me as we bundled up our collars and said, "Don't forget this, little brother. It might not be flashy, but Otto's life may be as good as it gets."

When I finished the story, Otto's dazzling blue eyes were serious. "Your brother's a good man," he sighed. "And you're a good egg, too. But you are lucky enough to *make* music; your big brother *makes it possible* for people like us to make music. Considering that he started out by wanting to be a singer, that's got to have been really tough for him, don't you think?"

Donna landed a job with "Big Apple Tours" and did long shifts riding around the city atop their big red double-decker buses serving as a tour guide. It was a decisive step away from music, but, if that's what she wanted to do, and it made her happy, I told her, then of course I supported her. I suspect that she made it through the fall largely by fantasizing about the European vacation she had planned for herself. Once she was in Europe and Bard was on break, I could concentrate fully on composing the brass quintet that the University of Wisconsin Madison commissioned in celebration of the 100th anniversary of the School of Music's founding. Next, I orchestrated the piano piece I'd written for Brubaker for the Milwaukee Chamber Orchestra and called it *Built Up Dark* at the request of its music director, Stephen Colburn, the Milwaukee Symphony English Hornist whose performance of the solo in the Dvořák *New World Symphony* had served as the catalyst for my birth as a composer.

I flew in September to Wisconsin to attend the Madison Symphony and Chorus' premiere of the *Taliesin: Choruses from Shining Brow*. I knew Father would visit the Green Room afterwards. The new music director John DeMain had just debuted the piece. We stood side by side in the reception line. Father was drunk. "Just who do you think you are?" Father asked me, smiling, as I signed a chorister's score. "I heard your pre-concert talk," he said, in the same friendly tone. I hoped that DeMain hadn't overheard the exchange. I pulled Father aside. He nearly pinned me against the wall. "Yes," I answered. "I saw you in the audience. It means so much to me that you were able to make it," I said, hugging him, inhaling the combination of sweat, booze, and pipe tobacco. "You said that you were broke all the time," Father hissed. "That's a lie." He was hurt. "I sent you money whenever you said you needed it. You didn't suffer. Why do you always make it sound as though nobody has helped you?" I hadn't seen him since the premiere of *Brow* three years earlier and had asked him for money only once. "Did I really say that I suffered?" I asked, on guard: "That's terrible. I'm sorry. Should I have thanked you? I didn't mean my answer to come out that way." Beat. DeMain's face froze in an embarrassed half-smile. "Are you staying here in Madison tonight?" I asked, opening the door to inviting him out to dinner after the concert. "What do you care?" said he, slamming it. I wasn't hurt. I wasn't angry. I was tired. "I wanted to know whether you were hitting I-94 back to Milwaukee half in the bag." I sighed. I recognized the smile he rolled out then from my childhood. It was his "I know something you don't know" sneer. "Oh, yes," he said. "I forgot. This is your *place of business*." His laugh.

I returned to Madison just a few weeks later to hear the Wisconsin Brass Quintet premiere my Concerto for Brass Quintet at Mills Hall. Donna hung out with college friends afterwards while the quintet and I celebrated with pizza and beer at Paisan's, an Italian joint in the middle of campus. As a student, I had bussed the table at which now we sat; Father had bussed the same table while a law student. After a while, I left them and took a walk along the shore of Lake Mendota. It was late November, and a few leaves still clung to the trees. The sun had just begun to set, and the sky and water were the color of wet bed linen, or of paper turned to pulp—a sort of dirty, snotty, mucous-gray. Drizzle began falling straight down. I thought of the afternoon that Mother had thrown out her manuscripts, the Royal typewriter, the tubes of paint, and the clay. Looking for a place to get out of the rain, I found myself, by accident, at an outcropping of land called Picnic Point—the spot where, when they were students, Father had proposed to Mother. Standing there, fists thrust into the pockets of my hound's-tooth blazer, I looked out at the Mendota Hospital for the Insane, perched atop an angry smear of rock, far off across the lake. Britt's voice came to me: "But you," he had said that afternoon so long ago that we spent in its ruins, "you're a selfish little fucker. We think that maybe that, and your musical talent, will help you to survive this shit." *Maybe*, I thought to myself—*maybe not.* My fingers, cold, wrapped themselves around the keys to the apartment on 98th Street back in New York that Donna and I shared. Without thinking, I threw them as far as I could into the lake. I'm sure it was just the wind in the trees, but I could have sworn that I heard Mother say, "Just let it go."

◆◆ 17 ◆◆

No Fear. No Hatred. Just Love
1996–1997

An old-fashioned carbon copy of Britt's January 1996 letter to Father arrived with a post-it stuck to it on which he had jotted, "Thought you ought to have a copy."

I have put off the writing of this letter for many years, for a variety of reasons. At first, I was too angry with you for the terrible things you did to our mother when I was a child—things only you and I and she know about. Then, especially after Mom's death basically dissolved the family, I came to understand what had driven you to be the capriciously brutal man you were when we were children. With this understanding came forgiveness.... Now I can remember back to my very early years—back to the man you were before whatever later tormented you began to change you—back to when you held me in your arms and I felt nothing but love for you. No fear. No hatred. Just love.

I let the page fall and looked up from the canvas deck chair in which I was sitting at the hundreds of apartment windows that surrounded the little roof deck behind the one-bedroom apartment on West 98th Street. I had, ironically, come out seeking privacy. Donna's brother, who had just moved to Manhattan to begin a career as an arbitrageur, and Robert La Rue, who needed a place to stay, had been sleeping for weeks on the living room floor. More irony: their presence made home life easier for me, since I preferred to quarrel in private.

Daron, wrote Britt in the letter to me that accompanied the carbon of his letter to Father, *one of the precious things that I have learned is that the child is the father of the man. Our childhood experiences color the rest of our lives. Our Dad formed much of the basis for the struggles in manhood with which Kevin and I have had to cope.... Since Kevin and I have reestablished contact, we have spoken for many hours about the impact of his childhood. Those experiences are at the core of what he refers to as the "devils" that drive him to drink. He has told me this, eye to eye, face to face and heart to heart, that when he is alone, with no family around, that these "devils" overcome him, and drive him to drink.*

My brothers had lived without speaking within blocks of one another in Springfield, Illinois for several years. Both were alcoholic, morbidly obese, and clinically depressed. So much pain. *We're still Little,* I mused ruefully, *and he's still Big. Jesus, what a mess we've made of things.* I shivered involuntarily as a gust of winter wind circled the courtyard. I rose, stuffed the letters in my pocket, looked up at the schist-colored sky, poured lees over the side of the deck, without thinking dropped the empty wine glass after it, listened to it shatter when it hit the walkway two floors down, sighed, shoved the door open, tripped on the ugly blue shag rug within, cursed as I fell forward onto the bed that I still shared with my wife, heard from the next room the sound of Rob practicing the *Marcia* from Benjamin Britten's third suite, buried my head in a pillow, and screamed.

Paul Kreider (then the Chair of the Music Department at the University of Nevada Las Vegas and now Dean of the College of Creative Arts at West Virginia University) offered me a multi-year artist-in-residence position and sweetened the deal with an official request for a chamber opera for his faculty and students to premiere. I leapt at the opportunity. Muldoon and I wrote an opera called *Vera of Las Vegas*—with a nod to Britten's Captain Vere and a billy (Budd) to the ribs of the American Nightmare. I felt as "dead inside" as my wife had said that she felt. And I wanted to write an opera about people who felt the same way; people who were desperately in need of personal reinvention. What better central driving musical metaphor for an opera about these people, I thought, than an "emotion-free" process piece built of musical cells? So, I erected the structure of the opera atop the structure of *Everything Must Go!* The brass quintet I'd written the previous summer at Yaddo. This allowed me to build a dramatic edifice atop and to conceal within a seemingly eclectic score the tight organization required to keep things from flying apart, musically. Paul and I ended up with a detailed treatment comprised of six ten-minute scenes. My musical strategy was to lure the listener into a musical amusement park to initiate them into hitherto unrevealed horrors.

We dreamt up the fantastical story together that autumn in his cozy office in Princeton. Early on, Paul deployed several characters from and references to his already-written one act radio play *Six Honest Serving Men*. I scrunched up in an easy chair with two legal pads on my lap—one had my architectural plan of six sections of ten minutes' duration each, and the other had on it a list of things I wanted Paul to address in the libretto. Paul sat with his feet up at his desk, periodically rising to walk around the room while talking, pulling books off the shelves, and fondling the spines, tucking them back in. It was grown up, fascinating, inspiring work. Now, after a dozen revivals or so, *Vera* seems to have earned a small, secure spot in the American fringe opera repertoire. I now believe that *Vera*, right down to the fact that the story begins and ends in the middle of a longer, unresolved narrative, is entirely complete unto itself.

Over the Christmas holidays, I first fulfilled a commission from Madison-pal David Lewis Crosby and the Moravian Music Foundation for a sprawling chorale prelude for trumpet, chorus and orchestra called *Stewards of Your Bounty*, then sank my teeth into composing the vocal score of *Vera*, completing it in early January 1996. It took about two months to revise and orchestrate; and received its concert premiere—I had insisted that Donna conduct—on 8 March 1996. Ironically, it was in the City of Sin that a voice on our answering machine at the hotel upbraided me: "Leave town, you fucking pervert. I read about your pervert piece in today's newspaper, I want you to know that there are God-fearing people living here in Las Vegas, and that we're watching you." Although *Vera* has since become my most frequently revived opera, only about a hundred audience members showed up for the performances in the 1800 seat auditorium. Over the years, I have received hundreds of touching emails and letters from people in the throes of personal reinvention who respond not just to the music but also to the libretto. It seems to resonate with its audience more deeply than all my operas except *Amelia*.

When Donna called from Venice, where an affair with a North African had turned sour, explaining that he had "forced her to sell her trumpets, hidden her passport, and was beating her and would I send her a plane ticket home," I booked her on a Pakistani Airways flight out of Orly. "Our marriage," she declared, "is over." Shock, relief, anger, exhaustion. I arrived an hour early at a café across the street from where we were to meet for dinner with two dozen roses; when she arrived at the restaurant an hour late, I left the roses on the café table, walked across to meet her, and proposed that we give our marriage a final try. She agreed. We went home together and continued, loveless. Periodically her lover would call. I'd snarl, *"Vaffanculo stronzo"* into the phone and hang up. One afternoon a few months later I returned from teaching at Bard and picked up a letter from her father waiting for her on the landing in front of our apartment. On a hunch, I opened it, and read his kindly, frank assessment of her options, his advice. Another cuckolding, and our marriage's futile little coda sputtered fitfully to an end.

Came the sad news that Louise Talma had died. Louise was born in France in 1906 and educated at New York University and Columbia. Her compositional voice owed most to her time at the Conservatory in Fontainebleau. Unlike Diamond, Louise—after working with Boulanger—remained a close friend and colleague to the great pedagogue. Once, sitting with her at a concert at which one of Lukas' pieces was being performed, I felt her hand close around my thigh like a vice as the work ended. "Oh, for God's sake, Lukas!" she ejaculated in the silence between the last note of music and the first beat of applause.

Who knows, I used to daydream, maybe the next Seabiscuit will emerge from the mist right in front of me, as on many mornings at Yaddo, I began the day very early by carrying a thermos filled with coffee into the forest that separated the estate and the Saratoga track. What cool, silent bliss it was in those days to sip coffee as the sun rose, and to watch through the chain link fence as the jockeys breezed the magnificent horses. Occasionally, Louise joined me. Pall Mall in hand, fascinator firmly perched in her thin, mouse-brown hair, paper-thin cotton sundress ironed and washed into within a memory of itself, Louise was as childlike as I ever saw her. Over dinner, she could uncoil herself in an instant when someone said something stupid. Lashing out, she remorselessly cut the offender dead with the fewest of stiletto-like remarks. With the slightest twitch of her upper lip, she would indicate to me that she wanted a light. Her "church lady" glasses were so old that they had gone out and in to fashion repeatedly. Dinner nearly over, dessert dispatched, coffee poured, nobody dared tell Louise to wait to light up until after dinner drinks were poured on the back porch. I was her favorite, summer in and out, at Yaddo. I'd pick up her bourbon at the liquor store, her chocolate at the Price Chopper, her smokes at the drugstore. Her music? Never much cared for it. But I adored her. Outgoing mail was placed in a communal basket in the linoleum room. "Dear One," she would say, using her pet name for me and handing me some letters, "will you take these into town when you buy hooch and mail them for me? I don't like other people knowing my business." In the end, on 13 August 1996, in her sleep in the Pink Room, after having spent many summers there and at the MacDowell Colony, Louise met the reality of death. Afterwards, many were astonished to learn that she had left a million dollars to MacDowell. I was not. It was like Louise to bite the hand that fed her. She left not a penny to the place in which, having for years composed and enjoyed her nightly bourbon and chunk of chocolate, she lay down for the last time. Laughing last over her bourbon in Paradise, my friend Louise left Yaddo, rather than a small fortune, her small body.

Kevin interviewed for the position of executive director of the New Mexico Symphony. The organization was in dire financial straits. "We were wondering how we could attract anybody good who could lead us out of our mess," Roger Melone, Kevin's good friend, former associate conductor and chorus director who served on the board of the directors, told me. "When we sat down and started talking, it was evident that Kevin understood the business inside and out." He was overqualified for the job, but he was an alcoholic, and had been honest with them about it. His performance there over the next few years was excellent. When he missed work, someone would come looking for him: he had a social safety net of people who loved him and cared about him that kept his binging to a minimum. There were extended periods of sobriety.

Britt telephoned. Instead of hello, he began by announcing, "I'll be dead within hours." He was furious with me, and coherent for frequent enough brief intervals to tell me that he was sorry that I was going to burn in hell. He forgave me, he said, for having "defiled" our mother's privacy by having set some of her words to music after she died. Oh, the pain my brother was in: bile, imprecations, the sort of vicious, venal stuff that should remain forever locked in the subconscious—it all spewed out of the telephone receiver like sewage. I assumed that he was high on pain meds. "I'll regret not having gotten to experience married life," he mused during a lucid moment. I told him that, so far, my experience had been … mixed. "Do you suppose Mom will be glad to see me?" he asked, voice breaking. Near the end of the call, he predicted, "If I check into the hospital, with my immune system compromised the way that it is, I know I'll catch pneumonia and that'll be that. I'm throwing everything away … then I'll get a taxi, go to the hospital, and die."

Thinking *one down, three to go*, I called Father and left a message on his answering machine to the effect that Britt was dying in a hospital in Illinois and that, if he wanted to see him, he had better jump in the car. Or something. I don't remember. I went to sleep in the pile of blankets that served as a bed—I hadn't the money, the time, or the interest in buying a new one to replace the one Donna had taken when she moved out—figuring that I'd be awakened by a telephone call from the hospital with the news of his death. I dreamed that night that Britt and I were wandering together through the ruins of the Mendota Hospital for the Insane again and that he did not have advanced cirrhosis of the liver, did not carry Hepatitis A, B, and C, was not morbidly obese. He was young, and beautiful, and the

Posing with my beloved brother Britt Arvid Hagen (left) in Milwaukee in August 1988. On the back of the photo he helpfully identified himself as a "Republican" and me as a "Crypto-Commie."

insides of his lungs—he was, like Mother, a chain smoker—were not black with tar. Lighting up a Newport and flashing that shit-eating grin of his, he said, "Little brother, Kevin and I worked hard to protect you from Dad. Don't let us down." Indeed, I was the sort of selfish man who could go to bed figuring that his brother would probably die sometime during the night. I wouldn't have boarded the next flight to Illinois to see him a final time even if I had had the money. He didn't ask me to come, and it never occurred to me to go.

Then I had the Green Room Dream again (only this time it was Britt who I hauled by the arm out of the toilet) until I was pulled out of the dream by a phone call not from the hospital but from Father. "Why should I care what happens to Britt?" he asked. An orderly had found my telephone number in Britt's wallet. He had called and given me the number of the ICU. "Because he's your son," I said, feebly. "You're his father." They hadn't spoken since Mother's death, but I felt that Britt's father needed to know that his son was dying. Father let out a long sigh. "What am I supposed to do?" he asked. "He's got no use for me. I haven't heard from him in years." "He's dying," I said, without emphasis. Already, I felt my heart hardening, the familiar icy repose setting in. He had taught me how to hate him. "Give me the number," he snapped. Beat. "Is it drugs?" "He called me last night, pretty out of it, saying that he was checking himself into the hospital to die," I replied. And then, cruelly, I threw Mother's words at him: "Who will care why after he's dead? Will you?"

> *I wish that my memories of Britt were as real as the memories of the last 18 months,* wrote Kevin later, *and especially of the last three days, and of the so sad, so tormented, so sick, so hopeless man I got to know at the end of his life. The last three days have been so terribly sad—seeing how he lived, in a hotel room at the Springfield Hilton, at the end, how he looked, and guessing how he felt and what he was thinking. And wondering how I could have been so self-absorbed as to have missed so much pain—or rather dismissed it—as Britt going through another Britt-like phase. I so wanted to believe he was making the comeback he seemed to be, and said he was.*

I remember Britt now not as he saw himself (or as he sought to be perceived by his brothers or friends) but as our mother saw him: nine years old, tenderhearted, small fists stubbornly balled at some injustice, fearsomely witty, intelligent, profoundly able to give love and even more hungry to receive it, back turned to the dark and for some unknown reason already the proud owner of a bruised heart. He was a willowy boy with long beautiful eyelashes and a smile that began tentative and blossomed almost with relief. His mischievous grin was an invitation to disaster, and not to be refused. He once emptied half a bottle of Mother's Chanel No. 5 onto the tummy of Kevin's teddy bear. Mother, furious, couldn't help but to laugh tenderly at the look of fury on Kevin's face. It took twenty years for Pooh to smell like a guy again. (Pooh lives now where Kevin would have wanted him to—with his friend JoAnn Falletta.) God, Britt could be funny. Mother loved him best because he needed it the most. Britt, our Father's image, worshipped her. Father loved Britt as much as he loved himself; he hated him the same way. Their violent fights were hair-raising. Britt was little; Father was big. The rest was, while not inevitable I suppose, classic. Mother understood her son as completely as she understood her husband. However, she wouldn't come between them, and she couldn't be there all the time, or for the rest of his life. Then she was gone.

As kids, we had a beagle named Cinnamon who, during the coldest winter days, preferred to relieve herself in the basement next to the furnace where it was warm rather than outside in the snow. During the week, while Father was in Chicago, these little accomplishments accumulated, since nobody went down there anyway and they were easier to clean up once they had dried. Friday afternoon after school and before Father's arrival, Britt was charged with the cleanup. He forgot. Sounded were the Three Taps of Doom and uttered the Dread Summons. Trooped to the basement, we were lined up next to the furnace. My God, he was furious, his pipe fairly vibrating between his small, yellowed, clenched teeth: "What do you think the neighbors think when they look in the windows and they see the floor covered with shit?" he hissed. The terrified silence was broken by Britt's tiny voice, sincerely looking for the bright side: "Well, at least they know we didn't do it!" Britt's relationship with Father—and Life—can be summed up in the emotions that filled the ensuing seconds, as Father first raised his hand to strike him and then let it fall as he was compelled to acknowledge the situation's painful absurdity.

During my first years in New York, Britt wired me hundreds of dollars to help me get on my feet. His letters were sentimental and sad, and his voice in them echoed his favorite authors—Fitzgerald, Wolfe, and Hemingway. He never got tired of—or grew past—them. There are good people in the world I have never met who loved him and understood him, yet he lived in the same city as Kevin for three years before meeting him for dinner. He reached out for help in various directions—to the Masons, to the Mormons, to worthy and unworthy associates. After a while, he stopped writing; we spoke only occasionally on the phone. The last few times it was clear that his demons were close at hand: he rambled incoherently, was abusive, angry, frustrated, bitter, and maudlin. At the age of forty, stretched out on a metal gurney when the coroner examined him, he had what she described as "the largest liver she had ever seen. This was slow suicide, and he worked at it for years," she said.

Winding sheet. Swaddling band. We are reminded each Easter in John 20:7 that the first thing that the resurrected Jesus did was to fold his *sudarium* before emerging from the sepulcher. In the last entry of the fragmentary diary that Kevin found in Britt's room at the Hilton, Britt described the pains he took in order not to depart this realm by tossing his wadded napkin on the table of life. Evidently, he spent his last hours folding his laundry. It would be comforting to believe that he did so as an expression of faith; but he wrote that he did it because he wanted to leave a good impression.

> *I wish you had shared your pain, Britt,* Kevin wrote, *because that helps make it go away. And when you were so sick I wish you had let someone know and accepted help. But I also say to you, my brother I love more than I ever realized while you were here, that I promise to take from this place tonight a resolve to learn from your pain and your sad life and not let my life be blighted as yours was. It can so easily be. It can so easily be. That is your greatest gift to me. A gift of life—and more valuable than the things that meant so much to you, the material wanting to impress your brother with your success— buying dinner when you couldn't afford it. Britt, you were a success. You were a success. Write it ten gazillion times on the blackboard, OK? And I love you. Bye, bro, I will miss you.*

Up until the spring morning when my soon-to-be-ex-wife sandwiched herself heavily into the booth across from me and I saw her for the last time, the Metro Diner at 100th and Broadway had been one of my favorite Upper West Side haunts. I spread the settlement agreement on the table in front of her like the plans to a house. "Let's get on with it," I said. "No. I want to order something first," she said, a cool Pan Am smile flickering across her lips. She glanced up to gauge its effect. I looked away. She gathered up the papers with elaborate care, piled them neatly to one side, picked up a menu, and deliberated. I stared at the ice in my plastic water glass. The waiter brought her a cup of coffee. She ordered, leaned back in her seat, and stretched. "How 'ya been?" she drawled.

I looked out the window. A pale, slender woman in a red dress only partly concealed beneath a royal blue pea coat sped northwards up Broadway with her head down, shielding her eyes from the intense morning sun. She reminded me of my violist girlfriend from Marseilles, dashing once through a drizzle to meet me near the Campanile in Venice. I looked back at Donna and thought about the violent North African with whom she said she had taken up. As a child, I had compulsively picked scabs when under stress. "How have I been?" I repeated the question vaguely, scratching at my arm. I examined the half dozen scabs on each of my hands. My arms and legs were covered with wounds. Sighing, the dermatologist had informed me, "I'm sorry, but there's nothing I can do for you. It appears to be psychosomatic: you are simply uncomfortable in your own skin."

My eggs came—sunny side up. They were runny, viscous, like snot. Next to the eggs was a pile of hash. I smothered it in catsup. A slice of blood orange serving as garnish was twisted like a set of filthy dentures. I fought back a wave of nausea. We both ate mechanically. What a mess. "I don't know," I said, looking at her squarely.

"So," she smiled thinly, "are you still a drunk?" "I drink a lot," I answered. "But I am not a drunk." "Oh, that doesn't matter," she said. I looked at her. "Because I'll tell the judge that you are." "Ah," I said, without inflection. I looked at the back of my hand. The largest scab there looked exactly like a fleck of the hash on my plate. I pulled it away from the skin and tucked it between the folds of my napkin. She got down to business: "I want you to know that I know that you got to be a better and better husband and I got to be a worse and worse wife."

Surprised, I looked up at her. She smiled brightly and crammed a slab of pancake in her mouth. I looked away again. Why had I made her end it? Why did I need to prove to myself that I had tried everything, everything possible to make it work? Why had it been more important to me to be right than it had been to be happy? She pushed her plate to the side, smacked her lips, and reached for the settlement papers. I signaled for the check. "You know," I said, "that you haven't any moral or ethical right to a dime." There was a sudden clatter of dishes in the kitchen and a sharp hiss as something hit the hot griddle. She slowly picked up the pen, lit up a malevolent, self-satisfied smile, and said, "I am legally entitled to it. I can get it. And I want it." As she signed the paper and I countersigned it, I felt nothing.

Twenty years later, I published the paragraphs above in the *Huffington Post* and somebody brought the piece to her attention. Her letter gave me the impression that I thought myself "the Great Man" who viewed her as a hanger-on. I accept responsibility for, and regret, my lapse in character in having married with such selfish, inhumane expectations; I am responsible for continuing to live with someone I no longer respected, loved, or even liked, who believed neither in herself or in me.

I have no memory of the premiere of *Stewards of Your Bounty* at the Moravian Music Festival a few days later. I only know I was there because of a flimsy memory of sitting at a bar in Winston-Salem, and because my Work Book says I was. Drunk or sober, there was nothing to do but go on, so, when Yaddo's president Michael Sundell asked me to dream up a musical event for March 1996 celebrating the relationship between Yaddo and Curtis, I suggested that Ned, Lukas, Lee Hoiby, and I—we were all Curtis alums who had spent time at Yaddo—perform our own music on a concert at Weill Recital Hall, I got right on it. Although I had long since disbanded the *Perpetuum Mobile* concerts, this remained a concert that I longed to present. When Mike's gracious and gifted wife Nina Castelli suggested that I ask Gary Graffman to host a repeat of the concert at Curtis, Mike asked me to coordinate both events. Yaddo hosted the Carnegie concert, which flowed seamlessly into an elegant reception masterminded by Nina that managed, despite the august surroundings, to feel both familial and intimate. The Philadelphia concert was fraught with defensiveness and discomfort, and was followed by an onstage talk hosted by Troy Peters that ended in disarray when, in a mic drop moment of deliciously bad taste, Ned characterized Pierre Boulez as "the Hitler of music."

The Green Room at Curtis, a few steps behind the jewel box concert hall, also served as a faculty lounge. I had arranged for Robert La Rue and Carolann Page to perform Ned's *Last Poems* with him. His playing was mediocre, his aggravation evident. Robert sat across the room, chatting affectionately with Lukas, who seemed so at ease that he might fall asleep. They had just performed Lukas' *Capriccio* together, and Rob's hand jumped up and down on the fingerboard of his cello like a spider as he silently demonstrated to Lukas an interesting fingering.

Soon, Ned, Carolann, and Robert swept past on their way onstage. I smiled at Rob, who rolled his eyes theatrically. The sound of applause filtered through the wall, then the first notes. Lee, a fellow Wisconsinite, and I sat together as Ned's piece unspooled. His bitterness was clear. He twisted the sheet music for his Violin Sonata in his lap. "I haven't been here in a long, long time," he observed, taking the room in. "Ned's faculty: neither he nor the school has never invited me to do anything. Ever."

I tried to change the subject by telling him stories as he waited to go on. "I remember," I said to Lee, "the November morning in 1983 when I arrived late, along with Ned's other pupils, to an American Composers Orchestra rehearsal at Tully Hall of Lukas' brand new orchestra piece. Lukas was hunched down in his seat about a dozen rows back from the stage, surrounded by his Boston University students. We sidled up behind Lukas, looming over his shoulder to follow the score. His discomfort was palpable. At the end of the piece, Ned said, 'What a sexual piece, Lukas'!" Lee groaned, smiling. "Oh, no!" he said, hugging himself. I finished the story: "Without turning around, Lukas flipped the score pages back to the title page, which read, "*Exeunt*, a piece about the imminent destruction of humanity by thermonuclear war."

"Oh, God, that's good," laughed Lee, wiping away tears. "Which reminds me," I continued, "of the time when, spending the weekend at David Del Tredici's house in Sag Harbor, I enthused for rather too long about opera. Tiring, David asked what my favorites were. I opined. He began asking what I thought of various 'great moments' in the repertoire. Swept away by my own enthusiasm and the sound of my voice, I overextended...." "So?" asked Lee. I paused for effect. "'So,' David asked, "what do you think of the overture to Strauss' *Elektra*?" (Of course, *Elektra* has no overture.) "Wonderful," I ejaculated without thinking. "Wonderful!," at which point David moved to the bookshelf and drew a copy of the vocal score." Lee laughed. "Oh, no, no, no," he said, laughing. "I'll bet you felt like a real asshole!"

A few moments later, I heard him begin his sonata through the wall. He was a terrific pianist. In time, the hiss of applause erupted like steam from an espresso machine, and Lee bounded backstage, clearly happy with his performance. It was my turn. My page-turner (one of Ned's current composition students) came to fetch me. "Toi times three," said Lee, smiling, relaxed. Nodding in return, I followed the boy out and onto the stage. Seating myself at the piano, I met Carolann's gaze and smiled. Robert sat in precisely the same spot he had when we had premièred *Three Silent Things* together on Friday the 13th of April twelve years previous. I looked at Laura Park, who was lightly touching the strings of her violin with the very tip of her bow to check the tuning. She glanced up, smiled, and nodded, yes. We launched into *Merrill Songs* (to which I had added one afternoon a few weeks earlier in Las Vegas violin and cello parts) renamed, for the occasion, *A Scattering of Salts*. Carolann sang beautifully. Was my playing any good, I wonder? I can't recall. Anyway, it wasn't dazzling, and anything but that onstage at Curtis was just a waste of time.

I developed chemical pneumonia, which took months to kick, as I trotted up and down the coast teaching: for two days each week I was Upstate at Bard; for one day I filled in for David Del Tredici at City College of New York (he was on sabbatical); and for one afternoon each week I taught at Curtis in Philadelphia. When I came up for tenure, part of me was surprised when Leon denied it, offering instead something he called a "limited-term appointment as composer in residence." It was a generous, appealing offer. I tried to accept it but, in the end, I knew it would be a relief to be free of what had become a toxic situation personally for me at Bard. In hindsight, had I been in Leon's position, I would have made the same decision. I met with Robert Fitzpatrick, Dean of Students at Curtis since my student days, as the school year came to a close, and asked him whether the yeoman service I had been doing there for several years teaching composition lessons to "non-composition" majors would ultimately earn me a studio of my own. When Fitzpatrick answered no I impulsively quit.

Marriage over, brother just dead, tenure denied, career stalled, massive debt, and no job, I bottomed out one chilly morning before dawn a few days later, sitting cross-legged on the floor, very much in the "rifled vault" I'd ended up in that rainy night in Venice again, slowly suffocating in the absolute silence, unable to move.

The next morning, I applied for a job as a barista at Starbucks and was grateful to be hired. The Starbucks in which I jerked coffee during summer 1996 had once been a Citibank branch. Paulie, the manager, a pinch-faced-troglodyte ten years my junior, had been clawing his way up the Corporate Coffee Ladder since graduating high school. "Listen, Hagen," he said, intentionally mispronouncing my name to rhyme with Reagan, "Maybe you think that you're better than me, but that doesn't change the fact that you pack the espresso too tightly when you make lattes."

Lincoln Center, forty blocks south on Broadway—it had only been four years since *Philharmonia's* premiere by the New York Philharmonic—had never seemed so distant. "Sorry, Paulie," I said, tamping down coffee into the barrel, attaching it to the espresso machine, and twisting it tightly to the right. "Mister Kelly," he corrected me. He was enjoying this. "Are you serious?" I asked. "Dead," he replied. "You need to act like you understand that I'm the manager and you're the junior associate," he continued.

My "coffee camerados" included a brilliant, painfully shy PhD in philosophy from Columbia nearly twice Paulie's age and an alcoholic writer with three widely praised published novels behind him. We didn't think we were "better" than Paulie was—just smarter, talented, and better educated. Nevertheless, he was our boss; we were the ones selling coffee to cell phone–wielding teenagers. I dreaded most when former Juilliard classmates stopped in; I didn't hate them, I hated their embarrassment and pity.

I was already late for work one morning when the phone rang. It was my good friend, tenor Paul Sperry. I loved performing with him. Joyous, and fearless on stage, when a note eluded him physically, he always found a fascinating, artful solution to the problem. His diction was superb; I learned from him every time we made music together—he remains one of the finest vocal coaches in the world. Sorbonne and Harvard trained, he studied with Olga Ryss and Richard Barrett, among others; but his chief influences were Pierre Bernac and Jennie Tourel. Longtime faculty at Juilliard, Manhattan School, Aspen, and former director of the vocal program at the Pacific Music Festival in Japan, he had premiered works by Stockhausen and Druckman, and, to my delight, Bernstein's *Dybbuk*, under his baton. His wife Ann, an eminent sculptor and feminist, gave Gilda and me an extraordinarily beautiful hand thrown bowl as a wedding gift that has taken pride of place on my piano ever since.

Paul remains a treasured friend. I loved reading through the songs that composers of all ages had sent to him over the previous months, but I had cancelled, at the last moment, a longstanding date with him to do so. "What's going on with you? Why didja cancel?" he asked. *I'm depressed, drinking too much, self-indulgent and self-loathing,* I thought, *but, otherwise, I'm fine.* "I'm working hard on a couple of things," I lied, "and I'm actually on the way to a rehearsal right now." In truth, I hadn't been able to get off work at Starbucks. Beat. "There's something wrong," he said. "I can hear it in your voice. Don't be bubble-headed: come over tomorrow. I'll fix us lunch, and then we'll look at some music together." There was no way out, so I said yes, rung off, and went to work. "Paulie," I said to my boss, "I'm going to need to take tomorrow's shift off." He sighed theatrically. "Why's that?" he asked. "I need to meet with a friend to read through some music," I said, not seeing the point of lying. "I can't let you out to pursue your hobby, Hagen," he said, amused. Instead of heading north to Starbucks the next morning, I headed south to Paul's apartment.

The penthouse apartment in which Paul and Ann had brought up their children, Ethan, Raphael, and Joshua at the Majestic on Central Park West overlooked Central Park—the panoramic view of the park and midtown made it a great place to throw parties. Indeed, together we'd recently done a fundraiser for Yaddo there at which my friend, poet and publisher Peter Davison, a protégé of Robert Frost, had read some of his poems, and then Paul and I had performed together some art songs by Yaddo composers, including a new setting of one of Peter's poems that I'd confected for the occasion. I threw my jacket over a chair in the kitchen, gave Ann a quick kiss on both cheeks, and headed straight into Paul's studio. On one wall hung the photographs of dozens of composers who'd written for, and who loved, him: he had commissioned and premièred works by a Who's Who of the 20th century: Dominick Argento, Bernstein, Robert Beaser, William Bolcom, Peter Maxwell Davies, Libby Larsen, John Musto, Stephen Paulus, Louise Talma, Charles Wuorinen, and on and on. I sat down at the piano and drew from the top of the pile of scores the sheet music for something by Larry Alan Smith. After I'd read through a few bars, Paul sailed briskly in, rubbing his hands together. "Oh, that sounds good," he said, referring to Larry's song. "I'm looking forward to digging into it."

After an hour or so, we headed for the kitchen; Paul threw together a salad while I drank a glass or two of a friendly dry white wine that he and Ann had run into in Tuscany and described to him a piece that I had in mind to write for him: *Songs of Madness and Sorrow,* a "dramatic cantata" for tenor and chamber orchestra based on a treatment written by Mother for me in 1982. Mother's diary entry about the "Golden Bird" that I had just set would serve as the emotional apotheosis of the piece. Still shattered and ginger, I worked on it for the balance of the summer. The piece addressed (by way of texts culled mainly from Michael Lesy's irreplaceable book, *Wisconsin Death Trip*) the two main responses to the childlike feelings of helplessness, panic and rage created by the inhuman ravages of simple bad luck (Acts of the Market Economy) and epidemic diseases (Acts of God) in small Wisconsin towns (Verona, Viroqua, and Black River Falls, towns from whence my family hailed) at the end of the 19th century. These two responses are both paranoid in nature. One manifested itself in Obsessive-compulsive behavior (which can make every person, from butcher to candlestick maker, more productive); the other was simple paranoia which arose from the realization that things had not turned out the way that everyone, even the newspapers, had said it would. This quixotic point inspired me, because this normally abnormal reaction was caused by the discovery of *truth,* not the creation of *delusion.* It seemed to me, during the hot summer of 1996, with HIV and AIDS as playing as stark a role as the epidemic diseases of 1896, that things hadn't changed all that much.

Salad eaten, wine drunk, pitch finished, Paul didn't make me ask him for a fee. He pulled out his checkbook and wrote a check, in advance, to pay for it. "I sense that you're in need," he smiled. I blushed. "Aren't I always?" I shrugged. As I folded the check in half on my way down in the elevator afterwards, I realized that it would enable me to quit the job at Starbucks. To tell you the truth, I never set foot in the place again.

I finished *Songs of Madness and Sorrow* in July and turned to a piece for the Waukesha Symphony, a semi-professional ensemble from a prosperous, conservative town just west of Milwaukee, to begin rebuilding my career, which I felt had fallen back approximately a decade—the exact duration of my marriage. I wrote, over the next few months, an orchestral suite called *Postcards from America;* I thought of it as a companion piece to *Occasional Notes,* the organ suite I had written a decade earlier for Leonard Raver. The commission fee from Paul carried me only so far, so I had to find another job.

Aware of my familiarity with the musical theater canon, composer James Legg referred his friend Broadway composer Donald Oliver to me for some lessons. Don co-owned the venerable music preparation office Chelsea Music, founded by Mathilda Pincus and her business partner, arranger Don Walker. When I mentioned that I needed work, Don Oliver was kind enough to offer me space at one of Chelsea's desks. For the next three years, I served there as a freelance proofreader and copyist for Broadway shows, films, recording projects, and cabaret acts.

The materials for a host of shows had been created (and were stored) at Chelsea— *Wonderful Town, Cabaret, The Most Happy Fella, The Music Man, Fiddler on the Roof, Silk Stockings, Company, Follies, Sweeney Todd, Evita, Chicago* ... and on and on. And *on.* The stacks were *incredible.* The list was staggering. I served as a member of the music preparation staff for Broadway productions of *Steel Pier, The Lion King,* and *Les Miserables,* as well as revivals of *Cabaret, Annie, Chicago,* and Andrew Lloyd Webber's *Whistle Down the Wind* for Really Useful's Washington production. I recall watching songs from the show, comprised of a melody line, lyrics by Meat Loaf, chord symbols, and a bass line, come in on the fax machine. Most of the other projects blur together in my memory.

The work was nerve-wracking, intellectually exhausting, emotionally and physically stressful—most copyists drank hard to let off steam. We knew even then that, despite the fact that work was still coming in, the era of hand copied music was ending. At Fleisher, and working for Arnstein, I'd worked on symphonic and operatic scores—that scene was tweedy. Chelsea's office fused Fleisher's disorderly-magic (think Ollivanders Wand Shop) with the Chaplin-esque, stubborn dignity of Stritch singing Sondheim's *I'm Still Here.* One wall consisted of grimy windows that looked north towards Columbus Circle. There was a battered, out-of-tune spinet, pictures of the composers and performers for whom the shop had worked on another wall, file cabinets filled with musicians' union invoices and contracts, shelves stacked with boxes of parts, conductor scores for hits and flops, and six desks for copyists. Dear comrades Brian Fairtile and Carol Retter were smokers, so a cloud of cigarette smoke blued the air. Swapping stories about copying parts for CBS and Sinatra with Norman Forsythe, stretches of shows that we copyists had actually written or re-orchestrated—all that oral history—combined with the smell of sweat, the dust generated by electric erasers, and the ammonia given off by the ozalid-printing machine in the corner—the air might have been unhealthy, but the atmosphere was grand.

Chelsea handled Liza Minnelli's musical materials. She was putting together a new Vegas show. Since she was a client of such long standing, Don and Paul Holderbaum led the team themselves. Brian joined them. I proofread. We all wanted to see Minnelli, so we piled into a cab and hand-delivered the charts to the rehearsal hall next to the Port Authority bus terminal where she was scheduled to read them with a band made up of crack New York freelancers. "How-do-you-do's" and so forth over, she settled on to a stool, and the players sat back in their chairs. For the first time, everyone started reading through the book together. John Kander had written something new for her. It clearly engaged her, because without warning she rose to her feet and became LIZA MINELLI. Everyone in the room experienced a sudden charismatic, emotional ripple effect. The hair on my arms stood up. Every player sat bolt upright. Unforgettable. Extraordinary.

Craig Urquhart (vice president at Amberson in charge of promoting the maestro's catalogue) had become over the years a dear friend and comrade. He threw me the chore of overhauling and redesigning the Leonard Bernstein website. The Internet was still very young; there were barely 100,000 websites in 1996. (By 2008 there were *160 million*.) Google hadn't yet been invented, and most people still used dial-up connections. My fluency in HTML coding (the simple hypertext markup language still used to create web pages) combined with the above average visual design skills that I'd learned from Mother during the 70s was a marketable skill—one could charge people who didn't yet understand the Internet for creating their websites. Along with music-copying jobs, I designed websites for Samuel Jones, William Rhoads, Ned, Paul Sperry, Craig, Virko Baley, and a dozen other colleagues and non-profits before hauling down my Cybershingle.

I was drinking one November evening at the Dive Bar at 96th and Amsterdam when I observed the bartender being fired for stealing from the till. I offered to fill in until they found a replacement. It wasn't the sort of place one came to for fancy drinks. Hired on the fly and paid under the table, I found myself behind a bar again for the first time since high school, decanting cheap well-liquor from a spigot, lighting people's cigarettes, talking down drunks, and drawing draught beer. The surreal, sodden, and sordid month-long stint ended when I boarded the Crescent for Virginia and a month-long residency at the Virginia Center for the Creative Arts.

Ebulliently-gifted composers David Rakowski and Beth Wiemann were there. Rakowski, a protégé of Milton Babbitt and Luciano Berio, was already serving on the composition faculty of Brandeis and was—as far as I could tell—universally admired and liked by his colleagues and performers because of his wide-ranging musical tastes, virtuosic compositional technique, and quirky sense of humor. An inspired and humane teacher, he also made the best pizza this side of paradise. His Music—on the surface, was modernist— exquisitely contrapuntal, deeply felt, unstinting in its architectural elegance, and shot through with humor; it made take-no-prisoners technical demands on performers and listeners that were lavishly rewarded. Wiemann, a graduate of Oberlin and Princeton, chair of the music division at the University of Maine, and a gifted clarinetist, wrote music every bit as compelling as Davy's. It fascinated me because I could not for the life of me locate a single note in it that was not crucial. They seemed happily married—something I found refreshing and grown up. They also both knew how to *laugh*—something I hadn't been doing very much of for a long time.

Lifted by Davy and Beth's non-judgmental kindness, I began drying out, running, and making better decisions. I *slept*. I reached out to music for a lifeline and received one in the form of a painstaking analysis of Maurice Ravel's magnificent Duo: inspired by it, I set to work on a new Duo for Violin and Cello of my own for Michaela and Rob, whose friendship I treasured, but whom I had for several years neglected.

I spent the last hours of the old year mincing toppings for Davy, helping him to make pizzas for our fellow colonists. After a few slices, I returned to my studio and began 1997 by concocting *Silent Night*, a collection of eight movements for chorus, cello, and overdubbed percussion. The intent was to create an alternative to the usual holiday kitsch; to create, as Brian Eno described his own work, ambient music that could "accommodate many levels of listening attention without enforcing one in particular"—that is, music "as ignorable as it is interesting." They were "premiered" in recording sessions at the Cathedral Church of St. Matthew the Apostle, Washington, D.C., on 20 April 1997 by the American Repertory Singers, conducted by their music director Leo Nestor, with La Rue, cello soloist. The final cello, synthesizer, and percussion overdubs were not finished until May 1995 at Bard, where I was in my final semester on the faculty. I've always been proud of what I always thought of as "the carol project," and wish that it had been easier for Bob Schuneman to market. Alas, they were highbrow; too elegantly constructed, a little too difficult and a lot too abstract for the general choral market in which E.C. Schirmer excelled. Even though I was no longer under contract, Bob agreed to publish all my music for solo strings. It seemed sensible to get them all into the can at the same time.

I was reading Annette Insdorf's book on Truffaut when Ned called. "Come over, I need you," he said. "How fast can you get here?" Outside, that dirty, midwinter Manhattan hard winter rain was falling straight down. A quarter of an hour later, Barbara Grecki let me in and went home to her place, next door. I kissed Ned on both cheeks and headed directly to Jim's bedside. Curled up in a rocking chair in the corner, a young hospice nurse named Gilda (no relation) sat, reading a Grisham novel. "I don't want to touch him," she said, voice lilting, scared. "Why ever not?" I asked. "He has the AIDS." Was she Jamaican, I wondered? I gave her forty dollars and told her to take a cab home. The airless bedroom smelled of stale sweat and dusty radiators. An untouched bowl of tapioca pudding sat on the side table, surrounded by pill bottles. He was dying, but his diaphragm was stubbornly bucking on. Ned, emotionally and physically exhausted by Jim's lengthy illness, slept fitfully on the pullout bed in the living room. I sat beside Jim's bed, held his hand, and watched his AIDS-dented cheeks puff and collapse. Sonny the *bichon frise* slept fitfully between his legs as my orange tabby Rimsky used to sleep between mine. One of the cats snuggled in his armpit.

After the streetlamps went out and before the sun rose above the skyline, brackish light—sort of a sickly, underexposed day for night, a reverse of *l'heure entre chien et loup*—streamed through the window. rose, moved as quietly as I could through the dining room and into the kitchen, pulled open the icebox, and used a nutcracker to break an ice cube into slivers. The refrigerator was empty. Two black bananas sat in a fruit bowl by the coffee maker I had given Ned for Christmas a few years previous. Passing the dining room table on my way back into Jim's room, I glanced down at a sheet of staff paper half-covered with Ned's characteristic handwriting. Thoughtlessly, I had placed the dropper bottle of morphine on it when I had administered the drug to Jim earlier that evening. There was a little stain where a tiny droplet had fallen onto the page. I placed an ice chip between Jim's parched lips. He moaned and squeezed my hand. Was there the very slightest hint of a smile? "My boy," he slurred, before passing out for the last time. Hours passed. When at last, the critical moment had come and gone and he had achieved that which the reflexive functions of his body had been fighting, I left him and summoned Ned. Frightened, child-like, he sat up groggily and threw his legs over the side of the sofa bed when I reached him. "Ned, I think you had better come," I said, as gently as I could. His shoulders slumped. I helped him up, steered him to Jim's bedroom, and closed the door behind him. As required, I called *les croque-morts*. They would arrive in a little while, put Jim's body into a plastic bag, hie him downstairs in the service elevator, lift him into an unremarkable station wagon, and ferry him away from the apartment on West 70th Street for the last time. I leashed Sonny, and took him for a walk in Central Park. Twenty minutes later, I stood, half awake and sad, a plastic bag wrapped around my hand, and waited as Sonny crapped under a honeysuckle bush in Strawberry Fields, remembering for some reason how, the afternoon Jim served Ned, Hugo Weisgall and me tea, Sonny spent the entire visit industriously humping Hugo's leg.

Shortly after dawn, I walked the obituary that Ned had typed up for Jim and a headshot uptown to Anthony Tommasini's apartment on Central Park West. After I relayed Ned's request that Tony "ask that it be run in today's *Times* as a personal favor," I observed to him that, to my surprise, he lived in the same apartment in which I rented a room when first I moved to New York—just three floors higher. "I can even tell you where your bathroom is," I pointed out, oddly. No matter how insistent we may be that they are not gone but merely absent, sometimes the quick can only perform mundane tasks for the dead.

I was unable to attend the January 1997 world première of *Songs of Madness and Sorrow* with Paul Sperry as soloist that Troy Peters conducted with the Tacoma Chamber Players in Washington. I ultimately paid for the Cleveland Chamber Orchestra, conducted by Victoria Bond, to record the work with Paul in April 1999. In the meantime, however, the recording of *Vera* had to be sorted out. Benjamin Milstein, a pianist and composer (then working as my assistant) known primarily for his electronica, and I worked our way through the dozens of VHS tapes containing the 42 tracks on which several live performances of *Vera* had been laid, creating first a production map, then a choreographed "live mix" combining all the chosen takes with numerous overdubs. As producer, I was after a supersaturated sound world, hyper-vivid and gauche, the musical equivalent to the imagery of Quentin Tarantino. Through extensive overdubbing additional electric bass, guitar, and synthesizer tracks (most of which were performed either by myself or by my Bard students), as well as subliminal vocals, Ben and I made *Vera* sound a bit like Nelson Riddle on mescaline. The resulting cast recording was ultimately released on the Composers Recording Incorporated (CRI) label. As it turns out, giving *Vera* to CRI was a mistake. *Vera* had the dubious distinction of being CRI's final release. As such, it received no promotion, never went into stores, and received no reviews. Otto Luening, Douglas Moore, and Oliver Daniel founded CRI in 1954. Dedicated to promoting new music and American composers, CRI released over 600 recordings on LP, cassette, and CD over its 49-year history. In 2003, the label was forced to go out of business due to financial pressures. (I was serving on its board at the time, was one of the people around the table invited on at the last minute—much too late, as it happens—to try and save the situation by proposing new models that reflected the enormous changes that were taking place in the business.) Ownership of the CRI catalogue moved to New World Records in 2006. Since then New World has worked to maintain the availability of many CRI titles that had gone out of print or never been put into digital format.

In April, I produced the recording sessions at Town Hall on 43rd Street that resulted in the Arsis release called *Strings Attached*. Robert, for whom I had written in 1985 a Suite for Cello and in 1987, the "editorial etude" *Higher, Louder, Faster!* was available to record the cello works. Since I couldn't reach Lisa Ponton (for whom I had written the Suite for Viola; she was living in Europe at the time) I asked west-coast-based Charles Noble to record it. Michaela arrived from Europe to record the Suite for Violin from 1984 and the new Duo with Robert. Suitcases, violin, and daughter in tow, Michaela decanted from her cab like *spumante* from a bottle. We hugged awkwardly. After making them comfortable, I invited Michaela out to the back porch around which the cocoon of apartment buildings flew up over twenty stories on all sides. As I poured her a glass of wine in full view of the over six hundred windows, I recalled dropping my glass over the porch's edge

Mel Rosenthal's Arsis CD cover photo, taken onstage at Town Hall in New York City on April 2, 1997, featuring treasured friends Michaela Paetsch (*left*) and Robert La Rue engaging with their instruments as I stand watch.

only a few months earlier. The absence of privacy was coolly apt. There were just discernable enough echoes of what we had once been together—or what I had wanted us to be—that our conversation stumbled inelegantly to its end as what the Irish call piss rain began to fall.

I also served during that time as artist in residence at Baylor University, and commuted every few weeks to Waco, Texas to teach, and to produce the record of wind ensemble works that Michael Haithcock and I were recording for Bob Schuneman's label. Mike and Rob recorded the new version of the Cello Concerto, which Rob had premiered with Leon and the American Symphony Chamber Orchestra the previous May, for wind symphony and cello, as well as other works, including a wind band version of the Flügelhorn Concerto I'd penned for Donna. To my surprise, there was enough left of my half of the divorce settlement to live off for the rest of the summer, during which I spent crafting a reduced orchestration for *Shining Brow* for the Chicago Opera Theater revival in August at the 1400 seat Merle Reskin Theater. The Reskin had risen, by way of the Blackstone, from the ashes of the Iroquois Theater, in which 571 lives were lost in a tragic fire in 1903. It was a perfect venue for director Ken Cazan's revival. Lots of tape rolled, and Bob spent a lot of time getting it into the can, but a recording was ultimately dished when Schuneman and AGMA (the American Guild of Musical Artists)—the union representing the chorus and cast— could not agree on financial remuneration for the chorus.

Paul flew out for the première of the new version of the opera, and I was touched that the Curtis Institute's Alumni Association booked a room at the Hilton and threw a small reception. (I realize now that I should have filled the room with luminaries, but back then, I sincerely thought that *other* people did that for one.) As the opera's composer, it was indisputably my Green Room, I thought, happy, secure, with Paul at my side. I wore my first tuxedo—purchased only a few days earlier at Brooks Brothers with some of the divorce settlement.

Father drove Wallace Tomchek, the beloved, charismatic chorus teacher who first introduced me to music as a religion when I was fifteen years old, and whom I had not seen in two decades, from Milwaukee to Chicago to attend a performance. We met beforehand for tea in the lobby of the Hilton. "You look like a young Napoleon in that tuxedo," observed Wally as he hugged me. His snowy white hair and beard, closely cropped, smelled of lavender soap. He wore a baggy blue sweater with coffee cups of various colors embroidered on it. I laughed, asked, "Did Napoleon wear tuxedos?" "It does look good," admitted Father. "Where did you rent it?" "Dad," I said, placing my fingertips to my temples. Wally motioned for me to sit down. I declined, motioning for him to sit down in my place. "Your father Earl dragged me down here," said Wally, half-serious. "He told me I couldn't miss a revival of *Shining Brow*." "You know," I told him, eyes tearing, "I think of you, Wally, every time the curtain goes up on one of my shows. Thank you for everything that you taught me." He removed his round, wire-rimmed glasses to wipe tears from them. "Well," he looked away, "you have no idea how proud your Father is of you. *No idea*." As I looked at Father I felt, gathering within, the familiar wari-

Standing in front of the Reskin Theater in Chicago July 2, 1997, with my librettist Paul Muldoon (*right*), on the eventful day that *Shining Brow* was first revived by Chicago Opera Theater, I bought my first tuxedo, and saw my father for the last time (photograph by Ben Milstein).

ness and emotional remoteness. *I do know,* I thought. *I do. And it means a lot, but just not enough, or in the right way. Not anymore.* Beat. "It's time to go," I replied.

I walked them across the street to the Reskin Theater and led them through the stage door. In the wings, I introduced Father to Ken Cazan, who led him to his seat in the house. With the stage manager's permission, I led Wally onstage. Hands clasped behind his back like a naval captain walking the deck of a colleague's new command, he looked up and scanned with a professional's eye and obvious pleasure the rows of Ellipsoidals and Fresnels; then he cocked his head, closed his eyes, and listened for a moment to the primordial sound of the orchestra tuning bubbling up from the pit. A quick smile, and a raised finger: "Ever notice," he said, "that the sound of the audience through the fire curtain is like the sound of rain in the trees?" Beat. We listened together for a moment, each in his own thoughts. Then, a look of completion on his face, he cleared his hands like a dealer leaving the table, pivoted, said, "Three *toi's*," purposefully crossed the stage, stopped to shake the hand of the stage manager, and disappeared into the darkness of the wings behind her. I never saw Wally or Father again.

◆◆ 18 ◆◆

Other, More Important Things
1997–2001

"What have I got? Resilience I've got," I wrote in my journal, sitting on a box filled with books, remembering the snowy night in Philadelphia when I had written, *"What have I got? Drive I've got."* I looked around me at the paintings stacked against one wall, the Baldwin up on its side like a beached whale, dozens of boxes of books, and allowed my gaze to rest tenderly on Clara, curled like a Nautilus shell in a pile of my dirty clothes and cleaning herself as cats do by licking her paw and then passing it as though worried across her brow. The front door opened on to the lobby; the building's driers vented just outside the windows, which looked out at a 45-foot-tall wall of schist. It was dark, and damp, and it smelled funny; nevertheless, it was a fresh start. A real-estate transaction involving my landlords (three brothers named Ho who each year sent out a Christmas card that read: "Ho. Ho. Ho.") and the one across the street in which my downstairs neighbors and I were pawns had landed me in a new place on 98th Street between West End Avenue and Riverside Drive. I pulled a daybook from 1981 out of a box, found the page, and read, *"Who knows what talent is? Inspiration? I know I've got my portion. I can't even imagine being alive at 30."* Somehow, I'd made it to 36. I wrote again the words I'd written at the age of 21: *"Whatever I lack in talent, I'll make up in hard work,"* slapped the pen down, picked Clara up, and began pushing things off the teak Javanese daybed I'd purchased from the lesbian couple in Albuquerque. *I'll be an Art Monk,* I thought, *and this shall be my Monk Bed.* I rarely slept for more than four hours anyway, so a bed was superfluous. A fulfilling personal life— hopes of one day having a family—these I determined to set aside until I felt that I was no longer a danger to myself or others. *Work works when nothing else works,* I thought. *Like Heaney's poem. I must ask Muldoon about that one. And nothing else has worked, so I shall work.* I sank down on the bed, tucking Clara in my armpit. *Am I "a dog barking at the image of his own barking?"* I asked, nuzzling her as she began to meticulously groom every square inch of my forearm. *There've been nights I only bothered to find home because of you, my tiny sack of bones.* I closed my eyes and dreamed this conversation: "You know, of course, that you are dead?" asked the Other Daron. "Oh?" I replied, "Do you recall how I came to die?" "Yes. You hugged your soul to death. You put your forehead down against one arm and you thought of yourself until you suffocated." "Is this, then, my resurrection?" "No. This is the coroner's report on causation."

A commission from the College Band Directors National Association (over a hundred colleges ultimately joined the consortium) for a full-length opera on a subject of my choice (using a librettist of my choice) came by way of a phone call from Michael Haithcock, then director of bands at Baylor University, and soon to serve a term as president of the CBDNA. I made a conscious decision to fight my "battle with symbolic collapse" by making an opera based on Shakespeare's *Othello* called *Bandanna*. I was all too aware that, as Julia Kristeva pointed out in *Black Sun*, "depression is the hidden face of Narcissus" and that Christian theology, in which I had been immersed since childhood, considered sadness a sin. Dante even consigned the melancholic to "the city of grief" in *Inferno*. "The loss of the mother," wrote Kristeva, "is a biological and psychic necessity, the first step on the way to becoming autonomous. Matricide is our vital necessity, the *sine-qua-non* condition of our individuation, provided that it takes place under optimal circumstances and can be eroticized."

I chose to treat *Othello* because I hoped that spending time as an artist working to transform my feelings of anger, betrayal, self-hatred, and guilt into art would provide me a way to escape the web of incomplete mourning—not just for my marriage but also for Mother—in which I felt trapped. I decided to recast the Venetian tale of the Moor (renaming Othello Morales) in a 1968 Texas-Mexico border town. The result was *Bandanna*, a two-act grand opera. The commission stipulated only that I could not use strings (except for contrabasses) in the pit. I asked Paul Muldoon to write the libretto based, as usual, on a detailed co-written treatment in which I stipulated the exact length and form of every scene. Also, as usual, I stipulated the structural underpinnings of every scene, aria, and ensemble.

Joseph McClain, general director of Austin Lyric Opera until 2002, when he resettled to San Miguel de Allende and founded Ópera de San Miguel, and I knew one another because of an opera treatment that Muldoon and I had written for him a few months previous about Lyndon B. Johnson. Music director (and company co-founder, along with McClain) Walter Decloux—whose son had been killed in action in Vietnam—had movingly demonstrated his trust in us as a creative team by signing off on a scene from that opera Paul and I had set at the Massacre at Mai Lai. Even though "in earnest" money had been wired to me in Venice while I was there with Donna, *LBJ* foundered when a major corporate sponsor (per Joe) feared a local backlash if the project was pursued. Still, I enjoyed working with McClain; so, when Mike Haithcock asked me to reach out to professional opera companies in November 1997 to see if one of them might be interested in producing *Bandanna*, I brought the project to Joe.

Only after the commission agreement was signed, my librettist engaged, and our detailed dramaturgical treatment co-written, did I begin discussing with Joe a side agreement that would make the ALO the "lead company" in a consortium that would—if he gave the go-ahead—produce *Bandanna* "no earlier than the 2000/2001 season." On the surface, at least, it appeared that I had succeeded in delivering, through Joe, a major company to present the opera CBDNA had just commissioned. Joe's position as both a consulting dramaturge and as artistic director of the ALO meant that anytime he disagreed with one of my creative decisions he could simply threaten not to produce the opera until I capitulated. Unfortunately for me, I don't work well when I feel as though I'm being manipulated, so I was forced to disconnect Joe and ALO from the project. To their credit, though disappointed, the CBDNA honored their contract with me, so Paul and I forged ahead. The CBDNA national convention was scheduled for Austin that year. I contacted Robert DeSimone, director of the UT-Austin Opera Program (now the Butler Opera Center) and asked him if he would stage the work, and he agreed.

I composed the prologue and most of the first scene of the first act at the MacDowell Colony during January 1998 in Chapman Studio, the most remote of the many cabins dotting the property—fully a mile away from Colony Hall. I would have completed the entire first act there but for the fact that there were 26 inches of snow on the ground. For nearly four hours each day, I slogged through the snow in a decidedly non-meditative frame of mind—the walk to and from the payphone, where I was jacking in to check E-mail and to send Muldoon requests for changes, took over an hour each way. Returning to New York, I wrote the balance of the vocal score in the new 98th Street apartment. My work routine consisted of rising at 7 a.m. drinking 7–8 espressos while composing until 5 p.m. at which point I would eat the same thing at a nearby burrito joint and speak Spanish with the waitress for exactly thirty minutes, return home, and copy out by hand the fair score for another two hours each evening while downing a bottle of viscous, leesy Antinori Montepulciano. The vocal score was completed in this fashion over a period of four months.

When Paul and I crafted the treatment for the last scene of *Bandanna* I was completely aware of the agonizing sequence of matricidal, fratricidal, uxoricidal, and suicidal acts that I wanted ritualistically enacted. Taken together, the sequence of dramatic beats constituted as comprehensive an expression of my emotional state at the time, as the ending of *Brow* was when I wrote it, and the apotheotic ending of *Amelia* when I wrote it. In her concluding *Willow Aria,* the music that Mona sang was written from the point of view that she already considered herself—as Mother in her final days had—dead; the strings that accompanied her were, throughout the opera, associated with death, since they—unlike the wind instruments featured everywhere else in the score—*did not breathe.* The transition from Mona's aria to her murder featured three violins, and it tracked Morales with cinematic underscoring as he crossed the stage with excruciating slowness, to her hotel room door. He was Charon, I wanted to say, and he was in *no hurry.* They were both already in the Underworld: Morales was Orpheus to Mona's Eurydice. In fact, both Mona and Morales intuited what *had* to happen—that Hagen Family fatalism—and were now simply going through the motions: once Morales opened the door, his deputy Cassidy appeared. Morales executed his friend. He then turned, as though in a dream, to Mona. He strangled his wife, who did not struggle, with the opera's eponymous bandanna. Then, without pausing, except to muse quizzically, and *without horror,* "Holy Mother of God," he killed himself by placing his service revolver in his mouth and blowing himself away.

Later, one critic complained that "the final scene—the climactic murder-suicide—is anguished to a grotesque degree." If I could have made it even *more* grotesque, *more* like a slow-motion nightmare, I would have, so focused was I on capturing my inner state. While composing it, I felt such an intense sense of closure that, at one point, I felt as though Mother was standing behind me at the piano, her hand resting on my shoulder. When the chorus crashes in, they sing *"Dona nobis pacem"* (pun intended) to anything but comforting music, the trombones, in fact, are marked *"fffff blaring like the horns of an approaching semi."*

In those days, I used to send a copy of the vocal score of whichever opera I had just finished to Jack Beeson, who would go through it and make marginal comments very lightly in pencil like "You buried a plot point here. This is an intrinsically slow word: why did you set it fast? Courageous! This is the Nieces from Britten's *Grimes!* Watch the *passaggio!*" Jack, published by Boosey and Hawkes and ensconced with tenure at Columbia University, was a major behind-the-scenes power broker during the years that I was coming up. I respected his opera *Lizzie Borden* and particularly liked *Hello, Out There,* a trenchant one act. Jack's knack for setting American English in a way that was understandable across the footlights I admired, though his scores rarely reached for broad lyricism. During spring 1998, Jack and I played and sang (and argued) our way through *Bandanna* one afternoon at his spacious Columbia University faculty apartment while his wife Nora kept the tea coming. "You're going to take a pasting from amateurs for the male ranges," he predicted. "The men are slung high. I get it: they are all being macho. I know you want them to sound that way. Moreover, I see you are saving up the sound of the female voice for the final scene. However, you are pushing the limits of *verismo* writing. Maybe too much."

A few months before the premiere, presenting the great conductor and promoter of the wind ensemble as a performing group Frederick Fennell with a copy of *Bandanna*, I asked Freddy how he thought the piece would go over in the band world. Eyes twinkling, he told me that he felt that there were three kinds of band conductors: "First, you have what I call the 'Educators': they teach high school band and play simplified arrangements of pop songs and movie themes. Then there are the 'Spit and Polish Men': they play marches, and for them music history stalled around the time of Holst. Finally, there are the 'Maestros': they could have been orchestra conductors but chose to conduct bands because they love them. These men and women are hungry for new repertoire and can have a better grasp of the symphonic repertoire than their colleagues can in the orchestra world. Almost none of them know anything about opera, my boy, so your opera is doomed."

The February 1999 staged premiere of *Bandanna* at the University of Texas Austin was conducted by Michael Haithcock and directed by Robert DeSimone. Several days into rehearsals, the alcoholic baritone singing Kane simply stopped showing up. I contacted Paul Kreider, who flew in from Vegas and learned the role of Kane in less than a week. A champion. With relief and gratitude, I paid his fee myself.

Muldoon and his wife Jean Korelitz flew in from the coast. David Del Tredici, who also flew in for the premiere, wept openly during the final scene and called me his "new hero." Ukrainian-American composer, pianist, and conductor Virko Baley, who had for years conducted the Nevada Symphony Orchestra and was Distinguished Professor of composition at UNLV, drew me aside after the final curtain and, sort of stunned, whispered, "These guys have no idea what you've given them. Watch out." A dynamic, thrilling artist, tough-minded thinker, and professional swashbuckler, Virko and I had had some great adventures together. I admired him: he knew life, and he wasn't afraid in his music to offend. He had entirely grasped the fact that *Bandanna's* score *meant* to push people's limits. "These characters are at the end of their shit," he told me later. "They're *in extremis.* That'll make people who like their opera tame uncomfortable. *The whole fucking score is unsettling.* You got what you wanted, tiger."

Kreider and Thomas Leslie, director of the UNLV Division of Wind Band Studies, felt as though *Bandanna* should be recorded. With Mike Haithcock's political and fundraising support, and Bob Schuneman's record label support as editor in Boston, they succeeded in surmounting the enormous organizational and financial challenges involved in getting the two-hour opera recorded in Las Vegas. Ben Milstein led the superb recording team, which included Joakim Goßman, a brilliant young tönmeister; Edwin Powell, a protégé of Haithcock's I'd first met in Waco who ultimately wrote his doctoral dissertation about the process of commissioning the opera from the band world's point of view; Eli Marshall, Ned's grandnephew and my former pupil; and Gilda Lyons, working on her doctorate in composition at Pitt at the time. Lynn Trippy, who had served as chief accompanist for *Vera*, prepared the singers and chorus, and Tom Leslie superbly prepared his UNLV Wind Orchestra before my arrival, so that I could hit the ground running as a conductor the moment we began rolling tape.

By controlling the casting of the recording, I could offset Paul Kreider's grainy, amber infused dramatic baritone as Kane with James Demler's rich, mellow, chocolaty lyric baritone as Jake (Iago). Travis Lewis, a gravelly bass baritone protégé of Kreider's as Cassidy (Cassio), underpinned the two higher voices agreeably. Honored as I had been by legendary tenor William Lewis' generous star-turn as Morales in Austin, he himself admitted that the role was better suited to a younger man. To my delight, Mark Thomsen was serving at the time on the UNLV voice faculty, and I could cast him. His ringing tenor was an absolutely perfect fit for the stag ensembles, and entirely plausible in Morales' several over the top arias. Darynn Zimmer was a plangent and burnished Mona and Lesley DeGroot a light, pure-toned mezzo Emily. Singers are my musical family. I love them dearly and appreciate deeply their putting themselves on the line for my music. In turn, I am faithful to them: Demler I'd first cast in *Brow* back in Madison; he ended up recording that work in Buffalo, and creating the role of James Joyce in *Antient Concert*. Zimmer had sung through the role of Mamah for me as I wrote it just as Kreider had sung the role of Wright.

The recording's accolades from major magazines like *Opera News* and industry experts like Henry Fogel, who understood what Muldoon and I were trying to achieve, went a long way towards invalidating the relative incomprehension with which the band world received the opera. "*Bandanna*," Fogel wrote in *Fanfare Magazine*, "is a poignant, dramatic, and moving new opera, one that belongs in the repertoire not because it deals with the politically hot topic of illegal immigration, but because it is powerful music theater." Since the band and opera worlds are in many ways mutually contemptuous, the constituencies most inclined to produce *Bandanna* cancel one another out. As Tim Page wrote, "neither fish nor fowl—as fierce as verismo but wrought with infinite care, [*Bandanna* is] a melding of church and cantina and Oxonian declamation." Even if I removed the band people from the equation by re-arranging it for orchestra, *Bandanna* will never find its niche, perhaps because people like categories and the music draws equally from jazz, musical, and operatic idioms.

Crushed by *Bandanna's* reception by the band world, I undertook a project celebrating love entirely out of love. With no commission in place, using Kenneth Branagh's 1993 film adaptation as my starting point, I hammered out, over the next three months, a libretto for my own, present-day gloss on Shakespeare's *Much Ado About Nothing*. I knew Hector Berlioz's *Béatrice and Bénédict* (1862), of course; I had played through the vocal score of Charles Villiers Stanford's 1900 opera at the piano. I joyously completed about ninety minutes of music—the first act, and the beginning of the second—interlocking love themes for Beatrice and Benedick, another pair for Hero and Claudio; a wildly ironic, cinematic, over-the-top horn fanfare for the ridiculous Dogberry and his pals. In my imagination, it would be staged at the Oriental, and the style of the music (Korngold by way of Max Steiner and Strauss) was of a sort I wouldn't return to until *A Woman in Morocco*, a decade later.

When Gary Graffman called to offer a commission for an overture commemorating the Curtis Institute's 75th Anniversary, I told him that my head was full of Shakespeare, and offered "an overture to *Much Ado About Nothing* along the lines of Barber's 'School for Scandal' overture." A few weeks later, he and Naomi took David Diamond and me to dinner. David graciously urged Gary that evening to offer me a job teaching composition at Curtis. It seemed like an audition, and, at the end of it, I felt as though it was only a matter of time before I received an invitation. The premiere of the overture of *Much Ado* by the Curtis Symphony brought me back to the Academy of Music for the first time since the 1991 premiere of Symphony No. 1. Although he had died in '93, it felt to me as though Bill Smith's spirit was everywhere.

Newspaper reviews still "mattered" to me back then. I was proud that Jay Joslyn had reviewed my *Suite for a Lonely City* for the *Milwaukee Journal*—prouder still, when Daniel

Webster had reviewed *Prayer for Peace* for the *Philadelphia Inquirer*. I wasn't naïve, but I *did* still believe that these writers of conscience and perspicacity had something to teach me. These writers were possibly the last generation of truly powerful, influential classical music critics in the States; thirty-five years later, only the smallest handful remain. When, a few years later, I took Tim Page's critical writing class at Juilliard, Tim gave me insight into the real personal and professional damage (for the artist *and* the writer) that a snidely-expressed erroneous assumption could do. When critic Donal Henahan simply did his job in January 1985 and described how my *Trio Concertante* was "a pervasively somber piece, [which] closed in an elegiac mood, with a long, carefully spun Passacaglia" (even now, I recall the squib from memory) it constituted my first mention in the *New York Times*; Diamond had pointed Henahan out at the premiere, and I got to experience the dread-filled excitement of going to bed that night knowing that it was at last my turn to be, as Sondheim's composer in *Merrily* exulted, "a name in tomorrow's papers." To me it had felt like arriving, and it had meant the world to me.

The audience gave *Much Ado* a rousing standing ovation. Over breakfast the next morning at Little Pete's, I thought I might enjoy a pass for old time's sake through the *Philadelphia Inquirer*. For some reason, I had forgotten that the concert would be reviewed. If I had remembered, I would have been prepared for David Patrick Stearns' pan in the paper in which his colleague Daniel Webster had helped launch my career by describing *Prayer for Peace* as "a welcome glimpse into [my] work's quality":

> Hagen's Much Ado *lived up to its title in all the wrong ways. The composer kept the orchestra extremely busy, but with musical activities that seemed third hand; one soaring french* [sic] *horn passage (the sort you hear in inspirational moments of corny movies) was repeated three* [sic] *times, even though once was enough to kill the piece's credibility.*

Stearns had decided, for whatever reason (or for no reason at all) to deal me a swift take-down for succeeding in doing exactly what I had set out to do. The part of me that still wanted to teach at Curtis realized instantly that musical politics in Philadelphia had swung in another direction. I had a luncheon scheduled with Gary, and was set to meet him at school, so I walked over, and settled into a chair next to the fireplace. As I waited, I focused steadily on the portrait of Mary Louise Curtis Bok. There was a beat of quiet. Although I maintained outwardly a pose of cool detachment, inside I was seething with hurt, and nearly blind with rage. The sense of betrayal I felt was somehow more profound, more existential than that I would have felt toward an unfaithful lover. I had chosen "the music world" as my arena for self-actuation and external validation. Fancying that I had joined what I viewed as a pantheon of Curtis composers had helped to steady me through some tough reversals and rejections.

I had fallen prey to a trap that anyone who had read *Jean-Christophe* should have known to avoid: I had trusted institutions and critics. Poisonous tittering broke out behind me. The hair on the back of my neck stood up. I felt as though a predator had entered the room. "Spano called it 'Secondhand John Williams' right on the podium," sniggered a young boy carrying a viola. Laughter. "Can you believe we had to play that shit?" asked another. A chorus of sheeshes mingled with chortles. I wanted to throw up. "That piece was a waste of our time," complained a girl. A composition student summarized my piece for them: "Talk about superficial!" My hands turned ice cold. Vera Breustle, Gary's secretary, came to fetch me. She stood before me. Coolly furious, I said quietly, "I'm sorry, Ms. Breustle, but I've gotta get back to New York." She cocked her head and looked at me curiously, not unkindly. "But what about your luncheon with Gary?" she asked. I squeezed my eyes shut and counted to three. Instead of meeting Vera's gaze, I looked past her at the portrait of Mary Louise. "I apologize, but something's come up," I lied to the picture on the wall. "Really?" Vera asked. I looked down at my hands. They looked like claws. I looked at the carpet. Although I had long since learned exactly how to be at ease in any situation, and, as an artist, mix comfortably with all classes; I would always be the sort of man who responded to people who played the class card by telling them a story about having tended bar, or copied music, or having wrung tunes out of a piano in a hotel lobby. "Really. I must go. Excuse me," I opened my hands, smiled, placed them carefully in the pockets of my leather flight jacket, and moved deliberately to the door, aware of my exact speed. I walked without looking back to Thirtieth Street Station, got on the first northbound train, went to the bar car, and ordered a scotch.

As I took my first sip, I realized that I had left the only existing handwritten manuscript for the entire first act of *Much Ado* in my room back at the Hotel Warwick. I didn't have a portable phone, so I had to wait until the train got to New York to call the hotel to ask after them. By the time that I reached the clerk from a payphone at Penn Station, the room had already been cleaned. "I'm sorry, sir." the clerk said. "There were no 'music papers' in the room. Perhaps you left them elsewhere." I remember that it rained, but I don't remember getting home that night. Somewhere during those hours now hidden from memory by alcohol, I hit a wall. I don't remember destroying over two hours of music, including what little remained of the vocal score of *Much Ado* and a completed Symphony No. 3, but, when I woke the next morning, I found the manuscripts, half-burnt and soggy, congealed into a pulpy pancake in the kitchen sink. Sixteen months of work.

Three days later, Ashley Putnam and I debuted *Phantoms of Myself*, a new cycle of songs based on poetry by Susan Griffin at the 92nd Street Y in New York City. Ashley had commissioned the cycle over drinks with stage director Ken Cazan and me after a rehearsal in Madison, Wisconsin of *Tosca* in April 1998. "For God's sake," she had admonished me, "don't write it *Tosca* high!" So, naturally, I ended the first song with a high C, which she sang beautifully. Tommasini dished up faint praise in the *New York Times* in the form of a putdown coupled with an admission that the audience had liked my piece.

My 39th birthday rolled around as I served a seventh day of jury duty—a nasty capital crime involving knives and cops. *Larkin Songs* was due in a week to Paul Kreider and the University of Nevada. (We ultimately premièred it together in February 2001 in Vegas.) I was doing double days—jury duty during the day, composing and practicing in the evenings—when the symptoms of appendicitis presented: severe pain in the lower right side of my abdomen, taut belly, and cold sweat. Like everyone without insurance, my only recourse was the emergency room. Fortunately, we wrapped up jury deliberations that day, and Doctor F. was scheduled for a composition lesson. He had me stretch out on the Monk Bed. Tapping my belly like a cantaloupe, he asked, "How long?" "A few hours," I replied. "Probably early enough to address with Cipro," he said, shaking his head doubtfully. Handing me the prescription, he said, "We'll walk to the pharmacist together. If it doesn't clear up within six hours, go straight to the E.R. You're taking a grave risk, Daron." "Why now?" I asked Doctor F. He sighed. "I believe you have brought this on yourself, Daron," he said. "People can make themselves sick. That's what you have done." I looked at the floor. "Why do you want to die?" he asked, quietly. I looked up at him sheepishly. "Change your life," he commanded, shaking his head.

In his memoir, *Palimpsest*, Gore wrote, "a memoir is how one remembers one's own life, while an autobiography is history, requiring research, dates, facts double-checked. It is more about what can be gleaned from a section of one's life than about the outcome of the life as a whole." Completion dates, premiere dates, opus numbers, names of publishers, the fading marginalia concerning commission fees, durations, venues, when a theme from one piece has been recycled for use in another—these are as close to "facts double-checked" as a composer gets. The list of works grows, as does the sense of the futility of "finishing" things, and, possibly, in time, an acceptance of the work as mandala. We learn, as Mother wrote, that "even the best of us are no more than fitfully inspired and successful fishermen and that most of us are, thanks to a compassionate God, contented shrimp reapers in isolated tide pools." I had access to little or none of this wisdom at the time, so I simply worked.

And I worked. First, I completed and conducted the premiere at the Canton Museum of Art of *Light Fantastic*, a 40-minute cantata for treble voices, soloist, and chamber orchestra commissioned to celebrate the founding of the Ohio Opera Theater by Ken Cazan, director of the Chicago revival of *Brow*, and Barry Busse, the plangent-voiced tenor who created the role of Louis Sullivan in it. For the finale I asked my particular friend, open-hearted anthropologist-artist Tobias Schneebaum—we had grown close during the early 80s at VCCA when I first nursed him through a malarial episode—to pen a brief reminiscence of his life with the Asmat. Then, I wrote *Suddenly*, an orchestral piece premièred by the Wisconsin Chamber Orchestra and Harvey Felder on the Capitol lawn in Madison, commissioned in memory of my friend, Wisconsin-based conductor David Lewis Crosby, who had premiered the Concerto for Horn With Winds and Strings. Then I wrote a suite for strings called *Angels* in honor of Yaddo's 100th anniversary which the Orpheus Chamber Orchestra premiered at the New York Historical Society, and a new song cycle commissioned by Paul Sperry called *Figments*, setting words by his childhood friend Alice Wirth Gray, which together we premiered in the Bruno Walter Auditorium at Lincoln Center before recording at Town Hall.

I wasn't surprised when, on 27 March, a New Berlin police officer called to tell me that "we found your dad several days ago. He had been ... um ... deceased for a couple of days and ... there was no indication of next of kin. So, um ... we had to track you down ... over the Internet. Nice website, by the way." Father's decomposing body had lain for several days before being discovered by a cop face down in his own dried vomit on the floor of the den in our Big Cedar House. The immediate cause was "arteriosclerotic cardiovascular disease," but, when I called the coroner for an explanation, he explained, without emotion, "Well, he was clearly an untreated diabetic, and the liver was cirrhotic, so there's that." *Two down, two to go,* I thought.

He had been failing for some time—his heart disease brought on by decades of untreated diabetes and alcoholism. I imagine that, since he was only slowing down, Father didn't see the point in paying a doctor to tell him to change his life. Father's emotions were volcanic. His thirst for expressions of love was impossible to slake. No gesture was enough, so his feelings were always hurt. During our conversation, immediately after Mother's death, he tried to explain himself to me by quoting the toast from *Citizen Kane*: "A toast, Jedediah, to love on my terms. Those are the only terms anybody ever knows—his own."

My brothers had promised their mother to keep trying to communicate with him, but it was naïve of her to expect them to just let go of the damage that a father can do to his son. Shortly after her death, each had an encounter with him that forced them to decide whether to carry on, or to make a new start, with him by telling him that he was forgiven— not that he particularly desired forgiveness, or felt that he deserved it, or understood the suffering and shame he'd inflicted on them with his actions, judgments, and words. The "unveiled secrets of their father," neither ever spoke to him again.

Partly because I rarely fought him, he never attacked me the way that he did them, so I remained—to a consciously calibrated degree—sensitive to the wounded love that motivated his anger. I never felt the need for an apology from him, or to offer him forgiveness. I accepted that he loved me, had done the best that he could, and that he was sick. To the end, being right remained more important to him than being happy. He taught me how to work; but his wife taught me how to love working. In the end, I kept in touch with him because I promised her that I would, and because not doing so would have made me feel guilty, and I didn't have what it took to accept that burden. We spoke on the phone. To avoid emotional manipulation, I'd hang up when he turned ugly. Conversations could be brief.

It was with a sort of relief that Kevin and I flew to Milwaukee to perform together the tasks of burying him, gathering up whatever was worth saving in the house and readying it for sale. In the garage sat the last in a long line of used cars and a lot of familiar, rusting gardening equipment. When we managed to get into the house, it was like a visit with Dickens' Miss Havisham. Enormous, ropy, decade-old webs hung from the soaring ceiling of the front room, in which buckets sat everywhere on sheets of plastic to catch the rain which had been working its way through the roof for years and in which cheap, remaindered furniture added after Mother's death cluttered the once elegant space. The kitchen whose floor we had scrubbed in our pajamas in the small hours as boys hadn't been used for anything except boiling noodles for what seemed a very long time. The pantry was empty. He had obviously been bathing in the sink. Between the kitchen and the library was an enormous, half-filled garbage can, which looked as though it had been placed there for our use in cleaning up after his demise. The third floor was deserted, the master bedroom with the huge bed at the foot of which Mother died was half-made, the sheet half-pulled off. It looked (and felt) like a crime scene. Once she had banished him, sometime in my early teens, he had never again slept there; he slept on a couch in the den, where he had clearly been living for years....

Father had converted what had been my bedroom into a sort of creepy storage room for teddy bears of various shapes and sizes, which he at some point had taken to giving out to strangers and acquaintances alike. There were dozens of them. The den, where he collapsed and died, was like the lair of some wounded animal. Stinking slightly of sweat, it was filled with broken electronic equipment, an empty Cutty Sark bottle on its side, and a single box filled with insurance papers. On a table sat a box containing what little he had elected to save of his and our family's history—letters, newspaper clippings, birth certificates, and a handful of faded photographs. He returned all my letters to me, tucked carefully back into the envelopes in which they had been sent. Like Britt a few years before, who emptied his Springfield hotel room before taking a taxi to the hospital one last time, father was determined to leave no Rosebuds sitting around for others to pick over. Nevertheless, it took us several days to cart away the garbage and the alarming number of broken vacuum cleaners and microwave ovens he had somehow accumulated, to knock the place into the barest shape before handing it over to a realtor who would then sell it after our departure "as is."

Mother's recipe box I rescued from the top shelf in the kitchen pantry and gave to Kevin, who handed it down to his son. Finally, I caught the kitten; Kevin's wife Judy adopted it. Kevin dealt with the realtor; I dealt with the funeral home and the local newspaper. Writing the obituary, I couldn't remember the names of his siblings, or any facts about his life.... We had his remains cremated. Kevin handled, as he had for Britt, the melancholy triage of Executorship. I arranged a memorial, to which neither of us went. Sometime later, a well-meaning relative sent a videotape of the service on which numerous familiar-looking people I have never met shared sad, kindly reminiscences of a man I never knew. When I told Father that "all we ever wanted was for you to be happy with us," his last words to me, in January 2001, a few weeks before he died, were, "I probably should have gotten psychological help when you were boys, but there always seemed to be other, more important, things."

◆◆ 19 ◆◆

The Virgin Mary Question
2001–2004

Composer, vocalist, and visual artist Gilda Lyons transferred into the music department from the visual arts department at Bard and, for a few months, studied with Joan Tower and me simultaneously. Within months of changing her major, she composed an orchestral song cycle, orchestrated it, and performed it with the orchestra. I deserved no credit for her astonishing accomplishment; she was simply extraordinarily gifted, a born composer. After graduation, Gilda moved with her boyfriend to New York. She worked for a while, as emerging composers do, as a proofreader for the New York–based music publisher Carl Fischer, as administrative assistant to the Lark String Quartet, and then, simultaneously, as personal assistant to David Finckel and Wu Han and to me.

I trusted Gilda's discretion and character so much that I asked her, during her duties as my assistant, to sort and file chronologically over two decades' worth of personal and professional written correspondence. Consequently, she observed from a distance (and without criticism) how lost I was. She observed the sad disarray of my personal affairs and the effect that they had had on me. An accomplished artist herself, she was aware of my struggle with alcohol and depression, did not judge me, seemed to accept me as I was, offered wise counsel, understood more about me than I did, and respected me enough not to try to fix me.

By 2001, Gilda had moved on to Pittsburgh, where she was in the middle of pursuing her doctorate in composition as a pupil of Anne LeBaron and Eric Moe at the University of Pittsburgh. Our relationship had long since modulated first from teacher-pupil to employer-employee, and finally to colleagues. Gilda called occasionally the way that I called Ned—to stay in touch, and to keep a professional relationship and friendship alive. One evening, Gilda called to ask my advice about how to handle an awkward situation into which a male composer I knew tangentially who had just given a master class at Pitt had put her.

I responded as a colleague and former teacher first—coolly, and with carefully calibrated outrage. It wasn't her fault, of course. We discussed gender politics, classical music's "glass ceiling," and so forth. Then I responded, a little more heatedly, as a friend—with anger that someone as manifestly good as she was should be put in the situation she had described. As I began to process the feelings being brought up, I heard myself responding with greater emotion. I recall clearly the moment when, in a beat of silence, I realized that what had begun as words of advice and consolation had taken on an unanticipated, unintended fervor. My feelings had, to my astonishment, shifted from friendship and collegiality to something deeper—I felt fiercely, atavistically protective.

Hanging up, I sat for a long time trying to sort out where all my emotional furniture had moved. Having decided that personal fulfillment was off the table, for me the conversation began a rolling back of Sartre's *nausée*, a reawakening of my soul to the epistemic possibility of actual happiness. We began chatting more frequently on the phone. The simple joy I derived from our friendship inspired a gradual reawakening to the art of direct, caring conversation. Talking to her was—and has remained—like standing on the deck of the Staten Island Ferry on a cold winter morning, leaning into the wind, looking

Composer, vocalist, visual artist, and mother to my sons: Gilda Lyons, in spring 2018 (photograph by Karen Pearson).

towards Manhattan as it nears, holding in one's bare hands a freshly-baked, warm loaf of bread; wholesome, nourishing, healthy, and good. I was astonished when it became clear to me that I had fallen in love with Gilda, the finest person I have ever known. There was no haste in our courtship, because we felt as though there was all the time in the world. We dated for a year (traditionally and respectfully); then we became engaged for another year; finally, Gilda moved to New York to finish her doctorate at SUNY-Stony Brook and we moved in together.

Written partly in New York and partly during my visits to Pittsburgh to court Gilda, the piece closest to my heart during this time was an oboe concerto for childhood friend Linda Edelstein. A protégé of the great Ray Still of the Chicago Symphony, and of Marc Fink, with whom she studied at UW-Madison while I was an undergraduate there, she had "played the A" for the other boys and girls the day I conducted *Suite for a Lonely City*. After graduation, she had continued to freelance in Wisconsin, but had also moved into orchestra management. That our lives had long since taken different paths didn't mean that we had forgotten riding to rehearsals together with our mutual friend the fine oboist (and now Australian-based zoologist) Channing Hughes in the back seat of Mother's Ford Granada, or having kissed once during a rehearsal break. I had a serious music-crush on her and swore to her then that one day I'd express my affection by writing a concerto for her. The three-movement piece celebrated Linda's sunny disposition, elegant technique, and great sense of rhythm. Linda premièred the promise kept—a concerto for oboe and string orchestra—with the Waukesha Symphony, for which she was then serving as executive director, conducted by music director Alexander Platt.

9/11, as everyone recalls, was an exquisite day that year—crisp, cool, and clear. Gilda had only just left for school: the subway took her from 96th Street Station down to the World Trade Center where she transferred to a train out to Stony Brook. My nephew

Ryan had just moved to New York to begin college, moved into his NYU dorm room. I finished my first cup of coffee at around nine, sat down at the piano to work. The phone rang.

"Baby, turn on the television. A man just got on the train and said that a plane has flown into the World Trade Center. They've stopped the train. The conductor said there are no trains behind us. I can see the smoke." "Are you okay?" I asked. "Yes." "Okay. Sweetheart: stay off the phone. Call me when you get out to Stony Brook." I squatted in front of the television and turned on CNN in time to see the second plane hit at 9:03. I called Ryan. "Where are you?" I asked. "I'm on the street, Uncle Daron," he said. "The air is gray." "Get up here as soon as you can," I commanded. "Start walking north now, fast." I sprinted out to the deli at 98th and Broadway and bought staples and three gallons of spring water. The sidewalk vibrated with the thunder of military aircraft streaking fast and low southwards over the west side.

Later: "I'm in Stony Brook. Everything's locked down: nobody's getting out or going in to Manhattan," Gilda said. "You're okay?" "Yes. I'm staying with Matt and Sally." I walked out to Broadway. Tractor-trailer trucks hurtled south in convoy through the dark at top speed, ignoring all the lights. I followed them on foot. Smell of steel. There was a superfine white film of grit on everything. Cabs with the back seats ripped out so that they could serve as makeshift hearses headed southwards like a fleet of ferryboats.

Like a lot of people, I was drawn south. Police barricades had been erected, a cordon drawn north of Little Italy. I approached a cop wearing a Kevlar vest and brandishing an automatic weapon as emergency workers struggled to move southwards between the blue sawhorses with NYPD spray-painted on them. "Where do I go to help?" I asked him. "Go home," he said, remote. Then, for a moment, he gave me his full attention. "Oh. For God's sake just go home to your family," he said, anguished. I stared at him, wringing my hands. He softened. "They're making sandwiches to send south in the park," he said, pointing. "Maybe they need a hand." I spent the rest of the evening standing stupidly at a broken folding Red Cross table, spreading bright yellow mustard with a broken plastic knife on one piece of white bread after another.

In 2016, Congress acknowledged that "over 33,000 first responders and survivors are living with illnesses or injuries related to the attack." Some of the illnesses (cancers, asthmas, respiratory diseases, etc.) were caused by airborne particulates. The air really was gray for a while; and we smelled the devastation on the breeze for weeks afterward. I still recall exactly how the air in Washington Square smelled that night. After the smoke cleared, the smell of molten metal and something indescribable—perhaps, if anything, the smell of blood iron one smells when one has a bloody nose—remained—pungent, crisp, sickly-sweet, and bitter.

Every city has its signature smell—there's the tropical fragrance of eucalyptus and burnt leña that greets you when deplaning in Managua; the dry, desert aroma of grilled chilies that hangs in the air of Albuquerque throughout the fall and clear up to the New Year. Gilda and I arrived for the December premiere of *Seven Last Words* by Gary Graffman and the New Mexico Symphony still disoriented and traumatized by the disaster in Manhattan. Kevin had helped me out—as he had with every orchestra with whom he'd worked—by committing his orchestra (he was then the executive director) to co-premiering the piece—Geoffrey Kalmus, a local patron, underwrote my fee; JoAnn Falletta had graciously volunteered the Buffalo Philharmonic, which played it a few months later. When we met, Guillermo Figueroa, the music director, was affable and aloof. Though he clearly wasn't a fan, I had three things going for me: first, my brother was his boss; two, one of the orchestra's major donors, the pianist Ralph Berkowitz, *was* a fan; and three, I could deliver Gary, a soloist of a caliber not normally associated with a small regional orchestra.

I had chosen the title *Seven Last Words* not because of the subject (which seemed a sensible and honorable one, even though it occurred to me not as a religious statement but as a narrative worth exploring musically) because I fully intended it to be my final composition. It has been played several times since—notably, in a chamber version by Joel Fan made possible by conductor Alexander Platt, at his Maverick Music Festival, in Woodstock, New York—but never again by Gary. Working with Gary had been an unmitigated pleasure. Comfortable in his skin, humane, and wise, he had, like me, spent his non-musical time as a teen and twenty-something devouring books. "What's my role in this concerto?" Gary had asked me during a coaching one afternoon at Curtis. "You're Jesus," I replied. "And the orchestra?" he asked. "They are the Holy Spirit," I answered. "Ah. Then who is the conductor?" he asked. "Why, God, of course," I explained. "But. Of course," he laughed. "How could it be otherwise?"

The performance over, Naomi, Gilda, and I found ourselves at the end of the receiving line in the featureless hallway that served as a Green Room at Popejoy Hall. At the front end stood Guillermo and Gary, relieved and fully-engaged in their roles as conductor and soloist. "The musician," I whispered to Naomi, "must behave appropriately, as though aesthetically superior to the patron, (hence, deserving of the fee), but also not behave as a social equal—right?" She pursed her lips for a moment, and then smiled sweetly. "What do you think tea time at Curtis is for?" she said, without inflection. "Practice, right?" I said. "Of course. And composers are either the worst at it or the best."

Ralph Berkowitz took Naomi by both hands and kissed her cheeks, "Hello, darling woman," he said, warmly. Then, matter-of-factly, "Gary was pretty good." A Curtis graduate born in 1910, Ralph was Gregor Piatagorsky's accompanist until the cellist's death in 1972. He was also a composer, arranger, and arts administrator, and was largely instrumental in keeping the Tanglewood Festival alive following Serge Koussevitzky's death. He looked over at me, eyebrows raised. "Did he play it okay?" he asked. I raised my hands, palms up, and then rotated them downward, then back up, smiling. "Of course," he laughed, "you guys, you're never satisfied." He winked at Gilda, and gave her a big hug. "Come over to tea tomorrow and we'll have a good, long visit," he said to her, conspiratorially. He shrugged a shoulder in my direction. "You can bring him with you." Kevin put his coat over Ralph's shoulders. "Time to go, Ralph," he said, affectionately. "Okay, dear boy," he said, looking up into Kevin's face. "Wait a minute, wouldja?" He wheeled around. "It's a good piece, honey," he said to me. "Remind me tomorrow to tell you about a dream I keep having about the Virgin Mary."

Kevin, Gilda, and I spent the next afternoon with him at his cozy southwestern-style bungalow. Ralph commissioned my Piano Variations, the music for which stood on the rack of his beautiful Steinway. I stole a glance at it and saw that he had covered the score with fingerings and had analyzed the music in several colors of pencil. Along with framed pictures of Bernstein, Copland, Jascha Heifetz, and the rest atop the piano there stood a picture of Ralph sitting in the balcony of Curtis Hall in the spot where Norman's parents had sat with Ned the evening of the performance of my memorial symphony for Norman. Ralph was seated with Menotti, Barber, and Rosario Scalero.

I picked the picture up and crossed to Ralph. "When are you kids going to tie the knot?" Ralph asked, hugging Gilda, eyes twinkling. "We're going to meet with a priest when we get back to Rhinebeck," I answered. Ralph grinned wolfishly. "Now, watch it, Ralph, she's my girl," I teased. "Atta boy," he laughed, releasing Gilda who gave him a peck on the cheek. "Listen, Ralph," I said, handing him the picture, "Can you tell me about those days?" "Oh, sure. Sure! They are all here with us right now. Look," he said, sitting in his chair, lifting his hand, and gesturing toward the other side of the room. The light faded as Ralph reminisced. As the sun set, he lit a cheroot, waved the match, placed it in the ashtray at his elbow, took a small sip from his scotch, and sighed. "I don't believe in regrets." He smiled. "Listen, honey," he said, leaning forward in his chair. "I want to tell you a dream I've had hundreds of times over the past sixty years. And you can tell me what you think it means: A long, dark limousine pulls up in front of my little bungalow. I walk out to the curb to see who it might be. Inside sits a beautiful young woman in a flowing white dress. She rolls down the window. 'Do you think,' she asks sweetly, 'that it's right that the Virgin Mary should have to pay for gas?'"

A few weeks later, we were granted an appointment with the Rev. Gerald Gallagher, an intelligent, humane Episcopalian priest and rector of the Church of the Messiah in Rhinebeck, New York. Underwritten in large part by John Jacob Astor (who had been born in Rhinebeck) and his family, the cornerstone was laid in 1897; it houses a serviceable Skinner organ donated by Captain Astor in 1921. Jerry met us at his office door. There was our man—brilliant, happy eyes; a firm, forceful handshake, an intelligent, warm smile. "Sit, sit, sit," he said, immediately pulling out a chair for Gilda. As she sat, I scanned the floor-to-ceiling bookshelves behind his desk, delighted by the familiar names: "Kierkegaard, Camus, Sartre, Hammarskjöld … Luther!" Jerry chuckled as he moved behind the desk. We sat down at the same moment. "So!" he exclaimed, hands together, smiling broadly. He suddenly spread his hands wide, looked at me, and asked, "What is the thing you love most about Gilda?" Jerry presided over our marriage on 22 June 2002 in what has since become our family's beloved home church. Elaine Valby (who, along with her wife, noted opera composer Paula Kimper, serve as Godmothers, or *madrinas*, to our sons) sang *Wild Mountain Thyme*; Robert La Rue performed Bach; Kevin read from *Corinthians*; and Gilda's brother Christopher read Rumi.

My Best Man was composer and arts administrator William Rhoads. Bill was a music and philosophy major at the University of Wisconsin Madison when *Brow* was being staged in March 1993. We met at a masterclass I presented about the opera, adjourned to a bar to continue the conversation, and immediately forged an intimate bond that remains to this day. He convinced me (as well as Gail Zappa, John Zorn, and several other composers) to sign an exclusive publishing agreement with Carl Fischer in New York for the few years that he ran the concert music catalogue. Currently Senior Vice President of the Esperanza Performing Arts Center, Bill served for a decade as vice president of the Orchestra of Saint Luke's before joining the Chamber Orchestra of Philadelphia as their executive director. I am proud to serve as godfather to his son Emerson.

Composer Paul Moravec, whom I had known since the early 80s, and for whom I had served as Best Man when he married children's book publisher Wendy Lamb, also stood for me.

For my particular friend Mel Rosenthal, photography was an instrument for social justice. His Leica thrust before him like Quijote's spear, he hurled himself into the back of squad cars in the South Bronx to raise awareness of social issues surrounding poverty and equality, into the Tanzanian countryside during the 70s to document medical care, into the Nicaraguan countryside to witness the effects of the revolution there. Mel was incredibly well-read, and taught English at Vassar for a few years. (We were both devoted readers of the Aubrey-Maturin books, which Mel could quote at length.) "Antonioni's *Blow Up* blew my mind," he told me once over Mescal one winter during the 80s at the Virginia Center for the Creative Arts. "I didn't have a damned clue, but I knew I needed to be a photojournalist." In time, Lisette Model mentored him. He was Susan Sontag's age and had a huge crush on her; he used to tease me about the fact that I, 22 years his junior, had one, too.

Mel joined the faculty at Empire State College in 1975 and added artist mentor to his folio. But he never considered himself an academic. "I'm a messenger," he told me once. "You touch people with notes; I do it with images. I take their pictures and give them back their image; you listen to what they say and give it back to them in music." He was a poet addled by one-hundred-too-many waltzes with malaria, kicks in the ribs in pursuit of a shot, and the broken heart of a man who couldn't—wouldn't—forget the things he'd seen. Another winter in Virginia, we wept together, tenderly passing pages of our mutual friend Jerome Badanes' just finished manuscript of *The Final Opus of Leon Solomon* to one another as Jerry sat, head in his hands by the fire, vulnerable and over-exposed.

Visual artist and professor Bobbe Perry probably saved us all from scurvy the summer we all met at VCCA, building soups from whence we all spooned wholesome lunches during a rocky period in the kitchen. She and Mel fell in love; they were one of the most beautiful couples I've ever known. They were like Dickinson's "two butterflies," in their questing hearts and profound understanding of one another. Both deeply-committed, sensitive artists who really knew one another. They lived around the corner from us on West End Avenue for years. They bought a country place. "Not enough pavement for me there," groused Mel when Bobbe tried to get him to go. "Trees make me tense." For years, we ran into one another at artist colonies, or late at night, or when their dog needed walking, or over produce at Gourmet Garage, or at friends' openings, and at funerals.

Mel—to our astonishment and trepidation—volunteered to photograph our wedding. In the event, Mel covered it like an infiltration of enemy territory. Shoulder to shoulder with my bride, ring poised over her extended finger, I looked into Gallagher's eyes and followed his gaze downwards to see Mel, flat on his back at our feet, framing up a Gregg Toland–style hero shot. Gallagher, a tolerant, intelligent man, whispered, "Mel, I'm not sure that this is appropriate." Swinging the camera away from his face with a lopsided-grin, Mel wasn't about to take orders from a priest: "I don't work for you," he replied happily, "…or God."

◆◆ 20 ◆◆

Espina
2004

Barbara Grecki, her short blond hair pulled tightly back accentuating her attentive, intelligent eyes, was fishing in her purse for her keys, late for a date, the September 1981 afternoon that we—appropriately for two whose lives have both been anchored in the theater—had our Wilder-Lubitsch cute meet. I, in a suit and tie, stumbled into her as I knocked on the door of Ned's apartment, which was right next to hers. She flashed the same sort of sudden, brief, dazzling smile that Mother used to, leaned over, twisted his doorknob, and pushed the unlocked door open. After singing, "Ned, dear, it's your new student," she gave me a quick hug, whispered, "Go on in; we'll get to know each other in time," gave me a gentle push inwards, another quick grin, turned, and disappeared into her own apartment. Beautiful and gamine in an elegant, Audrey Hepburn fashion that gracefully complimented Ned's public handsomeness, she and Ned were already great pals; she was also conversant with the names and work of the luminaries and artists with whom they mingled, and could hold her own with them socially. After Jim Holmes died, there was no longer anyone to call (as he had occasionally called me) people the next day to apologize for Ned's behavior and to smooth over any hurt feelings that might have resulted from something that he had said the night before. (Only half-joking, Ned told us both over tea once that he had a dream that Barbara and I married and had decided to take care of him. "Well, you both 'get' me," he said. "And, in the end, that's more important than love.") In time, Ned's grandniece Mary Marshall became his caregiver; but she did not fulfill for Ned the same social role that Barbara had. Barbara has remained true to Ned through his final years, always there when Mary is away, serving as a confidant to him, and performing the thankless task of smoothing over the rough spots for Ned with his friends that Jim once had. Had I known that 30 years in the future I would turn around and realize that we have been, quietly and consistently, treasured friends and collaborators all this time, would I have paid closer attention?

Barbara, an accomplished, singer, actress, director, and dramaturge, and I finished the first third of the slice-of-life anthology opera called *New York Stories,* during May 2004. *Broken Pieces* was first staged at the University of Southern California in March 2005. (I staged the professional debut for Kentucky Opera a few years later in Louisville.) Barbara's libretto concerned Pamela, a thirty-something divorcee, who lives alone in a small apartment on Manhattan's Upper West Side. She has been waiting for months for the tile man to come and fix the broken tiles in her bathroom. Antonio, a middle-aged Italian immigrant, arrives to do the work. During his visit, the two shards connect and share a lovely romantic moment.

For musical inspiration, I turned to two withdrawn pieces—*Lilly's Purple Plastic Purse* and Romance for Piano and Orchestra. It occurred to me that the character of Pamela was a lot like Lilly, an irrepressible little mouse created by Wisconsin children's author and illustrator Kevin Henkes. The music characterizing Lilly (written in 1998) I had placed in a drawer, not knowing when it would come in handy. (Promised by Henkes that I would be granted the rights by Hearst to have my musical version published, I foolishly went ahead without contractual permission, accepted the commission, and fulfilled it. Kevin was a lovely narrator, and did a marvelous job reading his own narration to my musical accompaniment with the Wisconsin Youth Symphony. Hearst in the end did not release to me the rights, so, I withdrew the piece. (Twenty years later, it was finally published by Peermusic Classical.) I repurposed Lilly's theme to underpin the more winsome aspects of Pamela's personality. I used the theme of the Romance as the climactic love duet for my fictional characters. In time, it served to underpin key moments in *New York Stories'* ensuing acts as well.

Producer Richard Marshall, executive director of the Center for Contemporary Opera, approached me about mounting that June staged premiere of *Vera of Las Vegas* at the Leonard Nimoy Thalia at Symphony Space. I leapt at the opportunity to reduce my orchestrations to sleek, schmoozy cabaret quartet. Robert Frankenberry, from the piano onstage, served as musical director. I reached out to Curtis classmate Paul Garment to perform the demanding reed book. (Although Paul and I had not remained in touch, his father Leonard (Len)—who had served as Special Counsel to the President for Richard Nixon and played saxophone in Woody Herman's band alongside Alan Greenspan early in his career—had over the years become—as a fellow Yaddo board member—a valued friend.) Charles Maryan devised no-frills stagings that helped to explicate Muldoon's words. Bruce Heath kept the stiletto-heeled Catchalls moving as sexily as any group of conservatory-trained new-music-specialists possibly could.

Mel decided that he wanted to document the show. Gilda stepped in heroically at the last moment to portray one of the Catchalls. Opening night, Mel and I sat beside Leonard Garment, Ned, and Gary and Naomi Graffman at a catwalk-side cocktail table in the Leonard Nimoy Thalia. During the "Strippers' Chorus," Mel's unerring sense of where the true story lay compelled him to document the following scene not in the opera but arguably more interesting: Gilda was staged with her derriere poised above our heads. Mel's camera snapped as Naomi observed, gimlet-eyed, to me, "And you're expecting her to count seven against five, for godsake." Len, peering up at one of the Catchalls, touched my arm and said, "you're a twisted man, Daron." Mel photographed Gary as he gazed at Shequida like a cobra hypnotized by a mongoose. "This," I replied to Len, "coming from Richard Nixon's lawyer." Sound of shutter clicking. "Yes, well," Len replied. Mel's camera clicking again, capturing Len's pride in his son Paul, playing a solo in the little cabaret ensemble as he absent-mindedly remarked, "The President didn't wear fishnet stockings." Beat. "That I know of." Beat. Shutter-click. Mel, in heaven, shooting every face, mapping each reveal. Ned, genuinely curious: "How can Gilda *sing* in that getup?"

Tommasini, in the *New York Times* (after taking me down a peg for comparing myself to Virgil in my program note), damned the show with faint praise, concluding that he "[could not] deny the theatrical audacity of *Vera*, which elicited many cheers from the packed house." A decade later, the opera world is awash in sixty-minute "post-genre, second-stage, socially progressive" chamber operas that share an awful lot of *Vera's* DNA. But God knows how to put you in your place even better than Tommasini. When, a few days after the premiere of *Vera* in New York, Kenneth Schermerhorn and I had lunch in Nashville before a concert on which he conducted my *Much Ado* overture with his Nashville Symphony, I asked him if he remembered the fan letter from the dazzled six-year-old boy who couldn't find a word grand enough to describe how moved he had been by hearing him conduct the Milwaukee Symphony Orchestra in the *New World Symphony* of Dvořák. He laughed and said no. I told him what I had written: "Dear Maestro, you were superfluous!" He exploded in grainy, rueful laughter, and, conflating Psalms 8:2 and Matthew 21:16, mused, "Truly, wisdom from the mouth of a babe." I laughed. "That certainly takes the piss out of me," he said, and began laughing anew. "How like coming home it feels to finally work together." "And how ironic, under the circumstances," I replied, "that the Largo was adapted into a song by Harry Burleigh called *Going Home*." "Indeed," he agreed, smiling. "I am neither a young nor a healthy man," he sighed, wiping his eyes, "but I am glad that we are finally sitting together now at this table."

Muldoon and I determined to follow *Vera* with another act and went so far as to co-author a detailed filmic treatment that put our characters on planes headed toward the Twin Towers on 9/11. Of working with Paul in Princeton that September on the treatment for *Grand Concourse*, I observed in my diary, "What a joy working with Paul and Ken Cazan; how delightful the quick intellectual exchanges; how effortless, like dancing; and how irrelevant the ego feels." I envisioned the stewardesses singing variations on the hymn *Down to the River to Pray* as the planes hurtled toward their doom and the drama on the ground unfolded. Despite pitching it steadily for about five years, I could not interest anyone in even producing *Concourse*, let alone commissioning it. (They were interested in doing *Vera*, but no more along those lines.) Was it still too close to 9/11?—Still too close to the bone?—My music?—Paul's words? As risky as *Vera* was, *Concourse* would have taken us further. I am very sad that the final act will probably never be written. Edgy and risky, *Grand Concourse* was a "show that got away."

A hurricane shut down the federal government the next month in Washington, D.C., when Gilda and I arrived to hear Leonard Slatkin and the National Symphony perform *Susurrus,* a short skit of a piece—that ultimately ended up in my Symphony No. 5—about the sound of wind through the trees. Ironically, the shuttered Kennedy Center having dished the second performance, for the first time, *not* hearing an orchestra piece was more fun than hearing it: Gilda and I walked down the deserted Mall and wondered at the uprooted trees, dined alone in empty restaurants, and retired to our hotel for pizza, relieved not to have to throw on high heels and fancy clothes. Of course, it was marvelous fun to return, after all these years, the next evening (once the lights in the Kennedy Center had been turned back on) to hear the piece. Handing Leonard a very expensive bottle of wine in the Green Room afterwards, I thanked him for the lovely performance. Thinking that he might say something kindly about my piece, I prolonged the moment. "Quite a show!" said Leonard at last, accepting the bottle and shaking my hand. "You mean my piece?" I asked. "No," he laughed, "God's—I meant the hurricane!"

As a matter of fact, Isabela—a Category 5 Atlantic hurricane—was the deadliest, costliest, and most potent of the 2003 Atlantic season. The effects were felt as far south as the Mosquito Coast, and rains throughout Central America were torrential. I've never gotten over the fact that Christmas is accompanied by rain in Nicaragua—though I've seen during the holidays a dusting of snow in Managua—tentative, sneaky flakes that skittered about like children who've just toilet-papered the trees.

Latin America is a bloody clot of Life and Death; a Gordian knot of Good and Evil, Wealth and Extreme Poverty, Man and God. For me, as it does for many folks, this continues to inspire a heightened awareness of possibility, an intensification of experience that renders emotions more vivid, the appreciation of the fragility of life more sanguine.

A few weeks after the premiere in Washington, we made our now annual trek to Diriamba, the birthplace of *El Güegüense*, where a traditional drama reenacted each January during the feast of San Sebastián, the city's patron saint, took place. Equal parts Malcolm Lowry (there are literally a dozen active volcanoes in Nicaragua at and given time) and Jim Lehrer (of the *Viva Max*, not the *PBS NewsHour* vein), I loved the unhinged madness of my mother-in-law's birthplace—where gun-toting lunatics fired off shots next to fuel pumps; people bought baggies of pastel-colored mystery booze from street vendors straddling the median strip; we slept with a machete in the bedside table; and the sunrises, every one of them, broke your damned Yanqui heart.

> *Either it was a discarded bone needle of the sort used by fishermen to repair their nets, or it a stingray's barb, a rusty nail—whatever, the four-inch-long* espina *passed through my Gilda's foot like a red-hot knitting needle through butter when she stepped on it in the Pacific surf.*

Diriamba, had a bank—or maybe two, I suppose; but, why in the world would one buy *córdobas* at a bank? The best rate to be had was at the gas station on the Carretera Panamericana. Gilda's mother negotiated the exchange rate with the *Coyotes*, scary-looking dudes who stood between the gas pumps, wearing crisscrossing ammunition belts, a wad of bills in one hand and an automatic weapon in the other. I felt intense, crazy pride, as I watched my fearless mother-in-law intimidate the *Coyotes* into giving her a better exchange rate.

> *Gilda turned chalky, one foot out of the water, the other in. "Don't move" I said. "I don't know what it is," she said. The pain moved across her face like a shadow. I bent down in the waves and felt for her foot as, reflexively, she lifted it.*

I love this family, every member of it, with the fierce, wild appreciation and gratitude of a man who never thought he could ever be anyone's son or brother or husband again. Gilda was born to the respected Alemán family; they operated Diriamba's department store, co-owned several small *Cinema Paradiso*–like movie theaters—and, as I learned the very first time I was shown the town, built the municipal Clock Tower—in nearby Diriamba. My father-in-law Bernie and Gilda met in Upstate New York, where they attended Woodstock, among other things, and earned their teaching certificates. Bernie taught English and Gilda taught Art to emotionally unstable children from troubled backgrounds at Pope Pius XII High School, in Rhinecliff, New York. Even after a stroke, Bernie can still handle himself and quote Shakespeare at length. They retired a few years before Gilda Marie and I married.

> *Blood poured out of both the top and the bottom of her foot and into the water, on my hands, all over her suit. I quickly checked the entry and exit wounds. Clean. Tore my shirt off and bound her foot. It stanched nothing. "I've got to get you to the house. Don't look at the blood," I said, trying to tie the shirt tighter.*

Our winter 2006 visit coincided with the weeklong festival of San Sebastian. We enjoyed a horse-drawn coach ride around the colonial city of Granada—a town dressed for wealthy travelers—and boated on the fresh water of Lake Nicaragua, prying monkeys off our shoulders—a lake so large that you could drop Puerto Rico into it. We trekked up the paths surrounding the active cone of the Masaya Volcano, made our way through the bustling markets of Masaya and Jinotepe, and spent our last morning in La Boquita on a ten mile walk on the beach to the shore's point (which revealed another point beyond that) at dawn. All the while, we were treated to incredibly lavish and sumptuous meals prepared by our Tia Leyla as well as delicious foods in fine Nicaraguan restaurants.

The patriarch of the family there, Ricardo Gutiérrez (Tio), was one of the preeminent horse trainers in Latin America. (In the Spanish style, once one become an eminence, one keeps horses.) The horse in Nicaraguan society served not just a beast of burden, but also as a mark of culture and prestige. One day we attended the Ipica—a huge equestrian festival—in Diriamba where $100 workhorses were ridden proudly next to $150,000 show horses. Because of his personal charisma, character, and his talent as a horseman, Ricardo seemed to know and be respected by everyone—from the peasant driving his burrow down the street to the President of the country, Enrique Bolaños, to whom we were introduced at one of the house parties to which Tio and Tia brought us during the festival.

The President had served as vice president under his predecessor, Arnoldo Alemán and just begun his term, which ended when Daniel Ortega and the Sandinistas came back to power in 2007. He has since retired from politics and runs a non-profit educational foundation. Casually dressed men loosely ringed him with automatic rifles propped against their hips and came to surround us as well as he—to our surprise—chatted with us for nearly twenty minutes.

"I'm okay," she protested. "I can walk." Putting weight on the foot, she nearly passed out. I looked back at the house, across a finger of water and far up the beach. There was no one for three hundred yards in any direction. "I'm going to ferry you, baby," I said.

The festival of San Sebastian celebrated the meeting of the patron saints of Diriamba (San Sebastian), Jinotepe (Santiago), and San Marcos (San Marco). Evidently, statues of San Sebastian and Santiago were *en route* from Spain when the boat carrying them capsized. Fishermen found the statues floating in the ocean, dry and safe in sealed boxes, as close to each of their intended destinations as they could have been. The folklore surrounding them is that, with this history, they must be traveling companions, and very close friends. Each year San Sebastian invites both Santiago and San Marcos, as he is from another nearby town, to celebrate with him in Diriamba.

"Sit down, brother," commanded Christopher gently, as I placed her in a chair on the porch of the little bungalow. He took over. The blood had by that time soaked everything we had on. "You look like you're going to pass out," he said, seizing my arm. "You should sit down." My tailbone connected with the ground as I nearly fainted from the sprint up the beach.

Faithful from each town carried the statues from Diriamba, Jinotepe, and San Marcos to Dolores, a town in the middle of all three Saints' homes, where the three met and then parade back to Diriamba. A huge Mass was celebrated in the basilica there and everyone processed, carrying the saints' statues, accompanied by extravagant, beautiful dances and music. Children as young as four years old—dressed up in elaborate costumes—threw themselves into the moment. Faithful of all ages walked on their knees to fulfill promises to the saints. The incredible smells of fresh—and delicious—festival foods like *picadillo, chicharrón, yuka,* and *nacatameles* as well as of horses, people and the spent gunpowder of fireworks—all overwhelmed.

Now that Gilda was safe, my mind began to fly off like a busted kite. "Like stigmata..." I shuddered, trying to steady myself by looking out to sea. The fist around my heart tightened. Blood still pulsed from the wound, but her color was returning. "Kierkegaard called it—what was it—a barb of sorrow?" I was going into shock. "If it is pulled out, I shall die," I half-remembered.

We attended Mass in the choir loft above the front door of the basilica with several priests, and five or six members of the family, leaning over the rail and looking down towards the altar. People were packed tightly in as the choir sang. At the customary moments in the Mass, probably three thousand voices inside the basilica, another several thousand outside in the square, sang. The cardinal finished, the procession began. The statues of the saints, covered in ribbons and silver Milagros were carried down the central aisle, preceded by dancers, huge waving flags, drummers, and flute players. The basilica trembled, and I felt what it is like when sound itself moves. Deafening fireworks exploded outside, thousands sang, and—a few feet away from us in the belfries—the bells began to peal. It was as beyond the pale as New Year's Eve in Venice in the Piazza San Marco, but even more intense, with a more fervent undercurrent of religion and danger.

> *"In this country," Chris observed as he wound gauze around his sister's foot, "Death sits right next to you at the bar without asking, claps you on the back, looks you in the eye, and buys you a Toña."*

Every hair on my goose-bumped arms stood on end in the heat as the procession passed out of the church through the doors below. I was guided to a rope like a blind person and directed to help toll the bells. Flying a dozen feet up and down, drowning in the sound of the singing, of the bells, of the blood pounding in my head, I looked first one way to see waves of people reaching up to touch the saints as they pass in the plaza, then another to see the Christ hanging above the altar, hands and feet nailed with barbs of sorrow to the Holy Rood. I looked another way and saw the huge clappers inside the bells, then another and saw the bullet holes pocking the belfry's inner walls, and then another to see Gilda's ecstatic face in song.

◆◆ 21 ◆◆

Pale Purple Line
2004–2006

Just when I'd begun to accept the likelihood that I'd be compelled to set aside my aspirations as a full-time composer for the sake of supporting a family, Speight Jenkins, general director of Seattle Opera, green-lit the major opera commission that I needed to maintain financial viability, thereby shelving the idea of going back to school for at least the next three years. In another life and time—say 1860-something—I might have met Speight squinting over a hand of poker in the saloon of a tumbleweed infested ghost town—he, the editor of the local gazette and local magistrate; me an itinerant alcoholic Lutheran preacher looking for lost sheep. Instead, a hundred years later, Speight graduated UT, Columbia Law School, served in the U.S. Army, and later became a music critic and journalist, helming *Opera News* for seven years, and then writing about music for the *New York Post* for another seven before a guest lectureship about Wagner's *Ring* brought him to the attention of Seattle Opera's board of trustees such that they offered him the post of general director of the company in 1983. As for me, life as a composer had been pretty much the same as what I imagine life as a drunken cleric would have been like—at least until I married Gilda. As it happens, on 5 November 2003, we met by Email:

> *I'm writing to you,* Speight wrote, *to find out if (A) you are interested in writing an opera for Seattle, and (B) what your ideas for such an opera might be. My first interest is in the music; the crucial factor in any opera is the music.*

Stephen Wadsworth, with whom I had remained very distantly in touch since I had asked the Madison Opera to engage him to direct *Brow*, had introduced Speight to it. Together they had gone through it and dozens of scores by composers from around the world. Speight chose me, and we embarked upon an 18-month epistolary working relationship, during which I pitched him more than two-dozen potential scenarios. He chose the last, a sprawling, *innig* piece in which I explored my preoccupation with flight as metaphor for life, birth for letting go and linking with the past, and the fact that the dead are not lost to us. Characters included the Wright Brothers (two male sopranos), Icarus and Dædalus, Neil Armstrong, Amelia Earhart, Leonardo da Vinci, and a little boy (me) laying on the floor on his tummy watching the moon landing on television. Once sold on my idea, Speight green-lit the project, James Kendrick began billing, and I began surveying my chickens, if not yet actually counting them.

My treatment consisted of a freely-associative assemblage of situations and tableaux held together by a purely musical narrative. Speight showed it to Stephen, who told him

Presenting the completed full score of *Amelia* to Seattle Opera's Intendant, Speight Jenkins (*left*), at the company's offices in May 2009.

that a stronger "through story" was required. (That through-story was, in fact, the true-to-life story of Gardner McFall, whom I had met Yaddo during summer 1984 and set one of her poems, *Sonnet After Oscar Wilde*, which closes the song cycle *Love Songs*. I loved her poetry. Gardner's flier father had been lost at sea during the Vietnam conflict, triggering a lifelong poetic fascination with his unknown fate. I determined to use Gardner's life experiences to hold together the narrative before asking her to write the libretto.) Speight told me that he wanted Stephen to direct, and that Stephen would require "story" credit for his help in weaving the events of Gardner's life into her libretto. Since Stephen seemed satisfied to be a member of the creative team and, publicly, at least, to be perceived as its leader, I contented myself with maintaining creative control privately—and by contract. This at least was how I justified draining the battery in my cell phone on the evening of 25 June 2004 talking for six hours with Stephen about the treatment on which I'd sold Speight. His role, Stephen explained, was to "strengthen the through-story and transform [my] oratorio into a dramatic vehicle."

Because I wasn't interested in doing a "take-down" of the military, but rather in exploring the human toll that military service extracts, Gardner's self-contained dignity and complete identification not just with my heroine's emotional state as an expectant mother (Gardner has a daughter) but also with her psychological makeup as a Navy junior guaranteed that the characters that she drew in the opera would personify the honorable rectitude that they do in real life. When I called her, later that day, explained what I had in mind, and invited her to write the libretto of *Amelia*, I took for granted that she would be willing to mine her past as I do mine, and to lay bare her most painful memories for the sake of telling our story. If I hadn't intended to strip myself every bit as bare in the process, I would never have asked.

Just before Gilda and I left for Italy that fall, Clara, aged 24—whose twilight years had been spent supine on a small cashmere pillow sewn for her by Gilda's mother, warmed by a lamp on my desk, exactly one year after our marriage, as though satisfied that I was at last in good hands—began to fail. She had but a single fang, and for supper each day gummed the single piece of sushi-grade tuna that Gilda brought home. I had her humanely euthanized in my arms by the vet.

Nothing had changed at the Rockefeller Foundation's Villa Serbelloni in Bellagio; I, however, was a new man—happy, at last, and filled with the optimism that only a sizable commission for a main-stage work can give an opera composer. The September breeze blew cold southwards off the Swiss Alps and into the open French doors of our suite. The golden morning sun warmed Gilda's sleeping face. Lake Como sparkled below, framed by the mountains where Benito Mussolini was brought to heel to the right, Bellagio itself to the left. I looked down on the villa in which my idol Giuseppe Verdi had composed *La Traviata,* another where Franz Liszt had composed the Sonata in B Minor, another now owned by actor George Clooney. The morning ferry sounded its horn as it pulled away from the dock; Cadenabbia's morning bells pealed. Gilda stirred. Menaggio and Varenna joined in. Her hand drifted to her face as she absently brushed from her brow a ringlet of hair. Bellagio's bells began to peal. Her eyes fluttered open. She smiled. "You are my home," I whispered.

Dennis Altman, working on *Gore Vidal's America* that autumn, asked Gilda and me to read a draft and respond to some of his commentary on Gore's musical associations. Dennis had deftly drawn a line from Gore's Myra to my Vera, and suggested that I consider making Gore's slender novella, *The Smithsonian Institution* into an opera. During a fistful of colorful phone conversations that I now wish I had recorded, Gore and I worked on the idea together off and on until his death in 2012. Another show that got away.

Is this how this story ends? I thought, as we stepped off the train from Bellagio, caught the vaporetto at the Santa Lucia stop, and threaded our way into the Grand Canal traffic. As we turned to port into the lesser canal and began heading out towards the Lagoon, I described to Gilda the rich counterpoint that the Casa Boccassini's opulent wisteria's "fire-fangled feathers dangling down" made with the chaste humbleness of its appointments. "It's like a time portal," I said. The boat turned in a broad arc to starboard and met some chop; the wind picked up, and the moon emerged from behind some clouds. "It feels like I could open the door and step back a decade, or a century, or two" I said, remembering *this is the same boat that ferried the Other Daron around through the night as he slept.* "Would you do it, if you could?" Gilda asked as the Cimitero di San Michele loomed, a deeper darkness in the gloom, off to port. "Go back? Oh, God, no," I said. I looked at the quay beside the vaporetto stop and thought, *there's the spot where, on my hands and knees, I wanted to stop but my diaphragm wouldn't.* Fondamente Nuove. The bar that served cheap rye. Electric, crazy relief, as though I'd just escaped being hit by a passing car. I took Gilda's hand and led us to Casa Boccassini. The sleepy night clerk showed us into the lobby decorated with small Murano glassworks tucked into backlit boxes. My Italian wasn't fluent enough to properly explain our late arrival or the fact that I'd called ahead to reserve my usual room, so I concluded the conversation in German, apologizing profusely. Muse, the cat now entrusted with Fellini's mousing chores—presumably with greater success, having the use of her eyes—rubbed her tortoise-shell flanks against my shins as, ritually reciting Roethke, I attempted to "climb the winding stair." "Be careful, honey," whispered Gilda as she gently disentangled Muse. *She winds between my ankles the way that Pra did when Mother was pregnant with me,* I thought. Gilda stroked her and placed her down in front of a broken teacup filled with milk. Muse so closely resembled Clara that she might have been her reincarnation. "She looks like..." I observed absently as I spun the familiar old-fashioned skeleton key in the door's lock. Throwing open the door, I could have been for an instant the man who did the same thing in winter '90 or '93. *That familiar feeling of icy remoteness. The feeling of being simultaneously there and not there.* I took a deep breath, and smelled Gilda's shampoo and ricocheted back to 2004. "Maybe she *is* Clara," replied Gilda, half-serious. "That would be nice," I said, taking in the same cheap furniture, the sink next to the bed, the lacquered Art Deco chiffarobe so like the one in the house at Rio Mar. Beat. "It's lovely, honey," Gilda said, when I—not knowing why—apologized, "let's go to bed." *I doubt that I'll ever return to this place,* I realized as, Gilda, in the crook of my arm, fell asleep. *Yes,* I thought, *this is how this story finally ends.*

A week or so later, Gilda and I attended in Dublin the Opera Theater Company's European première (and accompanied part of the Irish tour) of *Vera of Las Vegas*. Annilese Miskimmon directed; Jonathan Peter Kenny played Vera; Charlotte Page, Eugene Ginty, and Alan Fairs rounded out the principles. Irish audiences were entirely attuned to Muldoon's words. Countertenor Kenny's turn as Vera opened the role to an entirely new casting possibilities, because it taught me that it was the singer's *voice* (and vocal artistry) that made people believe in Vera, not the words she sang, and not her voice *type*, race, or gender-identification. Since then, the role has been movingly performed by, among others, Charles Maxwell (African-American male soprano), Shequida (Jamaican-born American drag artist Gary Hall), Jonathan Peter Kenny (Caucasian counter-tenor and Liverpudlian), Eduardo Lopez de Casas (Latino-American counter-tenor and Texan), and Brian Asawa (Japanese-American countertenor).

After the show at the Hawk's Well Theatre in Sligo one night, David Brophy, Ken Edge, Joe Cbisi, and Noel Eccles, the virtuoso quartet (an unfair description, since they all doubled and quadrupled instruments) for the touring production, steered Gilda and me past the attractive tourist trap near the theater. "We'll need a decent pint, now," said keyboardist and musical director David, slapping me on the back, "after all the work we've done tonight on that piece of shite of yours." Within minutes we were snuggled agreeably into a booth, the banter intelligent, literate, and humane; for the next few hours we were not permitted to pay our way. An influential music critic from England I'd done an interview with earlier in the day and who had just seen the show, joined us. Deep in his cups, he began to run his mouth about the Troubles. Gilda, sensing the boys' moods visibly hardening into that peculiarly Irish admixture of stoicism and suppressed cold fury, caught Joe's eye, raised her finger, and, in a quiet voice, commanded him to behave. Beat. Her cocked head. Their affectionate obedience—the sort every Hagen or Lyons boy immemorial has automatically given a woman who has reminded them of themselves. Their sheepish grins as I signaled for another round and Gilda ordered them all to put their hands on the table. Placing her hands gently on theirs, she said quietly, "Now, boys, you're not to pay for us anymore tonight. Let us take care of you." I hustled the critic and his girlfriend out the back door of the pub, saving the critic a black eye and *Vera* a bad review.

Muldoon graciously invited me to serve for a second time as composer in residence for the Princeton Atelier, the inter-disciplinary program that he and Toni Morrison co-directed. For the first residency, in fall 1998, I created and wrote the syllabus for a course called "From Art Song to *Parola Scenica*." Six singers, six poets, and six composers auditioned to undertake a regime that required everyone to collaborate with everyone else. Paul and I served as provocateurs and master artists. (I was amused when Toni, in her introductory comments to the class, assumed that Paul had crafted my elaborate syllabus.) The second time around, in spring 2005, we decided to create a chamber opera called *The*

Antient Concert that would receive a staged "workshop premiere" at the semester's end by Princeton students, directed by themselves. Paul stopped attending the sessions after a few weeks; the students and I were left—with the able vocal coaching and pianism of Jocelyn Dueck—to develop the piece on our own.

The story told by *The Antient Concert* (the chamber opera that resulted) concerned itself with the 1904 *Feis Ceoil* competition recital on 27 August 1904 in the Antient Concert Rooms in Dublin, Ireland. Legend has it that John McCormack and James Joyce competed that night in the Tenor singing competition. There is no documentary evidence of this; however, Joyce did win the Bronze Medal that year. Paul held that Joyce did not agree with the stipulation that competitors demonstrate their musicianship by doing some sight-reading and left the stage. I have since learned that Joyce could indeed read music but that he was too vain to wear his glasses, and therefore could not see the music well enough to read it. Many believe McCormack's 1903 win of the Gold Medal launched his career.

Once Paul and I had agreed upon the original lyrics of the songs we had chosen, I told him that he was free to write whatever he pleased. The lyrics would serve to generate his libretto just as the tunes would generate my score. Paul conceived of the piece as a torso, the first act of a larger work that would involve Samuel Beckett as a character in the second act. The libretto (which I set exactly as Paul penned it) for *Antient Concert* was as literary and static as Ronald Duncan's had been for Benjamin Britten's *Rape of Lucretia*.

I shared it with several producers. All felt it stood well alone; all thought that more along the same lines would be too much; none found it suitable for main stage production but thought it ideal for production in "site specific" and "second stage" venues. I'd love to write a second act for *Antient,* but—sensing as I composed it that it would be our last collaboration—I pressured Carl Fischer to publish the torso which I dedicated to Paul. (Indeed, in February 2018 Paul wrote to inform me that he was embarked upon a new *Antient Concert* with another composer that would include a second act. For my part, knowing that my setting of *The Antient Concert* would be rarely performed, I later recycled the variations I composed on the Irish ballad *Cailín Óg a Stór* to serve as the thematic basis for the first and last movement of my violin concerto, *Songbook.*) I finished the vocal score in February 2005 and began arranging it for string quartet. The first performance, at the Berlind Theater in Princeton, was billed as a "staged workshop" at Paul's insistence. I had the Borromeo Quartet engaged to perform, which they did, under my baton, on 17 April 2005.

The fourth wall—and my presence as conductor between the actors and the audience—diminished the work's ability to suspend disbelief. The concert premiere was broadcast live from Symphony Space in New York on Bloomsday XXVII (16 June 2007) as centerpiece of the annual festival at the invitation of neighborhood friend and founder of Symphony Space Isaiah Sheffer. It interested several producers, one of whom suggested that I stage it at the Century Association. In November 2007, I staged it there, and felt as though the piece finally played exactly as I intended it. I subtitled *The Antient Concert* "a Dramatic Recital for Four Singers," but it will be most effective when staged in a cozy Irish pub, the audience well read, slightly stoned, the piano slightly out of tune, and the singers intelligent and fearless.

David Alan Miller commissioned a double concerto based on Shakespeare's *Romeo and Juliet* for flute and cello for premiere by the Albany Symphony. I asked for Philadelphia Orchestra flautist Jeffrey Khaner and former Curtis classmate, cellist Sara Sant'Ambrogio of the Eroica Trio to be engaged as soloists. I also penned an orchestral suite commissioned by Troy Peters for the Vermont Youth Orchestra called *Gesture Drawings*.

On the telephone just now you asked me why, after 26 years, I continue to write so much music, I wrote to David Diamond in May 2005. I think that I finally have an answer for you. I write music compulsively, reflexively. How could you expect me to slow down or to stop any more than you could expect LB to settle down and to focus his energies on composing? I write so much because I write when I'm sad, and when I'm happy, married or divorced; when I'm broke, and (even better, I'd like to believe) when I'm flush. I compose whether I'm paid to or not, and whether I want to or not. I compose as I always have done: as I breathe—because the alternative, cher maître, *is unacceptable.... So please do come to Yaddo next month, where Michael Boriskin and I have put together a concert that will be performed in the Music Room at Elaina Richardson's behest that will feature your early Flute Quartet. I miss you and long to see you.*

The late afternoon light on the main lawn of Yaddo in June was stunning. David and I stood on the back patio, arm in arm, looking down towards the Sleepy Naiad statue at the foot of the hill. He had grown quite frail. "Before I forget," he said, "I want to tell you that Marc used to like to sit over there." He squeezed my hand and pointed at a spot far down the lawn near the rose garden. We turned around, and re-entered the grand hall. I guided him gently into the Music Room. Life-sized full body portraits of the Trask children loomed over us like gravestones. Late afternoon light streamed laterally through the leaded windows. I looked at David: his impeccably tailored gray serge suit hung loosely over his diminished frame. His blue shirt's collar was crisp. There was a large New Zealand-shaped liver spot on his scalp over his right eye. What remained of his hair was without color. His skin was papery and luminous. His rheumy eyes brimmed with tears. "Marc cared," he whispered urgently. "When he wrote *Regina* here, he could sing and play every note. He

Spending time with mentor David Diamond following a concert that Michael Boriskin and I had organized in his honor in the music room at Yaddo, Saratoga Springs, New York, in June 2005, several days before David died. Photo by Gilda Lyons.

knew words. You remember I told you once that he rewrote the entire libretto for Lenny's *Trouble in Tahiti* without needing to change a note of the music?" I stood up, walked to the front of the little ensemble, and addressed the audience. Comprised almost entirely of local high school students enjoying a rare glimpse of the estate's inner sanctum, they were attentive and excited. "A word about teachers," I began my memorized introduction:

> *I have been a member of the Corporation of Yaddo for many years, am in the middle of my career as a professional composer and have addressed many audiences and classrooms filled with students. It has been twenty years since I had a lesson with the amazing man sitting a few feet from me. Nevertheless, I am more nervous now speaking in front of him than I have been before any audience in the interim. Teachers that we admire and adore have that effect on us. That's a good thing.*

There was a smattering of laughter. I asked the audience to acknowledge David and they applauded warmly. "Thank you, Dear One," he said, sitting. "You know, I can actually *see* them all around us: Lenny, Aaron, Virgil, and Marc." He meant it. More tears. "I think that it is an illusion that the dead have left us, David," I ventured, as we posed. He smiled, squeezed my hand, and whispered, "Yes." I thought of our monthly telephone calls, my periodic visits to Rochester to see him as the years unspooled: "How are you David?" "Terrible. My heart, you know." "But Jerry is doing your music." "Yes, but he's the only one." "They're all here, Daron," he said, with conviction, "especially at Yaddo." And then, voice trailing off, "I've driven so many people away; I've lost so many...." A dozen schoolchildren from the audience surrounded us. They had loved his piece. He smiled radiantly, accepted their praise, and asked them their names. He died of heart failure a few days later.

Gardner began tentatively committing to some words for the libretto of *Amelia*. Each afternoon we met—again, I was in the Pink Room, and Gardner was down the hall—and talked about *Amelia* and the sort of opera we wanted to make together.

> *I wish,* I wrote to Speight on 8 July 2005, *I could express how excited Gardner and I both are by what we have come up with. When, at about two this morning, I slipped under her door (she has been lodged in the same house, down the hall) the tenth generation of revisions to the work we've done together here on Amelia before pouring myself a glass of wine and doing a little reading, I didn't expect to hear from her before her departure. But this morning I discovered that Gardner had slipped a note under my door, which read, in part: "Daron—I feel the Amelia project is such a Blessing—truly—and about our work together in the coming months I can only say: CAVU: Ceiling and Visibility Unlimited!"*

> *We did not begin in earnest until May 2006, again at Yaddo,* Gardner wrote in the "Afterword" of *Amelia*'s published libretto. *By that time, we had contracts with Seattle Opera and a final, mutually agreeable scenario.... Each morning, I sat down at my computer in Yaddo's High Studio to write, using the scenario as an outline but feeling free to invent key imagery to associate with the characters and to supply emotional motivation for their actions. When I completed a scene, I would share it with Daron, who processed the text by retyping it, sometimes making a deletion, or asking for an additional line or two.... By the time I left Yaddo in mid–June, I had finished the first two scenes of Act I.*

I began working out the opera's musical ideas by setting a sheaf of Amelia Earhart's public statements to music for treble chorus and string quartet. The Milwaukee Choral Artists and a string quartet made up of members of Present Music conducted by Sharon Hansen premiered the song cycle, called *Flight Music*, in November 2005 at the Cathedral of Saint John in Milwaukee. Most of the music of this cycle ultimately turned up somewhere in *Amelia*.

Sandy McClatchy, who in a few years would serve as librettist for my *Little Nemo in Slumberland* (he also penned libretti for *Miss Lonelyhearts* (Liebermann), *1984* (Maazel), *Dolores Claiborne* (Picker), and *A Question of Taste* (Schuman) among others), and I met when Bill Weaver commissioned me to compose the songs in memory of James Merrill—

Sandy was Merrill's executor. I admired his libretti and told him so. He telephoned and said that Tappan Wilder had agreed to loosen the bonds on the *Our Town* rights, and that he, Sandy, was looking for the right composer. How, he asked me, would I proceed if I took on the job? I don't recall now what I said, but I do recall ending the conversation by saying, "You know, the man you're looking for is really Ned Rorem. Ned's Quakerism provides the proper emotional repose; his age the appropriate cultural reference points. Most importantly, he's entirely secure in his own voice, and will be comfortable allowing Wilder's play take the lead." I doubt that Sandy chose Ned because of what I said, but I knew then (and now) that I was right.

Playing through the manuscript of the resulting vocal score with Gilda shortly after Ned finished his first draft later that winter, we pounced upon the opportunity of giving the concert premiere that December on her Phoenix Concerts series (Gilda's series, which she founded in 2005, had by 2017 presented works by over 250 composers) at the Church of St. Matthew and St. Timothy of Emily's aria—the only freestanding set-piece in the show. Ned attended the concert, and sat where he always had during the years that Jim Holmes had served as music director there, and for which Jim had hired Donna and her brass quintet to perform on holidays, and where I had sung for him and arranged music for his choir so long ago. In the aria, Ned's usual urbane ironic union of opposites were on full display—economy of construction, absolute, unwavering resistance to unnecessary emotionalism, frankly open textures, wisps of Poulenc at his driest, and the sort of stunning Protestant hymns that only an atheistic alcoholic Quaker whose life partner was a church organist can pen. Everywhere in the music there was a sort of cool, self-contained regretfulness—the regret so central to the play's initial impetus, a regret so intense as to border on dread—that perfectly underpinned and undercut the sentimentality of his characterizations.

Gilda and I rejoiced when we saw the pale purple line indicating that she had successfully conceived. The prospect of imminent fatherhood made the financial insecurity of my career as a freelance composer of concert music seem foolhardier than ever. Consequently, when bass player and foundation founder Gary Hickling reached out to me to ask me to serve as president of the Lotte Lehmann Foundation, to transfer it from Hawaii to New York, to professionalize and build it into something that might become self-sustaining, I saw an opportunity to learn on the job; I said yes. Named for Richard Strauss' favorite Marschallin, the international non-profit's purpose was to encourage young singers to learn and perform arias and art songs through sponsorship of an international singing competition, and young composers to write them through sponsorship of a composition contest. Secondarily, it maintained a fan-friendly database about the singer's career, gave awards to luminaries in the world of opera and song, and periodically sponsored recitals and master classes. I was an admirer of Lehmann's voice, but it had never stolen my heart. Her emigration to the United States in 1938 (her stepchildren's mother was Jewish), enabled her to continue her career until her retirement in 1951. She continued to give masterclasses at the Music Academy of the West, which she helped found in 1947. Her poetry and prose interested me little, her memoir, *Anfang und Aufstieg* a bit more, her painting not at all.

Donald S. Rice generously offered support and some advice. Don and his wife Genie, along with fellow long-term Yaddo board members Leonard Garment, Allan Gurganus, Nancy Lampton, Romulus Linney, Margo Viscusi, and several members of the Yaddo staff, had both watched and helped me to mature from an "affably pushy" teenager into a mid-career professional artist. A Trustee and Senior Vice President of the National Committee on American Foreign Policy and a former partner at Chadbourne and Parke, Don combined a Harvard man's grace and self-assurance with an attorney's mind and a poet's soul. He epitomized a gentleman who has earned respect through actions of substance, courtesy, and generosity toward people of all types. The day that he retired as Chairman of the Board of Yaddo I wept. I recall him leaning back in one of the baronial armchairs in the mansion's Great Room, blazer thrown over the chair beside him, two-toned shirt smartly cuffed with subdued but elegant links, crisp chinos suspended from blazing red stays, reminiscing for the gathered Membership about the great swatches of Yaddo's history that had unfurled under his watch.

Emulating as best I could Don's seemingly effortless *savoir-faire*, a copy of *Robert's Rules of Order* in my jacket pocket, I threw myself into building a board for the Lehmann Foundation. I drew upon my contacts in opera, publishing, recording, academia, and composition. Stephen Dembski, Scott Dunn, Lukas Foss, Margo Garrett, Speight Jenkins, Peter

As president of the Lotte Lehmann Foundation (2003–2008), it was my honor to cofound the ASCAP-LLF Art Song Composition Contest with Frances Richard, ASCAP's Vice President for Concert Music. Pictured on the first day of adjudicating scores in spring 2009 from left to right: Larry Alan Smith, myself, Frances Richard, Stephen Dembski, and Cia Toscanini at ASCAP's office in New York City (photograph by Michael Spudic).

Kazaras, Russell Platt, Bill Rhoads, Ned Rorem, Craig Urquhart, Brian Zeger, and others were enormously generous with their time and contacts. Dembski, Rhoads, and I had served together on the board of CRI as it went under. We laid the groundwork for a record label called VoxNova Media under the Lotte Lehmann Foundation's nonprofit umbrella to re-release out-of-print recordings and digitally-delivered sheet music—this several years before the major music publishers began offering it as an option to print.

One major benefit that I organized to raise money honored longtime-friend Phyllis Curtin. I invited Ned, to whom the Foundation had just presented its "World of Song" Award, to write an encomium to Phyllis. He delivered his touching speech to Phyllis and a gathering of over 200 dinner guests at the Century Association in New York. Afterwards, Brian accompanied some of the winners of our international, Internet-based, art song and aria contest in songs by Ned and by William Bolcom. It was the highpoint of my service. I was particularly proud of organizing, bolstered by a substantial gift from Margo, an art song composition contest, funded by the Lehmann Foundation and co-hosted by ASCAP, thanks to Fran Richard, that distributed to young composers about thirty thousand dollars' worth of commissions. Bob Schuneman, in another of his many supportive gestures, agreed to commit E.C. Schirmer to publishing the winning commissions.

After about two years, I realized that I needed either to engage the talents of a development officer for whom I could serve as a closer or begin searching for a successor who was better than I was at raising money. Kevin, when I told him that—just as David Del Tredici had once told me that teaching caused him physical pain—raising money for me did the same, replied that he only got good at it when he started having fun doing it. I invited myself to Albuquerque for what we both jokingly referred to as "Uncle Daron's Crash Course in Asking for Money."

Spending time with mentors Lukas Foss (*center*) and Ned Rorem (*right*) in my capacity as president of the Lotte Lehmann Foundation, at a benefit that I organized honoring Phyllis Curtin on May 10, 2005, at the Century Association in New York City (photograph by Mel Rosenthal).

A few days later, Kevin took me on a fundraising visit to the home of some symphony patrons. Perched miserably next to him on a plastic covered wicker couch in the slatternly sunporch of the ranch home of a retired naval aviator and his wife nestled in the hills above Albuquerque, I watched as the Navy Wife in her sixties flashed what once must have been a best-and-the-brightest smile, curtsied girlishly, and pressed into each of our fists a highball glass brimming with Ballantine's. "Lenny's drink," I murmured to Kevin. "Well, this sure isn't the Dakota," he muttered darkly.

"I sure do adore the symphony," she purred as her husband glowered malevolently at us over his bottle of Miller Lite. "I know," Kevin smiled warmly, "and the dinner was wonderful," he said, sipping the scotch. "Kevin," asked the pilot, "my wife's going to write the orchestra another big check. How does that make you feel?" "Just great, Wayne," replied Kevin, carefully. "Uh huh," he grunted, heaving himself up and walking into the kitchen to get himself another beer. As he walked away, he called out, "Tell me: how does it feel to be such a loser?" Kevin's smile, as he watched the woman's pen glide across the safety paper, did not shift. I wondered whether the players of the New Mexico Symphony knew that this sort of little ritualized humiliation formed an important part of what their executive director did to keep their orchestra afloat. "I do it for the music," Kevin said evenly, folding the check in two and placing it carefully in the breast pocket of his blazer. "Well, honey," she said, hard, to her husband's back, "so do I."

His business concluded, Kevin smiled warmly at Navy Wife, nodded to Pilot, and we saw ourselves out. Loosening his tie and sighing deeply, he turned to me and gave me one of the lopsided, rueful smiles we had both inherited from our mother. "Was it a lot of money?" I asked quietly. "The amount isn't the point," he said. We walked down the ship-shape pad of cement leading out to the street. In the end, despite all I'd learned as the artist member of fundraising duos, I hadn't Kevin's gift for closing—leaving the room folding a donation check and placing it in my blazer's breast pocket was something I did too infrequently to be a successful foundation president. Kevin's keys jangled in one hand. The other was free. I slipped my hand into it for a moment and said quietly, "I don't think I've ever admired you more."

I governed the Lehmann Foundation "like a composer"—the way that I used to perform my music—with complete familiarity and insufficient need for results. I took things as far as I could and began looking for someone with real business chops to take things to the next level. Since the board could not commit enough money to cover a three-year commitment to a dedicated fundraiser, I initiated a yearlong search for a successor of sufficient personal means to sustain the Foundation should funding fall short. The committee tapped soprano Linn Maxwell, whom I had met while serving on the Board of the Joy in Singing Foundation. (One of my final initiatives was to commit the foundation to collaborate on a concert of art songs with a fast-rising, ambitious young theatrical producer named Beth Morrison.) I remained on the board to support my successor. Sadly, Linn was unable to sustain the Lehmann Foundation's growth. One by one, my initiatives fell by the wayside, along with the board members who had supported them. In time, after having scouted composer Larry Alan Smith to assume the presidency, I too stepped off the board. I learned a lot, enjoyed the work, and—given a capable staff—would agree to run a Foundation again.

As President, cultivating the many older opera Intendants, singers, and teachers that Hickling had brought to the foundation in an advisory capacity was one of my chief pleasures. I received much wise and valuable advice from many of them. Some became friends—particularly legendary American soprano, and playback singer Marni Nixon, with whom

I used to enjoy martinis before the fire at the Century once each month. Marni supplied the singing voice for Deborah Kerr in *The King and I,* and for Audrey Hepburn in *My Fair Lady*. One February evening in 2007, I described to Marni watching *West Side Story* at the Oriental as a teenager and finding Natalie Wood desperately beautiful, but then finding myself oddly unmoved by her looks in *Rebel Without a Cause*. "Well," replied the "Ghostess with the Mostess," toying with the olive in her glass and smiling ruefully, "Natalie was a beautiful girl." "But now I *get* it, Marni," I enthused. "I realize now, after all these years, that it was not Natalie Wood at all. It was the voice—it was *your* voice that stole my heart."

Washington builder and philanthropist Pat Strosahl and his wife Joyce were, as a labor of love, renovating a former Church of Christ Scientist in the wine country town of Yakima to serve as a concert hall and had commissioned a (third, based on the tune *Wayfaring Stranger*) trio for the Finisterra Piano Trio to celebrate the founding of a fall music festival they were organizing to anchor their concert calendar. In March 2007, I flew out to Washington for the premiere. The Strosahls had renamed the church the Seasons Performance Hall and were looking for an artistic director and head of faculty to helm a three-week autumn music festival that they had decided to call the Seasons Festival. Over drinks, they convinced me to take the job.

It had been a hell of a cold Manhattan winter, and the rain that fell straight down in Managua when we landed there was smothering. Gilda and I were both nursing colds. The drive to Diriamba was dispiriting. By the time dinner was over, Gilda was running a fever. I lay down in bed next to her, a tense and watchful first-time-father-to-be, worried for both

Enjoying life with Gilda near our humble little house on the Pacific coast of Nicaragua, south of Casares, in winter 2004.

her and for the baby. We made it to Rio Mar the next day, and tried walked on the beach, but the cramping was acute, so we took to bed and planned to drive to the doctor's office in the morning. Within a few hours it was clear that we had to leave immediately. Around two, we climbed in the Trooper and drove—heartbroken, apprehensive, but determined— through the night from Casares to Jinotepe on a road that consisted mainly of potholes and ruts. Built by Somoza, it hadn't been repaired since the Sandinistas took control in '79. The trip had taken hours and had been from the start a complete, unvarnished fucking nightmare. The blood red Jeep burned oil; the gears ground and the clutch was tricky. Beside me, in the passenger's seat, excruciating pain shot through Gilda's womb with every rut and pothole I couldn't avoid. The truck's headlights hit the heavy tropical air and stopped dead, like a dull machete hitting a coconut. Exceeding 15 kilometers per hour was impossible; most of the time, hunched over the wheel, squinting into the darkness, I couldn't move any faster than the shambling *mestizos,* some of whom simply stood, staring at us, in the middle of the road, knowing that we would drive around them—which of course we did, but one sometimes wondered if anyone would notice if we didn't. The lurid, murky green light made them look like extras in a zombie flick. Halfway there, a row of men, arms looped together like those toy plastic monkeys, blocked the road. This was a common method used to stop *gringos'* cars to demand money. I touched the machete under the seat that Harold had given me before we set out for reassurance and hit the gas. Gilda moaned loudly and gripped the dashboard with both hands. The men looked like an unraveling strand of DNA as they disbanded, shouting "*cabrón*," and "*yanqui.*" The Alemán family— Gilda's relatives—had fought hard to improve education in Nicaragua and had been one of the few esteemed so universally for their good works that they had could weather both leftist and rightist regimes. Even though Gilda had dual citizenship, I was still a *"gordo gringo"* with an American passport, a manifestation of my homeland's condescending, strangely self-righteous, and meddlesome attitude toward Central America—particularly Nicaragua. A few days before, in Diriamba, Gilda had developed flu-like symptoms. It had become clear that the baby she was carrying was in trouble.

We arrived at the obstetrician's office in Jinotepe. On the dirt walkway in front of it stood a young *campesino* and his extremely pregnant wife. Inside, the linoleum tiles on the floor and the walls of the examination room were the green of old coke bottles, the mottled Green Room Dream green of the common bottle fly; the same awful, Mendota Hospital for the Insane medical gown bile-green vomit-color as the Sylvania House, the depressing Philadelphia SRO in which La Rue had lived, and in which I lived during summer 1982. Above the metal exam table hung, at an insane angle, a fluorescent lamp whose sole remaining working tube sputtered, buzzing, like a dying wasp, an intermittent B-flat. Behind a metal portable desk, on a huge cross, skin painted the color of a Barbie Doll, posed in the customary position, His blood, gleaming brightly, precisely the "Chevy Engine Red" Testors acrylic color eight-year-old boys used on plastic models, hung Christ. A young doctor shuffled in, rubbing his hands together, sat before a sonogram machine, and tapped his forehead lightly, saying, "Ah, this one does not work" to no one. The other machine, a Cuban model whose guts could be seen through its open back, hummed to life. Outside, in the street, a child screamed—or was it a monkey? I looked at Gilda questioningly, but her eyes were closed. I squeezed her hand as the doctor squeezed ultrasound transmission gel on her belly and slid the machine's wand back and forth. It was taking too long. He pushed, hard, into her side, and sighed as she grunted with pain. She opened her eyes and together we squinted at the tiny black and white monitor, not understanding what we were seeing. Again, he pushed. Gilda gritted her teeth, whimpered slightly, and squeezed my hand, hard.

He slapped a button and a picture, floppy, like an old Polaroid, began to slide out of the machine. The blurry black and white image looked like a stain, I thought, but it was the fetus, he said, in broken English, and then, with a quick look, he explained, "there is no movement." His finger fished around the tiny photograph. "Look," he said, pointing at something. "The heart does not beat. See?" I put my free arm around Gilda's shoulders as she slumped forward. The young doctor took a step back and began scribbling something on a prescription pad. Tearing off a sheet and placing it in Gilda's free hand, he said, in fast Spanish, "Get these antibiotics right away." He began to turn away. She dropped my hand and stopped him. Firmly, demanding his complete attention, she asked, "Dead?"

"Yes," he responded coolly, then, warming, "the fetus. It is not viable. I am sorry." Gilda looked at me and I hugged her. There was nothing left to do here; there was nothing more to say. We were for a moment unable to move backwards, unable to move forward. He moved briskly to the door. "I am late to my other office," he explained. "I must go." Then something I didn't understand in Spanish to his nurse in the other room and then he was gone. I folded the picture tenderly and put it in my breast pocket, and thought about how I should take some notes about what the doctor said for later and thought for a second of the Other Daron and then, ashamed of myself, got out of my head and got us moving. Hours later, in a private Cuban clinic in Diriamba far out of the financial reach of all but the wealthiest Nicaraguans, a young Cuban doctor and an anesthesiologist named Ascencion attended and I held my beloved Gilda's hand as she, semi-conscious on a gurney, miscarried.

◆◆ 22 ◆◆

Hamilton Heights
2007–2010

As I trotted past the Chicago Hilton's saluting doormen for a crisp-October-morning run, I whispered a little prayer of gratitude. Gilda had begun to recover from her ordeal in Nicaragua, and we had just seen together back in New York the first ultrasound images—little hands, feet, and an outsized penis—of what was clearly a little boy. Presently, I stopped and stood, panting, by the Belvedere Fountain. Drawing the fuzzy black and white sonogram image from my sweatpants and examining it, I thought of the night in 1977 when I had sat a few feet away, overcome, having just heard the Chicago Symphony perform Mahler live in Symphony Hall for the first time. Smiling, I looked over at the Hilton, where in the lobby I had met Tomchek and Father for tea in July 1997, when *Brow* was being revived across the street. That night I looked out over this spot to Lake Michigan from the Cliff Dwellers Club's terrace and silently mouthed the words, *just let it go,* scarcely able to believe that the previous decade of my life—especially the brutally destructive marriage that was the centerpiece of it—was finally past. I returned our baby's picture to my pocket, stretched, finished my run, returned to the hotel, freshened up, changed, and walked the few blocks to the great 1889 Dankmar Adler and Louis Sullivan designed Auditorium Building. Since 1947, it has been the home of the Chicago College of Performing Arts and Roosevelt University.

Gilda had joined the composition faculty of the Seasons Music Festival, and we'd begun to build, with the Yakima Symphony's music director, conductor Brooke Creswell, a fine program in which we paired conductors and composers for the duration of the festival. Pat Strosahl and his family had commissioned a fourth piano trio, based on the hymn *Angel Band*, for the Finisterra Trio to premiere in honor of the extraordinary Joyce Ritchie Strosahl, Pat's mother, and the Seasons Performance Hall's principal benefactor.

In addition to continuing to serve in Yakima, I had also been engaged to serve for a year as the Chicago College of the Performing Arts' composer-in-residence. Hence, the stints there. Lake Michigan sprawled to the right, the City of Broad Shoulders' soaring skyline to the left. I had been assigned a teaching studio a floor below where Louis Sullivan had kept offices on the sixteenth and seventeenth floors of the Auditorium tower. Outside the window and only a few dozen feet below, the El rattled northwards in a smooth curve. *I am standing,* I thought, *feet from where Sullivan mentored a young apprentice named Frank Lloyd Wright.* A stately Steinway grand dominated the space. I reflexively tap the orchestra rail in theaters; in rehearsal studios; likewise, I habitually run my hand along the piano's music rack before sitting down. I began to practice by playing extremely slowly through

As artistic director and head of faculty for the Seasons Music Academy and Festival (2005–2013) I particularly enjoyed giving master classes with fellow faculty members. The October 2011 class for conductors and composers featured, from left to right: Brooke Creswell, me, Donald Thulean, Robert Frankenberry, and Lawrence Golan. Don was a vibrant storyteller as our faces reflect.

Bach's *f# minor Prelude*, immediately beginning again when I reached the double bar. A knock at the door brought me to my feet.

Dean Linda Berna had scheduled a coaching of my anti-war song cycle *Dear Youth*. I admitted the student flautist, singer and pianist, and they introduced themselves as they tuned up. "What will you play first?" I asked. "*The Picture Graved in My Heart*," said the pretty soprano tentatively. I smiled reassuringly and sat in the room's remaining chair, ready to listen. When they finished, the singer sobbed. I opened the tattered copy of the E.C. Schirmer edition of the cycle I'd had since they first published it. "That line kills me," she said. "Which one?" I asked. "Oh, the wondrous manly beauty," she said. "I have a brother in the army. I can't stop thinking about him when I sing about the dying soldier." The pianist and the flute player looked away. "Let's talk about the technique of creating the moment as a singer," I said, and coached the songs for another forty minutes. A moment after the youngsters had left, the singer returned, cheeks wet with tears. "Thank you, sir," she said, squeezing my hand. Then, urgently: "I love the songs so much."

An elevated train rattled past on the Loop a few stories below. I asked myself how I could possibly take myself so seriously. As though in agreement, I heard a few bars of Schubert's *Der Winterreise* drift up from a practice room one floor below. As the young singer closed the door behind her and I was left alone, I recalled singing in an endless loop *The Happy Wanderer* at Father's command. *He was proud of me, right? Or was he making fun of me?* My ridiculous little penny whistle soprano voice piped on—*Oh, may I go a-wandering / Until the day I die! Oh, may I always laugh and sing, / Beneath God's clear blue sky.* Flowed the hot tears of a five-year-old—tears of embarrassment and rage and stubbornness coursed down my cheeks. I was terrified of what would happen if I stopped, ashamed of wanting to stop. *Wasn't that what being a professional composer had turned out to be? Singing, and singing, and singing?*

Commuting to Chicago to make money just as Father had forty years earlier reminded me that a thousand times growing up I had promised myself that I would not repeat his mistakes. I knew what Father's drinking had done to our family. I knew that Britt drank himself to death, and that Kevin was in the process of doing so. I had said far too many things while altered that I regretted, and far, far too many that I couldn't remember to people who were drinking companions, not friends. Perhaps, I thought, retracing his footsteps may help me to understand the man who had cradled me as a child. I would walk to the building in which he worked all week long. Once I reached the street, I telephoned Gilda, who was looking for a new apartment for us back in New York. We discussed her day as I walked down Michigan Avenue towards the Art Museum. The sun slid into the skyline. I pulled my blazer closed and hunched my shoulders against the wind. "These were the streets he walked," I thought. Looking up, I realized, "It's the same sky." I missed him. But I was missing not who he once was but who Mother had wanted him to be. Hadn't I come to miss not what they became as a couple but the young couple that for a few years they had been in a photograph?—The one of them striding arm in arm down 44th Street in front of the Majestic Theatre in New York after just having seen *South Pacific* there while honeymooning in winter 1952? It began to drizzle. I accepted the mundane truth that the presences that I had believed surrounded me with their absences were not the ghosts of the actual people I had known and loved but figments of my self-serving imagination— the people I preferred to remember them as having been. How convenient. I reached the intersection of Michigan and Wacker and turned left, followed the Riverwalk to Clark, turned right and began crossing the Clark Street Bridge. In the middle, I stopped, leaned over the rail, and peered down at the Chicago River. As Father had taught me to, I drew from my pocket a penny for Charon. Looking intently into the olive-green water, I said one final good-bye to him, and let it drop. "One," I counted, "…Two … Three … Gone." I looked up. Before me, the tall glass and steel building that had once housed the American Bar Association thrust up into the sky like a knife. I told Kevin about dropping the coins in the Chicago River on the telephone that night. "More than he deserved," he replied. "Remember, little brother, the coins were really placed on eyes only to prevent post death spasms from causing the eyelids to pop open."

In the Green Room after the concert at which the Amelia Piano Trio performed the triple concerto for piano trio and orchestra they had commissioned called *Orpheus and Eurydice* with the local youth orchestra in Corvallis, Oregon just before Christmas, a pale, slender youth of about fifteen dressed in black approached me with a book in his hand that he had liberated from a local library. It was Ned's *Nantucket Diary*. "Would you sign this for me?" he asked. "Why, for all love, do you want me to do that?" I asked. "Well, you're in here, a couple of times." "So?" I asked. "That means that you have met Ned Rorem." He was obviously creating his identity out of whole cloth. It was also clear that Ned's book had come to him at a crucial moment, and that it had helped him. That I existed meant that a Real-Life Ned existed somewhere, and not just between the covers of a stolen book. It meant that perhaps it might be possible to be who he wanted to be or become. "First," I said, drawing the boy aside and giving him a hug, "return the book to the library. Then, order a new one online. Send it to me. I'll take it over to Ned's apartment the next time I see him and ask him to sign it. Then I'll send it back to you." After I returned to New York, the book arrived, and I took it over to Ned's apartment to collect a dedication and a signature for the boy. Over chocolates and tea, I told Ned the story, and presented him with the book. Entirely without sentimentality, he inscribed it as though signing a credit card receipt, sighing, "Oh, Daron, I'm just so tired. Can you just take it away?"

A few days later, Gilda, and I sat with Lukas and his son Christopher, in the nearly empty Miller Theater at Columbia University. His *Time Cycle* had just received a superb performance. After his piece, the audience whooped and hollered. He asked, "But nobody knows I am here. Nobody remembers me. Should I go up?" His son said, "Yes, of course." He did. The audience acknowledged him affectionately. I reminded him that *Time Cycle* had not only transported me, made me forget where I was, the way he himself had when we first met, but that it had also made me forget what time it was, and he squeezed my hand, eyes shining. "How's Kevin holding up?" he asked. "He isn't drinking, is he?" I lowered my voice to reply, "I don't think so. But he left the orchestra, and I'm worried." "Me, too," he said, knitting his eyebrows and sweeping his hand through his hair. "Tell him to call me, will you?" he said, turning to Gilda. "How's the Little Man doing?" he asked her, patting her belly. "Pretty well," she smiled, hugging him. "Is it almost time?" he asked. "Very nearly," she smiled. His brilliant blue eyes lit up. "Oh, my! Another grand little opus!" he laughed, referring to what Aaron Copland had called Kevin's son Ryan over dinner in the house in Wauwatosa when he was a baby. Then he laughed deeply, from the waist, and easily. Not long after that, on 1 February 2008, Lukas died. Profoundly worthy of love, at heart a dear youth, the man was music. He believed (as I do) that Music should make you *feel* something; he felt that only critics and amateurs talk about style; he believed that music was *agape*, and that love is enough. Like me, he believed that having children was the best thing that he ever did. He always gave me the impression that he believed that. I miss him more than I can say.

Sixteen days later, at Beth Israel Hospital in Manhattan, Atticus crowned. I heard a near-cacophony of ecstatic voices in my head—so intense and brilliant that I saw blurry stars as I blinked back tears. Unimaginable joy. Gilda had just shouldered twenty-one hours of drug-free natural labor. It was time. When Atticus was born, he—like me—did not cry. The midwife immediately placed him on Gilda's breast. He lay there in her arms like baby Moses in his basket of reeds. The voices died away as the enormity of what had just happened sank in, leaving only Gilda's, murmuring to Atticus. Tranquil, perfect, and beautiful, Atticus smelled of freshly baked bread. He had swallowed a little meconium on the way out, so the nurses took him briefly to make sure he was okay. Only then did he whimper. When he heard my voice, he stopped immediately. In a trice, a nurse returned him to his mother's breast where he belonged. The child of musicians, he arrived at curtain time— exactly when Sharon Robinson and Jaime Laredo premiered my double concerto *Masquerade* with the Sacramento Philharmonic.

Gilda and I rented the place at 149th and Broadway in Hamilton Heights practically sight-unseen—workers were still sanding the floors and installing appliances in the three bedroom, pre–War fifteenth floor apartment. Kevin flew to New York to meet Atticus, and made a beautiful dinner for Gilda, which he served on moving boxes with a tarp thrown over them in the new place. Britt's death had chastened him, and he was attending AA meetings regularly.

Between stints in Chicago, I composed *Just for the Night,* the second act of *New York Stories*. Barbara Grecki's taut, sad libretto told the story of a schizophrenic advertising executive living on the street named Chip who barges in uninvited on his sister Babs one snowy Christmas Eve and asks to stay "just for the night" because the shelter in which he's been living is full. As Babs turns him away, the orchestra plays the tune of the popular Advent Melody *Away in a Manger*. The effect is superficially ironic, of course; but I also wanted to foreshadow the third part of the *trittico, Cradle Song,* the title of which refers to the title *Manger* is known by in England, and to *Mueller*, or *Luther's Cradle Hymn*, by James R. Murray, as originally published in 1887. The tune's tangled history in many ways manifests the relationship between the siblings.

I finished *Cradle Song,* the last of the three *New York Stories,* in August 2008 for premiere by the Finisterra Trio, Gilda, and Rob Frankenberry, at the 2008 Seasons Music Festival. It was entirely autobiographical: in search of sleep, Gilda and I had danced more than a few gavottes with Atticus and the baby monitor just as Mama and Papa do in the little opera. I dedicated it to Ned, eight bars of whose song *Early in the Morning* I used to underpin an aria sung by the parents to their infant. Nothing happened in it, of course, except that it involved the circular activity of trying to put a baby down for the night. It ended with the parents, thinking their baby has finally fallen asleep, being suddenly awakened by a final squall, transmitted by the monitor, from the nursery. Intertextual references abound in *New York Stories.* In the first act, Pamela's music ends up being associated with my music for Kevin Henkes' children's book character Lilly (the mouse); in the second act alludes to music penned by Bernstein for Sam and Dinah in *Trouble in Tahiti* and *Away in a Manger*; and the third act "cradle song" itself is an echo of Ned's setting of Robert Hillyer's poem about nostalgia and remembered youth.

Ned turned 85 that October. Gilda and I organized a concert of his chamber music on her Phoenix series at the Church of St. Matthew and St. Timothy—Jim's old parish. Ned mentioned that he'd written some short piano and cello pieces years earlier for Seymour Barab (married briefly to Shirley Perle, and cellist at one time for the Galimir Quartet and self-taught—though he claimed friends George Perle and Ben Weber as influences—composer of fairy-tale operas—including *Little Red Riding Hood,* the most-frequently-performed of any American opera) which had never been played. Like Michael Colgrass, who told Gilda and me over dinner in April of 2003 the story of how he decided to concentrate on composing during a stint serving as percussionist in the original *West Side Story* pit orchestra, Seymour—also a superb raconteur and mensch—explained to me that it had been during *his* time among the cellos in the same pit that he, too decided to concentrate on composing. I assembled a *festschrift* for the occasion which featured lovely tributes from a host of our mutual friends, including Mark Adamo, John Corigliano, Phyllis Curtin, David Del Tredici, Linda Golding, Frances Richard, Michael Torke, and Russell Platt, as well as former Rorem-pupils William Coble, Jonathan Holland, Daniel Kellogg, Eli Marshall, and Daniel Ott, among others.

The May 2009 air in Albany's cavernous old Palace Theater was crisp. Members of the Albany Pro Musica Chorus milled about us, donning sweaters, rubbing their hands together for warmth. Atticus, in my arms, reached out and shook David Alan Miller's hand gingerly. Then, David padded down the aisle to the stage and gave the downbeat for the final run-through of my Symphony No. 4. Atticus and I listened to the sumptuous massed sound of the first phrase: Whitman's "This is the hour for strange effects in light and shade...." I didn't particularly want even to be there. But I wanted keenly for the symphony to have been played for other people, and I wanted it to live on, to be played repeatedly. "Doesn't he sometimes wonder," the chorus sang as the movement ended with the same section of Clemens' *Life on the Mississippi* Ned had set 25 years earlier, "whether he has gained most or lost most by learning his trade? Something's lost." I didn't realize that I had been weeping until Atticus rubbed the tears on my cheeks in little circles with his index finger. "Are you okay, Papa?" he whispered. "I'm getting better, darling," I answered, hugging him close until he wriggled free, darted off, and zig-zagged down the aisle towards the orchestra.

A few days later, in Fort Worth, I slouched very low in a seat at Bass Hall, listening as some semi-finalists in the Cliburn International Piano Competition tore through the little Suite for Piano that I'd been asked to compose as a "required" piece. The audience around me, fierce musical partisans and industry professionals, listened knowledgeably with a tuned-in intensity one prays for as a composer. As Di Wu played the oscillating fourths with which the "Aria" begins, I looked at my hands. During a dinner party the night before, I'd placed them up against Van's and chuckled with delight at their cool immensity. "My word! You're as big as Sasquatch!" I teased. He smiled, courtly and gentle, and told me—probably out of simple good manners—that he had loved playing my piece "the other day, around two in the morning." I blushed. "I particularly liked the slow one; the one with the oscillating fourths...," he said, trailing off. "Oh, my *Billy Budd* aria," I laughed. His voice sharpened, and he shed his lofty distance. "Oh, dear! You're right. It's like Vere's music in the first act! Did you mean to do that?" "Oh, yes," I replied. "I'm paraphrasing the beginning of an opera I'm writing right now in which Amelia Earhart figures." His pale blue eyes lit up. "Another person lost 'on the infinite sea,' am I right?" he asked. "Yes, sir," I smiled. As Di finished the movement, I attempted to ball my hands into fists. Arthritis, with which I have coped since my early twenties, made it impossible. Despite the stiffness and discomfort, and a short-sighted penchant for binge practicing, I was a skillful pianist during my thirties, though (except when collaborating with singers) I always played like a composer, was painfully self-conscious, and easily bruised by colleagues' criticism.

Having finished orchestrating *Amelia* during the spring, I was free to choose and arrange music for a cabaret evening for Gilda and Rob Frankenberry and I to perform for the 2009 Seasons Music Festival. Gilda and Rob also premiered *Cradle Song*, the third part of *New York Stories,* accompanied by the Finisterra Piano Trio. The opening concert of the 2009 Fall Festival featured a set of new variations on *Amazing Grace* that I called *Just Amazed* that had parts for the entire faculty, including Dave Brubeck's son Chris, who had joined us as a guest composer.

I invited Bernard Jacobson to reminisce as the guest of honor at a benefit that I organized for the Festival. Like Maurice Abravanel, with whom I wandered, listening to him as he reminisced, the grounds of Tanglewood during my summer there, Bernard either knew everyone in the music world or knew a great story about them. Over the years, Bernard's adventures as a man living an Examined Life included stints as promotion director for Boosey and Hawkes, artistic director of the Residentie Orkest in The Hague, and artistic adviser to the North Netherlands Orchestra, program annotator and musicologist for the Philadelphia Orchestra, and music critic for the *Chicago Daily News*. He'd also been a translator, *bon vivant*, chef, and essayist—even a restaurant critic. Having never forgotten meeting him, and his kindness to both me and to Michaela in Philadelphia during the 80s, my long-term goal was to invite him to join the Academy's faculty, which the next year I did. I have always believed that I learned more from the oral history I had the honor of collecting from the notable artists like Bernard that I sought out and *listened to* than I did from books; as chair of the faculty and artistic director, I wanted to give my composition and conducting fellows the same opportunity I'd enjoyed when young.

That May I was in Milwaukee for twelve hours to appear on *Journal Sentinel* music writer Tom Strini's new public television show to promote *Amelia*. On my way to the studio, I stopped by the Big Cedar House for one final look. I reached the loop at the end of the cul-de-sac and stopped the car a few houses away. I did not intend to knock on the door. I thought maybe I would walk around the lot, peer into a window or two, and then go. Two large German Shepherds barked wildly. A huge Harley Davidson logo decorated the front of the house. Motorcycles parked in the driveway. Trespassing wouldn't be wise. There were two children playing within. "What the hell," I sighed, throwing the car into park and climbing out. I knocked on the front door. Their mother cracked it open. Awkwardness. "I'm sorry to bother you," I said, removing my tweed cap, "but I grew up in this house. Might I come in for a moment?" She was kind. "Honey," she called over her shoulder to her husband, "someone's at the door." The man who had bought the house "as is," a man who clearly could handle himself, climbed the stairs and wrapped my hand in his. No longer an overturned Viking Longship, the front room was simply that of a typical suburban tract house. Everywhere the cedar ("It was too far gone," the Father said, "we tried to save it, but it was too far gone.") had either been removed or painted over. The Lannon stone hearth still bore the pockmarks in it where Britt had lit firecrackers. Kevin's room, the library was now their little girl's room and was filled with dolls, a television, and homework. We walked the short flight of steps to the third floor. The father tapped on his son's bedroom door. A pale young boy looked up at me, curious and a little alarmed, opened it. This was the room Father had filled with stuffed animals after I had moved away, the room in which Britt had protected me the night I had peed myself, the room in which I had realized that it was our Father who was at fault, not us. Curtains now covered the enormous picture windows through which I used to watch the wind whip the trees back and forth. "The view frightens him," explained the boy's father. *I get that,* I thought. I looked at the door to the master bedroom, and imagined Father, drunk, pounding on it, braying "Let me in," and Mother's exhausted, "No." What had once resembled and felt like a crime scene was now just another room. I looked at the place on the floor just in front of the bathroom where Mother had died in my arms. Beat. My guide, the house's new owner, touched me lightly on the forearm and gestured toward the door. Together we walked down two flights to Father's den, now filled with exercise equipment. I imagined Father standing at the top of the stairs to the basement, the three of us boys standing in our pajamas in brown water up to our calves, pushing it around with brooms like tiny gondoliers, the rain falling so hard that the house vibrated. I thought of my beagle Cinnamon's dried feces scattered around the oil furnace, looked for the workbench at which I had built electronic gadgets with Father in junior high school. I swear I could smell molten solder; but I no longer smelled cedar. First, I saw Britt, Kevin, and me again for an instant, so young. Then, I mused, *Is this how this story ends?* I looked around a final time at the room where the man who was my father died. *Yes,* I thought, *this is how this story finally ends.*

At Ned's, a few weeks later, an afternoon of tea and backgammon: "You win," he remarked wearily as he swept the little discs from the baize and brown board. "But you win without finesse." My parents acknowledged that their style as a couple had been a combination of bludgeon and stiletto. "Again?" I asked. Wordlessly, we reset the board. "So, how are they—the little woman and your ... baby?" he asked. "Good, Ned, good," I smiled, poured us tea, and handed him a snapshot of Atticus. "Listen, having a son has made me think," I began, and then broke off. "Mmm?" I moved. It began to drizzle. Beat.

Ned moved. *What if something happened to the baby and I was not completely sober?* I rolled sixes and moved, rolled again, and moved without thinking. "You're distracted," Ned observed. I tried another tack. "Why did you stop drinking, really?" I asked. "Two and one would have been better like this," he instructed, drew a wavy line in the air with his right index finger, and lied, "I don't remember." The finger stopped. "Why?" I shook the dice, sent his piece Home, and waited. He pursed his lips and exhaled slowly. *Should I bother?* I thought. Jim had taught me years ago that, with Ned, one always had the option of simply not engaging.

Try the stiletto, I thought. "I can't square being a dad with drinking," I said. No reaction. So, I told him the unvarnished truth: "I'm afraid I'll repeat the cycle of abuse. You know?" For a moment, he focused, and then he slumped back into the white cushions. "I haven't even thought about drinking for years," he mused, airily. Beat. Hard look. He broke eye contact and looked out the window. "Besides, you're not a real drunk," he said to the air. I cocked my head. "You just want to be an alcoholic because I was one."

I looked at the board and realized, *when I beat Ned it is because he'd rather lose elegantly than win brutally*. This was the point at which Jim had always saved the day, armed with a tray of sweets, a tart admonishment for Ned, and a change of subject. I softened, remembering how we had played the day Jim died, how for years they had had their daily game, and that ours had been his first without him. Ned fidgeted with the dice cup for a moment, perhaps disappointed not that he had cut me, but that it had been felt. Perhaps he was deciding whether he had really meant what he said, or if he had said it just because it felt good. I'm no saint, either; so, I remained silent, observed him coolly, and allowed him to twist. He looked down into his lap. *I owe Ned*, I thought, sipping my tea, *and I made a promise to Jim.*

I counted to ten slowly, and chose grace: "Are you serious?" I asked, gently. "Well, I guess not," he said at length, choosing not kindness, but finesse: "If you say you are, then I guess that you are." I smiled thinly, and in return chose self-deprecation: "I guess I am what AA folks call a 'shallow bottomer,'" I said, shrugging. He smiled faintly, as though satisfied that I had told a mildly-amusing anecdote. In silence, I looked out the window and noticed, then followed the progress of, a rivulet of rainwater as it ran, snake-like, down one of the panes, pooling like blood on the sill, staining it. *We are who we are*, I thought as I accepted the cup, shook the dice vigorously, rolled a pair of sixes, and then another, and wielded them like a bludgeon. "Play me your new piece," he commanded, pushing the board away. Picking up the snapshot he had placed on the couch beside him, he said, "I want to look at this picture of Atticus while I listen."

◆◆ 23 ◆◆

Unmerited Favor
2010–2012

The Seattle Opera rented a house for me to live in a few blocks from Jerry and Jody Schwartz's atop Queen Anne Hill during *Amelia's* production in April and May 2010. I ate too much, drank too much, and began spinning out emotionally. I missed Gilda and Atticus intensely and felt cut adrift now that I should have been savoring the success of having even gotten this far. I was sober for staging rehearsals, which I attended because I wanted to learn from by observing Stephen direct, but there's really nothing for the composer to do at them, and so—even though it was fun to kibitz with Jerry, David McDade, Jocelyn Dueck, and assistant conductor Phil Kelsey during breaks—I felt over-exposed and irrelevant. After five weeks of staging, production moved from the rehearsal hall to the opera house. The orchestra read and rehearsed the score. The focus of production shifted to the realization of my larger compositional vision as the complex mechanism of the company lumbered to life. Technicians walked purposefully about, whispering. The lighting designer conferred with his assistant at the portable board set up in the orchestra. The enormous sets were assembled and struck, one after another, on the stage. This role was mine alone, and I relished it: I walked the darkened, empty house for hours, memorized the sightlines, and gauged what would "speak" to what part of the audience.

Opening night, the McCaw Hall curtain slid silently up to reveal *Amelia's* first scene. Jerry brought his baton down, and the Seattle Symphony began the first bars, intentionally redolent of Vere's music from *Billy Budd*—a blessing, homage, and a curse on this opera's characters. When Kate Lindsey, as Amelia, "saw" Icarus, Dædalus, and her dead relatives in the room, she was playing my reality. When Nathan Gunn cradled the newborn at the end of the opera, he was me. When, at the end of *Amelia*, she sings the incantatory phrase, "Anything is possible," Amelia is transforming sorrow into joy. I created the moment not only as a tribute to Atticus (to whom I dedicated the opera) but also as a transubstantiation of the grief that I felt for the baby that we lost in Nicaragua.

Walking hand in hand to the car with Gilda through fine rain after the performance I half-remembered a catechism from childhood: *In justice, we get what we deserve*, it began. I thought about Mother, on the back porch, hands covered with clay, sculpting the statue of the boy when I was a kid, saying, "I've captured my subject right down to the toes" while slicing off the boy's feet with a length of wire and tossing them into the clay bucket, only to start over. I knew what "a selfish little fucker" I'd always been. I accepted what a selfish husband I had been to my first wife. I had long ago accepted that it had been dumb luck that Ned invited me to Curtis so long ago. And I understood that few artists are fortunate enough to be given their "big chance," and fewer still have the talent required to capitalize upon the moment. *In mercy, we don't get what we deserve*, the catechism continued. That snowy night in Philadelphia at the age of 21 I'd written in my journal, *"Who knows what talent is? Inspiration? I know I've got my portion. I can't even imagine being alive at 30,"* At the age of 36, starting over, I'd written again the words I'd first written at the age of 21: *"Whatever I lack in talent, I'll make up in hard work."* Thirteen years later, at the age of 49, I wondered *What have I got? My Truth. Is it still enough? No. I wasn't the one who dumped the Royal typewriter, my manuscripts, paints, brushes, and clay in a garbage pail one rainy summer afternoon,* I thought. *Mother was.* Though not as good a person as she, I had developed into a better artist. And what I lacked in talent I *had* made up in hard work. I had finally gotten "it" exactly right and I knew it. By naming me after the Other Daron, she had as much as ordered me to *not* "just let it go." I had stuck with it. I'd grabbed the narrative that she had offered me and had run with it, unaware that the story was not about winning, but losing. *In grace,* I remembered, *we get what we do not deserve.*

Until now I had sustained the conviction that, as Rolland wrote, "there are some dead who are more alive than the living." I believed, as Vivian Gornick wrote in her reminiscence of a troubled parent-child relationship, that "release from the wounds of childhood is a task never completed, not even on the point of death." I had not expected, in conjuring all my spirits to form the finale of *Amelia* as I had, that I would also be—in the sense of Roethke's poem, *The Waking*—literally "waking" them. When I realized that that is what I had done, I also understood that, in the future, they would no longer be available for me to sing for and about, to remember as and when I pleased. Laughable as it may seem, it wasn't until that moment that I accepted that, as F. Scott Fitzgerald wrote to his daughter Scottie in 1940, "Life is essentially a cheat and its conditions are those of defeat." It wasn't that I had achieved at last my heart's desire and was confronted for the first time by the question, "now what?" The reviews by the dozen or so most powerful critics in the country—at the *New York Times, Wall Street Journal, Washington Post,* and so forth—had been good to excellent. I'd wept with Vietnam Conflict combat veterans moved to tears by my opera, already received the customary heartwarming letters of appreciation from cast members, but these were things I'd experienced before. I'd been aiming higher—whatever that meant. It was that I was sane enough to know that having done so had been an epiphanous experience for me, but simply another night in the theater—however fine—for the audience. Consequently, I found myself suspended as an artist between the moment when Mother tossed the terra cotta boy's feet in the clay pail, and when she started over.

Sandy McClatchy and Ned had been commissioned by Sarasota Opera to dramatize Winsor McKay's surrealist comic strip about a boy named Nemo. The *Little Nemo in Slumberland* project intrigued me because I was aware that McKay's work had influenced the most operatic of filmmakers, Federico Fellini, and because Victor Herbert had treated it around the turn of the century. "Sarasota Opera," explained Victor DeRenzi, artistic director and conductor of the company, when I first met him, "got more press when Ned backed out then we'd ever gotten for anything else." I called Sandy and asked to see the libretto, which was svelte and charming. When I asked him why he'd taken a pass, Ned said, "I don't have another opera in me," he said, "I'm just not interested." Reflexively, I pounced. I hied me to Yaddo for several weeks to finish the vocal score of the new opera. Sandy's charming libretto was, besides being a *fait accompli,* suave and entirely suitable. For the first time, I set a received libretto, and it was fun. I jiggered phrases here and there; but, really, the thing was ready to go, with no fat anywhere. One evening an odd performance artist in her early 20s presented what she called an opera. It consisted of snippets of YouTube confessionals from sad, lonely Humberts in response to her provocative, soft porn posts. Her major achievement so far as an artist had been a recurring role on an MTV realty show. I looked around the room at the respectful, rapt faces of the dozen or so thirty-something painters, writers, and composers and felt alienated. A few nights later, I showed a recording of *Amelia* and none of them came.

At Jerry's request, I provided a "farewell fanfare" commission commemorating his 27 years as Music Director of the Seattle Symphony. The title, *con gai: a greeting and farewell* ("daughter," in Vietnamese), I drew from Dodge's final words in *Amelia*. The music I based on a lengthy duet for two trumpets (Jerry's instrument, of course) and orchestra that I had composed on the fly during production to add time to one of the interludes so that the enormous sets could be trundled across the stage. The subtitle was "a greeting and a farewell"—appropriate to the opera (as it explored the character of Dodge, Amelia's father), and to Jerry, since he was retiring just as I had been given an opportunity to work with him. In addition, contractually obliged, I re-orchestrated the concerto *Seven Last Words* at Alexander Platt's request for the Maverick Concerts in Woodstock, and then crafted a motet for chorus and string orchestra for the Wisconsin Philharmonic and my high school choir called *Song of Gabriel*. I created a concerto called *Genji* for koto virtuoso Yumi Kurosawa to premiere in two versions—one with the Lark String Quartet and another with the Orchestra of the Swan in England. The idea of composing a piece for Michael Ludwig and JoAnn Falletta came up over dinner after the concert performance by the Buffalo Philharmonic of *Brow* on the night of my birthday in 2006. For inspiration, I turned to daily life: Gilda and I both sang spirituals and folk songs to the boys each night, embroidering and developing the tunes. Through the door, or over the baby monitor, as I tidied up the home we shared, I listened in. This to me was the musical manifestation of the musical fabric of our domesticity.

That winter I returned to Chicago for a production of *New York Stories* at the Chicago College of the Performing Arts. After drinks with the handful of young composers who had studied with me during my stint teaching composition there, I returned to my room. A heavy tumbler of single malt in my fist, I looked out of the floor-to-ceiling window at Lake Michigan, twenty floors below. I looked down at what used to be the Bar Association thrusting up into the sky like a knife, and brought the scotch to my face, and attempted to inhale its complex bouquet. The truth was that I hadn't been able to smell anything for months. My sinuses were swollen shut; I breathed now entirely through my mouth.

The next night, in Sarasota, a book in one hand, another tumbler of scotch in the other, I stood on the balcony of my hotel room in the moonlight looking out at the ocean while imagining the loving rhythms of bedtime back in the Hamilton Heights apartment. I raised the glass to my lips and tried to sniff but couldn't smell the peat. Even so, I sensed eucalyptus on the breeze, and the tang of chlorine wafted up from far below, where aquamarine light coruscated from the hotel pool. A pod of pelicans, their silhouettes as they flew past, accompanied by the flaccid clapping sound of their heavy wings, touched off a cascade of objective correlatives. *Oh no, not again,* I thought, dropping the book, pulling a handkerchief out of my pocket, and violently blowing my nose. I flared my eyelids open and spun seawards, where, far out, the birds were merging into the black horizon. *Breathe,* I thought, opening my mouth and taking in an enormous breath. I heard Gilda's voice, singing a line from *Angel Band: "O bear me away on your snowy wings!"* I spun around, looked back into the hotel room. Of course, she wasn't there; she was with Atticus in New York. *"Stop it. Stop it. Stop it!"* I heard Father bellow. *"Let it go,"* I heard Mother's weary voice reply. Less than fifteen seconds had elapsed. Beat. "I have a choice," I said aloud to no one, looking at the scotch in my fist. For an instant, the smells of Rosemary, juniper bushes, burnt leña, and … peat. I held it aloft, looked through it at the moon, and tipped it on its side, watching as the amber liquid ropily followed itself down sixteen floors and into the pool.

Still on Chicago time, I nearly missed my ride to the press conference set up by Sarasota Opera to introduce *Little Nemo's* new creative team. I fidgeted uncomfortably as Sandy spoke at great length about his vision for the piece. Victor came to the podium and hugged Sandy warmly. As the photographers' flashbulbs winked, the company's marketing director approached me and admonished me not to speak for too long—"composers always talk too much." DeRenzi left the room before I reached the podium. "I find that I have over the years become something of an expert on insomnia." People laughed. "Hence, it was a pleasure to compose an opera about a little boy who can actually sleep at night." Pleasant chuckles. I smiled at Sandy, who motioned to the door through which DeRenzi had just departed, raised his eyebrows, and shrugged. "An ambitious dreamer, I didn't learn to sleep at night until I married my wife. I accepted this project because I wanted to underscore its message for my son: we need the world of dreams. Without dreams, we have nothing left to us but hopelessness and the cold reality of our existence." I took three questions, and, within minutes, Sandy and I were on our way to the airport.

Arriving in Philadelphia by train later that spring, I meditated on the implications of a comment I'd just read by Ford Lallerstedt: *I'm thinking today of Curtis, of unmerited favor, of a sense of grace.* Curtis faculty member Ignat Solzhenitsyn, son of the great writer, was scheduled to play the piano, and two students—a clarinetist and a violist—were to join him, in the Philadelphia premiere of a suite called *Book of Days* that the school had commissioned. I checked in to the Warwick, where once the quizzical desk clerk had compelled me to drop Bernard Jacobson's name to check in—this clerk looked about fifteen years old—and then walked the short distance to the construction site of Curtis' nearly completed new rehearsal and dorm facility. Things had to change, of course; but I wondered what Mary Louise and Leopold Stokowski would have thought of the nondescript new building—entirely interchangeable with a thousand others just like it at colleges around the world—where once stood the Locust Club.

Emily Wallace and I dined together beforehand. We discussed her passion (and specialty) Ezra Pound, and how it might feel to set foot in the school again now that we were both former faculty members. Afterwards, we strolled together beneath the sycamores and across Rittenhouse Square. There was our beautiful school. I pulled on the heavy front door. The familiar cool objectivity set in—every bit as chilling as the refrigerated air that streamed out of Little Pete's into the swelter of my first night on the east coast. I took in the hauteur on the tender faces of the children—even younger than I remember ever having been. During the concert, next to Emily, I sat where Samuel Barber had sat—between Ralph Berkowitz and Gian Carlo Menotti—in the picture displayed on Ralph's piano in Albuquerque. I nodded a secret farewell to Ralph from the seat he so loved. At the age of 103, Ralph had only days earlier joined the Angel Band. *Perhaps he has already learned the answer to the Virgin Mary's question,* I thought.

Neither did I recognize a soul the next morning in the Common Room when I seated myself next to the walk-in fireplace on the chair in which Shirley Schachtel had taken my hand 30 years earlier. I thought again of Ford's comment, which had continued, *"A little boy gives all he has, everything he depends upon. No motive."* I looked around, remembering myself standing there for the first time, nervous excitement and exhaustion mingling, my stomach a-flutter, intuiting that the rest of my life was, all at once, opening before me. I could almost smell Shirley's delicate perfume. "So, you are brand new," I remembered her observing gently, and smiled inwardly. Brand new. *Yes. And now, I am here, but also not here anymore.* It felt like the early morning hours of that day—*entre les pays*—in the loft of the garret on Saint Mark's Place, listening to the rain falling in soft, peaceful, tiny handfuls on the skylight. Perhaps I looked in need of help, because a pretty child placed her hand on my shoulder. She reminded me of Michaela as a teenager. Like her, she smelled of rain. "Are you okay? Do you need something, sir?" she asked. Her innocent kindness. *To her, I am an old man*, I mused. I looked down at my arthritic knuckles. "No. Oh, no," I answered gently, looking up. She smiled sweetly, and sort of danced across the room toward a knot of friends. I rose, strolled to the painting of Mary Louise, smiled affectionately at it, and took a final look around. A young composer named David Ludwig (a pupil of Danielpour's and nephew of Peter Serkin) crossed the room and waved as he took my place. I smiled in return and pushed the heavy door open. After the stuffy owl light of the Common Room, the sunshine dazzled; the air was wintery dry. Across the street, a new café called Parc had opened since my last visit. The sidewalk in front of it bristled with little Parisian-style café tables. I crossed Locust Street and took a seat at one. I turned for one last look at the old mansion. *Is this how this story ends?* I asked myself. *Yes.* The last fragment of Ford's comment came to mind: "*No motive. Just unqualified love. The results are surprising, unpredicted. Tell others.*"

Presently the eager to please bearded boy that I once was—the one who met Ned for the first time in the tiny attic-classroom on the top floor across the street and intuited that he would have to be extraordinary to earn Ned's—and by extension, what he thought was the music world's—attention simply so that he could sing for them, joined me. I regarded the Other Daron tenderly. *You know, my little Mockingbird*, I said to myself, *you're the last of them.* He smiled back at me, secure in his essential goodness despite (and because) of the frog that he might as well have had secreted behind his back; he smiled the way that I once did, the way that my sons do, and have every right to. At length, he rose, reached for my hand, squeezed it fiercely with his small, strong one for a moment, smiled, nodded affirmatively, released it, turned, and walked slowly into Rittenhouse Square, never to return. He had never realized how beautiful he was.

◆◆ 24 ◆◆

The Deal with Fauré's *Ballade*
2012–2013

I'd not looked past the end of the Ouroboros' tail to its nose. In other words, when I observed to Mother as a teenager that Roethke's poem was about death she had corrected me: "Honey, it's a poem about rebirth!" Likewise, I hadn't looked past the waking that constituted the end of *Amelia* to my new life as a father. Seamus, already the spiritual shaman he's continued to be, arrived in May, and with his arrival, showed me the way forward. Gilda labored for close to a day with Atticus; Seamus was simply ready to arrive, and in enough of a hurry that his strong little shoulders caused a bit of tearing when he turned. Seamus gave her the natural, easeful labor she'd always dreamed of—Gilda and her Midwife Rebecca Crist McCracken discussed philosophy between contractions! *I am blessed with both loaves and fishes,* I thought joyously as I held Seamus for the first time. Atticus had smelled of freshly-baked bread. Seamus smelled like anchovies, and his little terra cotta red nose was squashed against his face, making him look like a little Aztec emperor.

That winter, I caught, while coaching singers for Buck Ross' winter 2012 revival of *Amelia* at the Moores Opera House at the University of Houston, the latest in a long line of sinus infections. Buck's terrific, sleek production proved that the show didn't need the huge scenic apparatus that Seattle had given it to be effective, and he had made a few changes—like bringing out the supers and doubling vocal parts in the final a cappella number—that clarified and intensified the effectiveness of the piece. Brett Mitchell, who the next season would become Associate Conductor of the Cleveland Orchestra, led suavely the new reduced orchestration that I'd crafted for smaller opera houses. Gardner, seated beside me, seemed pleased. Feverish, I bowed out of dinner and returned to my hotel. I'd made it through opening night, but, once alone, I began to panic. Finally, I dozed, sitting up in the bed. Around four, bathed in sweat, disoriented, I was awakened from the most fleeting of sleeps by the wheezing generated as I drew air through the congealing phlegm in my windpipe. Each breath sounded like the cries of the damned. I stumbled to the windows and drew the curtains, trying to remember which city I was in. It felt as though there was a sheet of Masonite in my face.

I have always loathed hotel rooms—even nice ones. If train stations are cathedrals to transience, then hotel rooms are rifled tombs. People, as far as I'm concerned, check into them to die. Uncle Keith swallowed Phenobarbital and vodka in one. Britt played out the last few years of his life in another. Kevin had been retreating to hotel rooms bearing crates full of booze since his 20s. Afraid of what would happen if I fell asleep, I dressed and spent the next five hours on the couch, panting through my mouth, waiting for a taxi to take me to the airport. I flew back to New York. As soon as his office opened, I went to see the doctor I'd known since first moving there. I watched Richard as he examined my file. "We're both gray now," he mused. I laughed. "Remember why we first met?" he asked. I did.

"It was the day you got back to New York from Tanglewood," laughed Richard. "I counseled you. You were afraid that Lenny had given you AIDS by french kissing you and your colleagues at a composer party at Seranak, I think." We both laughed. "Of course, you were fine," he smiled, flipping the chart shut and exhaling warm air on his stethoscope before placing it on my back. "Breathe in." I did. "Your lungs are congested. You're remarkably healthy for a fat man. Stop drinking so much. Lose some weight, okay?" He looked up to gauge my reaction. "I know," I said, wearily. "But the sinuses," he continued. "You've got to have them fixed. A man has to breathe." Beat. "Uh huh," I agreed. "It's hard not to interpret this as a metaphor," I quipped. "Maybe this is a sign. Maybe there's no air left for me in New York." Richard stared at me, unsmiling. "This isn't Art. It's Life," he said, coldly. I looked up at him, startled. "I know—," I began. "Listen. Let me remind you of something that you seem to have forgotten: art is important, but breathing is imperative. There's a membrane thinner than a sheet of paper separating your sinuses from your brain. I suspect that most of your sinus cavity is badly infected, necrotic even, and has been for a long time. All that has to happen is for that infection to cross through that membrane and—." I raised my hands up, and said, "I get it." He looked at me incredulously. "You've got to fix this," he concluded. I promised him that I would. "I'll refer you to a friend of mine. I trust him." He tore the prescription he had just scrawled off the pad and handed it to me. "In the meantime, maybe this will give you some relief." He looked up, half smiling. "Now, go away and write more music."

Not long after, a surgeon extracted from my sinuses "the most polyps [he had] ever seen." He pointed out, to my surprise, that he had also removed several turbinates, straightened my deviated septum, and excised an enormous amount of dead and diseased tissue—nearly the entire surface area of the interior of my sinuses. "So, was it like mowing my front lawn in there?" I asked. He wasn't amused. "This has been chronic for a decade or more," he said. "You were suffocating. You had use of less than five percent of your sinuses." I whistled. "So, it was like mowing the lawn of everyone on my street?" He looked at me queerly. "No," the specialist said, flatly. "It was more like napalming your entire neighborhood." My nose was stuffed with gauze; I breathed through tubes for weeks. Followed months of steroidal weight gain, antibiotics, bleeding, and more pain, as the tissue regenerated.

Somehow, through the steroids and pain meds, I musicalized the scenes of *Mawrdew Czgowchwz* that James McCourt sent me, completing about thirty minutes of a first act. The extravagant, intensely chromatic, hallucinogenic score—I was aiming for a sort of sonic equivalent of the paintings of Gustav Klimt—featured an extensive, druggy, electro-acoustic component derived entirely from cut-and-diced, processed brief snatches of Arnold Schoenberg's *Transfigured Night* and Richard Wagner's Prelude to *Tristan und Isolde* that manifested whenever her fans discussed her; only when she herself sang would the music "clear" and attain a sort of Debussyian post–*Pelléas et Mélisande* pan-tonal clarity. Some of the music has ended up in my Welles dream-opera, *Orson Rehearsed.*

I began shopping *Mawrdew* around. My astonishment at finding no interest from opera companies—except for a mild tingle from Brad Woolbright at Santa Fe Opera—was perplexing. I had to face the fact that either it was me that people didn't want, or that few people had heard of the ultimate opera lover's novel. Interest in the opera came not from the new young generation of executive directors at the small regional companies (who in truth I had not cultivated, as my relationships had been with their predecessors) but from the soon-to-retire generation that included David Gockley at San Francisco, and Speight Jenkins in Seattle, among others. I wrote to James with a heavy heart, telling him that I was compelled to put the project aside for "health reasons." In fact, I balked because I couldn't get any traction with producers.

In any event, *Mawrdew* had also to be set aside to reorchestrate *Vera* for the same instrumentation as Kurt Weill's *Mahagonny Songspiel* for a revival directed by Mark Streshinsky starring Brian Asawa in El Cerrito, a suburb of San Francisco. Brian, the nephew of sculptor Ruth Asawa, was an extremely brave, but not fearless artist; his tragic struggle with alcohol was clear, and he was clearly losing that struggle. Whether drunk or sober, he *inhabited* the role of Vera. He knew and loved her, he said, and his commitment to his performance was an inspiration. Brian's death at the age of 49, a short time later, in 2016, while heartbreaking, did not come as a shock to me; it came as a sort of unasked-for reminder of unfinished business.

Since the theater was dark the day before *Vera* opened, I boarded a ferry for the trip from Fisherman's Wharf to Alcatraz and back. To my relief, the Bainbridge Ferry meltdown in Seattle at which I had come perilously close to spinning out did not repeat itself. The Staten Island Ferry trip—my last—had left me unmoved. Facing Telegraph Hill, I flipped through some favorite images of Gilda and the boys on my iPod as the boat plowed into San Francisco Bay. I looked west toward the Golden Gate Bridge. Alcatraz bound, I drew the pristine, healthy Pacific air in through my nose and, for the first time in over a decade, I literally breathed freely.

I was genuinely astonished when Paul called to inform me that he intended to rewrite *Vera* with another composer. Wounded, when he asked me to withdraw the opera, I refused, explaining that, setting aside the fact that the copyright was owned by Carl Fischer and I couldn't do more than *request* that they withdraw it, I didn't *want* to. However, I had no objection in principle to his request to turn it into a new opera with another composer. ("Think of the dissertations comparing the two that will be written," I recall quipping.) Since I had co-written the treatment, I stipulated, I'd expect a token percentage of any royalties the resulting work generated.

Martha Collins' *Little Nemo* rehearsals at Sarasota Opera were—particularly after the high-flying intellectual and creative atmosphere that Stephen conjured during *Amelia* rehearsals—uninspired, so I absented myself, spending most of my time reworking another draft of the libretto that Barbara Grecki and I were developing for *A Woman in Morocco* based on her original play. As 200 kids sang about "a world of dreams" in the rehearsal hall, Ahmed and Teddy skirmished sexually in my hotel room whilst plotting Asilah's abduction. Opening night, sitting beside Sandy in Sarasota Opera's lovely jewel box opera house waiting for Steven Osgood to give the downbeat for the world premiere, I entertained myself by watching Victor DeRenzi, the company's conductor and artistic director, slowly making his way up the aisle like Don Fanucci through Hell's Kitchen, stopping here to hold a valued patron's hand between his and to chat, there to wave regally to a fan in the balcony, bending solicitously and handing a program to another patron, elaborately at ease, blooming where he was planted, the complete master of his chosen universe. He sat down a few rows away just before the house lights were set to go to half. All at once I felt a wave of panic. *What had I forgotten? The rail, the rail!* I handed my program to Sandy, lurched out of my aisle seat, and walked quickly down to the orchestra rail, where I tapped one-two-three-four-five-six-seven as the lights began to dim. Relieved, I turned around and considered the eyes of Steve's wife, artistic director of G. Schirmer's Peggy Monastra, who was seated in the first row with their young sons. Smiling, I looked up into the pretty little 1200 seat opera house and felt a sudden wave of pleasure—the exact opposite of anxiety. I was suddenly suffused for a moment with the wild idealism and excitement of those first exciting months in Philadelphia, when the whole world was opening for me. *Worrying once again my "barb of sorrow,"* I noted happily as the house lights dimmed. Whispering the most fleeting of prayers, I took my seat next to Sandy, squeezed his hand, and felt thankful as in silence *Little Nemo in Slumberland* was launched and the curtain glided upwards.

Atticus was now old enough for pre-school. The new apartment in Hamilton Heights was great, but Gilda and I agreed that our sons ought to have a backyard in which to play. Boarding the Staten Island Ferry for the first time since 9/11, it seemed natural to discuss leaving Manhattan for good. Standing at the rail with Gilda, the harbor the color of an opal, I could have been looking over the water at Seattle, San Francisco, or Venice. Any City. No longer mine. We strolled around Battery Park City before turning east towards Ground Zero. I recalled to Gilda how that day smelled—an unforgettable admixture of smoke, fused metal, aviation fuel, and … something else—the dead? The Freedom Tower, still unfinished, thrust into the mist on one side; dead ahead, the roar of falling water rose from the negative space of the World Trade Center's footprint. I looked up into the sky and remembered looking out the window of Jim Kendrick's Trade Center office, far, far down at the Staten Island Ferry and the Statue of Liberty, both rendered toy like; I remembered drinks at the Greatest Bar on Earth; I remembered a hundred trips to Erewhon and back on the Staten Island ferry, looking up at a skyline I felt mine.

As bone-chilling air swept up from the chasm there came the familiar objectivity, the feeling of no longer being there. "My thirtieth year in New York," I observed to nobody. Even after disenchantment with the art world had set in, I had continued to believe in the Jeffersonian notion that there is a "natural aristocracy" derived of talent and virtue. No more. "Wow," said a bearded Millennial in front of me. He clutched a copy of *The Fountainhead* and his ear buds throbbed with Björk's current single. Startled that he had overheard me, I made believe that I hadn't heard him. "You must be old," he said, meaning nothing by it. "Oh, I don't know," I replied. "Move along," a cop told me, misinterpreting my chuckle. I looked up from the memorial. Reflexively, I dug in, and gave him a hard look. The cop frowned back. "Listen, pal, a lot of people are waiting to take your place," he said. I chuckled ruefully, and said, "Yes *sir!* I really *know* that!" He shook his head, cocked his finger next to his temple as he shot Gilda a look, and turned away. I smiled at the hipster, who rolled his eyes, stuffed my hands in my pockets, and turned toward the Winter Garden. I thought of the Big Cedar House, which, of course, had been rather small and only special because I made it so in memory. It had just been like a lot of houses, on a street like a lot of other streets, in a suburb like a lot of other suburbs. We had played out our dramas just like countless other families just like us. I'd raced away from it as soon as I could, as hard as I could, and as fast as I could, to the coast. Thirty-three years later, as we crossed the West Side Highway, a cabbie leaned out of his window and swore at us in Punjabi. I was delighted. As I refused to relinquish my soul to the city, it had become time for me to relinquish my place in it.

Most weekends, we piled the boys into the car and drove to Rhinebeck, the safe, prosperous, quiet, picturesque village about 90 minutes north of the Manhattan in which Gilda had grown up, to look at houses. We found a beautiful, historic 3300 square foot 1858 Victorian and fell in love with it. To my surprise, my twenty-seventh application for a Guggenheim Fellowship to support the creation of the music and words for an opera about 9/11 called *9/10* was successful. I used the money to help Gilda's parents make the down payment.

Kevin's son Ryan was engaged to be married to Lily Sutton, a violinist and academic administrator then serving as director of admissions at the Bard Conservatory of Music, now Director of Student Affairs at the Jackson Institute for Global Affairs at Yale. (Many of the singers with whom I had worked had studied with her mother, Edith Bers, herself a student of Maria Callas and Stella Adler, and a member of the Juilliard vocal faculty.) That August, Gilda and I and the kids lived with her folks down the street as Gilda and I pulled wallpaper, rebuilt walls, painted, and cleaned the Big Victorian House for 16 hours a day.

Ryan and Lily's wedding was scheduled for the tail end of the month. When Kevin, who had promised to walk his son down the aisle with his mother Judith, did not appear on the train, I began making calls. At last I heard from him while bathing the children. *Shit*, I thought, trying to follow his slurred explanation, *I am so tired of playing the role of Charon. This time I'll be bringing it home to the boys.* Having binged for a several weeks, Kevin had stepped off the plane, and, detoxing, keeled over in baggage claim. "If you aren't willing to come to sign him out, then he'll be discharged into the social services system down here," the nurse explained. "It could be days before he's released." Since he was due Upstate for his son's wedding, I jumped in the car and drove to Queens.

Once there, I parked in front of the hospital. Lovers strolled arm in arm in the balmy, late night Queens air. The couples were sexy, chaste, nicely dressed; they marched up and down the street like the undergraduates in front of their dorms on sultry Texas evenings at Baylor University. Two paramedics shared a cigarette, lounging against the hood of their ambulance. After checking that he was stable and discussing his vitals with the head nurse, I went to him. Kevin shook involuntarily as saline dripped into one arm; a yellow "banana bag" filled with nutrients and lorazepam dripped into the other. Sorrow, pity, love, and anger. Unwilling to watch the symptoms of Wernicke-Korsakoff syndrome play out on his bloated, ravaged body, I left him there alone. I walked to the car and sat, listening to WNYC, too furious to think of anything at all worth saying during the drive Upstate. So, on the reverse of a grocery receipt, I assembled, with a crayon left in the car by one of the boys, a list of things to talk to him about: "(1) What's with Fauré's *Ballade in F Sharp Major for Piano and Orchestra*? (I had just heard it for the first time on the radio. Music was a safe topic.) (2) Are you physically capable of attending Ryan's rehearsal dinner tomorrow? (3) Did they give you Benzodiazepine, Diazepam, or Valium, or what? (I had been through this with others and knew the protocols.) (4) Have you eaten? What can you stomach?"

After a few hours, I returned to the ER and asked the doctor if Kevin, asleep on a gurney a few feet away, was ready to be discharged. "If he doesn't go into rehab, he'll be dead in less than a year," the young Asian doctor replied. "Yes," I replied, flatly. I woke him, asked if he was ready to go, and signed the release forms she reluctantly produced. He was too fat for the wheelchair. Another was called for. The orderly waited with him as I brought the Chevy around. Kevin barely fit in the passenger seat. I started the car and sighed: Thirtieth Avenue, Thirtieth Street, Thirtieth Boulevard—*oh, for Godsake, Queens*, I thought, *pull yourself together*. Kevin dozed for a few minutes, then jerked awake. "First, I've gotta cross town," I said, pulling into traffic and avoiding his rheumy eyes. "Then," I glanced at the fuel gauge, "we have to stop for gas. I'm going to drive across Harlem to get to the west side before hitting the Palisades." The lorazepam kicked in; he dozed off. The windows down, half an hour later, we eased down Martin Luther King Boulevard.

I listened to the pounding salsa and breathed in Upper Manhattan's unmistakable fragrance. After 28 years, I'd ceased to notice it, but I noticed it now—the exotic odor I'd thrilled to when Mother had brought us here as youngsters. I remembered standing with Kevin in Lincoln Center Plaza back then, not shaking from delirium tremens, but with excitement. I looked at my once handsome brother, Mother's precious first son, the talented Big Brother I had worshipped as a child, as he snored beside me in the passenger seat. Britt came to mind. I reached our old neighborhood and bought gas. As I manned the pump, Kevin awoke. I tapped on the passenger side window. "Do you need water?" I asked. He patted himself on the chest and coughed slightly. "I need to sleep," he said, and dozed off again. I drove under the soaring steelwork of Riverside Drive and into the Fairway Market parking lot, stopped the car, and climbed out. Leaning against the hood, I looked out under the West Side Highway, and over Harlem Piers Park at the Hudson. *How could I bring him into my home in this condition?* I thought. I studied him through the windshield. It may as well have been me scraping the conjunctivitis out of my eyes, tottering along at over 300 pounds on psoriasis-covered legs, struggling with night terrors and hallucinations, with no exit. He looked 85. He was broken. He was alone. He couldn't be fixed. *Then it will be three down, one to go. The point was,* I knew, *that by drinking I was already bringing "all this" home. I'd been in the middle of "all this" all my life. Astonishingly, and whether I have earned it or not, I have everything: a loving wife, two healthy, beautiful, intelligent sons, a home in the country in which they may safely grow up. I had Music to cling to, and, now, Gilda and the kids. How could I possibly endanger them? How can I possibly save him?* I got into the car and buckled the seatbelt. Before turning the key in the ignition, I turned to him. For a few minutes, then, we were alone together. I knew that it would probably be for the last time. As he slept, I promised him quietly, "I've had my last drink."

I kept watch for a little while, knowing that, for a few moments more, at least, anything was still possible, that we might still be okay, that this illness that we all shared wasn't going to take us all down. And then, because life is not an O'Neill play, there was nothing to do but to drive on. His son needed him. I had to help get him to where he needed to go. I started the engine and pulled gently out of the lot. For now, making sure that he rested couldn't be construed as "enabling" him. By habit, I edged the Chevy back on to the West Side Highway, headed north, and took the ramp up to the George Washington Bridge. We crossed into New Jersey and I headed north on the Palisades Parkway. Kevin stirred. "So," I began, taking a deep breath, "what's the deal with Fauré's *Ballade*? Do you know it?"

The fifth Seasons Music Festival got under way that October in Yakima, Washington. It was the best iteration yet. I'd assembled a good composition faculty: along with Gilda, who was now teaching composition at the Hartt School in Connecticut, I was able to add former pupil Miles Hankins, now a rising Hollywood film composer, and Luciano Pavarotti's protégé, Catalan tenor and opera composer Alberto García Demestres, who brought his perspective as a European and experience as a composition student of Berio's to the table. I'd also been fortunate enough to add Bernard Jacobson to the faculty. His charming performance of his own version of the narrator's part in Stravinsky's *L'Histoire du Soldat* was a highpoint of the festival, which also included the world premiere of my Piano Concerto (an uncompromisingly serious, technically challenging modernist blowout I'd composed in 2002 based on my Piano Variations for Ralph Berkowitz) by Tanya Stambuk and the Yakima Symphony, led by Lawrence Golan, the orchestra's new music director, son of Joseph Golan, whom I had grown up hearing in his capacity as principal second violin in the Chicago Symphony.

The repertoire that I programmed, the faculty and performing artist hired, and the composition fellows that I invited to participate all frankly promoted racial and LGBT equity. Pat Strosahl and I had integrated the jazz and classical arms of the enterprise well, and we, at least, were excited by the results. There had been no grant writing. Private funding had been tight, of course; but it had come. And money had been saved, in part by the donated service of Brooke Creswell, who had stepped in to serve as the much-needed on site executive director (after retiring as music director of the Yakima Symphony). But attendance at the concerts (and the small, though meaningful income that ticket sales represented) had been falling. In any event, the large migrant worker and Native American populations in the valley made *El Sistema* an irresistible program to support. Sagging demand for new homes was battering the bottom line at Pat's building company, which had been underwriting much of the festival; Joyce Ritchie Strosahl, the festival's primary benefactor, died. The decision to shutter came when Brooke, who had been serving as executive director, resigned to concentrate on *El Sistema*.

Amelia was revived in Chicago by the Chicago College of Performing Arts and Chicago Opera Theater in a tender production directed by Scott Gilmore and conducted by James Paul, who I first met as a child during his stint as associate conductor of the Milwaukee Symphony. A gentle, studious chap, our lunch at the Art Institute was a comradely quiet riot of musician stories old and new. Afterwards, I settled into my seat in the theater to observe his *wandelprobe* and wondered, throughout the first act, why I couldn't hear the low piccolo doublings of the violins (a useful commercial pit orchestrator trick that subtly firms up the pitch and plumps the tone of a small section of strings) and the very high, Britten-esque passages for two piccolos (they make orchestral climaxes for a small orchestra sound a lot bigger). When the musicians took a break, I walked down to the rail and leaned over, asking quietly, "Where are my flutes, James?" He shot a look at the flutes, both of whom were swabbing out their instruments and all at once attentive. "There was a lot of low piccolo that can't be heard, and a lot of very high piccolo that sounded shrill, so I had them play everything on the flute in the correct octave," he replied. "Ah," I said, "I understand. Thank you." I made quick eye contact with the flutes as I turned away. One nodded almost imperceptibly. Subsequently, they played their parts exactly as written. I'm proud of that moment, because it is the way I believe a mature professional composer should behave.

The Butler Opera Center gave the first fully staged theatrical *New York Stories* in Austin. During a slew of telephone conversations, Gore Vidal and I finally got serious about the *Smithsonian Institution* adaptation. After signing off on my treatment—Gore himself would make a "wheel-on, mute, cameo appearance" in a wheelchair, as a president, which tickled him—he encouraged me to begin devising dialogue myself, based on his prose. "Virgil wanted me to write him a libretto," he wrote to me a few weeks before he died, "and what I came up with was terrible. You do it." Stricken with pneumonia at 86, he died that July. Somewhere in his papers are whatever notes he made for our collaboration before pneumonia took him. I'm sure that some graduate student will unearth them someday.

For a true opera composer, the ink's not dry until you die. *Little Nemo in Slumberland's* successful premiere led to performances by the Tulsa Youth Opera, among others. Success with *The George Washington Suite*, a 20-minute opera skit commissioned by Opera Theater of Pittsburgh (Robert Frankenberry was the music director and composed, along with Gilda and Roger Zahab, other sections of the anthology of miniatures) led to their commissioning of a new orchestration and revision of *Shining Brow*. Jonathan Eaton and Rob approached me about creating a "pocket" version of *Shining Brow* that could be toured in schools and alternative venues. This would mean cutting out the choruses and eliminating all the secondary characters. Muldoon and I had intended that the choruses be the musical equivalent of structural pillars, so their removal didn't alter the drama, which was driven by the interactions between the major characters. Paul did not respond when I contacted him, so I cut the choral numbers and revised some of the libretto to make a new, pocket version myself. I mourned the loss of much of the prettier, more atmospheric stretches of the score. From a dramaturgical standpoint, the excision of the instrumental "fire interlude," however, seemed to intensify the psychological vacuum created by the offstage murders. The scene at the Cliff Dweller's club between Wright and Sullivan works as satisfyingly as a Chinese puzzle box. The result: the pocket version of *Brow* packs more punch than the original, main stage version. I also reorchestrated it for a third time, for small chamber ensemble suitable for pocket touring. Jonathan Eaton staged the "Fallingwater Version" of *Brow* that Opera Theater of Pittsburgh toured with great success in and around Pittsburgh. Rob, who had sung the role of Sullivan for the JoAnn Falletta's recording on Naxos, conducted (as he had *Vera* years earlier, on Broadway) a small but plush-sounding orchestra that was tucked on one of the house's balconies. Their site-specific production at Fallingwater, Wright's masterpiece in Mill Run, Pennsylvania, built for Edgar J. Kaufmann and his wife in the 30s, was a highlight of my life as an opera composer.

That July, unable to reach Kevin by phone, I asked a neighbor to stop by to check on him. "He's unconscious, sitting in a chair in the bedroom," he told me over the phone. "I knocked on the window, but he was unresponsive. I called him, and heard the phone ringing inside." Another binge. I called again, and Kevin roused himself. "Okay, it's time to sober up," I said, cruel. "I want you to check in with me every six hours, or I'll call the cops." He did as he was told for the next day or so, so I loosened the reins. His next call was late, his words slurred, his tone understandably resentful. Finally, unable to understand what he was saying, I had said, "I can't be responsible for you, Kevin; I have to take care of my sons." It took me a moment to realize that I had just betrayed him. Perhaps he had slammed the phone down in anger at that point and broken it; maybe he had signed off in relief. Maybe those were the last two choices left to him. In any event, the line went dead. I called Roger Melone, his conductor friend, in Albuquerque, and left a message begging him to check in on him. Then I went to bed.

Several days later (as the young doctor in Queens had predicted a year earlier) the police, carrying out the "welfare check" that I requested, found him. His solitary death— the point at which his spirit finally departed the body he had so badly abused, rather than just his sense of self—swimming in his own puke, came at the age of 57. Cause? A heart attack, due to unmedicated delirium tremens and, probably, a case of the flu—the autopsy found only trace amounts of alcohol in his system. He had been dead for several days, lying alone on the floor, like Father in the Big Cedar House, in the bedroom of the lovely little adobe home he kept on Alhambra Street in Albuquerque. His body was so badly decomposed that Ryan and I had to identify him from pictures at the Medical Examiner's office. I hope that he died quickly. I often wonder how long he suffered. *Three down, one to go,* I thought.

I flew to Albuquerque immediately and presently stood over the spot in his bedroom where he died. His childhood teddy bear Pooh was propped behind the chair. I picked it up and brought it to my nose: there it was, now mixed with the smell of death, the barely perceptible fragrance of Mother's Chanel No. 5.

There was everywhere evidence of both an interrupted life and a successful slow-motion suicide. The police had left the television on: it hissed and showed snow—the "cosmic microwave background radiation" left over from the Big Bang, the outermost ripple in the cosmic pond. Soiled bed sheets twisted grotesquely on the unmade bed. He'd taken his landline off the hook. The phone dangled from the side table like the orange furry tongue of a White Cemetery Iris. He had never heard the half dozen messages that I had left on the day he died on what I now saw was a broken cell phone, screen smashed, on the floor.

Kevin had long, beautiful fingers as a child; I loved watching their supple sweeps across the keys as he practiced Debussy's *Claire de Lune*. He wrote a book, which our Father typed and Mother illustrated, called *Sverre's Saga*. He was tall and slender, a determined long-distance runner; he edited his high school yearbook and starred in and directed plays. He had "baritone hair" before that was a thing, and sad hazel eyes that drove girls nuts, although he never put two-and-two together and realized that he could have been a cad if he hadn't been such a good man. He fell in love with opera as a teenager. Giuseppe Verdi was his musical hero. He loved how characters in operas expressed their feelings: openly, at the top of their lungs, like crazed animals. His own singing voice, an English horn-colored lyric baritone, was ideal for Sondheim and Mozart, but not large enough for the heavy Verdi roles that had inspired him to major in voice at UW-Madison. So, he turned to orchestra management. On a tip from Mother, he got a job with the Milwaukee Symphony, and married Ryan's mother, Judith, a violinist—she had studied with her father, and with George Bornoff, and with Raphael Bronstein, whose nickname for her was "Cookie," a play on her maiden name—in the Milwaukee Symphony.

Despite his addiction, he was by all accounts an excellent arts administrator. In 1997, after stints with the Milwaukee Symphony, Denver Symphony, Florida Symphony, Los Angeles Chamber Orchestra, and Illinois Symphony, Kevin landed in New Mexico, where he won a job as executive director of the now-defunct New Mexico Symphony Orchestra. The board hired Kevin knowing that he was an alcoholic. His staff was not just his professional but his personal support network—they were people who loved him who—when he disappeared to a hotel with a crate of booze—noticed his absence and went out to look for him. Orchestra and man kept one another alive for a decade, with Kevin as a maverick fundraiser, a key factor in his job. "You need someone who knows how to go ask people for fifty thousand and a hundred thousand dollars," conductor Roger Melone remarked after Kevin died. "That takes a very special person, and he knew how to do that. He had to inspire trust to get people to do that."

Grown acquisitive with the financial stability that Kevin's fundraising and stewardship had established, the musicians demanded a substantial pay hike. "The orchestra saved my life, and I saved its life," Kevin told me when they struck. "I knew that they were being unrealistic, but players usually are. I told them that if they got the board to give them the new contract, I'd retire, and predicted—without joy—that the symphony would be out of business within two seasons." The union's victory was Pyrrhic: the orchestra declared bankruptcy soon after the players won their contract negotiation.

Kevin took no satisfaction in having been right, but he did take satisfaction in having a hand in creating the symphony's endowment, the charter of which stipulated that, if it went out of business, then the money would endow Albuquerque-based symphonic music. "What this meant to donors was that no matter what happened to the symphony in the long run, their money would not go down the drain," Melone observed. Kevin turned to freelance consulting, and then served as executive director of Opera Southwest for a while, but the safety net of friends and co-workers that had helped save him from his own demons was gone. His binges increased in duration and intensity. In the end, his road became a river with only one terminus.

Kevin's cat Max came in and threaded himself between my ankles before stopping to sniff at the large rufous patch of carpet at my feet. I gathered him up and took one final look at the last things that my brother saw before he died, slung him over my shoulder, switched off the television, and walked to the living room. I found LP's of Verdi's *Otello* and placed the first disc on the record player, opened the windows, cranked the volume, walked out into his back yard, found a seat in a metal chair, cradled Max, and listened. The sun had set. A sliver of moon winked in the eggshell-blue evening sky. Even though a shower earlier in the day had ended a protracted drought, Kevin had ceased watering his garden: his beloved roses had died; the fountain was dry, the peach tree was desiccated, the flower beds had returned to desert. Max purred in my lap as I dug my fingers by habit into his supple flanks, caressing his fur. The atmosphere of loneliness and abandonment was almost tangible. Inside the little adobe house his son, comforted by his new bride, chose what to keep and what to throw away, performing the mundane task that the quick do for the still. *My brothers protected me*, I thought, as Jago sang, "*Ah! Bevi, bevi con me*" inside. *When it became my turn to protect them, I didn't.* Montano, separating Cassio and Roderigo, sang, "*Parole d'un ebbro....*" As the swordfight broke out, I thought, *No, I'm not Cain. Neither of them died because my last conversations with them ended the way that it did. But that doesn't change the fact that, in the end, like Peter, I denied them both: I didn't try to save Britt; I couldn't save Kevin; I only saved myself for the sake of my sons.* And yet, the great duet between Otello and Desdemona flowed on—"*Scendean sulle mie tenebre la gloria, Il paradiso e gli astri a benedir....*"

A satisfying narrative, yes; but how much of it is true? What we choose to believe to have been the truth trumps common sense. There's no empirical way to prove to yourself or others that you've acted humanely, or even that you've done the "right" thing; and it is just too, too easy to say that one addict died and another didn't one night because that's what he was on a day of the week that had a "y" in it.

◆◆ 25 ◆◆

People and Process
2013–2015

I had been in recovery since the night that I told Kevin as he slept in the Chevy that I had had my last drink. Recovery for me had been (and continues to be) centered on coming to terms with the fragmentary memories that have returned of things that I said and did while drunk. Like many highly-functioning alcoholics, there were many times when I was high that people didn't realize that I was; there were other times—many—that I didn't consider myself high, but I was altered—enough that my judgment was impaired. That man no longer has a place in my life, but I have come to understand the effect that he had on others, accept responsibility for my actions, and am ashamed. I acknowledge that I'll encounter people for the rest of my life that have every right to despise me for the person I once was. They know who they are; I do, too. I don't expect them to forgive me; I am aware that, in some cases, my behavior was unforgiveable.

David Roth, general director of Kentucky Opera, had tested me out the year before by engaging me to stage the three *New York Stories* pocket operas for his company. In retrospect, my evolving into an "auteur opera composer-director" was inevitable—Menotti had predicted as much that day over lunch at the Barclay. I had known all along that I possessed the skills and the inclination but had resisted the temptation to be a "one-man band" because I felt that the result would be better if a "full-time librettist" executed the libretto under my supervision rather than me "moonlighting" as one. After four operas with Paul, and several more with others, I concluded that, in my case at least, the benefit of being able to choose my own words resulted in better music, and, since opera is driven by the music and not the words, the way forward was clear. Having observed, over the span of thirty years—and to a large extent guided—Stephen Wadsworth, Ken Cazan, Mark Streshinsky, Robert DeSimone, and a dozen other directors as they staged my operas, I knew that I could do at least as good a job as they with my own material—better, in fact, since the long exploratory meetings during which I explained—and, to be fair, honed—my vision could take place in my own head, and the time spent instead on bringing the cast into the opera's world and empowering them.

I agreed in May to return to Milwaukee for four weeks to direct *I Hear America Singing*, a three-character musical commissioned by Skylight Music Theater's artistic director Viswa Subbaraman, the Masur protégé who I'd first met when he asked me to serve as a judge for an opera competition that his startup chamber opera company Opera Vista in Houston was holding. He'd gone on to conduct a stirring revival of *Vera* in a Houston strip club staged by Buck Ross. Skylight had nurtured the nascent directorial talents of both Francesca

Zambello and Stephen Wadsworth during the 80s, but it had also recently suffered a very public meltdown in leadership at the board and management levels that made it all the way into the pages of the *New York Times*. Entirely aware of what an extraordinary opportunity I had been given as a creative person to craft closure, I essentially wrote the show (*Together*, the "opus one" in my "Work Log,") that I would have written in July 1976 if I had known and lived everything I had since. The story, which took place in a Manhattan apartment during the 90s, concerned three middle-aged musicians grappling with their pasts: Robbie, a composer-pianist, Roger and his ex-wife Rose, singers. In it I blended new tunes, arias, and art songs by myself with my musical re-interpretations of American folk tunes to create the score, wrote new lyrics to new songs, and gave new lyrics to folk tunes, which dated from the Civil War era to World War I, to advance the show's story. Some of the songs also contained lyrics from the poems of William Blake, A. E. Houseman, Gertrude Stein and traditional ballads. Opening night, as the audience streamed into Skylight's 99-seat black box studio theater, I strolled onstage and tapped the grand piano that occupied the center of the set and tapped one-two-three-four-five-six-seven-eight. The 97-minute *roman à clef* annoyed self-appointed "Musical Theater Experts," and tickled genuine sophisticates. The reviews of the show itself were mixed, but audiences and critics all loved the cast, which included stalwart friend and champion Robert Frankenberry serving double duty as music director and playing the role of Robbie; and two local actors, Rick Penzich as Roger; and Carol Greif as Rose. I'm not sure if the script—hammered out in hotel rooms during productions of two other shows—was any good, but it was true to life. It played well with audiences, and I had fun directing it, despite having to be away from Gilda and the boys.

To my delight, Gilda flew out for opening night. I took her for the first time to a matinee at the Oriental Landmark Theater. The old place's magic coursed through me as we stood in the lobby and breathed in its faded, funky, faux opulence. As an organist fumbled loopily through an awful medley from *Carousel,* I shared without embarrassment the precious treasures of my youth. I introduced her to the golden-eared onyx lions flanking the broad staircase as we climbed to the low-slung, sweeping balcony, the Buddha's, the stage area with its massive dimmers, the dust hanging in the air just as it should. "I can't explain it, I just can't," I said, as we walked, hand in hand, up the main aisle. "I love this place the way I love Yaddo. It's what Allan Gurganus wrote … you know, 'some essence quorum of our souls' intensities.'" Gilda nodded. "This place," I continued, "is in my spiritual DNA. I feel as though I spent entire hours here suspended in that 'chanceful,' formative state where anything could still happen, safe, but questing; still a child, but on the cusp…." I stopped. She smiled. "I know, honey," she said. "It's what you and Gardner had Amelia say to her baby—'Anything is possible.'" The organist stopped playing. "Show me where you and your mother sat," she said, tenderly. Gilda had led me to within a few rows of where Mother and I had sat that cold winter afternoon in 1981. "Um," I said, looking away from her slightly so that she wouldn't see the tears that accompanied the smile on my face and gesturing. "It was just … over here." I placed the fingertips of my hand under her elbow, indicated with the other hand a nearby spot, and walked her the few feet. "We're here," I said, not believing it. "Well," I laughed, "if this isn't exactly the spot, then it should've been. How about here?" My God, I thought, as Gilda sat down and shook her hair in just that way and my heart leapt up and I couldn't help it I just choked and smiled and shook my head with love and awe and gratitude as she turned and flashed me the same sudden, sunny, dazzling, lopsided smile Mother used to. Gilda was more glamorous than Rita Hayworth, every bit the artist Mother had been and more. A vibrant, powerful woman in her prime, Gilda turned to me and—moving far, far past transference to transforming sorrow into joy in a heartbeat—remarked, "Honey, it's like your mom said: 'It's a poem about rebirth'!"

We returned, as usual, to Nicaragua during the 2015 winter holidays; the Pacific near Rio Mar that year was anything but. One day, Atticus and I headed out, hand in hand, for a walk along the beach to Casares. It was that time of the day in the tropics when the gravitational pull of the setting sun and the rising moon compete the most fiercely. The idea that the seventh wave is always the largest is a myth of course; but there is to the surf a stubbornly predictable, horrible rhythm of violence and surcease. The sheer tonnage of seawater thrown against the Nicaraguan coast will crush you like a rag doll if you're caught at sunset between the water and the lava cliffs.

Bolaños, the affable right-winger whom I had met at a party in 2007 was out. In the interim, Daniel Ortega had returned. He had thrown up statues of Bolívar and Chávez here and there, built homes for those *Managüenses* who had been living in *Las Ruinas*, accepted a treatment facility from the Germans to decontaminate Lake Nicaragua, began coming to terms with *La Cheureca*, and begun paying people to pick up the garbage around the highways. Closer to our little house, talk had finally given way to definite plans for the restoration of the Casares oceanfront, devastated by the 1992 tsunami. The road from Diriamba to Casares had been paved; the Chinese had fixed the one that ran south. There was even talk of running a municipal water pipe south to the Hotel Lupita, just north of *Rio Mar*.

As Atticus and I walked northwards along the beach, his small, strong hand—as little boys' hands must—began writhing wildly to get free. He was desperate to run into the Pacific, to throw himself into the incoming surf, and tired of his father telling him to be careful. Rendered breathless by the intensity of his own emotions, he cried, "Let me *go*, Papa. Let me *go*!" I gripped his hand all the harder as the seventh wave begin to rise to the west, Leviathan-colored, majestic, and horrible. "Ow, Papa," he said, pulling away. I lost my footing, fell, lost my grip, and he dashed into the water in pursuit of his flip-flop. He dove for his shoe just as the undertow was strongest and slingshotted seaward like an arrow, arms extended, head down, somersaulting like driftwood. My heart exploded. There was nobody around to call out to, no time to damn myself for being over 50 and out of shape. I pushed up from the sand and stumbled into the surf just as the next roller, horse head high, broke over him. *God, take me and not him* was my only thought. I was about six feet from him when the wave hit me head on and brought me to my knees. My arms were extended before me like a celebrant's arms to a congregation, half a broken Host in each hand. Water still up to my neck; I heard the roar of the wave breaking on the beach behind me. Suddenly, Atticus appeared before me, tossed skyward like flotsam by the wave, clutching his lost flip flop, a look of wild triumph on his proud, beautiful, magnificent, seven-year-old face. The ocean threw him into my arms and I grabbed him, hard, and held him for dear life as my heart burst a second time. *How could any father bear to look on as his son drowned? Right?* There was a knot in my throat, and a hot iron behind my forehead. *Death has slapped me on the back and bought me a Toña*, I thought, aware that I was going into shock. It was as though we had just been baptized. "Run up the beach," I commanded. "Get inland." With a passing, quizzical look, he did what he was told. *A father's dignity comes, Lord, from the fact that one of us will (and has a right to) completely forget that they were saved today, but the other will not,* I thought. A moment later, I caught up to him and, together we continued up the beach. I could scarcely breathe. Atticus had no idea how close we had both come to drowning. I watched him from the corner of my eye as—happy— he pointed his strong chin into the wind. After a while, whistling, he slipped his hand back into mine, and together we returned to the little house. "Want to watch Pelicans roost?" I asked, knowing that he would say yes.

As Father had in his house, and Kevin in his, when we returned from Nicaragua I crafted floor-to-ceiling pine bookcases in the library of the Big Victorian House. Once they were ready, I performed the respectful repetitive ablution beloved of bibliophiles everywhere—uncrating the thousands of books I'd been accumulating since 1979 and shelving them. Since this was a once-in-a-lifetime task, I took special care to open each, check for marginalia, note the date and place I'd acquired it, fan the pages to allow any papers to slide out, and wipe it down with a cloth before placing it tenderly between its brothers and sisters, there to stand for the rest of my lifetime.

It was time also for me to uncrate my brothers' and parents' books and to fold them into my library. But for those that he and Mother had acquired together in college, Father had thrown out or given away all his books and papers. How forlorn the books that remained in the Big Cedar House's library had looked, propped at crazy angles, cigarette-smoke-stained, moldy, some lolling open over the lip of the shelf like tongues. I fished a copy of *Leaves of Grass* from the crate and paged through it. Their marginalia, the handwriting so personal, so recognizable, was a testament to the seriousness with which they pursued their dialogue with favorite poets. It was possible to read their hearts and minds flowering for the first time. He wrote in the margin on one side of a page of Keats' *On First Looking Into Chapman's Homer*, "*Man cannot possess perpetual happiness; only momentary glimpses in intimation of beauty.*" On the other side of the page, she answered, "*Note how he makes nouns of adjectives & vice versa.*" Further down the page, he wrote, "*Every poet is contributing to a great poem; each poet is holding ground in his way—,*" to which she replied, with two brisk down-strokes of her pen beside Keats' lines, "*Of course, this is the function of a poet's role.*" Really, it's a love duet they're singing, with Keats' observations about Homer as the subtext. Beautiful. Keats had always been Father's solace, and John Milton; Mother loved Browning, and Baudelaire. A volume of Baudelaire, with Mother's corrections to the French translation interlaced with the published text, had a bookplate that read, "This book is the property of Gwen Johnson." They continued to sing together after marrying: Father picked up an anthology of British and American poetry during the 60s the bookplate of which read, "*Ex Libris* Gwen and Earl Hagen—*darling I knew you had to have this—Earl.*" A copy of Dylan Thomas' collected poems was inscribed by me, aged 13 in blue ballpoint pen, "*For Mama—a gift from your children, Christmas, 1974.*" When I die, my sons will inherit this library. Atticus already quotes his Uncle Kevin—"If you have a book, you have a friend"—and loves to read; it won't be long before my sons' jots join the choir of cryptic, witty, pensive, and wise voices that sings our family's duet with the past.

Cross-legged on the floor, dipping into books languidly and at random, I came upon Virgil's *Why Composers Write How* and re-read it for the first time since the early 90s. "Excellent music can be written on almost any kind of money," Virgil wrote, with that ringing certitude he was so good at conjuring—

> The composer who lives on music-writing invariably tends toward theater.... By and large, the theater is where the money is and where most of the composers are who have once had a taste of that money.... All I am saying is that the commercially successful professional composer (and by commercially successful I mean he eats) is likely to be a theater man. That is his occupational deformity, if any.

I'd commended Virgil's essay to a hundred private pupils over the past thirty-five years, from Dan Sonenberg to Tevi Eber, from Juhi Bansal to Karalyn Schubring, and had forgotten most of what he had said in it. Reading it again made me think of all of them. When I began, at Bard, I emulated the teaching styles of Ned and David in private: I was brutal, autocratic, and impatient with mediocrity. This didn't work very well for liberal arts college undergraduates, and so I relaxed my ways and became more nurturing and less demanding with all but the handful of extraordinary ones. With those I was as ruthless as my teachers had been with me: I was content to correct notation and spelling until they realized that they were wasting my time by bringing in mediocre work. Only when they gave me their best did I reciprocate. During my decade at Bard and elsewhere, I observed myself becoming increasingly didactic, and I began to believe that I knew what I was talking about. (In retrospect, it's clear to me that having been given tenure at Bard would have ruined me as a teacher.) Wherever I taught, I always taught at the piano, and played through and sang my pupils' work for them; or made them do so for me if they were able, and jotted on their manuscript, as my teachers had on mine. I prescribed books to read, and pieces to listen to, and still do. But I teach in a completely different fashion now.

The computer and the Internet have changed everything. Now, I vastly prefer teaching privately on Skype to lessons in person. Online, the student sends me the score file of her composition notated using the Sibelius notation program, and I open it on my computer, sharing my screen so that together we can manipulate their score as I teach. The midi playback makes hearing a reasonable realization of their intent easier. (I don't believe composing into music software makes for "glib" music any more than using a word processing program does when writing prose.) The student is free to make a digital video recording of the 60-minute encounter so that, afterwards, she can replay it for further study. I keep a sidebar open so that, when I mention a book the student hasn't read, I can Google it; I can throw up on the screen the biography of any composer, any composition, any performer or performing organization discussed. At the end of the lesson, I've left a list of key concepts in the sidebar, as well as links for further study, and return to them the annotated score file of their composition. What's lost for the student is the quiet time spent looking at one's teacher looking at one's music; what's lost for the teacher is the ability to require the student to play what they write. Nowadays, though, with so much music being beyond notation, what's gained by teaching this way far outweighs that which is lost.

Thirty-two years after our first meeting, I attended a reading of Barbara Grecki's new full-length play, *A Woman in Morocco* at a black box theater in Midtown. I couldn't force myself to wait even until the audience had left before taking her by the arm and imploring, "We've got to make this into an opera together." In the event, I served as stage director, and collaborated with Barbara on the adaptation of her script to libretto. Weary of contending with the usual producers' creative meddling, I decided to develop the work *ala carte*, granting a libretto reading to a small company in Philadelphia, the first staged workshop to Butler University in Austin, and finally, the professional staged premiere to Kentucky Opera in Louisville.

After the libretto reading, from which we learned nothing, Barbara and I gave the opera to Robert DeSimone, who produced an elaborate fully-staged November 2013 workshop production at the Butler Opera Center in Austin, site of the disastrous *Bandanna* production decades earlier. My challenging post–Korngold-ian, score glittered, thanks to Kelly Kuo's inspired leadership and the preparation of vocal coach Kathy Kelly; Robert's direction was honest—he'd agreed to "stage" *Morocco*, not to "fix" it, but to "stress test" the dramaturgy for the authors shielded from reviews.

Barbara came to stay in Rhinebeck for a few days and, together, we took what we had learned in Texas and spread red ink over what was left. I shared the revisions with Buck Ross (trusted head of the Moores Opera Center who had directed revivals of both *Vera* and *Amelia*) over breakfast at Café Luxembourg in New York. Buck provided invaluable feedback concerning the psychological verifiability of Clare's behavior in the final scene—advice for which I'll be forever grateful.

With Nancy Lampton's financial support, David Roth enabled me not only to stage-direct *Morocco* at the 350-seat Victor Jory Theater at the Actors Theater of Louisville for Kentucky Opera myself, but also to supervise every aspect of its design and execution. As a director, I staged the work in a way that capitalized on the performers', the situations', and the venue's strengths and minimized their weaknesses—I played the clarinet that was given to me. By necessity, I availed myself of the usual "poor theater" conventions—putting the singers' voices and bodies in first position, highlighting ritualistic, repeated gestures, and transforming props such as the knife, scarf, and stolen book, which doubled as Hitch-cockian MacGuffins into other objects, enhancing their significance. I instructed the singers not to "cheat" towards the audience when they sang, insisting that they concentrate as in film acting only on one another—particularly since the audience was practically on top of the cast in the three-quarter-thrust black box. Emulating Orson Welles, I staged every scene with foreground, middle ground, and background action. Characters rarely left the stage. But, contrary to Welles' tastes, I immersed the cast in the Method. The Greek Chorus of women doubled as Furies and moved sets; limited set pieces were assembled from what the company had on hand, and costumes were built from the gifted costumer's existing collection, with very few purchases. The theater possessed an ample compliment of lighting

A happy composer-director on May 15, 2015 (opening night), of Kentucky Opera's production of *A Woman in Morocco* at the Victor Jory Theater in Louisville with co-librettist Barbara Grecki (*center*) and conductor Roger Zahab (*right*).

instruments. Victoria Bain, just beginning her career, executed—and improved upon—the Jean Rosenthal–inspired lighting style. The result was filmic, fluid, and perfectly in sync with the musical and scenic shifts.

While directing *Morocco*, I received a note from Ford Lallerstedt. *"It seems,"* he wrote, *"that your life has been filled with every measure of good."* Interviewing to teach at Curtis, I had leveled with Ford about my drinking; he had been supportive and understanding and had hired me anyway. I had asked him if I had made a mistake all those years earlier, quitting the Curtis faculty. He wrote back, *"A so-called studio at Curtis, in light of your obvious success, is way down the list."* I heard Kevin say, *"You were a success, Britt: write it a gazillion times on the blackboard, okay?"* It had never occurred to me that Ford, for whom I had consummate respect and admiration, might consider me anything even remotely close to a success. I realized that what had held me back professionally in the past was not the accuracy of my estimation of my own talent—which I knew was great, but which never measured up to what I knew was possible, but my pride. It had been more important to me to be liked than it had been to be respected; Father had succeeded in making me the kind of man who kept his head down and his ass in the air. Despite Diamond's passionate admonitions, I had continued, year after year, to publicly minimize my own gifts as though either above them or ashamed of them—with the result that people unaware of, insensitive to, or in competition with, them were free to under-rate me as a man and as an artist—free to conclude the worst.

I'll forever be beholden to David Roth for giving me the opportunity to feel completely expressed for the first time as an artist making live opera theater. Members of my Yaddo family Don and Genie Rice and Elaina Richardson, among others, flew in to share the experience; Nana threw a marvelous dinner party at which we toyed with the idea of turning *Now, Voyager* into an opera.

Opening night, as Barbara and I held hands, I gently tapped—unbeknownst to her—one-two-three-four-five-six-seven-eight-nine with my foot as the lights dimmed. Both the production and the opera—even though it was in fact a jeremiad—were received with universal popular and critical praise; panels and conferences on human trafficking surrounded the première, and, as centerpiece of the 2016 Festival of Faiths, audiences included clergy and NGO workers from around the world. I found the labor completely satisfying as an artist and person, and entirely within my wheelhouse.

I had never had any interest in being a one man band, and I truly understood the alchemical nature of collaboration, but I also knew that I had now completed my apprenticeship in the lyric theater by performing every one of its constituent jobs, from catwalk to orchestra pit, from donor's luncheon and the board room to the Green Room: I'd budgeted, designed and helped build physical productions and sets, projections, and supertitles; I'd designed lighting and hung the instruments; I'd served as a grip, and stage managed, and "called" cues; I'd done make-up, designed costumes, and sound; I'd sung leading and supporting roles, albeit as a young man; I'd played piano in pit orchestras, conducted—and recorded the cast albums of—my own operas and others,' copied orchestra parts, orchestrated, and done extensive vocal coaching; I'd directed straight plays and choreographed musicals; I'd been "that composer" living through a soul-crushing flop, the one enjoying a career-making triumph, and the one who had learned the limitations of what could be achieved even when you've done everything right and it still doesn't matter; I'd written my own libretti, effectively managed through selective empowerment powerful, high-maintenance collaborators; I'd played for opera improvisation workshops in the Village during the early 90s; I'd "put my own shows over" by singing and playing their scores at the piano for commissioners, collaborators, and colleagues.

Through it all, I've just wanted to learn how to write a good opera. This is what I've pieced together, so far: one stages the opera that the people in the room can perform, not the one in your head; one performs the concerto the way everyone on stage can that day, not the one in your head. One's truth is useful to others only inasmuch as one has rendered it transposable; even then, "truth" and "love" are not enough. All this is true whether one wrote the thing or not. Art will take care of itself. Critics and colleagues will carp. Life will go on. One's "best" work will be met with skepticism and incomprehension. So, relax: concentrate on people and process.

◆◆ 26 ◆◆

We're All—All Here
2015–2017

Nova Scotia lox from Barney Greengrass on a fresh H&H Bagel and a cup of Zabar's coffee are the smells of the Upper West Side of Manhattan and grilled peppers are the smell of Albuquerque in the fall; a shallow bowl of borscht with a dollop of sour cream in the middle and a very cold shot of Stolichnaya is the taste of Coney Island and Managua's burnt leña in the winter; Red Star Yeast is Milwaukee's smell, evergreen and wood smoke are Aspen's in the summer. Ghenady Meierson's invitation to return to Philly to deliver a lecture about Alexander Pushkin, Tchaikovsky, and the libretto of *Eugene Onegin* to his Russian Opera Workshop at the Academy of Vocal Arts prompted a rare return to the clingy, moist low-tide tang of the Schuylkill River and the dry, metallic smell of air conditioners mixed with downtown's signature late summer notes of burnt scrapple and Gingko. As always, I walked from 30th Street Station to Rittenhouse Square and its exquisite canopy of Sycamores and looked toward the corner of 18th and Locust Street to Curtis. Instead of turning toward AVA my feet found themselves drawn for old time's sake to 219 South 17th Street, across from the Warwick Hotel—now called the "Radisson Blu," renovated, with a repulsively redesigned, pseudo-internationalist lobby.

There, unchanged, was Little Pete's! I pushed open the door, banged my fist on the cigarette machine just to the right for luck, breathed in the fragrance of congealed-grease and refrigerated air, took a swivel chair at the lime-green bar, slapped my newspaper down, noted with approval the tacky dust-covered plastic hanging plants, and looked across the horseshoe-shaped counter at a young woman. She was the picture of fierce determination, hunched over a thick pad of yellow Passantino music paper. Her mauve silk shirt, tucked neatly at her thin waist into faded jeans, hung loosely over her small breasts. Some sort of red bandanna was loosely knotted in her hair. *26*, I thought. No socks, cute red Keds sneakers. *No, more like 22 tops.* She glanced up at me, reached without looking for her coffee, took a sip, and returned to her composing. I unfolded the newspaper. There it was: "a wrecking ball is scheduled to fly through Little Pete's." *No!* The waiter approached me, flipping open his order pad. I pointed at the newspaper and grimaced. He shrugged. I gestured for him to come close. "Give me a coffee to go," I said in an undertone. "And give me the check for the woman at the counter. Tell her that someone just paid her tab and left." He shook his head, scribbled a few figures, ripped the receipt off his pad, dropped it in front of me, and poured me my coffee. He leaned over to her and said something. She looked up suddenly, looked around Little Pete's, smiled, and returned to her composing. He returned to me, wordlessly placed a to-go cup of black coffee in front of me and walked away. Happy, I rose, gave the slip to the guy at the register, paid, and turned to leave. "Do you want that in a bag?" He asked, pointing at the to-go cup in my hand. I looked at it— white, with blue stenciling on it that read in faux-Greek letters *We Are Happy To Serve You*—and felt happy.

Gilda and I drove with the boys to Virginia the next week so that together we could serve as the composition faculty for the Wintergreen Music Festival. As Erin Freeman led the Festival Orchestra in a performance of Barber's *Knoxville, Summer 1915* in the tent atop Wintergreen Mountain I sat, with Atticus on my lap, looking out over the Blue Ridge Mountains, thinking of how good it felt not just to be so intimately connected by school and tradition to Barber but also how much better by far it felt to cede my place in it and at Little Pete's to the girl in the red Keds. Now, somewhere in line after Ned and before her sat the bearded boy from Madison. As the undulating string figure with which *Knoxville* begins created the space into which James Agee's words flowed, I felt Atticus' finger gently touch the corner of my eye. "Are you okay, Papa?" he whispered, looking with wonder at the single tear that had collected there. "Never happier in my life," I whispered, hugging him close, and feeling more healed with each beat of my heart. I had come to serve as the Wintergreen Festival's chair of composition at the festival, for which I had created a piano concerto (my second) called *Chaplin's Tramp* that could be performed without the film being shown and remain viable as a concert work. Its formal elements derived from the structure of Chaplin's screenplay, of course; but the postmodern narrative the music conveyed also has its own rhyme and reason. That narrative was as follows: the piano (or, in live performance, the pianist her or himself) was Chaplin (who was, after all, a gifted tunesmith) as an

Following along, as chair of the composition faculty (2014–present), in the score with our composition students as Gilda Lyons rehearses arias from her opera *A New Kind of Fallout* with the Wintergreen Festival Orchestra, conducted by Erin Freeman, at the 2016 Wintergreen Music Festival, in Virginia on 17 August 2016. Seated, left to right: Britta Epling, Michael Laster, me, Eliza Triolo, and standing: Patrick Walker, Æden McEvoy, Meg Huskin, Chin-Shuo Wu (photograph by John Taylor).

old man, sitting alone in a screening room, watching a print of his film for the first time in many years. The audience watched the film with Chaplin and listened to his feelings and memories unfold as they watched the film. In a way, for a few minutes, we all got to become the Tramp. Atticus sat on my lap, Seamus on Gilda's. Erin, piano soloist Peter Marshall, and the chamber ensemble premiered *Chaplin's Tramp*. This time it was Atticus' turn to weep silently. "Are you okay, honey?" I whispered. "Yes, Papa, it's just—." "The movie, or the music?" "It's the music, papa—it's so happy-sad," he said, hugging me back.

I thought of that moment a few months later when, seated alone in the audience as Michael Christie conducted the premiere of my Symphony No. 5—Victoria Vargas was the soloist; the Phoenix Symphony played—I felt that familiar feeling of communion during the final movement. People around me were weeping, as they had at the end of both acts of *Amelia*, and at the end of *Brow*. The audience had been undeniably moved. I had connected with them, and yet I felt alone, acutely aware of what had and had not been achieved. People had had an aesthetic experience, Kevin had been memorialized, JoAnn Falletta's poetry had been set; I had reached an enviable milestone in my life as a composer; and I took quiet pride in having written a worthy piece. On the other hand, the professional "glass ceiling" that I'd felt for thirty years remained, and I understood that it would probably always be there, no matter how good my work was. Though her shoes remained unfillable, Fran had retired as Vice President for Concert Music at ASCAP, and her longtime protégé, my very dear friend since the early 80s, gifted composer-advocate Cia Toscanini (granddaughter of Arturo) had assumed her role; the sensitive and staunch Michael Spudic had

taken the role of composer liaison, but I no longer knew the faces of the workers in the offices across the street from Lincoln Center by sight. The American Academy of Arts and Letters awarded me a prestigious award, yet I couldn't help feeling that my time was passing, professionally. A new generation of excellent young composers had emerged, wishing, as I had at their age, that I would clear the stage so that they could get on with their lives, and management—always hungry for novelty and youth—could only approve.

Afterwards, the Green Room—which, as usual, was not green—held some staff members of the orchestra, and the dozen or so donors who had pooled their money to commission my piece. How different the world (and I) was from the day that I had sweated out my

It has been a pleasure to serve as co-chair of the composition program for the Wintergreen Summer Music Festival in Virginia with my wife Gilda for the past few years. Each year we bring our children, Seamus and Atticus, who took this photo in 2017 in the Blue Ridge Mountains.

first Green Room after the première of Symphony No. 1. Comfortably in control of the situation with a conductor I admire, cognizant of every thank you that needed to be tendered, every patron that deserved a nod, I knew my job, and how to help not just myself but the orchestra as an institution. "Thanks to you," I toasted the donors with seltzer, paraphrasing Boulanger's dying words, "the music will be without beginning or end."

Russell Platt, who had become a music editor at *The New Yorker*, curated a program at Bargemusic in Brooklyn in honor of Ned's 92nd birthday. Russell asked me to deliver Ned, if possible, to the event and, even though I knew he'd decline, I felt compelled to ask. "Yes," he sighed. "Do you think I *have* to?" "Of course not, Ned," I answered, laughing. "But you know that I have to ask." Ned's voice, faintly, over the receiver, turned away from the phone: "Mary, *Mary*, where's my book? *Get* me my red book." After a few beats of silence, he continued, "Come to my house the day of the event to pick me up, and I'll decide then whether I'm up to it."

Mary had gotten Ned to dress himself by the time I arrived. His clean button-down shirt fell loosely outside his baggy chinos. He had passed a razor across his cheeks, but a thin swatch of shaving cream still clung to a patch of throat near his jugular. "Are you coming to the concert?" I asked, kissing him on both cheeks and wiping away the shaving cream. "I still don't know whether I want to go," he said. "I went to an Academy thing a couple of days ago, and now…." He trailed off, his attention having shifted to a compact disc on the red dining room table of my piano trios that I'd given him a few years earlier. Absently pushing it across the tabletop a few inches with his index finger, he asked, "Did you write all these?" "Of course, I did, Ned," I smiled. Mary entered silently, carrying dinner plates from the kitchen. She shoved the various papers to the side and placed them out for the three of us. "Do you want water, Daron?" she asked quietly. "No, thanks," I said, looking at the five spears of asparagus, small piece of steamed chicken, and handful of iceberg lettuce on the plate in front of me. Ned put chicken in his mouth and chewed without interest. Suddenly alarmed, he picked at his sleeve and called into the kitchen, "Mary, why am I wearing a fresh shirt? I don't want to go anywhere!" Calmly, over the sound of

When Ned Rorem's grandniece Mary Marshall snapped this picture at his apartment in New York City on January 2, 2018, he had just observed to me (*right*) that we had known one another for over 35 years.

running water, she replied, "Ned, Daron's here to take you to Brooklyn to hear a concert in your honor." Without expression, he put a piece of bread in his mouth and chewed it. Swallowing, he looked at me, "What of mine are they going to play?" "*King Midas* I think," I replied cheerfully. "I'm looking forward to hearing it live. Do you recall the last time that *you* heard it?" He waved his hand in front of him as though sweeping away cobwebs. "Oh … I don't know," he said, wearily. He looked down, picked up his water glass and threw up everything he had just eaten into it. I looked away. There was a knock at the door. Barbara Grecki arrived, and we exchanged glances as I let her in. I took Ned's water glass into the kitchen and handed it to Mary, who accepted it without comment. "Barbara," I called into the dining room, "can I pour you a glass of wine before we go?" I peeked out. She leaned solicitously over Ned, and wiped his lips with a flour sack napkin. "No thanks, darling," she answered. Mary reentered, and asked, "Does anyone want dessert?"

When we arrived at the Barge, Barbara took the seat next to me. Paul Sperry, on the other side, touched my arm and drily observed, "It would have been nice if someone had actually come to this thing." Indeed, about twenty people sat, scattered like fallen leaves, among the empty chairs. Of Ned's nearly four decades' worth of students, only Russell and I were there; of composers under the age of fifty there were none. "Look at the skyline," I said, squeezing Barbara's hand. "Can't you just *see* the Twin Towers?" Seated next to me, she looked out the picture windows facing Manhattan and squinted her eyes. "If I squint, then I can sort of remember," she sighed. "I didn't see you at the Century the other week," Sperry said, smiling. "I wanted to ask you whether you can come and give a presentation to my American Song Rep class at Manhattan School again." I thought of the adventures we'd had together over the past 35 years; the pleasurable afternoons reading through the tall pile of manuscripts in his music room in the apartment on Central Park West that he shared with his sculptor wife Ann; how afterwards he would throw together a salad and pour me a glass of good dry Orvieto afterwards; the cycles, including *Figments, Songs of Madness and Sorrow,* and *Muldoon Songs* that he commissioned. Ann was dead now; he had moved to a smaller place near Riverside Park and, for the most part, ceased performing in public. "Of course. I'll email you tomorrow. Shall we have lunch together on 43rd Street?" I asked. "That sounds fun," he said. We sat together and listened to music by our friends. Russell, clearly disappointed that

My particular friend Paul Sperry and I at the Century Association in 2018. Paul, who commissioned several of my song cycles, and I have read through so much music and given so many performances together that I can't remember it all.

Ned was not with us, had included on the program a handful of his own elegant, tasteful settings of poetry by my old opera camerado Paul Muldoon. Russell graciously included my *After Words* cycle, movingly performed by Joseph Gaines, Justine Aronson, and the Brooklyn Art Song Society's artistic director Michael Brofman. Ned's *King Midas*, written the year of my birth, served as the finale.

"Look at the time! Oh dear! Oh, dear I shall be too late!" I thought, knocking on David Del Tredici's door at Westbeth a few weeks later. If Ned had slowed down with age, David seemed somehow to have manipulated time to the extent that he was more active than ever. David—perhaps our time's finest time twister—once sat down at the piano and played the entire 45-minute score of his opera *Dum Dee Tweedle* for me at his Sag Harbor home and I would have sworn that only fifteen minutes had elapsed. Now, nothing's more precious to an older composer than time. To give another composer's work time is to take it from one's own. I try not to think about all the years that, like Ben Weber, I copied "other men's music" for money. That's why I was deeply grateful when David gave over the entire afternoon to listening to *A Woman in Morocco* with the score. His current boyfriend let me in. After visiting for a while, I put the CD in the machine and took a seat. I watched him as he listened. (When you think about it, it is very weird the way composers watch one another listen to their music.) Now 78, prone to fading out and recovering with a jerk, David sat on the red leather couch across from me with *Morocco's* vocal score in his lap. His white hair was cut very short; his olive colored cargo pants and polo shirt were freshly washed. We'd seen each other yearly at Yaddo, and I had observed as his partner had died, the Sag Harbor house was sold, and new relationships had burst into flame and mellowed into warm friendships.

Presently I recalled to him a memory of breakfast at Yaddo during summer 1988 with Richard McCann, filmmaker Sharon Greytak, and painter Michael Flanagan. I related how I had just looked at him across the table and just … *marveled* at his talent. "I realized that being surrounded by talent," I told him, "simply gives me … *joy*." 27 years later, David now wore orange-rimmed glasses, moved more slowly through his Westbeth apartment and composing lair, and was on the very verge of retirement, but he still threw himself into his work like Leda to Music's Swan, composing and playing the piano for hours and hours every day—like Mother "*feeling* what a foot is like, not just *seeing* it," David has always preferred to "*feel* what the music is like, not just *hear* it." I wondered, as my old friend *what will Del Tredici do? Cheat time*, I hoped. *Rob time*, I prayed. *Beat time*, I knew. *Bend it; possibly even trick time into giving him more*, I had to believe. *It has all unfolded so quickly! Too quickly!* I thought. *He still has so much singing to do.* With a rush of tenderness, I thought, *look at the time!*

That October I reluctantly accepted Martin Bresnick's invitation to speak to the young composers at Yale. Beforehand there was the customary composition faculty luncheon. "When did we last see one another?" asked Chris Theofinides when he arrived. "Wasn't it at Paul Moravec's 'Pulitzer Party'?" "Ah," I laughed. "I had forgotten Paul's party. But I had not forgotten the pleasure of seeing you." When Aaron Kernis hugged me, I recalled fondly to him when he used to accompany the chorus at New York University that I used to conduct. Our performance of the Mozart G minor Mass together at the end of the semester was enthusiastic if not stylistically coherent. I recalled to composer Kathryn Harris the summer morning at Tanglewood thirty years ago when she, Bright Sheng, Eric Sawyer, and I stripped to our skivvies and danced from one edge of the meadow below the Seranak patio at Tanglewood to the other, hoping to ruffle the composure of the numbingly proper WGBH announcer Robert J. Lurtsema as he broadcast live from the patio. "It was Grieg I was playing on the flute, wasn't it?" she asked. "*Peer Gynt*, yes," I smiled. "Oh, that was *fun*," she smiled.

After signing a release handed to me by someone at the Yale Oral History of American Music project, I wrote. "*Art = Life,*" on the chalkboard. "I had a teacher once who began a class by writing that," I said, thinking of Doerf. "What does it mean to *you*?" Blank stares. "*Live an Examined Life,*" I jotted. Cool resistance. "*Craft Sets You Free,*" I scrawled. "What does that mean to *you*?" I asked. Nothing. Holding forth to these young composers, I had come a long way from the brash young creature with a song to sing who had burst through the heavy front doors of the Curtis Institute. In the back of the room, a pale graduate student raised his hand and asked, "Um, why do you frame everything you say in male hegemonic language?" I thought of the story Bernstein told me about how Copland, backstage after the premiere of *Connotations* at Avery Fisher Hall, wondered where all the young composers were. I turned my back on them and walked to the chalkboard, picked up a heavy chunk of chalk and wrote "*SING,*" in large block letters on the chalkboard. Beat. "Sing," I said, underlining it, "and *sing,*" I repeated, underlining it again, heavier, "and *SING,*" I finished, vehemently scratching a jagged scar of chalk under the word a final time. *Wasn't that what being a professional composer had turned out to be? Singing, and singing, and singing?*

I met Aaron for dinner. The waiter came by with a glass of wine for him. I turned my glass over. "Sober, now," I explained. "Ah," he said. "Do you mind?" "Of course not," I said, "enjoy it." By most measurements, Aaron's success as a composer of serious concert music had been as complete as is possible: Pulitzer prize, Yale professorship, decades of prestigious commissions, critical esteem—even a family. Gentle, rambling conversation about children, wives, mutual friends, and looking for meaning. I described leaving New York for Rhinebeck, feeling like Jean-Christophe ending up in a remote corner of Switzerland. "You know," I said, realizing it as I said it, "I am hoping that I have come out the other side." He put his knife and fork down and looked at me closely. "What do you mean?" *Shall I, in a decade or two, return to New York in triumph?* I teased myself. *No. There's no longer any triumph to be had there. For me, with my* soupçon *of talent, there probably never had been. I wonder if Muldoon feels like a success?* I mused. *Probably. As for me, I had begun my career identifying with Frank Lloyd Wright and his boulder and ended it identifying with Edwin Cheney and his little potsherd.* "I feel like I'm ready to start," I mused aloud. "Or maybe you're getting ready to finish!" Aaron chuckled. "Maybe," I agreed.

Atticus and I drove to Albany for the world premiere by the Albany Symphony under David Alan Miller's baton of Michael Torke's sumptuous new piano concerto. Atticus sat beside me, every inch the serious concertgoer in his freshly pressed button-down shirt, cradling a stuffed animal. I touched his shoulder lightly, gestured toward Michael, and whispered that he was just above us. Atticus looked up, then at me, and flashed Mother's sudden smile. Gilda never cared for fishing; but she loved it when her father when he took her out in his boat. I think that Atticus and I both feel the same way about symphony concerts.

I glanced upwards at Michael, sitting alone, handsome in his keyboard-side box, dressed in a jet-black "dead man's suit." He listened; coiled as though to spring, chin thrust out, eyes fierce, intent-filled and vulnerable. The couple in front of us stole admiring glances at him. "I'll have to tell him about that," I thought. There would be some sort of "mixer" for Millennials after the concert at which the attractive young soloist would make herself available and Michael would perform his Green Room duties. But we were slipping backstage during the intermission so that we would be able to sidestep all that. "Papa, I'm scared," he said. "Everyone looks at me." "Backstage is part of our world," I told him. "They're looking at you because you are beautiful, and younger than everyone else." We nosed through a knot of players as we had a few weeks earlier, with Seamus, to JoAnn Falletta's dressing room. "There's no need to be afraid," I said. "This is your world, too, if you want it to be." I stopped at the player's refreshments table and chose a cookie for him. "Where's David?" I asked the concertmistress. We followed her instructions and soon found the correct dressing room. Warmth. David reached out his hand to shake Atticus.' "This is the boy who disrupted your rehearsal of my Fourth," I said, mock stern. Atticus shook his hand gravely. "Ah," said David. "Mine are all about to leave the nest. You have another, right?" "Yes, there's my Seamus," I replied. "Such names!" David exclaimed. *"Such names" indeed, I thought—the one already manifesting the character of his namesakes Cicero's correspondent and a certain fictional lawyer, and the other already displaying the poetic nature of his namesake, Seamus Heaney.* We continued our Green Room shorthand. I hugged David, and then Michael. "It's a gorgeous, emotionally-rich piece," I gushed. "I loved it, just loved it." Michael leaned over to Atticus, and said, "Thank you for coming to my premiere," and shook his hand. Turning to me, half arch, half serious, Michael asked "Are we the old ones now?"

I needed someone new to negotiate the licensing for my theater works with whom I could also begin building a long-term publishing relationship. I turned to Todd Vunderink, vice president of Peermusic Classical. It looked as though I had finally found in Todd as a man, and in Peermusic as a house a partnership that exactly matched my needs and temperament as a composer. Signing with manager and agent Scott Levine, I formally began my second career as a professional stage director. During summer 2016, while I was at the Wintergreen Festival, Daniel Visconti (a rising composer to whom I'd been instrumental in awarding the Douglas Moore Fellowship and who I'd subsequently mentored a bit during

Directing *Orson Rehearsed* at the Studebaker Theatre in Chicago, fall 2018 (photograph by Elliot Mendel).

production in Seattle, who was serving as director of artistic programming for a group of musicians that called themselves the Fifth House Ensemble in Chicago) called and asked if I'd like to write something for them. I had already founded the New Mercury Collective to produce *Orson Rehearsed*, a multi-media exploration of the interior of Orson Welles' mind during his final moments I had been developing for nearly a year—shooting and editing film, collecting sounds and crafting a libretto from snippets of Welles' scripts and public comments, and composing trial arias. As stage director for the project, it seemed sensible to fold Fifth House in as a collaborating ensemble, since, for this iteration of the work at least, their inclusion had the potential—provided the players were up to the challenge of singing, moving, and playing all—of elevating the customary role of orchestra to on-stage characters. Atlas Arts Media provided technical support for the projection of the 48 short films in performance at the Studebaker Theater; Robert Orth, Robert Franken-berry, and Omar Mulero played the role (split into three avatars) of Welles, and Victoria Bain, with whom I had collaborated so well in Kentucky on *Morocco*, returned as lighting designer.

Like a child attempting to summon *gravitas* by killing everyone off at the end of their tale, I had believed that my work was inspired by what Kierkegaard described as the "barb of sorrow lodged in [my] heart." Sentimentally, I'd subscribed to the idea that its cessation would eliminate my need to create. Of course, life after *Amelia* had taught me what nonsense that was. My obsessive-compulsive circling back into memory to close loops had never been sentimental; rather, it had fed my fatalism and sense of being both defined and trapped by my own spirits. I now understood that a biographer pursues his subject's truth by march-ing facts down the page after it like little soldiers, while an artist interlaces life's storylines and dreams, pleating and plaiting memory and associations until one's truth emerges as a braid.

That "pleating and plaiting" was foremost in my mind as I gave the downbeat of the Bernstein "Jeremiah" Symphony in Presser Hall on the Temple University campus in Philadelphia on 4 November 2016—my 55th birthday. The faces were older and wiser; the smiles were warmer and tinged with nostalgia—I'd known some of these Orchestra Society of Philadelphia players since I made my debut as a conductor with them in April 1983. I remembered giving the same downbeat during fall 1979 during my fifteen minutes of podium time with the university orchestra as a student of Catherine Comet's in Madison. Unable to afford the rental fee, I had copied out the parts by hand. This night, Craig Urquhart and Boosey and Hawkes had loaned the parts for the piece to me for free as a professional courtesy. Then I thought of Jay Joslyn's *Milwaukee Journal* description of my debut with the Park Promenade Youth Symphony in 1978. He wrote that I must have felt like Moses atop Mount Pisgah, looking down from the podium into an orchestral Promised Land—and I did. The memory triggered by this, the physical repetition of long-since mem-orized and internalized musical cues, I recalled the insecure, nervy, frightened, yet exhil-arated very young man weathering Comet's stern observation I was then. I observed myself now—self-assured, teaching, pensive, stronger and more useful because of the many expe-riences that had shaped me since then. I glanced over at Gilda and cued her. To listen and to accompany the love of my life as she sang the solo part in the third movement originally composed for Jennie Tourel was to feel her heart and mine folded together, and to weave her into the very fabric of my musical identity. Standing back in the percussion section, a recent Curtis graduate who had just entered my composition studio pinch hit; and, at the piano, veteran of many shared musical adventures reaching all the way back to tea time with Madame de Lancie, dear Hugh Sung, tactfully doubled the struggling strings. After the break, I rehearsed and recorded a new orchestra piece by one of my current private students—marrying the present to the future, since his successful submission of the recording we were making would enable him to continue his studies with my dear friend Anne LeBaron at Cal Arts. I couldn't imagine a more meaningful way to celebrate my birthday.

It felt surprisingly easy that fall to detach from a major project I had been developing for nearly a year—an opera based on Edward Lewis Wallant's novel *The Pawnbroker* that was first pitched to me by a west coast lyricist. After I had crafted a new treatment, composed several arias, and—based on those materials and my reputation—successfully pitched it to Susan Danis, Intendant of the Florida Grand Opera, with whom I had enjoyed serving as a panelist for the National Endowment for the Arts, the librettist (through whom flowed the rights) unexpectedly insisted that she have veto power over my music.

The world at large had never seemed so fraught, yet I couldn't help but summon Charles Sprague's poem, which James Fenimore Cooper had used as the legend for chapter seven of *Wyandotte: "Bless then, the meeting and the spot."* It was Thanksgiving. I was seated at the head of a long table in the living room of our Big Victorian House. *"For once be every care forgot,"* I thought, poised to tap on my glass to tell everyone that Gilda and I would perform some songs together before the meal was served. Tomorrow there would be a new crisis, a new illness, a new bill to pay, but, for the moment, the next line came to mind: *"Let gentle Peace assert her power."* Looking around the table at people I loved so very much, I was humbled, grateful, and astonished: dearest Matthew Wright and Karen Pearson—their children Calder and Lark; Al Boutin and Lindy Wright, Matt's mother; Matt's brother Adam and his wife Jessica Ann; our dear friends Rabab Haj Yahya and her husband Talal El-Jabari and their children; my beloved father-in-law Bernie and his bride, Gilda's mother; our boys, Atticus and Seamus; and, standing beside me, her hand on my shoulder, Gilda herself, radiant. *"Let kind Affection rule the hour,"* I remembered. *I was a selfish man,* I thought, *but I was self-aware, and I worked to be more.* I wanted to fall to my knees. Instead, I tapped twice, rose, and crossed wordlessly to the piano. "We're all—all here," I thought, as I took my seat on the piano bench.

I teased out the first few notes of Copland's dignified, soulful setting of the great hymn *Shall We Gather at the River*, looked up at Gilda and waited, contentedly, for her to begin. She raised her hand slightly as she often does when she begins a song. I thought of the countless times I've held that hand; I thought about the anticipation of restoration, and how her love and acceptance has transformed my sorrows into joys. After ending the hymn with her, I placed my hands in my lap, the better to listen as she sang *Aatini nay wa ghanni*. Rabab's eyes glistened as Gilda sang *"Give me the flute and sing / for singing is the secret of existence"* in Arabic. Talal's brusque expression softened, and he swayed a little; his eyes met his bride's and she smiled beautifully. *"For people are lines Traced with water"* Gilda sang, and closed her eyes. I raised my hands without pause and eased through the few gently throbbing beats that prepared a space for Gilda to sing Barber's exquisite setting of Agee's poem. She looked at me for an instant, smiled, and turned to our guests. *"Sure on this shining night / Of star made shadows round,"* she sang with a sureness of heart and an emotional accessibility so authentic that her sons rose from their seats at the table and rushed to her to protect her. *"Kindness must watch for me / This side of ground,"* she continued. I glanced past her and cherished the shining pride in her parents' eyes. Matt looked down at the napkin that he held in his hand, listening intently; Karen's clear gaze was fixed on Gilda as she continued, *"All is healed, all is health."* I cadenced, and as I began the final phrases I saw Al reach for Lindy's hand. Gilda's face turned slightly downward, her hand raised to her temple, eyes closed, listening, as I played the concluding measures of the Barber. In the silence that ensued she opened her eyes, which sparkled, and gave our sons, both at her feet now, the same dazzling smile Mother used to give me, and launched into *Angel Band*, a hymn she'd sung to the boys a thousand times: *"I know I'm near the holy ranks / of friends and kindred dear,"* she sang as I thrummed away beneath. *"O bear me away on your snowy wings...,"* she sang. I felt then as I had at the age of seven when I determined to *be* Music. Our sons gazed up at their mother, ecstatic; my extraordinary wife was perfect. *There's nothing to be ashamed of,* I thought, *and everything, everything to be grateful for.* As she repeated the last phrase, *"O bear me away on your snowy wings / to our immortal home"* the hair on my arms stood on end, and there came a lump in my throat, a profound sense of longing, the feeling of being tugged out of myself and suspended in midair. At long last—even if only for a time—I knew that I was entirely among the quick.

Postlude
Two Dawns

Rio Mar, Nicaragua, 30–31 March 2018

Oh, my beloved, benighted Nicaragua, I think, watching countless metric tons of sea-water hurtle into and over *las Cortinas,* or curtains—named for the cascade the Pacific makes when it thunders over them and the slab-like shape of the volcanic rock formations themselves—thrusting out of the Nicaraguan shoreline south of Casares with the weight and sound of a doomed jet. It is *entre chien et loup,* the hour between dog and wolf, when the light parts the veil between day and night in a part of the world comprised of attracting opposites: priceless natural beauty and heartrending poverty; profound generosity and the expedience of necessity; life, and the other.

I look to the sun, a somniferous blob of mercurochrome, far out to sea. Atticus and Seamus build a sandcastle in the surf a few feet from me with Nicole, conscious of the place's beauty, but still untouched by its menace. I reassure myself of their safety by observing that Gilda and her mother are close by.

A swimmer who looks to be about twenty-two, slender, swarthy, and breathtakingly reckless, thrashes in a shallow, rocky *posita* at the base of the curtain of frozen lava on which hammers the deafening tide. He strokes piston-like, joylessly, against the incoming rollers, his arms pumping mindlessly in the confined space like a diaphragm providing air to a dying brain. When his head disappears among the razor-sharp outcroppings, I think, *he's going to die,* and commence the mental calculus—distance from me to him, him to the rocks, boys to their mother, next wave to the shore, time required to cover the distance between us, distance I can go without leaving my sons fatherless. His head reappears, and the wave flicks him backwards. At this point, he can either get out or dive into the next wave.

Out of the corner of my eye I note in an instant both my oblivious children's joy and the horror on the women's faces. I halve the distance between myself and the swimmer in case I am compelled to decide whether or not to try and save him. At that moment, with difficulty, he climbs out of the surf. *So, he is going to live,* I think. Shaking my head, I turn to Gilda. Her eyebrows rise; wordlessly, she indicates with her finger that I should look back.

He has scaled an immense slab of frozen lava and now stands, back to us, arms thrown wide like waxen wings, facing the ocean; haloed by the ruby sunset; dazzling in his youth, his arrogance, his foolishness; and his proximity to his own destiny. *He's invited Death in,*

"Fully among the quick" at last, with my soulmate and wife Gilda, sons Seamus (*on my lap*) and Atticus, father-in-law Bernard J. Lyons, and mother-in-law Gilda Alemán Lyons, August 2018 (photograph by Karen Pearson).

I think. There isn't even time to call out to him. In one beat, his legs are swept from beneath him and he disappears. Sucked inland, not seaward, between the Charybdis of water and Scylla of stone, his head reappears for an instant as it hits a shelf of rock six feet under where he had just been standing. His legs follow as the waves cascade over and around him, pushing him into the *posita* another six feet down, where he disappears again. I begin towards him. His head reappears. I determine to drag him out of the water and begin CPR. Comes the next wave, which pushes him under and expels him, raking his legs against the barnacles. I think, *if he's unconscious, then it's going to be easier to serve as Charon; if I can reach him before he's carried out to sea.*

As I make for him a third time, he hauls himself out of the water, and strides decisively to a log on the beach, pulls a phone from a bag, and begins texting. I stop and observe him. Stabbing at the phone, he seems unaware of the blood streaming from the deep cuts and abrasions on his legs. If he has been concussed, then he hasn't yet gone into shock. He doesn't seem drunk, altered, or fatally injured—there seems even to be a slight caper in his step. (Or is that my imagination?) *Is he suicidal? Has he stupidly taunted Death in some sort of sideways-macho-bullshit Hemingway stunt, or is he just a fool? What is his story?*

The children, concentrating on their sandcastle, seem to have missed it all. I inhale deeply, noting with a trace of guilt that I feel no compassion for the boy, and feel relief that I haven't really been called upon to decide whether or not to risk my life to save him.

Seamus sings quietly as he pats the wet sand; the ladies are still processing their astonishment. Atticus looks up at me. "Did you see that?" I ask him, indicating the swimmer, his back to us, sloping up the beach in the starlight, talking animatedly on the cellphone. "Hmm?" He replies. "The boy who nearly met Death just now," I answer. "No," he says, sunnily. "I was watching my sandcastle get swept away."

That evening, in the rancho, I hear in ecstatic counterpoint the songs of a dozen birds in only ten seconds as they roost in the neem, eucalyptus, palm, and mango trees that surround Bernie and me as we swing like a spider's dinner in hammocks strung up in the rancho at Rio Mar. I think, *there were at least thirty different bird calls in the air. I can only differentiate a dozen. Even though I know that I missed them, I don't mind, and I can accept not having heard them all. Is that what aphasia is like?* All at once, the singing stops. Silence.

In the gathering dusk, three stately palomino *chanchi* sashay down the middle of the deeply-rutted dirt road outside the gates past the *"Huevos de Yankees"* (a useless, stalky plant that pops up uninvited all over Nicaragua that gives inedible, tennis-ball-sized green fruit just below its crown) on their way to what used to be Cuban Pete's place up the hill. Released by Iveth from their pen for the night, the dogs streak past us, mewling, to the outcropping of *sonsiquite* on the river side of the house, there to stream like champagne over the rocks and out to the ocean where the tide runs very, very high. The first sound to return, now that the sun has set, is that of the surf. It pounds like distant artillery; the roosting birds' feathers rustle as they jostle for position; the northern wind's whoosh blends with the ocean's deep song; and the drone of winter cicadas joins the rhythmic, hollow, thumping sound of iguanas on the house's metal roof fucking.

Bernie is asleep in the hammock next to mine. Aphasic from the post-operative stroke that he suffered six years ago, his world no longer makes much sense to him. The obsessive web-spinning to which I've subjected the skein of my memories in an effort to construct from them a meaningful narrative is the equivalent to him of a man brushing cobwebs from before his eyes. The stroke took away his ability to read his beloved Shakespeare, Melville, and Joyce; to consistently recognize his children; to identify my sons; to know with complete certainty, even, where he is.

His eyes open, he pitches forward slightly, and waves his hand before his face. "All these people I love were looking at me and I was dead!" he says, still in a waking dream. "You were there; the woman I live with; my sister—. Do you get it?" He asks. "Yes," I reassure him. "That was your wife Gilda, your sons, your sister and her husband … and your daughter." He smiles suddenly, "the one who sang!" He cries. "You were waking up after your stroke," I explain. "They wouldn't talk to me," he continues, "but I could hear her singing, and I knew she wanted me to come back." "You did. You did," I reassure him. "And the first thing I thought was that I was dead and that every second now is a bonus," he says. "Do you get it?" "Yes," I promise him. "But I didn't make it all the way back," he says. "We've got the best parts, Pappy," I say.

"Our coordinates, according to my phone," I tell him, "are: 11°38'11" N 86°20'59" W. We are two old, white-haired, gringo Quijotes painted red by the sun worrying about our wives and children who've gone shopping in Masaya and Diriamba." "So, *that's* where we are," he chuckles. *There is no comfort in exactitude.* "Are you hungry?" I ask him. "No," he answers out of principle. "Maybe a cup of coffee." "I'm putting some eggs and cheese on a tortilla and making a fresh pot of coffee for myself," I say, airily. "OK," he says, and falls asleep.

Since there's no time here except for the enormous seasonal rhythm of the stars and tides, he picks up where he left off when I help him out of the hammock and place the good, hot coffee in his hands. Digging into his eggs with a will, he observes, "They love us here, kid. I really don't know why. But they do." I don't answer. Tearing a warm tortilla in half, I hold it to my nose and inhale its wholesomeness—so like the way my son smelled when he was born. I hand it to him, observing, "We're very lucky guys, Pappy." He takes it and uses it to scoop up his eggs. We finish the meal in agreeable silence.

Just when we start missing them most, Mama calls Iveth's phone with the message that they're all fine and that they will be home in a couple of hours. We don't discuss it, but each feels the other's relief. We're free to pretend for a few more hours that we're self-sufficient. After we wash the dishes, Bernie climbs back into his hammock. Just as he's about to nod off, he observes, "I don't know why I'm still here. I can't really do anything anymore except love all of you." He's suspended again in the web between waking and dreaming, between life and the other. I clear my throat lightly. He opens his eyes. "Orson Welles is supposed to have written, 'We're born alone. We live alone. We die alone. Only through love and friendship can we create the illusion for the moment that we are not alone,'" I tell him. "Well put," he says, closing his eyes, for the moment mollified.

It's so late that it's early. "The eggs were good," he says. "Gramma made them. I only heated them up," I say. We're quiet. Long after I think he's asleep, he rolls over and mutters, "*Huevos de Yankees.*" I chuckle. He winks. No more sounds of birds, iguanas, livestock, or even children. Just the gentle heartbeat of the crickets, the occasional surge of the breeze, and the sea comfortingly caressing the shore.

Bernie is fast-asleep, and I'm half-awakened by the well-thumbed copy of Joshua Slocum's *Sailing Alone Around the World* that slips from my hand when Harold steers the Trooper in. Atticus carries in the groceries—*pastelitos, picos* and local coffee from Diriamba; Harold shoulders in a six-gallon jug of potable water; the women ferry in presents to take back to the States. We let Seamus, who has fallen asleep during the drive home despite the wild roads, sleep on in the jeep. Gilda turns down the boys' beds; her mother begins stowing things in the kitchen; Iveth closes and locks the gate; and I awaken Bernie and guide him inside.

Returning to the jeep, I gather Seamus in my arms and bury my nose in his fine, long, straight hair—exactly like mine at his age—and smell the burnt leña and dust of the market in it as I carry him to bed. *Before we return, Bernie may die,* I think, *Nicaragua may be engulfed by another civil war.* I climb into bed with the boys, pull them close, and sing them their secret songs. A few hours later, disentangling myself, I rise. Alone, I stroll to the ocean with a cup of coffee and honor the dazzling full Blue Paschal Moon—the first to be followed the next day by Easter Sunday since 1714. The surf intensifies as the sun begins its ascent behind the trees; the pelicans begin to rustle; and there's the staccato nicker of a horse. As dawn breaks, instead of the sound of the rooster's call, comes the plaintive howl, nine beats long, starting low, rising, and dying as it falls, of a lone hound, from across the estuary where the sweet water of the river meets the salt of the sea.

Rhinebeck, New York, 14–15 November 2016

It is the hour just before dawn. *Well, Britt, Kevin, Mom, Dad, I'm still here,* I say to myself, standing in the back yard of the Big Victorian House with the gray slate mansard roof, holding a cup of coffee and looking at the Supermoon. Leonard Cohen wrote that "Success is survival." *None of you survived,* I muse. *But, having learned what I have about life, I refuse to believe anything but that your lives were all success stories anyway—though probably not one of* you *thought so.* Nimbus clinging around the bare branches of the trees makes them look like a clipper's rigging. The streetlamp across the way flickers pinkly, sputters, and dies. I consider the fact that I've outlived my entire family—thanks, as Britt pointed out the afternoon in 1980 in the ruins of the Mendota Hospital for the Insane—to their support, and the fact that I've always been "a selfish little fucker." I have been lucky, resilient, industrious, and blessed with a passion—in my case, for music. *Don't call me Charon,* I muse; *call me Ishmael. Like him, I'm the rejected older tradition, still here, not yet quite ready to make an exit. Like him, I'm an undependable narrator, because no one is left to contradict my testimony—I can choose to remember you any way I please. And I have.* In the same way that, standing at the rail of a theater, I turn around to take in the house, I turn around to take in the Big Victorian House. Above it hangs the Supermoon—the closest it has been to Earth since 1948. *What hour? What country's this? What day? What season?* I muse, recalling the moon scene from the Rostand play. *And thanks to you*, I say, toasting it, thinking of Gilda; *you, who know everything about me, have made my story transposable.*

Like its owner, there will always be things to fix in our Big Victorian House that were broken long ago, and things that break that need somehow to be mended. I love that there's not a line in the house that's "not somehow askew." The roof renders every outside wall on the second floor parabolic. Light pours into the first floor through a massive, anachronistic picture window emplaced because, forty years ago, a car careened off Route 308 and barreled through the wall. The house is sinking, but the hickory headers have aged to petrification, and are as strong as steel. The house's age and history, like the mansion at Yaddo, comfort me. I love it all: the gouges in the walls, the dozen layers of wallpaper, the evidence of one remodeling and renovation after another, the gobs of caulk left over from the work of one untalented carpenter chockablock to the expert craftsmanship of another. There's a brass plaque next to the front door that says it was built in 1853. The meticulously restored heavy nineteenth century floor planks, pinned to the rafters below with huge, handmade penny nails, all swoop up towards each room's center and then down towards the walls like a sloop's to the scuppers. Periodically, a nail will simply work its way out of the board its married to and snag a sock. A silent traversal of any room is not possible: some boards whistle when you walk on them; others bark like a dog, or groan like a ghost.

While I have not experienced a manic episode like the ones in Venice, Seattle, and Chicago in nearly a decade, I still must claw my way back to the surface during periods of severe depression. I am aware that it is hard on my family; but at least I am sober and have not used alcohol since a year before Kevin's death. I accept that many of my old friends and I are now on a different wavelength.

I have rediscovered—and derive fulfillment from—a thousand unremarkable, yet comforting gardening, carpentry, and maintenance skills taught me by Father in childhood that I thought as a Manhattanite I'd never use. I teach Atticus how to hold a rake and do not need to dwell on how Father, frustrated for some reason, broke Britt's finger while showing him how to hold one. I watch as Seamus inadvertently walks through the garden, undoing all the deadheading I've done, and don't fear that I'll slap him in a fit of pique the way Father once slapped Kevin when he did the same thing. I'm at least fifteen years older now than he was then, and I've had a lot of time to work things out. I often demand respect from my sons when I ought to concentrate on earning it instead. But, although I'm far from an ideal father, I acknowledge that between the fathers and sons in the Hagen family there exists a suicidal chain of abuse that must be openly discussed, dissected, and severed. *I will not ruin these boys,* I swear, pouring the last of my coffee out onto the lawn and beginning to walk back to the house.

To my amazement, a young deer strolls fearlessly up to our picket fence and looks at me. *"He makes my feet like the feet of a deer; he enables me to stand on the heights,"* I recall from Bible Study. The deer is a sacred animal. It is a shaman, and often the bringer of tidings. It embodies the spirit of softness combined with strength, grace crossed with power. *Why have you come on this, of all days?* I wonder. I reach into my robe for something to feed it. I expect the creature to bolt, but it remains, stoic, self-assured and brave, a beautiful thing. I pull a bit of bread from my pocket, smiling as I remember the night in Venice when, at the apex of my selfishness, as "evidence of things not seen," the girl in a blue pea coat emerged from nowhere to place a crust of bread in my hand and I had reversed my course, taken my first, fawn-like steps back towards home.

I toss the bread. It lands between the deer's hooves. It blinks, twice. It cocks its head over its shoulder as though listening for the *ferne klang*, dips smoothly to scoop the biscuit up in its mouth, and walks slowly, with the stately grace of a queen, to the split rail fence dividing our yard from the neighbor's. I look away for a moment. When I look back, the deer is gone.

Moved, I walk slowly across the bedewed lawn, aware of my exact speed, to the kitchen, turn on the coffee pot, and read the ledes and major stories in *Le Monde, Deutscher Allgemeiner Zeitung, Los Angeles Times,* and the *New York Times* on the Internet while the first new pot of the day brews. I pour a cup and sip it while quickly scanning the fifty or so emails that shall have come in during the night, deleting nearly all of them, setting aside a dozen or so for attention later in the day. I finish as dawn breaks.

Kevin's sideboard, serving platters, and dining room chairs came to us. I still catch a whiff on very hot days of the fetor of his decomposing body emanating from their upholstery. Richard and Tim Lewis gave us a pair of lovely pelican-backed chairs, end tables, and bookcases; Barbara Grecki gave us some beautiful cabinets, lamps, and the rugs upon which the boys now play. I accept these gifts on behalf of my family—the people they love, and I accept my own small part of that inheritance. Accepting without guilt this generosity of spirit on the part of others is new to me, but it as a part of my life now. I also smell freshly mown grass, and good, freshly baked bread. I hear the wind, and the occasional whoosh of a passing car.

The significance of the statue of the boy that I modeled for as a child—the one that Mother sculpted a half century ago which still sits on the top shelf of a bookcase in my sons' bedroom is manifest by the many ways that she looked at me as she fashioned it. Every time our eyes met, it was different—the probing, impersonal stare of an artist, the loving look of a mother, the appraising look of a critic, the self-contained look of a woman I never knew, but would have liked. I understand now how she found it possible to stop saving rejection slips—how she had no more use for the typewriter. How she eventually discarded the tools and the clay. I understand now that it had always been for her the Process of sculpting the boy, not the Finishing. The Qur'an tells us that God created man from clay. If so, how could He possibly be done with us, or we with Him? As a boy discovering the frog that she had hidden behind the boy's back, I had only grasped the statue's most superficial secret. As a mature artist disclosing the nature of my reality at the end of *Amelia*, I had anticipated a similar shock of recognition on the part of the audience. When it did not come, I was at last compelled to accept the deeper truth that my "truth," carried along with me for all its charm for so long, just wasn't all that important to others, and that it was beyond my gifts—after all, I am not a God—to make it so. After all, a sermon is not an opera, though an opera can be a sermon. In the end, whether I had had anything truly original to say had never been the point; the point had been in the trying to make the point, the process of the process. I realized then that the sculpture had never been of me at all. She had sculpted the Other Daron—the brother who had been born immediately before me who had died after only a few days. In sculpting the boy, and in giving me his name, she had both memorialized him in clay and transfigured him in flesh.

I rise from the table to pour some more coffee from the pot. Gilda and the boys are still asleep. I can imagine at these moments without regret what things will be like here after I am gone. My sons' tears, and laughter of operatic intensity, will issue forth like feathers from burst pillows. Bath times and bed times will meld into one bright, thrumming, activated chord. Hair will be tousled, favorite books read, lullabies and secret songs sung. Screen doors will get slammed and mended, weeds pulled only to return, hair will be cut, pebbles pulled out of nostrils, ticks removed, leaves raked, gutters cleared, shutters painted, memories forged, wounds cleansed and Band-Aids applied, nascent personalities shaped and encouraged. My sons will know the childish comfort of having observed that their parents love them and one another. Despite the wickedness, the unfairness, and the madness of the world at large, they will feel for a few wonderful years that their world is safe, and that nothing will ever change it. My sons will grow up in a village where they may walk home after dusk illuminated by the soft, peaceful, flickering golden light streaming from the windows of the homes of neighbors that know, love, and will help to protect them. They will feel good, clean dirt between their toes. They will run in the grass barefoot without the risk of stepping on a used syringe or slipping on used condoms. They will feel over-ripe tomatoes burst in their hands when on a soft summer afternoon they pick them from our garden. They will experience languid summers, grow loopy with sunshine; enjoy the healthy silkiness of their own skins. They will spend entire days building dams across the brook behind their Grandparents' house, drawing treasure maps, catching and releasing bugs, making believe that they are *La Longue Carabine* in the woods, crying "My death is a great honor to the Huron, take me!" to no one. Dog day cicadas will sing their burring songs by day, crickets their chirrups by night. My sons will run into the middle of the lawn, close their eyes, lean their heads as far back as they will go, feel the sun on their faces, spin around, and imagine they are swimming in the hot, lively air above them, awakened after a seventeen-year-long slumber. At the end of those days, they will sit around our big, inviting dinner table, the late summer night air flowing through all the open windows and doors making them groggy. They will have the space, the time, and the safety, to learn from their extraordinary mother how to revere the imaginative spirit as I learned to from mine. They will fall in love at the age of eight with the pretty girl on Alfred Street, endure the breaking and mending, mending and breaking and growing of the heart freely and completely given. My dream is that I shall have somehow succeeded in transmitting to them the best parts of me, that they will use the tools that I gave them as children to learn how to be the "humane and mostly happy" men that Mother hoped that I'd someday be after I am gone. In time, like their parents, each will discover his bliss, and derive fulfillment from the struggle. They will sing their own secret songs. They'll grapple with the Art versus Life paradigm and reach their own conclusions. One day they'll even realize that the struggle itself shall have been the point.

Crossing to the piano, coffee in hand, I am comforted knowing that my children stand as good a chance of growing up as strong and true and as undamaged by me as any loving father could have desired. That means more to me than anything else in the world. I sit down at the keyboard in the living room of the Big Victorian House, place the coffee on the trivet that used to sit on Mother's desk when I was a kid, close my eyes, and gently lower my fingers to the keys. *I've always assumed that I am a failure*, I think. *I'm unwilling* to think of myself in any other way. For, as Browning wrote, "a man's reach should exceed his grasp, Or what's a heaven for?" The feel of the ivory pressing against my fingertips makes me smile. I cock my head to the side and listen. The whoosh of a car passing by on Market Street. I open my eyes to see the bare winter branches of the trees outside and remember the boy whose fine, straight hair his mother used to trim by placing a soup bowl on his head and cutting around the rim; the boy who sat, trying so hard to be still for the light of his life as she sculpted him in clay; the boy whose dream of becoming music has been fulfilled; the boy whose path has led him here, to a small village in Upstate New York, his sons and wife asleep upstairs; the boy who, like his brothers and Mother, always harbored a deep, fatalistic conviction that he would, as the Other Daron had, die before his time. *You are like a rich man entering heaven through the ear of a raindrop,* I think, remembering my son's namesake's poem, realizing that I won't die before my time, after all. As Gardner had Dodge, Amelia's dead father, explain to his daughter (and as Mother once observed to me): "Living is hard; dying isn't any easier." *Life may be fair, but there is nothing "fair" about it.* I recall vividly being taught that "people in their right minds never take pride in their talents." *But I did succeed in becoming Music,* I muse. *I can warm a little to the nascent dignity that derives from that promise met.* Quickly, before the slender insight can evaporate, I jot a note to my priest—

> *Richard,* I observe, *I am music. I breathe it and the alternative silence is at this point still unacceptable to me. My sons need a father; Gilda needs a foil and helper. But I have come to understand that music was always just the score, not the performance. You are a performer of magic, bringing to my life for me each time I observe your movement through the mass, the score with which you've been provided, the reminder that more than self-actuation is at stake here.*

Hearing the pounding of little boy feet above me, I smoothly notate the phrase of music hanging like an echo in my mind like a magician winding up an illusion. As I rise from the little Baldwin grand piano, I feel a gentle tug, pause, and affectionately run my palm along the lid. *Of course, I'll continue to compose,* I tell myself, *because now comes the good stuff.* My bare feet fish for and then find the slippers parked beneath the piano. As ever, I think of the Roethke poem as I move to the base of the stairs and look up. *As the hymn proclaims, "The holy ranks of friends and kindred dear" are still near,* I think. *And I feel—and take comfort in—them; but I no longer need—nor can I spare—to spend my remaining time waking the dead and seeking the quick.* My quick, Atticus and Seamus, fresh from bed, and still in their pajamas, appear at the top of the stairs, rubbing the sleep out of their beautiful eyes. As dawn breaks, they descend, encircle me with their arms, and look up into my face. *How could I possibly, under the circumstances, have regrets?* I think, holding them to me. *I hope that I will be here to observe one day as they take their own reins, veering away off course in the matter of an occupation or profession, someday experience the almost superhuman compassion and sorrow of seeing them gallop off hell-bent to damnation without crying foul.* The happy / sad of being a parent is that you can't keep your child in your arms forever. They have already begun to squirm away. When I release them, my heart sings as I watch them explode not into my time, but their own.

List of Works and Premieres

Withdrawn works are, by and large, not included. Publishers are Burning Sled Music (+), E.C. Schirmer (*), and Carl Fischer (^). Works licensed by Peermusic Classical (~).

The works are listed chronologically by completion date.

1981

Prayer for Peace **for string orchestra+**
 Philadelphia Orchestra / William Smith / Academy of Music; Philadelphia, PA / 18 January 1983

1982

Overture to the Andersonville Trial **for orchestra+**
 Santa Cruz Symphony Orchestra / JoAnn Falletta / Santa Cruz, CA / 12 November 1989

Wind Songs **for oboe, bassoon, and horn+**
 Katherine Greenbank; David McGill; Shelley Showers / Curtis Hall; Philadelphia, PA / 6 April 1982

Echo's Songs **for voice and piano+**
 Karen Hale; Daron Hagen / Curtis Hall; Philadelphia, PA / 7 January 1983

1984

Three Silent Things **for soprano and piano quartet+**
 Karen Hale; Michaela Paetsch; Lisa Ponton; Robert La Rue; Daron Hagen / Curtis Hall; Philadelphia, PA / 13 April 1984

Divertimento for viola, harp, and vibraphone+
 Lisa Ponton; Therese Elder; Charles Ross / Curtis Hall; Philadelphia, PA / 13 April 1984

Piano Trio No. 1: *Trio Concertante+*
 Shames-Paetsch-Jaffe Trio / Michaela Paetsch; Claudio Jaffe; Jonathan Shames / Saint Joseph's Church; New York, NY / 4 December 1984

Suite for Violin*
 Michaela Paetsch / Carnegie Hall / New York, NY / 7 May 1985

A Walt Whitman Requiem **for soprano, chorus & string orchestra***
 Long Island University Post Chorus / Mark Shapiro / Interfaith Chapel; Long Island, NY / 22 April 2018

1985

Vägen **for mixed chorus and piano+**
  Madison Festival Choir / Eric Townell / Oscar Mayer Theater; Madison, WI / 4 December 1993

The Voice Within **for mixed chorus and piano+**
  Madison Festival Choir / Eric Townell / Oscar Mayer Theater; Madison, WI / 4 December 1993

Occasional Notes **for organ***
  Robert Gallagher / Saint Paul's Chapel, Columbia University; New York, NY / 28 March 1985

Suite for Violoncello*
  Robert La Rue / Paul Recital Hall; New York, NY / 11 March 1998

Flute Sonata No. 1^
  Su Lian Tan; Elena Ruehr / Paul Recital Hall; New York, NY / 11 March 1986

String Quartet No. 1+
  Festival Quartet / Tanglewood Music Festival; Lenox, MA / 25 August 1985

1986

Grand Line: a Tribute to Leonard Bernstein **for orchestra+**
  Denver Chamber Orchestra / JoAnn Falletta / Trinity Church; Denver, CO / 9 November 1987

Love Songs **song cycle for voice and piano+**
  Perpetuum Mobile Series / Carol Chickering; Robert Kopelson / Columbia Artists Management Hall; New York, NY / 29 April 1988

Six Love Songs **for cello and piano+**
  Robert La Rue; Daron Hagen / Trinity Church; Denver, CO / 6 November 1987

Piano Trio No. 2: *J'entends***+**
  Lehner Piano Trio / Alice Tully Hall; New York, NY / 7 April 1987

Suite for Viola*
  Lisa Ponton / Paul Recital Hall; New York, NY / 2 December 1986

1987

Higher, Louder, Faster! **etude for solo cello***
  Robert La Rue / Paul Recital Hall; New York, NY / 31 January 1987

Little Prayers for mixed chorus*
  NYU Washington Square Chorus / Daron Hagen / Florence Gould Hall, Alliance Française; New York, NY / 15 January 1986

Occasional Notes **for organ, or eleven players***
  Present Music Ensemble / Daron Hagen / Vogel Recital Hall; Milwaukee, WI / 20 March 1987

1988

Symphony No. 1: *Short Symphony***
  Philadelphia Orchestra / William Smith / Academy of Music; Philadelphia, PA / 19 April 1991

Harp Trio for flute, viola, and harp+
  Debussy Trio / National Federation of Music Clubs Convention; Philadelphia, PA / 1988

The Presence Absence Makes for flute and string quartet+
  Music of Our Time / Robert Stallman, et. al. / Alice Tully Hall; New York, NY / 1988

Rapture and Regret **diptych for soprano, cello, and piano+**
  Bill Douglas Dancers / Karen Hale; Robert La Rue; Eric Sawyer / Cunningham Dance Studio; New York, NY / 4–9 December 1987

1989

Muldoon Songs **for voice and piano^**
   Friends & Enemies Concert Series / Paul Sperry; Daron Hagen / Greenwich Music House;
   New York, NY / 12 February 1992

Heliotrope **variations for orchestra***
   Brooklyn Philharmonic / Lukas Foss / Great Hall, Cooper Union; New York, NY /
   24 October 1989

Sennets, Cortege, and Tuckets **for band***
   University of Wisconsin–Milwaukee Symphonic Band / Thomas Dvorak / Vogel Recital Hall;
   Milwaukee, WI / 20 April 1989

Jot! **for clarinet, marimba, and piano^**
   New York Youth Symphony Chamber Music Program / Merkin Recital Hall; New York, NY /
   1 June 1989

1990

Heliotrope Bouquet **for theater orchestra (arr. Of Scott Joplin / Louis Chauvin)***
   Orchestra Society of Philadelphia / Daron Hagen / Presser Pavilion; Philadelphia, PA / 1990

Dear Youth **song cycle for soprano, flute, and piano+**
   Sonus Trio / Dumbarton Methodist Church; Baltimore, MD / 10 March 1991

Philharmonia **fanfare for four trumpets and orchestra***
   New York Philharmonic / Michael Morgan / Avery Fischer Hall; New York, NY /
   15 October 1992

Symphony No. 2: *Common Ground**
   Oakland East Bay Symphony / Michael Morgan / Calvin Simmons Theater; Oakland, CA /
   3 April 1993

1991

Shining Brow **opera***
   Madison Opera / Stephen Wadsworth; Roland Johnson / Oscar Mayer Theater; Madison, WI /
   May 1993

Fire Music **tone poem for orchestra***
   Long Beach Symphony Orchestra / JoAnn Falletta / Music Hall; Long Beach, CA /
   22 March 1992

1992

Everything Must Go! **For brass quintet+**
   Brass Ensemble of the Orchestra of St. Luke's / Bryant Park; New York, NY / 15 September 1992

As Watchmen Look for Morning **for mixed chorus and piano+**
   Madison Festival Choir / Eric Townell / Oscar Mayer Theater; Madison, WI / 4 December 1993

1993

Concerto for Horn with Winds and Strings+
   Wisconsin Chamber Orchestra / Sören Hermansson; David Lewis Crosby / First
   Congregational Church; Madison, WI / 1 November 1996

Music from Shining Brow **for brass quintet***
   Millar Brass Ensemble / Chicago Botanical Garden; Chicago, IL / 13 August 1994

Joyful Music (version 1) for mezzo, trumpet, chorus, and orchestra+
   Madison Symphony and Chorus / Kitt Reuter-Foss; John Aley; Roland Johnson / Oscar Mayer
   Theater; Madison, WI / 21 December 1994

Joyful Music (version 2) for mixed chorus, brass, and organ+
   Festival Brass and Chorus / Eric Townell / Overture Center; Madison, WI / 26 September 2004

1994

The Waking Father song cycle on poetry of Paul Muldoon+
   Kings Singers / Ozawa Hall; Tanglewood; Lenox, MA / 27 July 1995

The Elephant's Child (withdrawn) a cappella opera for seven singers
Concerto for Flügelhorn (version 1) for string orchestra*
   Woodstock Chamber Orchestra / Donna Hagen; Luis Garcia Renart / Woodstock Concert Hall;
   Woodstock, NY / 28 February 1993

Concerto for Flügelhorn (version 2) for wind ensemble*
   Northwest Washington Wind Orchestra / Donna Hagen; Carolyn Vian / Olympia Concert Hall;
   Olympia, Washington / 21 May 1994

Lost in Translation (version 1) song cycle for voice and mixed ensemble+
   Michael Sokol; Frederick Hammond, et. al. / Olin Auditorium, Bard College; Annandale-on-
   Hudson, NY / 21 March 1994

Lost in Translation (version 2) song cycle for voice and orchestra+
   American Symphony Chamber Orchestra / Kurt Ollmann; Leon Botstein / Vassar Concert
   Hall, Vassar College; Vassar, NY / 6 May 1994

1995

Stewards of Your Bounty for mixed chorus, trumpet, and orchestra (or organ)*
   Moravian Music Festival Chorus and Orchestra / David Lewis Crosby / Wachovia Concert
   Hall; Winston-Salem, NC / 21 June 1996

Concerto for Cello (version 1) and orchestra*
   American Symphony Chamber Orchestra / Robert La Rue; Leon Botstein / Olin Auditorium;
   Annandale-on-Hudson, NY / 3 May 1996

Concerto for Cello (version 2) and wind ensemble*
   Baylor Winds / Robert La Rue; Michael Haithcock / Baylor University Concert Hall; Waco, TX /
   18 November 1997

An Overture to Vera for mixed ensemble+
   Present Music Ensemble / Donna Hagen / Rennebohm Auditorium; Madison, WI /
   7 September 1995

Merrill Songs song cycle for high voice and piano*
   Charles Maxwell; Daron Hagen / Danny Kaye Playhouse; New York, NY / 31 October 1995

Taliesin Chorus from Shining Brow for mixed chorus and orchestra*
   Madison Symphony Orchestra and Chorus / John DeMain / Oscar Mayer Theater;
   Madison, WI / 16 September 1996

Built Up Dark for chamber orchestra+
   Milwaukee Chamber Orchestra / Stephen Colburn / Cathedral of St. John; Milwaukee, WI /
   11 May 1995

Concerto for Brass Quintet+
   Wisconsin Brass Quintet / Mills Concert Hall; Madison, WI / 6 September 1995

1996

Hope **for mixed choir, and any three single line instruments***
American Repertory Singers / Leo Nestor / studio recording / Fall, 1996

Postcards from America **for orchestra+**
Waukesha Symphony Orchestra / Richard Hynson / Shattuck Auditorium; Waukesha, WI / 15 October 1996

Songs of Madness and Sorrow **dramatic cantata (version 1) for voice and mixed ensemble+**
Pacific Chamber Soloists / Paul Sperry; Troy Peters / University Place Presbyterian Church; Tacoma, WA / 31 January 1997

Songs of Madness and Sorrow **(version 2) for voice and piano+**
Sequitur / Paul Sperry; Sara Laimon / Merkin Recital Hall; New York, NY / 9 April 1987

Vera of Las Vegas **nightmare cabaret in one act^**
Opera Theater (Ireland) Dublin, 2004 (seven cities) / David Brophy; *American Staged Premiere:* 26 June 2003 / Thalia Theater at Symphony Space, NYC / The Center for Contemporary Opera / Robert Frankenberry; *Concert Premiere:* 8 March 1996 / Ham Concert Hall, Las Vegas, Nevada / UNLV Opera Theater / Donna Hagen

1997

Night, Again **for band***
Baylor Wind Ensemble / Michael Haithcock / Baylor University Concert Hall; Waco, TX / 19 November 1997

Symphony No. 3: *Liturgical***
Waukesha Symphony Orchestra / Alexander Platt / Shattuck Auditorium; Waukesha, WI / 28 April 1998

Silent Night choral cycle for mixed chorus, solo cello, synthesizer (or vibraphone) *
American Repertory Singers / Robert La Rue; Leo Nestor / Cathedral Church of St. Matthew the Apostle; Washington, D.C. / 20 April 1997

Duo for Violin and Cello*
Michaela Paetsch; Robert La Rue / Sulzberger Parlor of Barnard College; New York, NY / 18 April 1997

1998

Bandanna Overture **for band^**
Small College Intercollegiate Band / H. Robert Reynolds / Bates Recital Hall; UT-Austin; Austin, TX / 24 February 1999

Bandanna **opera^**
Premiere: 25 February 1999 / McCullough Theater, Austin, Texas / University of Texas Opera Theater / Michael Haithcock. Notable Performances: *American Concert Premiere:* 3 March 2000 / Ham Concert Hall, Las Vegas, Nevada / UNLV Opera Theater and Orchestra / Daron Hagen; *European Concert Premiere:* 26 April 2006 / Parr Hall, Warrington, UK / North Cheshire Concert Band; Manchester Chamber Choir; RNCM Soloists / Mark Heron

Forward! **For brass and percussion+**
Madison Symphony Orchestra brass / Daron Hagen / South Portico of the State Capitol; Madison, WI / 29 May 1998

1999

Suddenly (version 1) for orchestra^
Wisconsin Chamber Orchestra / Harvey Felder / Capitol Statehouse Lawn; Madison, WI /
30 June 1999

Suddenly (version 2) for band^
Washington Winds / Edward Peterson / in studio / 12 February 2000

Much Ado overture for orchestra+
Curtis Symphony Orchestra / Robert Spano / Academy of Music; Philadelphia, PA /
1 May 2000

Light Fantastic cantata for tenor, treble chorus, and mixed ensemble+
Ohio Opera Theater Orchestra and Children's Chorus / Barry Busse; Daron Hagen / Canton
Museum of Art; Canton, OH / 26 November 1999

Love in a Life song cycle for voice and piano^
Paul Kreider; Daron Hagen / Ham Concert Hall; Las Vegas, NV / 14 June 1999

Serenade for Ten Instruments+
Oakwood Chamber Players / James Smith / First Unitarian Society; Madison, WI /
3 October 1999

The Heart of the Stranger song cycle for voice and piano^
Paul Kreider; Daron Hagen / Ham Concert Hall; Las Vegas, NV / 11 June 1999

Qualities of Light for piano^
Jeanne Golan / Weill Recital Hall; New York, NY / 21 January 1999

2000

Larkin Songs song cycle for male voice and piano^
Paul Kreider; Daron Hagen / Ham Fine Arts; Las Vegas, NV / 18 February 2001

Concerto for Oboe (version 1) and string orchestra+
Waukesha Symphony / Linda Edelstein; Alexander Platt / Shattuck Auditorium; Waukesha, WI /
7 November 2000

Oboe Quintet (version 2) for oboe and string quartet+
Stephen Caplan, et. al. /International Double Reed Society Conference, Rando-Grillot Recital
Hall, West Virginia University; Morgantown, WV / 9 August 2001

Angels for seventeen solo strings (or string orchestra)+
Orpheus Chamber Orchestra / Ethical Culture Society of New York; New York, NY /
7 May 2000

Figments song cycle for voice and piano on words of Alice Wirth Gray^
Paul Sperry; Daron Hagen / Joy in Singing / Bruno Walter Auditorium; New York, NY /
24 April 2002

Nocturne for Piano and String Quintet (or string orchestra)+
Marc Peloquin; Bloomingdale School of Music Faculty Quintet / Tenri Cultural Institute;
New York, NY / 6 February 2016

Phantoms of Myself song cycle for voice and piano on poetry of Susan Griffin^
Ashley Putnam; Daron Hagen / Theresa L. Kaufman Concert Hall, 92nd Street Y; New York,
NY / 10 May 2000

2001

Seven Last Words (version 1) for piano left hand and orchestra+
New Mexico Symphony Orchestra / Gary Graffman; Guillermo Figueroa / Popejoy Concert
Hall; Albuquerque, NM / 14 December 2001

Seven Last Words (version 2) for piano left hand and mixed ensemble+
Maverick Ensemble / Joel Fan; Alexander Platt / Maverick Concert Hall; Woodstock, NY /
3 August 2010

2002

Piano Variations^
Marc Peloquin / Bloomingdale School of Music; New York, NY / 21 June 2005

We're All Here (version 1) for mixed chorus and mixed ensemble+
Present Music; Brookfield Central High School Chorus / Phillip Olson / First Unitarian
Church; Madison, WI / 23 October 2002

We're All Here (version 2) for mixed chorus and piano+
Wisconsin Chamber Choir / Robert Gehrenbeck / Trinity Lutheran Church; Madison, WI /
11 May 2008

Snapshot No. 1: Gwen and Earl's Wedding Day, 25 December 1951 for string quartet+
Elements String Quartet / Merkin Recital Hall; New York, NY / 18 November 2003

Piano Concerto No. 1+
Yakima Symphony Orchestra / Tanya Stambuk; Lawrence Golan / Seasons Performance Hall;
Yakima, WA / 16 October 2010

2003

Flute Sonata No. 2^
WGDR Studios Vermont (live broadcast) / Su Lian Tan; Chris Molina / 31 July 2004

String Quartet No. 2: *Alive in a Moment for* **baritone and string quartet+**
Amernet String Quartet; Paul Kreider / Greaves Concert Hall; Highland Heights, KY /
8 October 2003

Susurrus **haiku for orchestra+**
National Symphony Orchestra / Leonard Slatkin / John F. Kennedy Center for the Performing
Arts; Washington, D.C. / 18 September 2003

Letting Go **song cycle for voice and piano^**
Claire Vangelisti; Alfredo Carerra / Auditório do Departamento de Comunicação e Arte da
Universidade de Aveiro, Portugal / 11 December 2002

Chamber Symphony for mixed ensemble+
Albany Symphony Chamber Players / David Alan Miller / Albany Institute of History and Art;
Albany, NY / 6 March 2003

2004

Sappho Songs **song cycle for two female voices and cello^**
The Phoenix Concerts / Gilda Lyons; Elaine Valby; Robert La Rue / Church of St. Matthew and
St. Timothy; New York, NY / 23 September 2005

I Had Rather **for mixed chorus a cappella^**
The Presidential Singers / Judith Clurman / Library of Congress; Washington, D.C. /
26 October 2004

Romeo and Juliet: **concerto for flute, cello, and orchestra+**
Albany Symphony Orchestra / Sara Sant'Ambrogio; Jeffrey Khaner / Palace Theater; Albany,
NY / 16 January 2005

2005

Flight Music **for treble chorus and string quartet (or piano)+**
Milwaukee Choral Artists; Present Music Ensemble / Sharon Hansen / Cathedral of St. John; Milwaukee, WI / 20 November 2005

The Antient Concert **a dramatic recital for four singers^**
World staged premiere: Phoenix Chamber Players / Daron Hagen / Jocelyn Dueck / Century Association; New York, NY. Notable Performances: *staged workshop:* 17 April 2005 / The Princeton Atelier / Borromeo String Quartet /Daron Hagen / McCarter Theater / Princeton, NJ; concert *broadcast premiere:* 16 June 2007 / Bloomsday on Broadway XXVI / Peter Sharp Theater / Symphony Space, NYC

2006

Songs of Experience **song cycle for voice and piano+**
Wintergreen Summer Music Festival / Steven Condy; Kelly Horsted / Wintergreen, VA / 17 July 2007

Piano Trio No. 3: *Wayfaring Stranger+*
Seasons Music Festival / Finisterra Piano Trio / Seasons Performance Hall; Yakima, WA / 2 March 2007

Snapshot No. 2: *Wayfaring Stranger* **for string quartet+**
Sweet Plantain String Quartet / The Knitting Factory; New York, NY / 23 February 2006

Orpheus and Eurydice: **concerto for violin, cello, piano, and orchestra+**
Chicago Youth Symphony / Amelia Piano Trio / Allen Tinkham / Symphony Hall; Chicago, IL / 11 November 2007

Gesture Drawings **four sketches for orchestra+**
Vermont Youth Symphony / Troy Peters / Long Music Center; Colchester, VT / 5 May 2006

2007

Agincourt Fanfare **for brass and timpani+**
Fargo Moorhead Symphony Brass / Rourke Gallery; Moorhead, MN / 25 October 2007

Amelia **opera+**
Seattle Opera / McCaw Hall / Stephen Wadsworth; Gerard Schwarz / 8 May 2010; *Reduced orchestration premiere:* Moores Opera Center / Buck Ross; Brett Mitchell / Moores Opera House; Houston, TX / 27 January 2012

Piano Trio No. 4: *Angel Band+*
Seasons Music Festival / Finisterra Piano Trio / Seasons Performance Hall; Yakima, WA / 29 September 2007

Icarus **for solo clarinet+**
Susan Martula / Albany Museum of History and Art; Albany, NY / 4 March 2007

Masquerade: **concerto for violin, cello and orchestra+**
Sacramento Symphony Orchestra / Jaime Laredo; Sharon Robinson; Laura Jackson / Symphony Hall; Sacramento, CA / 16 February 2008

2008

Symphony No. 4: *River Music+*
Albany Symphony Orchestra; Albany Pro Musica / David Alan Miller / Palace Theater; Albany, NY / 9 May 2009

New York Stories **three one act operas:** *Broken Pieces*^
   Staged premiere: 8 March 2005, by the University of Southern California Opera, Los Angeles, CA. *Concert orchestral premiere:* 19 February 2007 by Music on the Edge, Pittsburgh, PA. *Cabaret premiere:* 13 February 2008 by Boston Opera Underground, Boston, MA

Just for the Night+
   premiere: 7 April 2008 by Prism Ensemble, New York, NY. *Semi-staged premiere:* 17 June 2009 by Long Leaf Opera, Chapel Hill, NC

Cradle Song+
   Semi-staged premiere: 21 October 2008 by University of Puget Sound, Tacoma, WA. *Concert premiere:* 26 October 2008 by the Seasons Music Festival, Yakima, WA

New York Stories **(complete)**~^
   Site-specific staged premiere: 30 October 2010 by Kentucky Opera, Louisville, KY. *Semi-staged concert premiere:* 1 November 2011 by Chicago Opera Theater / Chicago College of the Performing Arts, Chicago, IL. *Theatrical premiere:* 24 February 2012 by the Butler Opera Center, University of Texas, Austin, TX

2009

Northern Light **haiku for orchestra+**
   Youth Orchestra of San Antonio / Troy Peters / San Antonio, TX / 31 January 2010

Three Celtic Songs **for three solo women's voices or treble choir+**
   The Phoenix Concerts / Gilda Lyons; Elaine Valby; Ruth Cunningham / Church of St. Matthew and St. Timothy; New York, NY / 20 November 2009

Four Irish Folk Songs **for two voices and piano+**
   Gilda Lyons; Elaine Valby; Daron Hagen / Hudson Opera House; Hudson, NY / 18 April 2009

Just Amazed **seven variations for string septet, piano, trombone, and two voices+**
   Seasons Festival Ensemble / Daron Hagen / Seasons Performance Hall; Yakima, WA / 11 October 2009

Suite for Piano+
   Van Cliburn International Piano Competition / Mariangela Vacatello; Kyu Yeon Kim; Di Wu; Michail Lifits /Bass Performance Hall; Fort Worth, TX / 28–31 May 2009

2010

Genji: **concerto for koto (version 1) and string quartet+**
   Yumi Kurosawa; Lark String Quarte+ / Tenri Cultural Institute; New York, NY / 19 February 2011

Genji: **concerto for koto (version 2) and small orchestra+**
   Orchestra of the Swan / Yumi Kurosawa; David Curtis / Stratford-on-Avon, UK / 28 May 2011

Genji: **concerto for koto (version 3) and large orchestra+**
   Hawaii Symphony Orchestra / Yumi Kurosawa; Naoto Otomo / Honolulu, HI / 17 May 2014

Con gai: a greeting & a farewell **for orchestra+**
   Seattle Symphony Orchestra / Gerard Schwarz / Benaroya Hall; Seattle, WA / 14 October 2010

The Song of Gabriel **motet for mixed chorus and string orchestra (or piano)+**
   Wisconsin Symphony Orchestra; Brookfield Central Chorus / Phillip Olson / Sharon Lynn Center for the Arts; Brookfield, WI / 7 December 2010

Little Nemo in Slumberland **a magic opera in two acts+~**
   Sarasota Youth Opera / Martha Collins; Steven Osgood / Sarasota Opera House; Sarasota, FL / November 2012

Book of Days **for clarinet, viola, and piano+**
Curtis on Tour / Kelly Coyle; Ayane Kozasa; Ignat Solzhenitsyn / Mondavi Center; Davis, CA /
19 March 2011

We Few **scena for male voice and piano+**
Agincourt Duo / The Rourke Art Museum; Moorhead, MN / 25 October 2015

2011

After Words **song cycle for soprano, tenor and piano+**
Lyric Fest / Justine Aronson; Joseph Gaines; Laura Ward / Academy of Vocal Arts;
Philadelphia, PA / 28 January 2013

Vegetable Verselets **a vegetarian song cycle for voice and piano on words of Margaret G. Hayes+**
Caroline Worra; Tracy Cowden / Virginia Tech Auditorium; Blacksburg, VA / 27 April 2011

The New Yorkers **song scene for two voices and piano+**
Five Boroughs Songbook / Martha Guth; David Adam Moore; Jocelyn Dueck / Galapagos Arts
Center, DUMBO; Brooklyn, NY / 6 October 2011

Songbook: **concerto for violin, string orchestra, harp, and percussion+**
Buffalo Philharmonic Orchestra / Michael Ludwig; JoAnn Falletta / Kleinhans Auditorium;
Buffalo, NY / 13 May 2011

Intensive care **for violin, cello, and piano+**
Beijing New Music Ensemble, Beijing, China and Finisterra Piano Trio, Seattle, Washington
(simultaneous) / Ullens Center; Beijing, China; Benaroya Concert Hall; Seattle, WA /
9 December 2011

Three Sky Interludes from Amelia **for orchestra+**
Seattle Symphony Orchestra / Gerard Schwarz / Benaroya Concert Hall; Seattle, WA /
26 April 2012

2012

secrets my mother told me **for koto+**
Yumi Kurosawa / Sumida Toriphony Hall; Tokyo, Japan / 11 July 2012

Five Nocturnes for Piano+
Teo Gheorghiu / The Louvre; Paris, France / 22 November 2012

Angel Band **for voice and orchestra+**
Yakima Symphony Orchestra / Gilda Lyons; Daron Hagen / Seasons Performance Hall; Yakima,
WA / 21 October 2012

2013

Early, Later: **90 for Ned for clarinet and piano+**
Thomas Piercy; Judith Olson / Bargemusic; Brooklyn, NY / 18 October 2013

A Woman in Morocco **opera+~**
Kentucky Opera / Daron Hagen; Roger Zahab / Actors Theater of Louisville; Louisville, KY /
23 June 2015

2014

Valse Blanche **for violin and piano+**
Livia Sohn; Benjamin Loeb / in studio / concert premiere: Livia Sohn; Andrew Armstrong /
South Windsor Cultural Arts Center; Windsor, CT / 1 November 2015

Valse Noir for cello and piano+
> Phoenix Concerts / Adrian Daurov; Di Wu / Church of St. Matthew and St. Timothy;
> New York, NY / 27 March 2015

Speight (Jenkins Leit) Motif for four Wagnertüben, or Tubas, or trombones, or trombones and tubas+
> Seattle Opera Gala / Members of the Seattle Symphony / McCaw Hall; Seattle, WA /
> 8 August 2014

Symphony No. 5: *Desert Music*+
> Phoenix Symphony Orchestra / Victoria Vargas; Michael Christie / Phoenix Center for the
> Arts; Phoenix, AZ / 9 October 2015

Four Dickinson Songs for voice and piano+
> Lyric Fest / Joseph Gaines; Laura Ward / Goodheart Hall, the Music Room, Bryn Mawr
> College; Philadelphia, PA / 15 July 2014

I Hear America Singing musical+~
> Skylight Music Theater / Daron Hagen; Robert Frankenberry / Broadway Theater Center;
> Milwaukee, WI / Spring 2014 run

2015

jaik's songs song cycle for voice and piano+
> Stephanie Weiss; Christina Wright-Ivanova / Doc Rando Recital Hall; Las Vegas, NV /
> 25 January 2017

Heike Quarto #1: Appassionato for koto, voice, and cello+
> Duo YUMENO / Yoko Reikano Kimura; Hikaru Tamaki / Tenri Cultural Arts Center;
> New York, NY / 15 March 2015

Hymn of Forgiveness for mixed chorus and organ+
> Chorus of Church of St. Matthew and St. Timothy / James Holmes / Chorus of Church of
> St. Matthew and St. Timothy; New York, NY / 13 September 1996

Piano Concerto No. 2: Chaplin's Tramp (version 1) for piano and mixed ensemble+
> Wintergreen Music Festival / Peter Marshall; Erin Freeman / Dunlop Pavilion; Wintergreen,
> VA / 24 July 2015

Piano Concerto No. 2: Chaplin's Tramp (version 2) for piano and orchestra+

2016

Anniversary in Memoriam Leonard Bernstein for piano+
> Lara Downes / CUNY Graduate Center Elabash Concert Hall; New York, NY /
> 2 December 2017

Heike Quarto #2: Cantabile for koto, voice, and cello+
> Duo YUMENO / Yoko Reikano Kimura; Hikaru Tamaki / Nakashima House and Studio;
> New Hope, PA / 1 May 2016

Blake Songs (version 1) for voice and mixed ensemble+
> IonSound Ensemble / Robert Frankenberry / Bellefield Auditorium; Pittsburgh, PA /
> 20 March 2016

Blake Songs (version 2) for voice and orchestra+
> University of Pittsburgh Symphony Orchestra / Robert Frankenberry; Roger Zahab / Bellefield
> Auditorium; Pittsburgh, PA / 20 27 February 2018

A Handful of Days song cycle for female voice and piano+
> Berlin Song Fest / Stephanie Weiss; Christina Wright-Ivanova / Knutson Studios; Berlin,
> Germany / 25 January 2017

2017

Dante Fragments **for voice, violin, and piano+**
Virginia Center for the Creative Arts / Adelaide Muir Trombetta; Domenica Luca; Unknown / Mt. San Angelo; Sweet Briar, VA / 4 June 2017

Sonata for Cello and Piano+
Wintergreen Music Festival / Sarah Kapps; Peter Marshall / Dunlop Pavilion; Wintergreen, VA / 27 July 2017

Heike Quarto #3: Misterioso **for koto, voice, and cello+**
Duo YUMENO / Yoko Reikano Kimura; Hikaru Tamaki / Kennedy Center for the Performing Arts; Washington, D.C. / 1 April 2017

Piano Trio No. 5: *Red is the Rose+*
Prometheus Piano Trio / Helen Bader Recital Hall; Milwaukee, WI / 13 February 2018

Chaplin Suite for **mixed ensemble+**
Wintergreen Music Festival Chamber Ensemble / Erin Freeman / Dunlop Pavilion; Wintergreen, VA / 28 July 2017

Lilly Sketches **for woodwind quintet+**
Wintergreen Music Festival Quintet / Erin Freeman / Dunlop Pavilion; Wintergreen, VA / 6 August 2017

Piano Trio No. 6: *Horszowski+*
Horszowski Piano Trio / Kimmel Center for the Performing Arts; Philadelphia, PA / 26 November 2018

On the Beach at Night **scena for baritone, cello, and piano+**
Seth Keeton; Karl Knapp; Robert Elfline / Augustina College; Rock Island, IL

2018

A Chaplin Symphony **for mixed ensemble+**
Wintergreen Music Festival Chamber Ensemble / Erin Freeman / Dunlop Pavilion; Wintergreen, VA / 20 July 2018

Heike Quarto #4: Grandioso+
Duo YUMENO / Yoko Reikano Kimura; Hikaru Tamaki / Kosho-ji Temple, Kyoto, Japan / 17 June 2018

Orson Rehearsed **a multi-media prestidigitation+~**
New Mercury Collective; Fifth House Ensemble; Atlas Arts Media / Daron Hagen; Roger Zahab / Studebaker Theater; Chicago, IL / 15 September 2018

Select Discography

Operas

Bandanna, University of Nevada Las Vegas Opera Theater and Wind Orchestra, Opera Theater Chorus, and soloists Lesley DeGroot, James Demler, Paul Kreider, Mark Thomsen, Darynn Zimmer, conducted by Daron Hagen (Albany TROY849/50, 2006)

Shining Brow, Buffalo Philharmonic Orchestra and Chorus, and soloists Matthew Curran, Robert Frankenberry, Brenda Harris, Gilda Lyons, Robert Orth, Elaine Valby, conducted by JoAnn Falletta (Naxos 8.669020–21, 2009)

Vera of Las Vegas, University of Nevada Opera Theater Orchestra, and soloists Patrick Jones, Paul Kreider, Charles Maxwell, Carolann Page, conducted by Donna Hagen (CRI / New World 902, 2002)

Concertos

Concerto for Flügelhorn and Wind Ensemble, Baylor University Wind Ensemble, Vern Seilert, Robert La Rue, conducted by Michael Haithcock; also includes the works *Night, Again; Sennets, Cortege and Tuckets;* and *Cello Concerto* (Arsis Audio CD112, 1999, 2015)

Koto Concerto: Genji (also includes works by Schlefer), Orchestra of the Swan, Yumi Kurosawa, conducted by David Curtis (MSR Classics MS 1429, 2011)

Masquerade—Concerto for Violin, Cello and Orchestra (also includes works by Danielpour and Ludwig), Vermont Symphony Orchestra, Jaime Laredo, Sharon Robinson, conducted by Troy Peters (Bridge 9354, 2007)

Songbook for Solo Violin, Strings, Harp and Percussion (also includes works by del Aguila and Ewazen), Buffalo Philharmonic Orchestra, Michael Ludwig, conducted by JoAnn Falletta (Beau Fleuve 610708–094951, 2014)

Song Cycles

Daron Hagen: Songs of Madness and Sorrow, Cleveland Chamber Symphony, Wisconsin Brass Quintet, Oakwood Chamber Players, Paul Sperry, conducted by Victoria Bond and James Smith; includes *Songs of Madness and Sorrow, Concerto for Brass Quintet,* and *Serenade for Ten Instruments* (Arsis Audio CD127, 2004, 2015)

Daron Hagen: 21st Century Song Cycles, Lyric Fest soloists Justine Aronson, Kelly Ann Bixby, Suzanne DuPlantis, Joseph Gaines, Gilda Lyons, Daniel Teadt, Laura Ward; includes the cycles *After Words, Songs of Experience, Phantoms of Myself, Four Irish Folk Songs,* and *Four Dickinson Songs* (Naxos 8.655434, 2017)

Daron Aric Hagen: Love in a Life & Other Works for Voice & Piano, Paul Kreider, Daron Hagen; includes the cycles Muldoon Songs, Love in a Life, and The Heart of the Stranger, and the arias *And her scent, was it musk?* and *Why do you shrink from Señor Kane?* (Arsis Audio CD119, 1999, 2015)

Dear Youth (selections; includes works by Berg, and Platt), Tobé Malawista, Jane Shelly, Margaret Kampmeier (Albany TROY1032, 2008)

Figments (also includes works by Larsen, Moravec, and Cipullo), Paul Sperry, Daron Hagen (Albany TROY654, 2004)

Hagen: Songs, Susan Crowder, Bradley Moore, Sara Stern; includes the cycles *Love Songs, Echo's Songs, Dear Youth,* and *Merrill Songs* (Arsis Audio CD106, 1997, 2015)

Larkin Songs (also includes works by Boyle, Altman, and Hennessy), Elem Eley, J.J. Penna (Affetto Recordings AF1501, 2015)

Letting Go (also includes works by Cipullo, Eddleman, Hennessy, Hundley, and Hoiby), Elem Eley, J.J. Penna (Albany TROY1050, 2008)

Instrumental Works

Anniversary in Memoriam (for Lenny), for piano (also includes works by Bernstein, Corigliano, Schwartz, Sandresky, Abels, Blitzstein, Foss, Gordon, Ran, Urquhart, Bleckman, and Rorem), Lara Downes (Sony Classical 84284011251, 2018)

Daron Hagen: Complete Piano Trios; includes Piano Trio Nos 1–4 Finisterra Trio (Naxos 8.559657, 2010)

Hagen: Strings Attached; includes *Duo for Violin and Cello, Suite for Violin, Suite for Viola, Suite for Cello,* and *Higher, Louder, Faster!* Robert La Rue, Charles Noble, Michaela Paetsch (Arsis Audio CD111, 1999, 2015)

Harp Trio for flute, viola & harp (also includes works by Mathias, Kibbe, and Bondon), The Debussy Trio (Sierra Classical 5001, 1995)

Qualities of Light (includes works by Barber), Jeanne Golan (Albany TROY324, 1998)

Red is the Rose, for piano trio (includes works by Bansal, Roven, Donato, Lyons, Martin, Leyman, Sonenberg, Carol, and Oteri), Entelechron Trio (Roven Records 55518, 2018)

Valse Blanche: How Love Comes, Tangiers, October 1958, for violin & piano (also includes works by Verdi, Tchaikovsky, Sarasate, Kreisler, Hubay, Martinu, Handel, and Berger), Livia Sohn, Benjamin Loeb (Naxos 8.5734303, 2016)

Band

Daron Aric Hagen: Seduction and Prayer; includes *Bandanna Overture, Seduction Scene, Mona's Prayer, Forward!,* and *The Heart of the Stranger,* Baylor University Wind Ensemble, Paul Kreider, Linda Keith McKnight, conducted by Michael Haithcock (Arsis Audio CD123, 1999, 2015)

Wedding Dances from Bandanna (includes works by Young, Grantham, Welcher, and Daugherty), North Texas Wind Symphony, conducted by Eugene Corporan (Klavier Records CD11099, 2000)

Choral

Daron Hagen: Silent Night; includes *Lullay; O Come, O Come, Emmanuel; God Rest Ye / O Come; Silent Night; Once in Royal David's City; Sussex Carol; What Child is This?; At Bethlehem Proper; Hosanna,* American Repertory Singers, Robert La Rue, Daron Hagen, conducted by Leo Nestor (Arsis Audio CD107, 1997, 2015)

Index

Numbers in **bold italics** indicate pages with illustrations